LETTERS

1905 – 1965

Macmillan Publishing Company
New York

Maxwell Macmillan Canada
Toronto

Maxwell Macmillan International
New York   Oxford   Singapore   Sydney

ALBERT SCHWEITZER

LETTERS

---❧---

1905 – 1965

Edited by Hans Walter Bähr

Translated by Joachim Neugroschel

Published in German as *Albert Schweitzer: Leben, Werk und Denken 1905–1965 Mitgeteilt in Seinen Briefen,* © 1987 by Verlag Lambert Schneider GmbH, Heidelberg.

Macmillan Publishing Company   Maxwell Macmillan Canada, Inc.
866 Third Avenue   1200 Eglinton Avenue East, Suite 200
New York, NY 10022   Don Mills, Ontario M3C 3N1

Macmillan Publishing Company is part of the Maxwell Communication
Group of Companies.

Library of Congress Cataloging-in-Publication Data
Schweitzer, Albert, 1875–1965.
    [Correspondence. English. Selections]
    Letters, 1905–1965 / Albert Schweitzer; edited by Hans Walter Bähr;
translated by Joachim Neugroschel.
        p.   cm.
    Translation of: Leben, Werk und Denken, 1905–1965.
    Includes bibliographical references and index.
    ISBN 0-02-607171-1
    1. Schweitzer, Albert, 1875–1965—Correspondence.
    2. Missionaries, Medical—Gabon—Lambaréné (Moyen-Ogooué)—
Correspondence.   I. Bähr, Hans Walter.   II. Title.
R722.32.S35A4   1992
610'.92—dc20   91-47881
[B]   CIP

Macmillan books are available at special discounts for bulk purchases for sales promotions, premiums, fund-raising, or educational use. For details, contact:

Special Sales Director
Macmillan Publishing Company
866 Third Avenue
New York, NY 10022

Book design by Maura Fadden Rosenthal

10   9   8   7   6   5   4   3   2   1

Printed in the United States of America

CONTENTS

TRANSLATOR'S NOTE

Some of these letters were written in German and some in French. To simplify the problem of spelling the place names, I have consistently used the French (and normal English) spelling for Alsatian place names: that is, Strasbourg rather than Strassburg. On the other hand, for places that were German when the letters were written but are Polish today, I have stayed with the name used at that time, since the present Polish form would sound anachronistic: Kattowitz instead of Katowice. My choices are based on historical and not political considerations—just as the use of Istanbul or Constantinople would be determined by the historical context and not by any ethical preference.

EDITOR'S NOTE ON THE TEXT

Albert Schweitzer's life and work, his story, his thoughts and deeds, his experiences constitute the theme of this book. It is based on Schweitzer's letters and the personal accounts they offer throughout the phases of his life. A few of these letters are complete; some are excerpted to focus on the main topics.

The structure of this book and the formal principle of including both complete texts and excerpts are dealt with in the preface. We must reemphasize that this is not a collection of letters in the strict sense; rather, it is a documentary presentation to the extent that it can be achieved with the extant sources in Schweitzer's correspondence.

Most of Albert Schweitzer's letters were written in German, some in French (indicated by [f]). A few of his letters were sent in English translations of his original German texts. They are indicated by an [e]. Although the phrasing and syntax of these English-language letters are sometimes awkward, we have not revised the original texts.

Salutations have usually been retained whenever they have a personal character. Names and locations of recipients have been affixed before the respective texts. Multiple periods (. . . .) constitute a typical device of Schweitzer's; they do not indicate omissions.

Schweitzer, especially in early letters, integrated French sentences or phrases in German text or German ones in French text. These have all been italicized.

Often, Schweitzer had to write numerous letters—accounts—within the space of several weeks, so a few of them contain similar material. In some cases they have been left as is in this volume; in other cases such repetitions appear superfluous.

Any comments by the editor or the translator within the texts are placed in square brackets; parentheses are to be found in the original letters. If a word appeared to have been left out, the editor made the appropriate addition in brackets.

The editor of this volume had at his disposal the various collections of letters at the Schweitzer Central Archive, which is located in Schweitzer's house in Gunsbach, Alsace (see the preface). Owners of other letters provided him with their contents; the Central Archive has copies of the editor's own collection. Some letters or excerpts were found in literary sources or through personal tips.

The texts used for this publication were either the original manuscripts, photocopies, or handmade copies; in some cases they had already been published (see the source citations in the notes).

PREFACE

A large-scale correspondence, maintained for decades, can reveal the writer's thoughts and actions in both their history and their reality. Such documents are valuable sources for research and for a more general understanding. Emerging with the developments that characterize them, they belong to the very phases of that evolution. This holds true for Albert Schweitzer's letters which, on a personal level, demonstrate his lifework amid the social, intellectual, and spiritual problems of his time. They highlight his wishes and goals, his daily activities and their wider context, his methods of coping with reality, and his overall life story.

Albert Schweitzer wrote these letters in Africa or Europe; in Lambarene they were often his only opportunity to communicate with distant places. They contained his reports—one of the features that made the plan of this book possible. Along with letters that he regarded as crucial for his project, there are poignant dialogues with close friends and individual replies to many people who approached him. We also find the thank-you notes for donations to his hospital, the hospital correspondence itself, and the necessary explanatory letters about his work—often in difficult moments.

As for Schweitzer's early years in Strasbourg, there are few extant letters written by the young theologian as a New Testament scholar, a preacher at the Church of St. Nicholas, and an expert on Bach. Soon his correspondence is marked by his decision to serve the Mission Society by going to the African jungle. His resolve is laid out in his letter to the Mission (in Part One of this book): He asks to be sent to the Congo area of Central Africa after a term of preparation. It was from missionaries who visited his parents at the Gunsbach parsonage that the boy learned about the serious illnesses and the general conditions in these regions. Now, along with his theological profession, his sermons, his numerous Bach recitals, and his literary labors, he studied medicine. The stress and strain of this life-style triggered health crises. Then in Africa, in the primitive conditions on the equator, his situation began to change radically.

In Lambarene, Schweitzer, as he explains in his letters, sought the "outpost of the Kingdom of God." In his desire to serve the commandment of Jesus, he found the place of his profession of faith. According to his letters, Schweitzer was following the orders of Jesus the Lord, in whose name he took up his work in Lambarene, often communicating and acting in almost unmanageable quandaries. During those first few years his wife, Helene Schweitzer, née Bresslau, was the only trained person who could help him, along with native assistants. During subsequent decades Schweitzer, fulfilling the dictates of faith, developed his project in Lambarene—as depicted in his letters. He set up his facility near the Mission station and, even after World War II, he kept adding buildings that he himself planned and constructed; architecturally they fitted in with the tropical climate. Here, as described in his letters, he kept coping with the jungle landscape, treating countless patients, holding church services for them, writing his letters and his manuscripts, and facing what he saw as ineluctable demands.

Every few years Schweitzer would go to Europe to speak on behalf of his project, give talks, deliver theological and philosophical guest lectures at universities, check scholarly sources, gather money for Lambarene by means of organ recitals in churches, see friends, conduct negotiations, and promote an understanding for African needs with his hands-on knowledge of the situation. The events and demands of these travels as well as the European concert tours for Lambarene are frequently mentioned and documented in these letters. Schweitzer stayed with his early decision to spend most of his time in Lambarene, but these periods were punctuated by his visits to Europe with their duties and encounters. By adhering to this plan and disregarding many other things, he felt he could achieve the results he was hoping for.

More and more groups emerged in his correspondence, as shown by examples culled from the various periods. At the same time, he devoted his evenings and nights in Lambarene to continuing his scholarly research. He wrote texts with his characteristic scholarly rigor—studies on theology, philosophy, intellectual history. He deepened his knowledge of Bach's scores detail by detail; after his early discovery of the ethical principle of reverence for life, he kept refining it, staying abreast of current events, especially the problems of peace, civilization, and the future, which are thrashed out in many of his letters.

Albert Schweitzer's life, as revealed in his correspondence, took shape in the various domains of his thoughts and actions. In both Lambarene and Europe he always confronted the problems he saw, their possibilities, their difficulties, their dimensions. This involved self-control and self-sacrifice, which are only hinted at in the letters, while his difficult crises of fatigue are never concealed. Occasional passages tell of certain inner struggles; normally, however, they were not recorded by a man who was taciturn about such things.

His correspondence was often a burden on Schweitzer, as he explains in some letters, but he kept up with it all the same. If we look at his writings and manuscripts, then, from a literary standpoint, we must regard his letters as part and parcel of his lifework. Any man who develops the epistolary medium as Schweitzer does is following a propensity for this form of communication and establishing his own presence in it, especially in the letters, long or short, that reveal the creative writer, the historian.

The reader of these letters, most of which are linked to Schweitzer's project, also becomes aware of features that bring out his individuality—features that, as in any person, are unmistakable, indeed unique. *Individuum est ineffabile*: This saying is applicable to any human being and thus to the man who wrote the texts in this book. They contain nuances, aptitudes, basic attitudes of a unique and special character—outgoing or retiring, passionate or neutral, but always in its true intrinsic nature.

The job of collecting Schweitzer's letters began at his house in Gunsbach, the European center of his project. The directors of the archive asked anyone in possession of Schweitzer's letters to notify them. To the extent that the recipients could be located, the directors managed to obtain originals, photocopies, or copies, so that thousands of texts written by or to Schweitzer are now preserved at the Central Archive, with further letters being added now and then. Several detailed groups are fully available here or from owners with whom the archive is in contact.

Since this correspondence had to be squeezed into a single volume, the editor was faced with the problem of carrying out such a plan within this limited space. The simpler solution would have been to include only complete texts of a small number of letters; the other possibility was to include excerpts along with entire letters. This latter alternative was chosen in order to make the book more comprehensive, so that it could include more letters—many texts whose information might otherwise have been omitted. Along with the letters picked for this book there are numerous ones that are comparatively important for the theme—whole series and single items of every kind. Consistent with its goal, this volume strives to give an overall picture that demonstrates the context of Schweitzer's life and the directions he moved in. The form is not meant to be that of a typical edition of letters.

Instead, the book presents its determining and structuring theme, which is sought in letters and treated with the immediacy that is possible in letters; in other words, this book offers letters germane to Schweitzer's project.

While some letters are not preserved here, as indicated at appropriate points, the selection pays heed both to certain thematic aspects and to the size of the book, in terms of the entire volume and the information it transmits. Such a narrative of work and life is also contingent on the number of letters that have survived, so that considerable gaps may crop up in the chronology. This problem does not loom large in Schweitzer's correspondence, except from 1905 to 1912 and during wartime. However, another formal feature had to be dealt with: Because of the large number of letters that Schweitzer had to write, often in a short time, some of them contain similar sections or texts. They are represented in this volume but not always included, and the omissions are indicated.

Albert Schweitzer always wrote his letters by hand—a principle that he persistently observed even as his correspondence kept growing, especially after 1949. If one of his assistants replied to a magazine on his behalf, then Schweitzer would always add a few lines to the response.

Schweitzer's autobiographical books, *On the Edge of the Primeval Forest* (1921), *Memoirs of Childhood and Youth* (1924), *Out of My Life and Thought* (1929, 1931), constitute a literature that the writer has molded according to his blueprints. However, Schweitzer talked about his later life not in books but frequently in the circular letters, which contained news from Lambarene. Unlike his books and his circular letters, Schweitzer's personal letters, both in their goals and in their contents, are individual documents about their times. Nevertheless, for any discussion of Schweitzer and his work, his books, particularly *Out of My Life and Thought*, remain fundamental—even for the periods after 1931, which are recorded in his letters. Thus the reader will see that the letters have their own intrinsic function in illuminating Schweitzer—a function that differs from that of his autobiographies.

The editor of this volume is aware that any such collection involves a personal approach, subjective elements, as in any scholarly process. Still, a scholar always pursues the goal of locating and presenting the "thing itself." Despite vast differences, this book aims at understanding letters that express realities of life.

II

In Albert Schweitzer's writings, all areas of his work and thought are characteristically expressed; here we find them within the context of his correspondence. In his books, especially the scholarly ones, his treatment of themes and problems had more closure; but in his letters, he approaches them over the years in a dialogue revealing resolute precision of themes and statements.

Thus countless letters are devoted to religion and its issues—faith, ministry, and theological research. Throughout his correspondence, from his very first—and crucial—letter to the Mission Society, he expresses the conviction that dictated his Christianity. God's will is experienced in Jesus' tiding, in Jesus' religion of love, which endures beyond time and is active for the Kingdom of God. After years of serving the Alsatian Church, Schweitzer deals with that faith in services and evening devotions in Lambarene, using verses from the Old and New Testaments. In his letters, as in his sermons at home and in Africa, he talks about the liberating foundation of faith and its consequences. The Gospel, the Sermon on the Mount, sums it up in the Beatitudes of mercy and peace: Schweitzer refers to them in his letters and quotes those words of faith.

His scholarly theological works, which are mentioned in his letters, deal with biblical writings and basic themes of theological research, laid out historically and systematically—a demand that Schweitzer made on himself and on others. They also deal with the presentation of phases of modern theology. Then come Schweitzer's own opinions, from his student days to his manuscripts, about his ideas of the Kingdom of God, which are mentioned in his letters. These investigations have a lasting value in their approaches to problems and in their conclusions. And simultaneously they are part of a development of the theological field, revealing various positions and viewpoints.[1] Schweitzer's writings, as a crucial part of theological literature, continue to have an impact; for instance, his studies of the quest for the historical Jesus; then *The Mysticism of Paul the Apostle*, which was published in 1930 after long years of work; and finally *The Kingdom of God and Primitive Christianity*, which came out in the 1950s.

In his own personal way Schweitzer combines biblical scholarship with the power of the Gospel; as theological realms, the two form a unity in his letters. He professed his faith in his words, sermons, and letters as well as in his actions. Thus, in their communications of faith

---

[1]See the group of essays by various theologians in *Albert Schweitzer: Sein Denken und sein Weg* (Tübingen, 1962) and Erich Grässer, *Albert Schweitzer als Theologe* (1979).

and their deep Christian justification, his letters can help us understand
Schweitzer the theologian. As a spiritual, intellectual, and active figure,
he is a witness in the history of Christianity, concentrating on the
Tiding in a specific ecumenical sense.[2]

In his early memoir, *On the Edge of the Primeval Forest*, Schweitzer
wrote a chapter on the Mission as he lived it in Lambarene; these
were experiences that he shared with other missionaries in that region.
He says that he immediately senses "the victoriously elementary quality of the thoughts of Jesus" during his sermons in Lambarene. These
words resemble his depictions in the circular letters and his opinion—
explained in those same letters—that one should speak about Christian faith in the African conditions in order to show that faith to the
audience and relieve it of demonic compulsions. In his addresses
during services at the hospital and in the devotions, Schweitzer presented exegeses, some of which were recorded afterward. In contrast,
the archive contains manuscripts of some 150 of his Strasbourg sermons, a number of which were published in two collections, 1966 and
1974.

In regard to his medical practice, Schweitzer's accounts are to be
found chiefly in the printed circular letters dispatched to the hospital's
patrons and to parishes that sent donations. Some portions of his
correspondence concur with other letters on medical themes in this
book. Schweitzer records the experiences of the practitioner and simultaneously knows how to observe as a scientist, especially when
analyzing the origins and manifestations of illnesses in the tropics.
While the diseases are the same as in Europe, they may have different
causes in Africa, which in turn affect the choice and length of therapies.
The circular letters mention those disorders that afflict his patients,
but it is especially the African epidemics, such as leprosy and sleeping
sickness, that he copes with from the very start. They sweep across
the interior of the continent like natural forces, spreading farther and
farther. In Lambarene, Schweitzer used new medications to fight
them.

As his letters point out, a great number of operations had to be
performed at the hospital. The doctor had to operate in tropical heat
and avoid infections, and often urgently and quickly since the patient
had been brought from very far away. Schweitzer's correspondence
presents the broad spectrum of surgical problems burdening the de-
fenseless patients. For miles around the inhabitants knew they could
visit the hospital and be treated there.

---

[2]See *L'Evangile de la Miséricorde*, published for Schweitzer's birthday (1965).

French letters that Schweitzer wrote to local figures and authorities are part of his African correspondence, and they contain information about the kind of help that his patients needed. For such letters Schweitzer used pads with carbons in order to keep copies; a few from the 1930s have been preserved. Numerous letters in this volume discuss medical and human problems that a helpful person has to confront in this region.

A growing number of patients kept getting admitted, and others in the surrounding area had to be taken care of. As a result, more physicians were required. At Schweitzer's behest, two Alsatian doctors were the first to arrive; subsequently many physicians, male and female, practiced there over the years. Native assistants were trained, and female assistants, inspired by the idea of helping in Africa, likewise came—at first from Alsace. Thus, as Schweitzer reports, a team was formed under his aegis. Later on even more patients arrived, putting a great strain on the therapy and the food supplies. In regard to Schweitzer's female assistants and the physicians, our choice of letters is also meant to indicate their great achievements. They worked along with him, as Schweitzer repeatedly emphasizes.

In Lambarene, Schweitzer wrote long manuscripts dealing with issues of civilization and ethics; they were continuations of his philosophical labors, which had begun earlier in Strasbourg, with his book on Kant's philosophy of religion—indeed, Kant had a lasting impact on Schweitzer. In the letters picked for our volume, the philosophical texts are first introduced during those months when the more definitive draft of a book crystallized. The themes recur in the further development of Schweitzer's critique and philosophy of civilization as well as his writings on the ideas of other civilizations. He dealt in detail with the process of civilization in modern societies, summarizing his studies in *The Decline and Restoration of Civilization*, the first volume of his philosophy of civilization. Regarding the social, spiritual, and scientific conditions, he tries, after a critical analysis, to discern the elements of a renewal of civilization in an approach that "thinks toward mankind." In his own fundamental conception of the reality of Being, Schweitzer reflects on the phenomenon of "life" and also, as a historical human task, the problem of ethics, ethical conduct, and responsibility for life. With the demand for "reverence for life," Schweitzer verbally summed up the ethical principle that he created and developed as fundamental for the individual space and the collective standard. This principle addresses primarily the individual person, his consciousness and his decisions, just as Schweitzer assigns the individual a special place in ethics. But then he resolutely demands an obligation that encompasses the entire society, indeed the whole of civilization.

Schweitzer's ethical principle also applies to human conduct toward living creatures in nature, which involves an open ethical situation; in his letters he sees his task as expanding ethics in that direction, both theologically and philosophically. In his opinion, ethics must confront this problem, and human beings must therefore behave ethically toward animals as well. He realizes that limits can be placed on such conduct, but in many letters he expects people to have this ethical desire to seize opportunities sensitively and to use them consciously. It is only through this expansion that ethics, according to Schweitzer, can become "complete ethics"—which, for him, is an existential position. In a 1975 lecture at the University of Strasbourg, celebrating the Schweitzer centennial, the editor of this volume discussed the conception and dynamics of this theme in Schweitzer.[3]

Albert Schweitzer's letters, especially after 1950, emphasize the further social implications of this ethics, which is now confronted with its sharpest antithesis, the nuclear test explosions, an epoch-making challenge to be treated below. And further challenges come from other processes flouting the commandment of reverence for life.

Schweitzer keeps his scholarly disciplines apart; for his philosophy of civilization he does not insert theological concepts into his structure of proof, nor does he invoke philosophical concepts for his theological works. However, this separatist approach does not imply that no profound connections exist between those two disciplines to the extent that they share contents; their inner rapport is likewise demonstrated by the letters in this volume. As an ethicist, Schweitzer, in a crucial passage of his autobiography (chapter 21), writes that the ethics of reverence for life is the ethics of Jesus—an ethics that has been recognized as necessary for our thoughts. That same year, 1931, he states in a letter (page 123) that the ethical principle of reverence for life is "nothing but Jesus' great commandment to love—a commandment that is reached by thinking." Schweitzer leaves the theological and the philosophical discussions of ethics within their respective precincts, but the cognizant person experiences them beyond that separation.

A theme recurring through every phase of Schweitzer's correspondence is his treatment of music, especially the works of Johann Sebastian Bach, their interpretation and performance, which he per-

---

[3]H. W. Bähr: "L'Ethique cosmique d'Albert Schweitzer et les problèmes de l'éthique naturelle."

sonally demonstrated in numerous organ recitals. He also played compositions by Felix Mendelssohn-Bartholdy, César Franck, and Schweitzer's organ teacher Charles-Marie Widor. A focal point of his musicology was his efforts regarding organ building and its reform. For years and years, as he himself said, he wrote hundreds of letters advocating the preservation of organs built from the seventeenth to the late nineteenth centuries.[4] As a consultant he took part in organ restorations and new constructions. Even during World War II letters from Lambarene to people in Palestine and the United States illuminate tempo problems in performing Bach's organ works and in building organs. From his second letter in this volume to his letter of July 1965 to a Czech expert on Bach, the sequence of Bach letters covers numerous issues, including performances of choral works and organ recitals. Schweitzer published the first versions of his Bach book at the age of thirty-one. His work on this book, which has been translated into many languages, is detailed in some revealing letters. Along with a presentation of his compositions, it offered new insights into their character and motives. Several longer letters, from 1953 to 1962, refer to the eight-volume annotated edition of Bach's organ works, which Schweitzer put out, first with Charles-Marie Widor and later with Edouard Nies-Berger; it was published in New York, and a few of the volumes have been translated into French and German. Volumes one to five, with the preludes, fugues, sonatas, and concerti, were completed before Schweitzer's first trip to Lambarene. Volume six (1954) contains the choral preludes and organ chorales, as do the final two volumes, which were coedited by Nies-Berger.

In the jungle zone of Lambarene, Schweitzer managed to maintain and practice his organ technique and to continue studying the compositions. He was able to do so because of the Paris Bach Society. When he first sailed to Africa after years of collaborating with them, they gave him a piano with organ pedals, which was specifically built for tropical conditions. Thus, during his visits to Europe, he could soon go on concert tours to benefit his hospital. However, beyond research and practice, Bach—as Schweitzer describes it in his letters and in his book—became a spiritual world for him, down to the theological and artistic dynamics of the compositions. In 1947 this fundamental experience for Schweitzer was expressed in his letter to the Dutch Bach Society.

---

[4]See Albert Schweitzer, *Deutsche und französische Orgelbaukunst und Orgelkunst*; also instructive in this connection is Bernhard Billeter, "Albert Schweitzer und sein Orgelbauer."

Schweitzer's letters about peace and humanity,[5] the demands he made on the present-day world, became more and more numerous, especially after 1950. In regard to the political issues of the world situation, Schweitzer held back from publicly expressing his views until the time of the Korean crisis. Then he began stating them more and more emphatically in his letters and also in his radio talks, with their sharp arguments and warnings against nuclear testing. As Nobel peace laureate, Schweitzer, as explained in a 1953 letter to the Nobel Prize Committee, wanted his acceptance speech in Oslo to deal with reverence for life or with "the problem of peace in our time." The latter suggestion was chosen. For decades Schweitzer, in his correspondence and conversations, had repeatedly advocated international understanding. As an Alsatian, Schweitzer, even in difficult political situations, also championed French-German cooperation, which was consistent with his own ideas. Schweitzer's letters show his growing awareness of the worldwide problem of peace, and in concluding his 1954 Oslo speech, he quoted the apostle Paul: "Insofar as it lies within you, be at peace with every man." Here his political ideas fused with the Christian commandment of peace—as in his long response in 1952 to Stockholm's *Svenska Morgonbladet*, which had asked him, "What does mankind need most today?" The fight against nuclear arms, the dangers of radioactive damage to mankind, nature, and the atmosphere were constantly discussed by Schweitzer, and this correspondence added greatly to his workload.[6] In these appeals he pointed out the nuclear peril in the international situation, the effects of atomic testing, and the possibilities of peace. Every conceivable solution should be tried in an earnest and relevant way. In an essay and also in a letter included in this volume, Schweitzer welcomed the pact on banning aboveground nuclear tests; he saw this as a first step. In dealing with all these issues he reconfirmed his self-image, as described in his acceptance speech for the 1928 Goethe Prize in Frankfurt; in it he stated that he experienced the "destinies of our time and the anxiety about mankind" profoundly and vividly.

In the Gabon jungle it was possible to receive and dispatch mail thanks to the location of Schweitzer's hospital; he had built it on a sloping hill, near the Mission station on the large Ogowe River, which winds through the dense tropical forest. From Port-Gentil, which lies

---

[5]In 1959 the philosopher O. F. Bollnow, to whom Schweitzer wrote in 1960, wrote "Menschlichkeit in der Kulturkrise der Gegenwart" (The humane in the crisis of present-day civilization), also published in *Albert Schweitzer: Sein Denken und sein Weg*.

[6]See Benedict Winnubst, *Das Friedenskenken Albert Schweitzers* [Albert Schweitzer's ideas on peace], Verlag Rodopi, Amsterdam, 1974, 219 pages (also contains documents).

on the ocean, a small mail freighter chugged through the vast, almost impenetrable jungle, reaching Lambarene some 150 miles inland. Lambarene could be reached only by way of this river, and whenever Schweitzer returned to the African coast from Europe, he would board a steamer that brought him close to the hospital. The baggage—all the mail and medical supplies—could reach Lambarene only along this river, with the bulkier transports often requiring complicated unloading maneuvers. A network of roads was not built until much later. During World War II the French army set up an airfield across the river from Lambarene, and it is now used for civil flights as well. Later on, in the southern region, the new native government built the first railroad in this country, the Transgabonaise, after expanding the road system.

Schweitzer's letters frequently contradict a harmonious concept of his life in Africa—a notion that some people may have formed in distant areas. Like his writings, these letters evoke the reality of the work and the situations. They concretely show the strain, the climatic and medical difficulties, the endless chore of obtaining food for the patients, the building of more hospital rooms—to cite just a few examples. Schweitzer also had to worry about the economics of running the hospital, which was supported by donations from relief groups, from numerous patrons in their homelands, from church parishes, as well as from Schweitzer's income from his books and organ recitals—a thoroughly risky aspect. Anyone familiar with Schweitzer's writings and circular letters knows about these problems; their persistence is reconfirmed year after year.

To comprehend the circumstances of Schweitzer's work in Lambarene requires knowing the social, regional, linguistic, and ethnic conditions of the people living along the Ogowe River, between Central Africa's mountain plateaus, the vast, damp, tropical jungle, and the estuary near Port-Gentil on the coast. The letters assume knowledge of this overall environment, and we hear that prior to 1960 this area of the Congo was under the French colonial administration and then became part of the sovereign Republic of Gabon.

Schweitzer's *On the Edge of the Primeval Forest* (1921) includes a long chapter, "Social Problems in the Jungle." Another portion deals with the situation of the native logging workers who were employed by foreign private concession firms. Abused and exploited in the swampy areas, the workers fell ill, and some of them wound up in Schweitzer's hospital. The social and economic processes in the country, the incipient industrialization, had profound implications for the substistence economy of the peasants. Referring to Schweitzer's book and his observations, H. O. Neuhoff reports on the situation in

Gabun—Geschichte, Struktur und Probleme (Gabon—History, Structure, and Problems), 1967; and the Gabonese government is also in
possession of documentation and statistics. Profound changes were
triggered by the discovery of raw materials along the coast and in the
south. Today, Gabon, eighty percent of whose surface is covered by
the jungle, exports not only okume wood—which used to be its
dominant item—but also oil and ores. For many years Schweitzer
observed this economic restructuring and its impact on Gabonese society.

A special difficulty in the everyday workings of the hospital was
the variety of languages spoken by the patients—Bantu dialects that
were translated by Schweitzer's French-speaking assistants in the medical practice. One can readily imagine the kinds of problems that
cropped up in the medical interviews with patients and the therapeutic
measures. For the sermons Schweitzer, as described in the circular
letters, used his helpers to render his words into the main languages
of the region.

In his letters, especially during the middle period, Schweitzer lovingly talks about the Gabonese landscape, its isolation and grandeur,
even though the hot, often oppressive climate and the jungle required
constant resistance. Depictions of its seasons, tornadoes, atmospheric
moods, plants, and forests recur throughout the letters.

Schweitzer's hospital was originally set up with the help of his wife
Helene. Today, with new buildings in the vicinity of the Albert
Schweitzer Hospital, it is administered by a joint commission consisting of the country of Gabon and relief organizations. In 1961 and
1963 the new state and its government honored Schweitzer for the
fiftieth anniversary of his hospital. After the emancipation of Africa,
the hospital became part of the present structure of the country. Its
efforts on behalf of the population have never been denied, and in its
new form it has become a medical center. Today it helps people in
further developing the region, which involves its own health services;
indeed, the hospital unites the efforts of African and non-African
professionals within Gabon.

At this point I would like to thank all the people who have supported
my work on this book with their interest and cooperation. Mrs. Rhena
Schweitzer-Miller of Atlanta, Albert Schweitzer's daughter and heir,
was particularly helpful with the publication of these documents,
which reveal her father's goals and wishes. Schweitzer's nephew,
Professor Gustav Woytt of Strasbourg, also read the text for this book,
supplied information for the notes, and at the editor's request, provided German translations of the French and English texts for the
German edition. I am particularly grateful for this crucial assistance.

At the same time I am obligated to various individuals and institutions whose work was crucial to this book. The gathering of Albert Schweitzer's letters was begun in Gunsbach by Emmy Martin, who is Schweitzer's representative. She meticulously compiled his correspondence as a documentation of his project and was supported and advised by Schweitzer's friend, Robert Minder. Ali Silver, who spent two decades in Lambarene working closely with Schweitzer, is the successor and director of the Central Archive; through her intense activities she increased the collection, expanding it and giving it its present structure. Tony van Leer, at first Schweitzer's long-term assistant in Lambarene, likewise provided valuable long-term assistance with the tasks of the correspondence archive, dealing with the intricate problems and the constant sifting of the material. Hermann Baur, M.D., of Basel, chairman of the Commission for Schweitzer's Spiritual Work, in his helpful and friendly way accompanied the genesis of this volume for many years. For a number of years Ingeborg Abromeit of Tübingen transcribed the handwritten letters precisely and reliably. Lothar Stiehm, a publisher, an expert on Schweitzer's ideas and writings, and coeditor of the volume of his sermons (1974), prepared the publication of the letters with the thorough and painstaking care that is characteristic of all the books he publishes.

I would like to thank Natalie Chapman at Macmillan, New York, for her outstanding editorial work on and sympathetic handling of this book. I am also grateful to the American translator, Joachim Neugroschel, for taking over the difficult task of translating this book, with its wide variety of themes. He has succeeded in recognizing the nuances in Schweitzer's language and creativity and admirably translating his correspondence. While preparing this book, I received a great deal of advice, for which I am very grateful.

I am especially grateful to my father for taking me, a young boy, to a church performance of J. S. Bach's cantatas in the presence of Albert Schweitzer; that was my first impression of him, long before I started reading his works.

During the 1950s I managed, as a young scholar, to have several conversations with Schweitzer in Gunsbach; he also spent two days in Tübingen in 1959. This helped me to familiarize myself with certain problems and their context. This volume is a product of scholarly research, but it also expresses my personal gratitude to Albert Schweitzer for our encounter. Subsequently planned and developed on the basis of his correspondence, it is intended to contribute to a solid and subtle knowledge of Schweitzer's work.

HANS WALTER BÄHR

PART ONE

———∞———

1905 - 1912

~

To the Reverend Alfred Boegner, director of the Paris Mission Society,
Paris

Strasbourg, Thomasstaden 1
Sunday, 9 July 1905[1]

[f]

Dear Reverend and Colleague,

I am writing you today to inquire whether you might need someone
for [missionary work in] the Congo. I would be delighted to place
myself at your disposal.

Allow me to introduce myself and to describe my qualifications. I
have a doctorate in philosophy and a *license* [teaching degree] in
theology, I am the preacher at the Church of St. Nicholas, the supervisor of studies at the School of St. Thomas, and a lecturer at the
theological faculty. I am thirty years old.

My plan to become a missionary is no sudden whim. I used to
dream about it even in my childhood when I donated my pennies for
the little African children. After completing my studies of theology
and philosophy, I intended to devote myself to being a teacher and
to training pastors; but in the back of my mind I have always envisioned that I would not remain a lecturer and supervisor at the school
forever. I have held this position for two years now, and my contract
does not run out until 1910. I feel very happy, for it is a blessing to
train pastors, and my students like me. But from year to year my
desire to serve as a missionary keeps growing, virtually pulling me
away from my present activity. During my lectures I keep telling
myself: Others could perform this job just as well as you can. You
could easily be replaced here, but there is a shortage of people over
there! I cannot open the *Journal des Missions* without regretting that
I keep lingering here, even though I am determined to leave in several
years. Four months ago, after long and serious considerations, I re-

solved to finish my work here earlier, as soon as possible. Since I wanted to let my plan ripen, I waited four months before writing to you. Tonight I mulled over everything once again, combing the innermost recesses of my heart; my mind is made up, nothing can change it.

I realize that the General Union of Missions is seeking missionaries who have completed a thorough study of theology. Let them seek. I will make myself available to them only if you do not want me, for of all the mission associations, I love the Paris Mission best. During "mission lessons" in my childhood, my father, who is pastor at the Church of the Valley of the Vosges, told us about the reminiscences of Casalis.[2] The impact of those reminiscences has remained with me. I feel that in working with the brothers of the Paris Mission I would give it my all. And I likewise believe that despite everything, it is the duty of us Alsatian Protestants to be part of French Protestantism. Germany is rich enough in Protestantism.

I am completely independent. My parents[3] are still living: My father is a pastor in Gunsbach, near Munster in Upper Alsace. I have two sisters who have made good marriages, a third sister who lives with my parents, and a brother who is an engineering student. I believe I have already told you that I am thirty years old. I am in very good health, I have never been sick. I am a teetotaler. I have kept from marrying so that I may remain free for service in the Mission and avoid being forced to change my plan against my better judgment. If I can endure the climate, I will marry; until then, I would not like to bind a woman's lot to my own so that I may be completely free to serve our Lord.

If by any chance I failed to endure the climate or if I became an invalid as a result of the vicissitudes, I would not become a burden to the Mission Society, for I can always return to the pastorate in Alsace where I will be welcomed with open arms. Herr Curtius,[4] the chairman of our board of directors, is a very good friend of mine and attends my sermons regularly.

You may have seen my name recently in a newspaper or a journal, for a great deal has been written about my book on Bach,[5] which was published in February of this year. I neglected to tell you that I am also an artist, a close friend of Widor, who asked me to write this book for him. This work netted me a profit of seven hundred francs. I have held on to this money and put it aside; it will pay for my trip to the Congo so that the Mission Society, which already has so many expenses, may have a few less.

Please do not be alarmed by my activities in theological and philosophical scholarship or by my writing about music. Yes, I have experienced it all: scholarship, art, the joys of scholarship, the joys of art. I know the elation of success, and I felt true pride when I delivered my inaugural lecture at the age of twenty-seven. But all those things have failed to quench my thirst; I feel that this is not everything, that it is nothing. I have grown increasingly simpler, more and more childlike, and I have come to realize more and more clearly that the sole truth and the sole happiness consist in serving our Lord Jesus Christ wherever he needs us. I have mulled it over hundreds of times; I have meditated. Absorbed in my thoughts about Jesus, I have asked myself whether I could live without scholarship, without art, without the intellectual environment in which I now exist—and all my reflections have always ended with a joyous "Yes."

That is why I ask you to accept me. I am focusing on the Congo because I am particularly drawn to working there. But if you need me somewhere else, I am likewise at your disposal.

I have a secret hope that I will not remain alone, that one or another of my students will follow me sooner or later, and that the time will come when Alsace will again present its contingent of missionaries for the Paris Mission.[6]

I am writing you these lines with deep and joyful emotions, and I pray that our Lord may bless my decision and make me worthy to labor in all humility for the coming of His Kingdom.

∼

To the Reverend Alfred Boegner, director of the Paris Mission Society, Paris

[Paris, October 1905]

[*f*]

The Mission Society refuses to commit itself to me. It has available an Alsatian theologian who, it knows, will be completely at its disposal in a while.

After talking to the missionaries and breathing the air of the chapel, I know that our theological views are in marvelous harmony. And when you say that the French mission emerged from the Revival movement at the start of the nineteenth century, then I know what a revival is, for I feel that Jesus revived me when I was immersed in my scholarly research and He said to me, "Go where I need you." And I *will* follow Him.

~

To J. C. B. Mohr publishing company, Tübingen
                              (temporarily) Grimmialp
                              Spiez, Switzerland
                              [1905]

For the moment I could offer you a manuscript that has grown out
of my lectures: "From Lessing and Reimarus to Wrede. A History
of Research on the Life of Jesus."[1] It is made up of (1) a systematic
elaboration of the problem in accordance with the literature; (2) a
vivid summary of the literature, so that my book saves one the trouble
of reading the originals. To explain all this more clearly, I am enclosing
an outline of my contents. I was able to write this work because the
Strasbourg Library has a unique and complete collection of writings
on "the life of Jesus." You see, after [18]70, all publishers donated
their publications in order to replace the losses suffered by Strasbourg
when its library burned down. These resources have enabled me to
be exhaustive.

Nevertheless, my presentation is lively. Unimportant things are
simply mentioned in passing. Everything should be vivid; the book
as a whole is marbled with lively and sweeping ideas and planned in
such a way as to be a textbook for pastors and students but also of
interest to the general public.

~

To Anna Schäffer, teacher, Mulhouse
                              Strasbourg
                              Monday [October-November 1905]
                              [f]

Dear Mademoiselle,

I am up to my ears in work, but I am intent on giving you the
explanations that you have requested, for, as a good teacher, you have
the right to hear them.[1] However, I will keep them short.

I nursed this plan for years, along with a second plan that would
have led me to working in the Inner Mission. However, I opted for
my first plan. All of you knew only my critical spirit, but behind it
there was another, a quite simple spirit, known to only two or three
intimates who were aware of my plans. It is so simple. When a
lieutenant joins the army, he commits himself to going to battle, if

necessary, all the way to the border and, if need be, to distant colonies. And we, who follow our calling to join the host of the invisible Lord— we have to prick up our ears: he may be sending us to the borders in order to save people, to do good in His name. And we listen to Him so rarely. We all huddle in a group, we wear ourselves out in arguments and discussions, but fail to realize that the true life springs from simple actions and that the true religion consists in truly serving our Lord, no matter how we may construe the word "serve." I am leaving the seminary but remaining a lecturer and vicar, and earning money on the side by writing. I intend to study medicine and will complete my studies in five years! Then I will place myself at the disposal of the Congo Mission.

~

To Music Director Gustav von Lüpke, Kattowitz [Katowice]
Santa Margharita Ligure
Sunday afternoon, April [19]06

Dear Herr von Lüpke,

Three days ago I received *Der Kunstwart* [1906] and read your[1] article on my *J. S. Bach, le musicien-poète.*[2] Now I am taking advantage of a quiet Sunday afternoon by the blue sea to converse with you. I am very tired, and I ought to get back to my work for this semester and especially to the German version of my Bach book. Your lines have helped me to forget my weariness and given me courage, for aside from a very few intimate friends, almost no one else has so thoroughly grasped the basic concept of my book; I would like to talk to you for hours on end.

My book has already gone through two editions within six months, and our Paris Bach Society has been performing cantatas every two weeks—and already in German as well; however, this is still on a small and modest scale, for the thought of a "snobbish" Bach cult in France makes my hair stand on end. My friend Bret is traveling through Germany, familiarizing himself with the various interpretations. He is going to be a capable conductor of Bach. His mentor was César Franck.

Several weeks ago I told Breitkopf und Härtel I'd be willing to have my Bach book published in German and in English. However, I intend to rework it totally. The first two "nonautonomous" sections will be compressed, perhaps even reduced to two chapters; on the other hand, the chapters on aesthetics and the discussions of practical issues will be more detailed. I feel that this would be more appropriate.

If you have any comments or corrections, I would be delighted to hear them.

Once I regain my full energy, which I have lost by burning the midnight oil, I hope I can have the German version of the Bach appear by Christmas.

For me, art is Never-Never Land. I cannot always tarry there because I devote a great deal of work to the philosophy of religion. But when I sit at the organ, accompanying passions or cantatas at Sankt Wilhelm's[3] (during the past ten years, Professor Münch and I have jointly performed around one hundred Bach cantatas and also one of the two passions annually), I am all organist.

As an organist I went through the German, then the French school. You may be interested in my comparative study, "The Art of German and French Organ Building and Playing," which is in the current issue of [the journal] *Musik* and will be published separately by Breitkopf und Härtel.[4] My essay will probably raise a few hackles, for it states that our German organ building is on the decline. This is because the prices have been reduced so sharply that artistic work is no longer possible, and the unbridled increase in the wind pressure has led to thoroughly inartistic intonation. The sound of our organs may have become more intense, but at the price of a poorer and less beautiful tone.

I am also writing to *Der Kunstwart*, which would like a specialist to take a position on these matters. Let me send you an offprint as a friendly memento.

Meanwhile, my heartiest thanks to you for the tremendous good you have done me in my state of fatigue. I cannot tell you how much courage this gives me.

And if ever you happen to pass through Strasbourg, I would be delighted to have a good talk with you and play Bach for you on old, unrestored Silbermann organs.

My address: Dr. Albert Schweitzer, Thomasstaden 1/III.

~

To Gustav von Lüpke, Kattowitz [Katowice]
Strasbourg, Alsace
2 January 1907

Please don't forget that I am a preacher so that vacations are not rest periods for me.... And it is very difficult preaching with a tired mind. . . . I am worried about next Saturday morning; I have not written a single line as yet, but the sermon is prepared in my head: "Worry not!"

From the bottom of my heart,

Albert Schweitzer

~

To Gustav von Lüpke

Gunsbach, Upper Alsace
[1907]

[This letter about the Bach book was penned, as Schweitzer writes, "in my office at the parsonage in Gunsbach."]

On Saturday I concluded my lectures, then I put things in order. For three weeks I kept putting all my incoming mail in a huge envelope, and today I opened it. Naturally, you have top priority. You cannot imagine what a relief it is to know that you are checking the galleys [of my Bach book].[1] The passages to which you have raised stylistic objections have been revised.

I am eager to know how you feel about the phrasing and the crucial chapters: "Bach and Aesthetics," "Poetic and Pictorial Music," "Word and Sound in Bach."

But first come the instrumental works and *The Art of the Fugue*. I am utterly exhausted from the great strain that this book has caused me. But then again I am happy because I believe that my new efforts were not in vain. If I am capable of working another four weeks in order to complete the final chapters, the greater portion of which has been written, then the most difficult part will be behind me.

My very best to you! A pity that Tübingen is so far away; otherwise, you could come and spend a few days at the Gunsbach parsonage. In any case, the address is Gunsbach, Upper Alsace, District of Colmar.

Very gratefully yours,
Albert Schweitzer

~

To Music Director Gustav von Lüpke

Strasbourg, Thomasstaden 1

All Saints Day, 1 November 1907

Dear Herr von Lüpke,

Today I can actually relax a bit and take a holiday. I am using my free time to send you a sign of life.

First of all: "News." My mother and my sister are convalescing.[1] I am still somewhat peculiarly tired, yet I am looking forward to the winter. During the next few days, everything in my life will resume its orderly routine. On Sunday I am accompanying four Bach cantatas: *Schauet doch und sehet, Die Elenden sollen essen, Ein feste Burg*, and *Gott soll allein mein Herze haben.* The soloists are Walter[2] and the Philippi girl.[3] Orchestra and conductor, Professor Münch, and choir [are] first-rate. A true pleasure. On Tuesday I start lecturing[4] [at the Theological Faculty]. On November 27 I will be accompanying the *St. John Passion* in Paris at the new concert hall on rue de la Boëtie. A glorious organ (Cavaillé-Coll, designed by Widor). And the woodwinds there! Only the choir is not *à la hauteur* [equal to the task]. It is impossible to discipline these Parisian women. But glorious voices.

Despite the dazzling conditions, I have turned down two Bach organ recitals in Paris that an impresario offered me for late October: I must avoid wearing myself out. . . . And besides, I need time to think again, to concentrate. For eighteen months now I have been living purely for my work without being able to gather my thoughts. I have experienced nothing with my few friends, discussed nothing with them. I have been an anxiety-ridden drudge. . . . Now I want to "live," talk, dream, read again, devote a lot of thought to my sermons. . . .

Once my Bach comes out, I will tell you about my plans for the future. You will be somewhat astonished, for I am determined not to become a professor, and indeed I have informed my faculty about my decision.

Many thanks for your comments. In our rehearsals we have tested your idea about "Ach, wo ist" at the beginning of the second part of the *St. Matthew Passion*; the effect is tremendously natural. All in all, everything I have said about the *St. Matthew Passion* is based on the experiences I have gained by accompanying this opus eight times— four of these times I studied it thoroughly under the baton of Professor Münch. However, because of your observations I have expressed some things differently—in a mellower and more unequivocal fashion.

To Alfred Boegner, Paris

Strasbourg
Friday, 24 January 1908

[f]

Dear Mission Director and Friend,

I have received the paper for Mission Sunday. Three days earlier I asked my church for permission to devote two Sunday afternoon services to the Mission and to send the collections to the Paris Mission.

I am scheduling the second of these services for next Sunday, and I hope to gather a nice little sum. On Sunday night I am leaving for Paris to play the organ at the Bach Society recital next Wednesday. If the first rehearsal, on Monday, ends early enough, I will pay you a visit at 6:30, for I have to shake your hand and report to you about my medical studies. Things are progressing!

From the bottom of my heart,

Your very devoted
Albert Schweitzer

~

To Hans Pfitzner, Strasbourg

Strasbourg, Alsace
Thomasstaden 1 A
Saturday, 19 July 1908

Dear Herr Pfitzner,

I do not have the honor of being personally acquainted with you . . . I know you only from your works.[1] You may have possibly heard my name as the author of the most recent Bach book and also as a writer on problems of organ construction.

Professor Ehrismann[2] tells me that you are keenly interested in the organ at the Sängerhaus. I have been dealing with this subject for over a year now. It might be of some benefit to the matter if you and I could get together before Tuesday's decisive meeting. Professor Adler in Vienna, on behalf of the General Society for Musicology, has assigned me the task of preparing the discussions of the Subdivision for Organ Construction at next year's Haydn Congress in Vienna; he has also asked me to give the lecture. Now I would like the organ at Strasbourg's Sängerhaus to be the paragon of a concert hall organ with a beautiful tone, and I believe I could present my ideas to you more effectively in a private conversation than at the public session. At the same time I would like to give you the opportunity to glance through my piece on organ construction,[3] in which I have laid out my thoughts on the artistic organ. I am looking forward to getting together with you on this occasion.

Please let me know if you have a moment next Monday when I might speak to you. The best time for me would be between eleven and one or between five and seven, at your convenience. I would also like to show you a model organ that I set up in the suburb of Kronenburg; it will probably be put on the agenda of the discussion.

~

To the Reverend Louis Schweitzer and Adele Schweitzer, Schweitzer's parents in Gunsbach

> Barcelona
> Wednesday, 2:00 P.M.
> 22 October [19]08
>
> [f]

My dear parents,

The worst is behind us! That was last night's organ concert and the lecture preceding it. Quite frankly I was somewhat worried about this lecture since I am not used to giving long talks in French . . . and the hall is enormous: three thousand people. But to my amazement I discovered that I felt as much at home in French as I do in German, and that it was easier for me to speak loudly and clearly in French than in German! I stood there without a manuscript, and within three minutes I sensed that I had captured my audience more surely than I had ever done before. I spoke for fifty-five minutes, and next came an organ recital that lasted for one hour. I have never been so successful. When the program ended, they all remained in their seats: I had to go back to my organ and play for another half hour; the audience was sorry to leave . . . it was half-past midnight!

Here, the concerts are announced for 9:15, but at that time there's not a soul in the auditorium; toward 9:30 the first few people arrive, strolling about in the hall and the lobby, and toward ten o'clock, after three rings of a bell, the people deign to finally take their seats!

On Saturday, a grand concert with organ and orchestra is scheduled in the morning, and I have long rehearsals in the evening, for the organ is very difficult to play since the sound is always delayed. Luckily, I am well rested, and I am managing to overcome the difficulties. Absolutely *everyone* addresses me as *"cher maître"* [dear maestro]; the art critics settle down in the auditorium during rehearsals; my portrait is displayed in the music stores. It's such fun.

I am staying with Walter[1] at the premier hotel on the grand square with splendid palm trees. I have a view of the square and the entire city all the way to the big mountains forty minutes away from here; they are as high as the Hohnack.[2] I walk over to them every afternoon; [it takes me] a total of two hours.

The weather is the same as at home on a lovely June day. The men who were waiting for me at the railroad station roared with laugher when they saw Walter and me in overcoats.

As I am writing to you, the square below my window is filled with a terrible din. The king is arriving in an hour, and the troops are now taking up their positions. Tomorrow evening there will be a grand gala performance at the theater. I have been invited, but I am not going; I want to rest, for I feel too well to risk my excellent condition.

I will close now, otherwise the letter won't go off tonight. It has to be at the post office by four o'clock. There is no night train to France.

Please forward this letter to the Ehretsmanns and to the Woytts.
Hugs and kisses,

                              Albert

[in pencil:] The cuirassiers are just arriving. Papa would be charmed by the sight of their wonderful horses. Barcelona is gigantic, eight hundred thousand inhabitants. It is one of the most beautiful cities that one can see. [in ink:] If you write me, address the letters to

                    13 ALT DE SANT PERE
                    c/o Senor Millet.

A letter takes three days . . . so it's not possible. I'm leaving Sunday morning, and I'll be back in Strasbourg by midnight on Monday.

                              ~

To Schweitzer's parents in Gunsbach
                              Barcelona
                              Friday, 23 October 1908

                                             [f]

I have just been asked to participate in the gala concert that will be given on Monday evening in honor of the king and queen. I have accepted. I am to play a Handel concerto for organ and orchestra and the organ part in the Bach Magnificat. The tickets are horrendously expensive. Some of the boxes cost one thousand francs! The net receipts are earmarked for the Catalonian orphans. I am the only soloist in this concert.

I get no chance to write because so much time is wasted here; yesterday's rehearsal dragged on until 12:30 A.M.! Today from 2:00 to 6:00! No one ever hurries, and they all smoke constantly. No sooner have we rehearsed for ten minutes than the conductor sits down, rolls himself a cigarette, and smokes it, and the instrumentalists do likewise . . . and they don't continue rehearsing until the cigarette has been smoked. Paul[1] could see fiddlers galore here, each fiddling away with a cigarette in the corner of his mouth. At first I was annoyed at the waste of time, but now I am quite domesticated, and I smile.

The newspapers have reported very positively on my lecture and my recital. On Saturday evening the auditorium will be sold out. I live very sensibly. I have just taken a big two-hour stroll along the large ring street, which runs from the hotel to the mountains. No rehearsal tomorrow morning! I'll sleep, write . . . and take a walk.

If anyone had ever told me that someday I'd be sending Bach's music flowing into the ears of the king of Spain! I am mailing the program to *Der Bote vom Munsterthal* . . . if only because of Mademoiselle Immer.

Yesterday I was amazed to see that they don't take anything like the same security measure for the monarchs as in Germany. The crowd thronged around the king's carriage, so it could advance only at a walking pace. Freedom reigns here. They did not even clear the streets for the military parade. A woman with a donkey cart held up an entire regiment; it was too comical. We went to the harbor— immensely huge—to see the French squadron.

The city and the people generally make the best impression. Everything is clean, everyone works.

It is ten-thirty at night. I am writing to you by the open window . . . the large palm strees are swaying in the wind.

I embrace you with all my heart,

Albert

⁓

To the congregation and the new confirmees of St. Nicholas's Church, Strasbourg

Sunday, 4 April 1909

[In the sermon on Palm Sunday afternoon:]
St. Mark, 8:36: "For what shall it profit a man if he shall gain the whole world and lose his own soul?"

Our thoughts on this day are with the confirmees, a number of whom have accepted my invitation to join us for a brief devotional.

The beginning of the biblical verse that is meant to sum up our thoughts signifies something very different to them and to us. So much of what they are feeling today is echoed in the words, "gain the whole word." After all, this day is an event not just in their religious lives but also in their purely human existence. Life is opening up before them; it is as if they had discovered a door opening to the outside world and were gazing at everything that awaits them. They have a feeling of power, such as one possesses only in those years; they have confidence in their abilities, in the things they want to learn, in their work, their health; and however modest they may be, they are certain that they shall gain a piece of the world and a piece of happiness; and this confidence is aglow with dreams of personal progress and good ambition.

Deeply moved, I recall having this wonderful feeling myself, and I do not wish to dampen it with a single word. Let them feel it fully.

However, may their joie de vivre include the verse, "For what shall it profit a man if he shall gain the whole world and lose his own soul?"

You, however, are seeking hours of concentration at home and, with the pealing of the Sunday bells, here between these silent walls, so that your souls may speak to you and not be drowned out by the noise of daily life.

And persist in action. You cannot fathom what action is and what it means for your spiritual life.

So many people lapse into the misery of indifference because they have not been strengthened by action from the very outset. But you should not forget that from now on you must keep your eyes open in order to become active human beings in the Kingdom of God.

～

To Gustave Bret, Paris

[Strasbourg, 1909]

[*f*]

My dear Bret,

Tired as I am, I still have to drop you a line to express the amazement
I felt when I heard your choir sing the Mass [Kyrie and Gloria of
J. S. Bach's B-Minor Mass].[1] I am not talking about the nuances and
tempi that you chose: they are entirely consistent with my ideal; rather,
I am talking about the manner in which your choir carried out your
intentions. I have heard this mass at various times, performed by
famous choirs, but never have I had such a sublime sense of perfection.

I will never forget the "Et in terra pax" . . . If your choir goes on
in this way, it will soon become one of the premier choirs in Europe,
not because of the large number of performances but because of their
artistry.

You know that I am not yet Parisian enough to flatter you. What
I am telling you is the pure truth.

I wish you good health and good cheer in the further training of
your delightful choir. Is it clear that the final chorale of "Wachet auf"
must be sung *fff* [fortissimo] from start to finish? That is the correct
approach. You will receive the notes for the program. By when do
you need them?

My best wishes to you, your wife, and the Bach Society.

Albert Schweitzer

To Elizabeth Stern, Derendingen by Solothurn

Strasbourg, Thomasstaden 1 A

27 April 1909

I hope you have the opportunity to be very active, at least for the
present. Fräulein Kronmayer will, I believe, be sending you a sermon.
Please send it back to me soon.

I am somewhat rested. The new semester starts the day after tomorrow; how shall I get through it? Well, good night. Let me know
how you are, even if I cannot always respond.

To Fritz Härpfer, organ builder, Bolchen, Lorraine
Strasbourg, Thomasstaden 1 A
Monday, 5 July 1909[1]

Dear Herr Härpfer,

You looked so tired and so depressed on Saturday that I simply have to send you a friendly greeting for the coming week. There are moments in life when we think we cannot go on and everything appears gloomy, but eighty percent of this feeling is due to fatigue. So take heart. And take care of yourself. Avoid unnecessary excitement. You did not look as good as I would have liked.

I, too, experience such moments of despair; that is why I can sympathize with you. No shoptalk in this letter. Let it be merely some friendly lines. I will write to Dalstein[2] about the matters at hand.

Very sincerely yours,
Albert Schweitzer

To Luise Lenel, Kiel

[Strasbourg]
Sunday evening, 15 August 1909[1]

Dear Frau Lenel,

I meant to send you a wire, but it was such a busy day at the clinic that I have not managed to get away until now, toward evening. Several doctors were taking the day off in order to enjoy the beautiful Sunday, and so we "apprentices of my caliber" were needed. But I did think about you and everyone else all day long: I can see Mademoiselle Edith in a lovely white baptismal frock. I have the following godchildren: (1) my niece, Suzanne Ehretsmann, in Colmar; (2) Hans Münch, Münch's youngest son, in Strasbourg; (3) A. Herrenschmidt, the niece of Tata [Herrenschmidt]; (4) my nephew [Louis] Woytt. I did not plan or want to be a godfather ever again, but now I have become one anyhow. So please give Edith the list to which she has been added.

What moves me so deeply is that I know so well how this child will be raised. You and Walter give one a feeling of such pleasurable confidence that you are the kind of parents who are bringing their children up for the serious time to come, not as people who try to gain a place for themselves with the belligerent use of their elbows, but as people who gain substance from noble, ethical convictions. I feel this deeply in both of you.

What will become of my sponsorship? I fear that by the time Edith has grown up and reached the age when she and her godfather could achieve a fine human relationship, I will have finally succumbed to the fevers [in Africa], no matter how valiantly I may resist. But the present nevertheless makes it worthwhile being a godfather ... the thoughts I have about her future.

~

To J. C. B. Mohr publishing company, Tübingen
                              Strasbourg, Thomasstaden 1 A
                              5 April 1910

Dear Sir,

Some time ago you wrote to me inquiring whether I could fit the work on a new edition of my Reimarus to Wrede book into my schedule for the immediate future. Please forgive me for not responding right away. I was very tired and overworked.

I would be very glad to revise my book, taking note of writings that have come out during the past few years. By when would it have to be done?

Now for other matters. I am currently revising a work, which is completed in manuscript. It is a sequel to my history of the investigation of the life of Jesus and is written in the same manner.[1] It offers a history and summary of the studies on St. Paul, from Semler (eighteenth century) to Völter and the hypotheses of the Dutch. I would estimate its length to be fifteen sheets.

Would you like to publish this work? I am certain we could come to an agreement. The revision of the manuscript will be completed during the summer. It is very readable and lucid, like the others you have received from me.

~

To Edith Lenel, Schweitzer's godchild, and to Frau Luise Lenel
                              Gunsbach
                              Tuesday after Pentecost, 1910

Dear Edith,

I am laboring with medicine and am simultaneously immersed in my edition of Bach's organ works for an American publisher. On Friday,

Widor, who is collaborating with me on this project, is coming to Gunsbach from Paris so that we can settle the details. It has to be ready by noon on Monday since I must then leave for a rehearsal in Freiburg. Next, on Sunday, I will be going to Strasbourg to preach,[1] but I then have to return to Gunsbach immediately because the afternoon is set aside for working with Widor. This is what is known as Whitsuntide vacation.... Your friendly invitation has reminded me how overburdened my life is and how unsocial my life is during this period—so that I cannot even attend your birthday party.

~

To the Reverend Alfred Boegner, Mission Society, Paris
Thomasstaden
Saturday, 20 May 1911

[f]

I am placing myself at [your] disposal because I would like to serve Jesus in regard to the great tasks that are incumbent upon us ... to carry out our obligations to those who are far from Him and disinherited [in the colonies].

After reading the Mission newsletter, which has won me over to the cause, I am firmly convinced that I can work with you in the fellowship of the spirit.

I studied medicine in order to be as useful as possible to you all. My fellow students at the Strasbourg Medical Faculty were very kind to this theologian, who requested their hospitality for five years.

May I ask you, dear Monsieur Boegner, to convey the details of our plans to the committee, in accordance with the ideas that we have exchanged since our four-way conversation.

The main point is that I want to attach myself in some way to the work of the Paris Mission. You will show me where I can be of help. I, for my part, will turn to the world of my friends in music and writing and to my audiences in Strasbourg (St. Nicholas's) in order to try to obtain the funds for my equipment and my livelihood. If this is only partially possible, you will help me. However, I believe I will find a good portion of what I need.

~

To J. C. B. Mohr publishing company, Tübingen
At present Gunsbach
Munster Valley
26 August 1911

Dear Sir,

I can also tell you that my manuscript of *Die Geschichte der paulinischen Forschung*[1] is completed and will be available to you by September 1. This is the continuation of Reimarus to Wrede, only this time I have separated the history of research from my own presentation. My presentation will appear under the title *Die Mystik des Apostels Paulus*.[2] This work, too, a sequel to the first, is almost finished.

In regard to Reimarus to Wrede, I would like to know if you are planning a new and *completely updated* edition, for I would have to tackle this work fairly soon. I would make sure that the overall size of the book remains the same despite the additional material. We would then drop the title *Von Reimarus zu Wrede* and simply call the book *Geschichte der Leben-Jesu-Forschung* [The Quest of the Historical Jesus].

~

To the Reverend Karl Leyrer, Schirmeck, Lower Alsace
Gunsbach
Saturday, 26 August 1911

Dear Leyrer,

Here is the manuscript! My penmanship is poor at the beginning because last spring I fell on my arm in the hospital, injuring my elbow joint, so that it was terribly difficult for me to write. Thank you so much for being so obliging. I'm extremely anxious to hear your[1] verdict on whether the book is lucid, reads well, and so forth. I'll be here until the end of next week (Saturday). After that, in Strasbourg!

~

To Anna Schäffer, teacher, Mulhouse

Tarascon

18 November 1911

[f]

Dear Mademoiselle Schäffer,

I have a ten-minute stopover at the railroad station in Tarascon, a name that conjures up the evenings of my boyhood when I heard you reading *Tartarin de Tarascon* and you and my aunt laughed so hard that tears came to your eyes.[1] So I have no choice but to send you a souvenir. On the other hand, this place is not very amusing. It is raining, it is cold. I've been on the train all day . . . and [I'll be traveling] all night as well . . . but then . . .

Sunday, 5:00 A.M.

I had to quickly stuff the letter into my pocket. The train was pulling in. I have just woken up. The day is dawning over a grand and exotic landscape. We are still two hours from Barclona. I will spend ten days there for my farewell concerts. In Paris, where I played the day before yesterday, I had a talk with the colonial minister[2] in order to clear away any difficulties that may arise from my German citizenship [in regard to future activities in Africa]. He was charming, and everything is in order.

My very best wishes to everyone around you who asks after me.

⌒

To the Orféo Català Choir, Lluís Millet, Barcelona

Strasbourg

9 January 1912

[f]

My dear Catalan brethren,

How kind of you to write to me through your great leader![1] And how happy I am that the mass [J. S. Bach's B-Minor Mass] was so successful!

If you intend to perform the mass again, I will be entirely at your disposal, but please answer me as soon as you receive my letter and let me know if it is certain and on what date I have to be in Barcelona. I am needed in another place toward mid-March, and I would like to plan my schedule as soon as possible. Naturally, you have a much higher priority.

A crucial point: Please don't forget to write me whether you are doing the mass with C# or without C#. If it is the one with C#,[2] it will cost five hundred francs more since this requires a great deal of practicing on my part. The English Bach[3] is already packed up and will be going off to you in the next few days. Some other news that may interest you: I am not going to the Congo alone this summer; I am taking along a charming young girl as my wife and my medical assistant. Her name is Helene Bresslau,[4] and she is the daughter of the professor of history at the university. She worked with me on all my literary labors and has extensive medical knowledge from spending two years as a nurse in hospitals. We have been good friends for years.

That is all I have to offer in the way of news. Don't forget to write me soon about the dates.

And all my best wishes for the new year.

With my heartfelt wishes,

Your very, very tired friend, who loves you all very much and is greatly looking forward to seeing you again . . .

Albert Schweitzer

[In Barcelona] I will be staying at the small square with the palm trees.

~

To the director of the Paris Mission Society
Strasbourg
23 February 1912

[f]

Thank you for the good news. I am happy that it will be Lambarene. It fits in with my initial idea, but you know that I was willing to follow any advice given by these gentlemen. Tonight I finished drawing up the baggage list. My medical supplies are chiefly a gift from a professor of medicine at the University of Strasbourg.

~

To Dr. Heinrich von Recklinghausen, Strasbourg
Barcelona
14 March 1912
[postcard]

Dear Dr.,

Once again on the musical road. Many thanks for your kind and friendly lines. I'm sleeping a lot here! But ten hours like Goethe—no chance of that as yet.

Yes indeed, I'd like to stay here longer and study surgery, but this interim situation is becoming untenable. . . . I want to break off with everything at once, then learn a lot of necessary things on my vacation.

à vous de coeur [with all my heart]

My best regards to your mother,

Albert Schweitzer

PART TWO

———— ⌘ ————

1913 - 1918

~

To Jean Bianquis, director of the Paris Mission Society, Paris
Gunsbach, Upper Alsace
18 January 1913

[f]

Dear Monsieur and Friend,

No, please do not deprive me of the pleasure of writing you what is,
I grant you, a brief note, for I must share with you all the joy that
overcomes me now as my departure approaches. I can feel my health
returning! I no longer fear work as I did two months ago, my pulse
is back to normal, my mind clear.... It's an indescribable feeling.

Thank you for your friendly card. It's all set, we're leaving on
March 25. We are starting to pack. During my illness I lost the
addresses for sending my crates as freight to Le Havre and the luggage
to Bordeaux. Would you be so kind as to send me the addresses again
(written very legibly).

Thank you for *Daily Bread*, which you sent me with a lovely
dedication. I have been familiar with this little book since my adolescence. In Mulhouse, passages were read aloud every morning at
the home of my uncle, who raised me.

~

To Dr. Heinrich von Recklinghausen, Strasbourg
[Postcard written during Schweitzer's first voyage to Lambarene]
[April 1913]

This is our ship.[1] We are on the equator, and we are well despite the
heat. My best to your family and the Spiegelberg family. We are
learning a great deal on this trip. The African coast is beautiful. The
economic situation is dismal in many ways. We hope to be in Lam-

barene on the nineteenth. My wife sends her best. I'm homesick for
St. Nicholas's.

～

To Adele Woytt [Albert Schweitzer's sister], Oberhausbergen by
Strasbourg
                              [April 1913][1]
                              [After the arrival in Lambarene]
                                                          [*f*]

Dear Woytt,

Just a few heartfelt lines. You'll get the news from Helene's journal.[2]
You'll also be receiving a photograph of us. Show it to the circle[3] and
give everyone my best. Tell them all the news about us.

I'm really happy. I feel I've done the right thing in coming here,
for the misery is greater than anyone can describe.

First of all, there are all sorts of terrible abscesses. They are treated
with iodoform and other methods. Then there are all stages of leprosy.
This requires a very long, drawn-out treatment with chaulmoogra oil
or other remedies. I won't see the result for ten months. Leprosy is
very difficult to diagnose in its early stages, and yet this is very important, for treatment should commence before the abscesses develop.

I see a great deal of sleeping sickness. It is very painful for these
poor souls, and until I am fully set up, I must be satisfied with giving
them sedatives. And elephantiasis . . . that constantly increasing swell-
ing of the limbs. It is dreadful; eventually the legs are so thick that
the people can no longer drag them about.

Many heart cases; the people are suffocating. And then the joy
when the digitalin works! Evenings I go to bed dead-tired, but in
my heart I am profoundly happy that *I am serving at the outpost of
the Kingdom of God!*

At present it is especially tiring because we are still living in the
chaos of unpacking, and I often don't know where to look for the
medicine I need. I also still lack an interpreter and medical assistant.
He is due to arrive on the twenty-fifth.

Night is setting in. It is annoying: Night falls daily at 6:15; the
final rays of the sunlight are still coming at 6:00.

I kiss you all, including my historiographical brother-in-law.[4]
                              Albert

Lots of luck with history! My very best to Anna when you see her.

≈

To J. C. B. Mohr publishing company, Tübingen
Second letter
[Lambarene—April 1913][1]

Herewith the mailing list for copies of the galleys of the new edition of *Geschichte der Leben-Jesu-Forschung*, which you were kind enough to copy for me.[2] I am not certain of several addresses and am unable to find them in the chaos of unpacking. We can simply send them through the respective publishers.

I am very busy setting up my medicine hut, but once this is done, I have my evenings after 6:00 P.M. to myself because it is always dark at this time and nothing more can be done outdoors. Since everything comes by river, it is not difficult for me to obtain books.

The suffering among the Negroes is really immense. This afternoon a man came who had been bitten in the foot by a giant spider, and his limb was already completely swollen. Every third Negro has gangrene in his toes, so one is not useless here.

≈

To Anna Schäffer, teacher, Alsace
Lambarene
18 May 1913
[f]

Dear Mademoiselle Schäffer,

We have only one day left to take care of the mail. The river steamer is sailing back downstream tomorrow. That is why we'll be writing all night.

This letter is merely a sign of life to tell you that we have arrived safely and are now in the process of setting up, and that things are going well for us! Our house is located on the banks of a branch of the river (a branch as wide as the Rhine), and we can see two hundred kilometers of water and jungle. There is a mountain chain in the distance. The jungle starts ten meters behind the house, and the equator lies eighty kilometers from here! Believe me, it's hot. What misery for a doctor! Abscesses, leprosy, sleeping sickness with their dreadful pains. I am profoundly happy that I can help where there was no one else. And how grateful they are when their abscesses are bandaged! But mountains of bandage are needed! Beg wherever you can for old linen, no matter how tattered, and send it to Frau Professor Fischer[1] in Strasbourg, Thomasgasse 15; she will forward it to me here.

My wife asks you to also send Frau Fischer the patterns for the native clothing, which you told her about. She has things sewn for us. She is my plenipotentiary, managing all my affairs.

In haste. The pirogue is waiting to take the letters to the post office. The moon is rising over the river.

Best wishes to both of you. A thousand kind thoughts to your circle of acquaintances. Also to Theophil and Nast, when you write them, and to the Münches, to Maisch, Keller, and so forth.

I do not regret coming here. It feels good to help, to be at the outpost of the Kingdom of Heaven. If Aunt Sophie[2] had only suspected that her shiftless nephew would someday be serving the Mission!

From the bottom of my heart,

Albert

〜

To Suzanne Ehretsmann, Schweitzer's niece
Lambarene
Sunday, 18 May 1913

[f]

How overjoyed I was by your account![1] If you only knew how good it is to mentally reexperience everything that has happened. In reading your letter I felt as if I were walking to the Kanzrain [cliff and lookout point near Gunsbach]. Please go there a lot in my stead—I'm homesick for it! I can't write you a long letter because we are still busy setting up, and we get thirty patients a day! All the medicines have to be prepared here! Don't forget to go to the Kanzrain on Midsummer Day.

Here comes the thunderstorm. A storm every day—it's very exhausting. And each time we feel as if the palm-frond roof is about to fly away.

Don't forget to go to church every Sunday!

I kiss you.

Your
Albert

〜

To the Committee for Schweitzer's Work in Lambarene, Strasbourg
[with the notation: "To be circulated"][1]

Lambarene
16 June 1913

I am now in a position to judge which medications are the most important. They are quinine; sodium sulfur; chaulmoogra oil, which is effective when blended with olive oil (to treat leprosy); sulfur (for scabies); potassium iodide (for a number of skin diseases); all cardiotonics (since the number of people suffering from heart disease and pneumonia is shockingly high); anything required for the preparation of soothing and desiccant ointments; bromine (epilepsy) and arsenicals. During the past few days I have ordered *huge* quantities of these medications (suitably packed for the tropics) since I have run out of the ones I brought along, and I have had nothing for two months now. It always takes *three months or more* for an order to arrive here.

As long as the medicine barracks is incomplete, working here is an arduous task. I spend my days in an old chicken coop *without windows*. Its roof is riddled with holes so that I have to wear my pith helmet all the time, which is agonizing. Even the most minor operation in this space is extremely cumbersome, but the favorable outcome is worth the trouble. The people are very grateful for what we do for them. The misery is enormous.

It is strange how quickly the worst abscesses clear up after a somewhat sensible treatment. It is almost miraculous at times. Likewise, the outcome of most pneumonias is surprisingly positive if they are not complicated by malaria or sleeping sickness, which, alas, is often the case, especially among the loggers who are exposed to all infections and are paid in alcohol. All civilizing work is futile as long as liquor (and what liquor!) may be imported into the colonies.

I can think seriously about treating leprosy, sleeping sickness, and elephantiasis only when the barracks is finished. I have likewise avoided absolutely all hernia operations in the henhouse. But please tell everyone participating in the work how necessary it is and how grateful the people here are.

To the Reverend August Ernst and the Reverend Robert Will, Strasbourg

> Lambarene via Bordeaux
> Cape Lopez
> 16 June 1913

Mes chers,

Well, I'm fine. And when you[1] receive this letter, around July 14, it will be hot on Thomasstaden, but not as hot as here. And you'll be looking forward to going on vacation, but there's no vacation for me since I can see no possibility of stemming the torrent of patients coming from far away. So for two years I'll be working day after day, and then I'll take one long vacation in old Europe.

Frau Fischer can tell you a lot about the state of things here. I'm very glad to be here since the misery is enormous, indescribably enormous. This morning alone I saw eight cases of leprosy. Finally, I viewed a six-kilogram elephantiasis growth between the legs of a Negro. The poor man can no longer drag himself about.

Living far from the world is bizarre. Receiving no newspaper, nothing ... only the murmuring of the jungle and the surface of the gliding river. Each day passes very monotonously. At the end of the day you are amazed that you are still on your feet after all the misery you have seen.

So now greet the Circle,[2] and when you drink a good cool beer, toast my health. Cool beverages are lacking here. The water temperature is 28° [82° Fahrenheit].

> With the very best wishes from both of us to you and yours,
> A. Schweitzer

~

To the Paris Mission Society, Paris

> Lambarene
> 18 June 1913

> [*f*]

The two months I have spent by the river in the midst of our dear missionaries have been enough for me to make a final decision: I will continue to serve the work as long as God grants me life and health and also as long as the Evangelical Mission offers me its hospitality.

Essentially, you should know how devoted my wife and I are to the work, how happy we are that we can be a bit useful to the Mission on the Ogowe, and how harmonious we feel with all the people working along this river for the coming of the Kingdom of our Lord Jesus.

~

To the Orféo Català Choir, Lluís Millet, Barcelona
In a canoe on the Ogowe
23 July 1913

(My address: Lambarene.... Departure of the mail steamer on the 23rd of the month in Bordeaux)

[f]

My dear Catalan brethren,

Now you've retreated to a quiet corner in beautiful Catalonia to enjoy your vacation, and I am gliding along in a canoe (carved out of a single tree trunk) on the mighty river, which is framed by the jungle ... under a blazing sun. How marvelous this landscape is: water, jungle. Nothing, no one. My canoe, with the paddlers singing their ancient melodies, alone on the mighty river, lost in an unknown world. I spot a monkey perched on a huge liana. He sends you his best. Several hours ago I canoed past a half-dozen hippopotami. But you all probably want to know how things are going with the sister [Helene Schweitzer] and the brother of the Catalan musicians. The answer: dazzlingly. No fatigue, no fever. This is due to our very sensible way of life and the wonderful location of our house. It sits high up on a deforested hill, towering above the river. Almost no mosquitoes, and one of the most beautiful views in the world. I am now mentally improvising a counterpoint to the motifs of the paddlers.

I can tell you that we are happy. Our life is hard and monotonous. From seven in the morning until six in the evening we belong to the patients. I often have fifty or sixty cases a day, people who have traveled over a hundred kilometers by canoe. Oh, this misery.... It is indescribable.

And while I am bandaging the abscesses, my ears can still hear the Bach mass coming from you,[1] and I feel as if a few of the solemn words of this text were resounding in the midst of these wretched people, to whom good is being done in the name of Jesus: ... *Benedictus qui venit in nomine Domini* [Blessed is he who comes in the name of the Lord]. ...

The evenings belong to music (if I am not too tired). My pedal piano arrived in very good condition, and I am in the process of doing finger exercises and revising my entire repertoire ... and the accompaniment to the *St. Matthew Passion*. Yes, I am counting on it. No day passes without my dreaming of the moment when I can be with you again, rehearsing. And the sister of the Catalan brethren is also looking forward to it. Walter [the Berlin Bach singer] is quite prepared to sing in Catalan. He can do it if you send him his part in time.

I'll be sailing to Europe a year from April, that is, April 1915. Could you shift the performance to November? That would be the most convenient date for the soloists because they are overworked in February and quite exhausted. Aside from Walter, you ought to hire only Catalans. The paddler at the bow of the boat is shouting: Watch out, the *carlecarle* (snake)! We are traveling along the shore, and the trees offer us shade by stretching their branches out over the water. And snakes are lying on these branches. We mustn't bang our heads against them. You can see that life here is not without its charms. Your sister will be sorry that she hasn't accompanied me on this trip and that she therefore cannot send you her best wishes with mine.

～

To Madame Noël Christol, missionary
[Recuperating at the N'Gomo Mission Station]
                                        [Lambarene]
                                        25 August 1913
                                                            [f]

Dear Madame Christol,

I'd like to scold you for going to the trouble of writing us when you should be resting. We both know very well how much you have to do, and we know each other well enough not to require the rules of etiquette but to fully understand each other.[1]

Nonetheless, your letter was very valuable to us because it brought us a touch of affection and informed us that H. Champel[2] is sick. *If you see that he is not improving, do not stand on ceremony; send us a brief message*, and I will come straight down in a pirogue. We canot take these things lightly, given H. Champel's weakened health. My wife is putting away the things we have unpacked today. It is very late. We both send you our best wishes and ask you to give our regards to the Pélots and to H. Soubeyran, without forgetting Monsieur and Madame Faure.[3] Whenever I think of the name Soubeyran, I see myself going to La Belle Jardinière[4] to select my tropical clothing.

～

To Ida Luise Wernicke [in the Strasbourg parish]
Lambarene
6 October 1913

Things are still going well. No attack of fever as yet! Of course we have to live very carefully. By now you must have received my printed account, and you know something about our life. The things you've written to me about St. Nicholas's [the Strasbourg church] are lovely. Every Sunday morning I am not here but there, and I can see many dear faces in front of me.

The worst things here are the leprosy and the sleeping sickness. Last Thursday morning *all* my new patients had the latter disease. I observe all safety measures to avoid infecting myself, and I hope that a year from May [while visiting Europe] I will be safe and sound when I mount the pulpit of St. Nicholas again. I would be horrified at the thought that I might fail to carry out my plan and that these people would have no one to help them. My wife, too, is very happy.

Yesterday a trading post owner sent a motorboat for us so that we could dine with him forty kilometers from here. In the evening, as we were [heading] home, an angry bellowing suddenly erupted very close by, and two gigantic hippopotami surfaced forty meters ahead of us and, luckily, swam off without wreaking vengeance on us for disturbing them.

Say hello to all our mutual acquaintances. My wife sends her best regards. Our best wishes to you and yours.

Albert Schweitzer

~

From Schweitzer's circular letter to the Strasbourg supporters and friends of his work: *Bulletins* [printed in Strasbourg][1]

The patients start arriving at 7:00 A.M. and instantly receive a round piece of cardboard with the daily number, which determines the sequence in which they are seated and called in for examination. Joseph [native assistant] cleans the pharmacy and oversees the disinfecting, the washing and boiling of bandages and the other medical fabrics; at the same time he serves as an interpreter since he is a more skillful translator than N'zeng, who is fully occupied with keeping the journal anyway. My wife is in charge of the instruments, and she makes the preparations for surgery, acting as my assistant at these operations.

The wooden skeleton of the barracks has been up since mid-June. The river level went down. When I saw the sandbanks emerge, I was encouraged, but then came the news that there are no fronds left to cover the roof and no bamboo poles for rafters because the natives neglected everything else in order to chop down trees.

We had even more trouble with the medical supplies. To avoid wasting money I had refrained from taking along too many supplies. I first wanted to see what was really necessary here. After familiarizing myself with the situation and gaining an overview of the use of medications, I ordered more supplies by the June mail. But deliveries take three or four months.

However, as limited as our resources are, we do a lot with them. It is worth working here just to see the joy of the patients whose abscesses are finally cleaned and dressed and who don't have to keep running around in the dirt with sore feet!

After looking back at my first two and a half months of working here, I can only say that a physician is very, very necessary, that all the natives within a radius of 150 kilometers require his help, and that he can obtain disproportionately huge results with relatively meager resources.

I hope that these initial reports to my donors and friends will bolster their conviction that they are participating in a necessary and fruitful work and that we may convey at least a feeble echo of the gratitude of many of the poorest of the poor.

~

To Walter Lowrie, doctor of theology, American Church of St. Paul, Rome

> Lambarene
> 15 October 1913
> (Strasbourg address:
> Thomasstaden 15)

Dear Dr. Lowrie,

It is a great joy and honor to make the acquaintance of the translator of my favorite book among my juvenilia.[1] You cannot imagine how delighted I am that my views will now become known in America and England in the terse form in which they first appeared. May I thank you and Dr. Worcester from the bottom, the very bottom, of my heart.

Now I am here for two years, the only physician in an area four hundred kilometers long, wide, and deep, to battle against leprosy, sleeping sickness, and the other evils. I intend to alternate between two years here and one year in Europe.

The days are devoted to helping in the name of Jesus, to fighting for the Kingdom of God—actions that I call "practical eschatology." The long, silent equatorial evenings are devoted to scholarship and art, as much as the day's fatigue allows. I have my lovely pedal piano, and Bach's fugues pour out into the jungle, which runs by ten meters behind my house. Enclosed is a postcard showing the view from the window where I am writing to you.

Also, many thanks for your friendly invitation to Rome.[2] My wife is thoroughly delighted and is trying to figure out some way we could take the trip during a visit to Europe. I hope to meet you via Rome. But one more request. I would love to have a photo of you and one of Dr. Worcester. Could you send them to me with your respective names on them? For now, all I have is this small picture of the two of us, which I have clipped out of a magazine. Every three or four months I mail reports on my activities here to acquaintances. I shall take the liberty of sending them to you and Dr. Worcester as well.

My very best to you, and from my wife too.

~

To Dr. Fritz Haas (a senior government official) and Frau Haas, Strasbourg

> Lambarene (Ogowe—Gabon)
> via Bordeaux, Cape Lopez
> 13 December 1913

Dear Fritz, chère madame,

The Schweitzers were very touched by the letter from the Haases. It was like a lovely fragrance wafting to us from Strasbourg. And we were delighted that the *petit* Haas is cheerfully growing and will be attending the Latin School. Your mention of Langenbruch evoked childhood memories, and Maulbronn Monastery reminded me of wonderful days. We have just taken our first stroll in many days: We walked along a narrow path to a Negro village, twice crossing the path of dangerous army ants. I took our young puppy into my arms, and we hopped over those places. This is one of the most sinister things I have ever known. As we fall asleep in the evening, we often think: If only these creepy-crawlies don't sneak across our throats!

They can kill a chicken in two minutes. A person who can't move is doomed within minutes. I have also gotten to know more than enough hippopotami. During a nocturnal canoe trip to a sick white man, two gigantic fellows surfaced fifteen meters ahead of us in a canal that is barely forty meters wide, and for a long time they glared at us suspiciously, accompanying us *à distance*. To make matters worse, we were in a treacherous current in which sunken trees were tossing about.

There are patients galore. I am finally able to deal with sleeping sickness properly. Treating this and leprosy offers the best and most visible results, but we have to make enormous effort. Operations still have a terrible effect on me. These are generally cases of very complicated hernias.

Luckily, tomorrow is Sunday. I'll have a little time to write letters, for the departure of the mail is getting too close for comfort.

Please make my excuses to your mother for my failure to say goodbye to her in person. I was so awfully tired that I paid no farewell visits before shipping out to Africa.

〜

To Katharina Birgert-Matter, Gunsbach
                              Lambarene
                              24 January 1914

Dear Katharina Birgert-Matter,

Your donation for the poor, sick Negroes has given me much joy, and you have my deepest thanks. Recently I told the blacks that some of the money for the medical supplies comes from whites who have to work hard to earn it. They found this incredible, for they believe that whites are all rich and well off. However, they are grateful for everything that is done for them. If memory serves me, we attended the same school in Gunsbach. Is that correct? Best regards from my wife. And I send you my most grateful wishes. Ah, if only I could breathe some fresh air in Gunsbach. We suffocate here.

〜

To Gustav von Lüpke, Kattowitz [Katowice]

[Lambarene, before August 1914]
[postcard]

Dear Friend,

How are you? I haven't heard from you for such a long time. I was greatly interested to read about your performance of the *St. Matthew Passion* in the *IMG*.[1] In 1915–16 I will be spending a year in Germany, immersed in the second edition of my Bach, which I frequently work on here.[2] I also have to travel a lot for Bach and organ matters, and I hope to look you up if I am anywhere near Kattowitz. In Africa "near" can mean two hundred kilometers! I am working and practicing a great deal on my pedal piano and studying my entire Bach from beginning to end. Ah, it is wonderful to have the evenings all to yourself, no going out, no visits, no newspapers! You can work to your heart's content. My wife sends you her best.

~

To Robert Kaufmann, Zurich

[Lambarene]
5 August 1914

Dear Friend,

At this moment, as the mail is going off, we hear that there is a war in Europe. There is a possibility that our letters to our parents may not arrive if ever there is war between France and Germany. So please do us a favor [from neutral Switzerland]:[1] Write to my parents and my wife's in a closed letter and tell them that we are well and that our letters are en route.

Addresses: (1) Reverend Schweitzer, Gunsbach/Upper Alsace, near Colmar; (2) Herr and Frau Professor Bresslau, Strasbourg-Ruprechtsau, Alsace, Mengesstrasse 6.

Tell them that we are well and are awaiting precise news before deciding whether to return to Europe.

In haste,
Albert Schweitzer

~

To Robert Kaufmann, Zurich
                                    Lambarene
                                    28 December 1914

Many thanks for your lines of 6 October 1914, which I received on
Christmas Day! It is so kind of you to do us these favors![1] Enclosed
is a letter for my parents. I am writing in terrible haste; a steamer is
unexpectedly whistling on the river, and I am scribbling these lines
and sending them to the ship by canoe—I hope it can overtake it.
Health: satisfactory because of the great heat! Food: sufficient. Treatment: decent. We are enjoying our relative freedom of movement.[2]
Our letters are no longer opened. They've stopped harassing us. *Happy
New Year!*

⌒

To Romain Rolland
                                    [Lambarene, 1915]
                                                            [*f*]

Dear Friend,

You may know that I have been interned here. After being closely
guarded by black soldiers for three and a half months, my situation
has eased up. They have given me some freedom of movement and
allowed me to resume my medical practice. Health: fairly good. Food:
sufficient. But I can feel my two and a half years under the equator,
and so can my wife.

I am writing to you simply to tell you that from time to time I
read your writings. The [Swiss] newspapers reach all the way into
the solitude of the jungle, and your ideas are among the few comforting ones in these dismal times. Given what you know about me,
you must sense how often our minds meet. And I must tell you how
greatly I admire you for your courage in fighting against the vulgarity
to which the minds of the fanaticized masses have sunk in our time.[1]
Please do not respond to this little greeting from the jungle. You must
have a lot of writing to do. But if you should respond, then please
bear in mind that others may read the letter before it reaches me.
Good-bye. . . . For how long? And be courageous in waging the struggle in which I join you with all my heart, although in my present
condition I am unable to assist you.

From the bottom of my heart,
                                    Albert Schweitzer

~

To Dr. Paul Siebeck, J. C. B. Mohr publishing company, Tübingen
[Lambarene, August 1915]

Dear Dr. Siebeck,

Many thanks for your kind lines of June 9, which arrived surprisingly
quickly. I am glad that the business with the American has been
settled.[1] I had written him immediately that there must be some kind
of misunderstanding on his part. The translator is an extremely kind
man who has gone to a great deal of trouble, proving to be very
selfless.

Meanwhile, I am keeping up my spirits by working on a history
of philosophy (in my leisure hours). I have been sketching it for years,
and now it is taking shape; in fact, the first draft is complete except
for the final two chapters.[2] When will the time come when I can
submit it to you in small script on large sheets of paper?

For now, be well, you and all your near and dear. We send you
our heartfelt wishes.

~

To Schweitzer's family in Gunsbach
[Cape Lopez and Lambarene
November-December 1915]

Both of us still feel the effect of the sea air. I feel so fresh at my work
that I am amazed at myself and am starting to believe that the work
[cultural history] I have written under the equator will turn out well.
This is pineapple season—I wish I could send you a basketful! Our
life is very monotonous, but we are glad to be living very quietly.

We feel fresh. There's enough food, but the heat is becoming
dreadful. Don't worry about us; we can survive here for a long time
if necessary, and then we can have a rest at the parsonage. But if the
pastor is tired, he should not reserve the place for us, as beautiful as
our reunion at the parsonage would be. In these times we are learning
to do without a great many things. But I believe that now the pastor
should be with his congregation, and that is fine too.

~

To Robert Kaufmann, Zurich

                          Lambarene
                          26 May 1916

Dear Friend,

On May 25 I received your kind letters of March 28, April 6, and April 7, including the enclosures and newspapers. My deepest thanks for everything. When you write to me about music, I am extremely interested. And if anything interesting is published about music, please send it to me. At present I am reading Goldschmidt's *Musical Aesthetics of the Eighteenth Century*.[1] It is a miracle that one can still think rationally in this heat, but I am managing. At the moment I am busy tending patients who had to go to Cameroon as bearers and returned with the most serious kinds of dysentery and lung diseases. What misery! They rode by rail from Duala to Edea, and since they had never seen a train before, they call it "the steamer that travels by land." The misery caused by the African war is quite extreme.

We are still surviving, we have enough to eat, and we are trying to live one day at a time so that we do not have to think about too many sad things. Our best regards to your dear wife, and our thanks and best wishes to you.

                          Affectionately,
                          Albert Schweitzer

⁓

To Robert Kaufmann, Zurich

                          5 July 1916

                                              [*f*]

We are still surviving. . . . But you cannot imagine the physical fatigue one feels after almost three and a half years under the equator. Nearly all the people who came here at about the same time as we did have returned home, several of them seriously ill. We are still surviving. For now there is a lot of fish; this simplifies the food problem. Otherwise, our life goes by in a monotony that you can no more imagine than our fatigue under the equator. My philosphical work is advancing and so is my practicing of the Bach organ works down to the last detail.

Note:

Lambarene
July 1916[1]

This is the dry season. Evenings, we stroll on the large sandbanks in the riverbed, enjoying the puffs of fresh air that waft downstream. Nowadays the hospital is quieter than normal. I am using my leisure hours to record my impressions of the mission. I have been living at a Mission station for over three years now.

≈

To the director of the camp for interned civilians, Garaison, High Pyrenees
[As an interned Alsatian, Schweitzer and his wife were taken from Africa to Garaison in the south of France in 1917]
Garaison
24 December 1917[1]

[f]

Dear Monsieur,

I was deeply moved by your kindness concerning me, of which you informed me several days ago. May I please ask you to express my profound thanks to the responsible authorities. In the conversation in which you allowed me to participate after you told me about the new orders concerning me, I spoke to you about the increasing activities opening up for me ever since the prefect of the [department of the] High Pyrenees was good enough to authorize me to provide medical care to the countless sick people in the large internment camp. You agreed with me that some very useful work could be done here, and you understood when I told you I was wavering between the offer of freedom of movement outside of Garaison and the good things I could do inside the fence of the camp.

Today, I would like to tell you that I want to opt for my duty. At this time all French physicians, some of whom are close friends of mine, are devoting every last bit of their energy to the tremendous task they have to bear; I would therefore find it egotistical to do nothing when I see that I can accomplish something useful and assume a small share of the burden (my health permitting).

Acquainted as you are with the situation in Garaison, you have given complete approval to my decision, and this reassures me that I am acting properly. For four and a half years I have been doing

humanitarian and medical work in French Colonial Africa. The unexpected improvement in my health and my wife's—thanks to the
good air of Garaison—enables me to become somewhat active again.
I would like to use this opportunity to accomplish similar work in
France, where fate seems to have assigned me.

That is why, sir, I would like to ask you to notify the authorities
who have jurisdiction over me and to ask them if they would have
any objections to my carrying out the task that you and I are envi-
sioning.

Could you yourself perhaps reflect on how far my situation here
might be eased if I remain in Garaison in order to make myself useful
here in some way? I would be especially interested in being able to
take walks and correspond with my family[2] and friends without
having to limit the number of letters or being subjected to the harsh-
ness of the delays caused by the camp censors; I would also be interested in receiving packages from my suppliers and having access
to some of my deposited money in order to make purchases in the
area. . . . In a word: I would be interested in everything that you
consider useful and practicable.

Rest assured that you will never have cause to complain about any
abuse or any tactlessness on my part. In asking you to transmit my
deep thanks to the authorities and more effectively presenting my
case, I remain,

Sincerely yours,

~

To Adele Woytt, Oberhausbergen, Alsace
Camp for interned civilians
St. Rémy de Provence
Bouches du Rhône
[June 1918]

[f]

My dear sister,

Tell old Münch that no day passes without my thinking of him, that
I am truly looking forward to seeing him again, and that I am
marvelously maintaining my finger technique by practicing the organ
on a tabletop so that I will be fit for the performance of the cantatas
that we are going to play. If he could thoroughly study [J. S. Bach's]
Gottes Zeit[1] and include it in the program, I would be delighted.
Sometimes I get to play something on an old harmonium (when I
accompany the mass in the camp chapel, which has been set up in an

old monastery), and I see that I am advancing rather than regressing. I would never have dreamed that one could play the organ so well on a table.[2]

Is your husband still writing calendar stories? Please forward these lines or excerpts from them to the Ehretsmanns and to Paul. Our best to all of them.

Also give our regards to Curtius and tell him that good letters have arrived from Gerda and Olympia.[3]

~

To Robert Kaufmann, Zurich

Strasbourg, Thomasgasse 15
2 August 1918
[After Schweitzer's release from internment]

Dear Friend,

I am at such odds with my memory that I don't know whether or not I have already written to you and thanked you for your kind reception in Zurich.[1] So if I have already done so, as I believe I have, you can blame this second letter on my stupidity, which I hope is only temporary. We cannot tell you how moved we were to meet you and the others for the first time. Also, many thanks for your kind donations. Those moments will remain as a fantastic memory. At present, we have to deal with a lot of red tape regarding our papers. Everything is complicated because we were gone for such a long time, and we have to straighten out so many things, but we hope to have the most important things taken care of within a few days and can then visit my father for several weeks. After that I will probably become a doctor in uniform. In any case, you will get more news from us very soon. Our best to Strohl,[2] to whom I will also be writing, and to Mathieu.[3] Our best regards to Frau Kaufmann, and we hope we can get together for a long meeting in the not-too-distant future.

We both send you our grateful wishes.

Always your
Albert Schweitzer

~

To Alice Helmbold, Strasbourg

Gunsbach
27 August 1918

Dear Frau Helmbold,

For now, let me be brief;

(1) In regard to playing the organ, I have forgotten nothing; in fact, I learned a lot at the internment camp by practicing on the table for hours on end. I've studied numerous organ pieces in detail and can now perform them from memory. When I returned to my organ, I felt as if I had left it only yesterday.

(2) My residence is Strasbourg, Alsace, Thomasgasse 15; I will be there as of September 15 when I will be assuming a position as doctor at the clinic for skin diseases, from which I hope to draw great benefits for my new tropical practice.

(3) At the moment we are in Gunsbach.

(4) Our health has suffered from our exceptionally long stay in the tropics and our subsequent internment, but, I hope, not permanently. Currently we are still so tired that I find it strenuous just to write a letter, which is why I am limiting myself to short notes, although I would prefer to write lengthy accounts and ask lots of questions.

Yesterday, I walked along the road to Munster, thinking about that spring evening when we strolled with the two of you. Well, our very best to you and your husband. My wife asks for a bit of room to add a few words.

For our old friendship,
A. Schweitzer

Dear Frau Helmbold,

May I also express my congratulations and my warmest wishes to you and your husband! We are grateful to be at home again and are delighted at any news about old friends—despite the many sad things that we learn and with which we deeply sympathize—and we are especially delighted when the news is as good as this! Best of luck for the future! I hope that we will get to hear more eventually.

In friendly remembrance,
Helene Schweitzer

〜

To Dr. Ernst Kurth, Berne

Strasbourg, Thomasgasse 15
29 September 1918

Dear Dr. Kurth,

Back from French internment, I am reimmersing myself in Bach, at my splendid Silbermann organ in St. Thomas's. And at the same time your wonderful book has come out, lucidly articulating things of which I had only inklings.[1] I cannot tell you how much I admire your achievement. For now, I have greedily skimmed through your book: I have time because, after undergoing a (successful) operation on September 1, I still need lots of rest and am spending part of each day in bed. My first impression of your book is that you have plumbed the very depths of phenomena that consitute the essential and intrinsic nature of Bach's music and are also crucial to the nature of all music per se. You present the metaphysics of Bach's counterpoint in the broadest sense by unifyingly tracing these various phenomena back to great basic ideas and fathoming the essence of "sound movement" more deeply than anyone else has ever done. This metaphysics not only spells progress in understanding Bach's art, it is also bound to influence artistic creativity in our time. It strikes me that your book will exert all kinds of tremendous effects.

The confines of my own creativity are narrower: I am dealing with the problem of how to perform the works appropriately when so much nonsense about them is circulating. As soon as the war is over, I will have to get to work on the new edition of my Bach.[2] At present I have been drafted as a medic.[3] But I have time to practice and philosophize. My health suffered somewhat in the tropics and the prison camp, but not permanently, I hope. I do not have to tell you that I am looking forward to making your acquaintance and that I will do everything I can to bring our meeting about as soon as circumstances permit. We will then sit down on the organ bench together.

PART THREE

———— ∞ ————

1919 - 1922

~

To Robert Kaufmann, Zurich

Barcelona
21 October 1919

These days in Barcelona are my first refreshment in some time now, for I am amid artists with whom I have been friends for a long time and I have an audience that is extremely receptive to art. Otherwise, I can relax only when I am alone with my wife or several friends at my organ in St. Nicholas's or absorbed in my philosophical work. The future is completely obscure for me and full of health concerns and economic worries. But the main thing is for me to remain fresh in order to definitively complete the works that I have sketched out. I hope to visit your city in the not-too-distant future and see you for a few hours. I am especially looking forward to meeting your dear wife. Let us also spend an evening at an organ.

In Barcelona I have played two programs—only Bach, Mendelssohn, and César Franck.

So ... *auf Wiedersehen*. My very best to you both.

Albert Schweitzer

Best regards to my student when you see him.

~

To Herr and Frau Robert Kaufmann, Zurich

Strasbourg
7 December 1919

Dear Friends,

First I have to thaw out. Sometimes I really fear that a great deal in me is frozen. And when I was so happy with you, I had sad thoughts because my wife was not sharing my happiness. I had to give her a detailed description of everything. So thank you a thousand times; you have no idea what those hours in your home meant to me.

I am scheduled to return in January to give a lecture to theologians and one to the general public. We will then arrange an organ evening with a large group of guests. I am looking forward to it.

I have no lack of work. Often I write until late at night. At present I am working on the final volumes of the American edition of Bach's organ works. Unfortunately, I accepted a very bad contract. I'm not even earning ten centimes an hour. I hope to be done with this project in two months. My wife and my daughter[1] are well. They send their best regards. I saw my father and my sister Marguerite a few days ago. Both are fine and send you their best wishes.

> Your always grateful
> Albert Schweitzer

~

To Ford, a missionary, Libreville, Baraka

> Strasbourg, Nicolausstaden 5
> 12 February 1920

> [f]

Dear Mr. Ford,

Thank you for your long, dear letter of January 9. It is so kind of you to go to such trouble about my things. How happy I am that the manuscript [on the philosophy of civilization, written by Schweitzer in Africa] has been found.[1] Thank you for looking again. I would be even happier if I had my manuscript here, for I have to lecture on this topic next summer at the University of Uppsala, and I am burning the midnight oil trying to recreate my entire book. But perhaps this will make it better.

I fully agree with you: The manuscript titled "Sketch" could be mailed as a registered package, or two or three packages if it is too big for one. Please be kind enough to do this as soon as possible. Please also send me the rest: the typed manuscripts of the chorales, the sermons, and everything else.

Once again: Please mail me the manuscripts in a package as soon as you can. I will be infinitely grateful to you. You have probably handed the other things over to Morels. I am writing in haste; I have only just returned from Switzerland, after giving two lectures and playing the organ in Zurich. In two days I have to leave for Spain, for Barcelona, where I am giving an organ recital.

My thoughts seek you in Samkita, where you are now at the conference [of missionaries]. I am sorry to hear that, with such an exhausting life, you also have to worry about your health.

Please open all the manuscripts to make sure you are mailing me the ones that say "Sketch." Contrary to the title, these are the most advanced drafts of the book. Thank you for the portion that you have already sent me, which is the first chapter.

We often think about you all, and we hope that we will meet again someday. May God lead us, all of you and us, on the path that He has chosen for us.

Very sincerely,
Albert Schweitzer

My wife sends you a thousand best wishes.

～

For the readers of the Evangelical newspaper *Kirchenbote* for Alsace and Lorraine
[In the early postwar period]

Strasbourg
[1920][1]

From the old year to the new.

Genesis 32:26: "I will not let thee go, except thou bless me."

Luck and happiness mean, first of all, success. But whenever the human spirit thinks not only its own thoughts but also those of God's spirit, then it asks both less and more of the year: It wants the year to be not only lucky and happy but, more than anything, blessed.

Every year is given to us to bring us forward not only in the time of our lives but also spiritually. It leads us toward eternity and is meant to prepare us for eternity. But preparation means experiencing the vicissitudes and storms of life and growing spiritually through them. Understand this and reflect upon it.

Leave the bustle of the world and climb the still, high mountain. Call your purest thoughts, call Jesus, call God, and then come to terms with the year.

Your spirit is in quest of higher things, and whatever it makes of the year, that is what the year is for you. "All things work together for good to them that love God" [Romans 8:28]. May those words strengthen and comfort you and help you to enter the new land, as one tried but blessed, as one made spiritually happy.

～

To Prof. Dr. Gustav Adolf Anrich
                              Heidelberg
                              16 March 1920

Dear Herr Anrich,

First, my best wishes. I am spending twenty-four hours in H[eidelberg]
and have received your friendly card.[1] I am touched by your interest
in my future plans. However, nothing is so obscure to me at the
moment as these plans. All I know for sure is that I can make no
plans for now. You see, I am a man with debts. The funds for my
Congo enterprise were deposited in marks at a German bank in
Strasbourg. The outbreak of the war prevented me from paying the
firms in Paris that had supplied my equipment and boat tickets. The
Mission Society advanced me the money. Likewise, I had to borrow
francs in France during the war since I was cut off from my own
funds in Strasbourg. Now I owe over twenty thousand francs, and I
only have marks, which have no value because they are in a German
bank. . . . So I have to make money in order to pay off my debts.

To do so I am giving lectures and concerts in neutral countries.
Until I wipe out my debts, I have to remain in the country with
French currency, especially because whatever instruments and equipment I possess in the Congo are still sequestered. It is tragic that after
five years of my doing such work, the final results are a heavy burden
of debts, only because the actual cash, which would have been enough
to cover everything, has been devalued to one-sixth or one-seventh of
its former value. But since, contrary to all expectations, my health has
improved marvelously after my second operation, and I am becoming
quite robust again, I have the courage to take up this struggle for
money. The day will come when I will be free to make plans and
launch a new activity without being tied to any specific location.
Naturally, I have no idea how long I must wait.

I hope to find something in Sweden when I go there in May to
lecture under the aegis of the Olaus-Petri Foundation.[2] I will be talking
about the philosophy of religion ("The Ethical Problem in the Religions of the World, Philosophy, and Modern Civilization"). This is
a paper that I drafted in the stillness of the jungle.

My very best to Grafe and Frau Schumm. I hope that your mother
has settled in nicely. My very best wishes to your esteemed wife.
                              Always your devoted
                              Albert Schweitzer

In [St.] Nicholas [Church in Strasbourg], I sometimes think I ought to see you walking through the door. A lot has changed there.

~

To Cathedral Dean Pfannenstiel, Lund
                    c/o Archbishop Söderblom
                    Uppsala
                    13 May 1920

You must forgive me for having others write to you on my behalf, but I had to concentrate very hard in order to complete my lectures, which are now done.[1] My big problem was cutting my twenty-hour manuscript to seven hours. Meanwhile, you have received contradictory information about me, which no doubt has caused you trouble and worries—much to my regret. That is why I am writing to you in my very first free moment, to give you an idea of my situation.

I was slated to speak at the Mission festival in Lund on May 26. I still have to go to Stockholm and give a few lectures, some of which have been postponed to the week after Pentecost because of the memorial ceremonies. However, as I learned by telephone, the Mission festival will be ending on May 26, before I am to deliver my lecture. As a result, I prefer first to wind up everything in Stockholm and then go to Lund with a clear mind. Otherwise I would have to head right back to Stockholm on May 27.

So I shall be finished in Stockholm at the end of the week after Pentecost and will be going to Lund on Monday, May 31. The archbishop feels I ought to spend two days in Lund; that is, first give a lecture on my activities as a Mission doctor in the sleeping-sickness area of Equatorial Africa, and then play a recital the next day, repeating this recital in Malmö. What do you think?

If you prefer my lecturing on the *Sunday* evening after Pentecost (that is, Trinity Sunday, May 30), I could manage to do so. First, let's talk about the lecture. I am rehearsing my lectures with a good Swedish speaker, a theology student named [Elias] Söderstrom,[2] who instantly translates every sentence into Swedish. Practice is making it perfect. He accompanies me everywhere. I would prefer to give my lecture in a church, *gratis*, and I request permission to end with a modest collection for my work in Africa.

You see, because of the war and the collapse of the mark, my medical practice is burdened with debts, heavily burdened, and I am liable for these debts but do not have enough personal resources to cover them. All the funds for my enterprise were in marks, and during the war I was entirely cut off from my money since I was in a French colony and my money was in German Strasbourg. By the time I gained access to my money, the mark had fallen, and I have to pay in French francs. Hence my destitution.

The topic of the lecture: "Four and a Half Years as a Mission Doctor in the Sleeping-Sickness Area of Equatorial Africa."

[As for the lecture tour:] The archbishop[3] is encouraging me to do it and must bear the responsibility. So which would be more convenient for you, Trinity Sunday and Monday, or Monday after Trinity Sunday and Tuesday? And would you be kind enough to put in a good word for me in Malmö, where I will venture to do the same, and please tell me to whom I should address myself. Believe me, it is only the urgency of my work among the poor, abandoned people in the jungle that gives me the courage to trouble people with my affairs.

～

To the Chairman of the Conference of Protestant Missions in the Ogowe District

Strasbourg, Nikolausstaden 5
24 July 1920

[f]

I believe that in Sweden, Denmark, and Alsace I am certain to find the wherewithal to continue my work on a very modest level. Pastors at these northern churches, especially in Stockholm, Göteborg, and Copenhagen, have assured me that they and their congregations will not abandon me when I muster the courage to resume my work. Countless Alsatian pastors have given me the same promise. Jean Monnier regrets that I plan to give up teaching altogether, but in his deep feelings of friendship for me, he wishes to support me with his entire circle of friends.

Before taking any steps I want to ask all my friends in the Ogowe District whether you approve of my returning to the Ogowe, to Lambarene, and once more laying claim to the hospitality of the Mission in order to help it to the best of my ability. I believe that your memories of me are the same as my memories of you, that we are fraternally united in the task that we have to perform along the river.

For me it would, of course, be worthwhile in my new activity to utilize the experience I have gained on the Ogowe and to capitalize on the trust I have acquired among the natives.

My wife cannot accompany me this time. She has to remain in Europe with our delightful little daughter. Her health is not strong enough for her to spend long periods in Africa ever again. The lack of her precious help will inevitably restrict my work, but we have no choice.

In Sweden, by giving concerts and lectures, I needed only three weeks to earn the eighteen thousand francs that I owed the Paris Mission. I have now paid off all, or nearly all, my Congo debts.

Best regards to you and to all missionaries. Please give my best wishes to the catechists and to the teachers who remember me.

Your very devoted
Albert Schweitzer

~

To Robert Kaufmann, Zurich

Strasbourg, Nikolausstaden 5
1 October 1920

Dear Friend,

I'm tired because for ten weeks now I have concentrated intensely on completing the final draft of the first volume of my philosophy of civilization. The title of this first volume, which corresponds to my Uppsala lectures, is *Civilization and Ethics in Human Thought.* It will be done by Christmas.

From Zurich I am going to Lausanne, where I am to perform on an organ based on my designs (the church was built by Mademoiselle de Loys).

My wife is coming along to choose the stops and meet my Swiss friends. Is it really true that we are going to be your guests? ...

With a thousand heartfelt regards to you and yours,

Always your
Albert Schweitzer

Please hold on to the list of church fees. I have written to D. Surber, the administrator of church property, telling him that you and he may someday have to discuss something about me.

~

To Robert Kaufmann, Zurich

Strasbourg
21 October 1920

Dear Herr Kaufmann,

Well, it's all set. Here is the program as I envision it, together with
the layout. If it is inconsistent with Zurich conventions, then please
change it.

⌒

Fraumünster, Zurich
Sunday, 28 November
5:30 P.M.
Spiritual Concert
Organ: Herr Albert Schweitzer (Strasbourg)
Violin: Herr Willem De Boer (Zurich)
Program

1)	Prelude and Fugue in E Minor for Organ	J. S. Bach
2)	Choral Prelude on "Jesu meine Freude," for Organ	J. S. Bach
3)	Chaconne for Unaccompanied Violin	J. S. Bach
4)	Fantasia and Fugue in G Minor	J. S. Bach
5)	Adagio for Violin and Organ in E Major	Albert Becker
6)	Adagio in A-flat Major for Organ	Felix Mendelssohn-Bartholdy
7)	Theme and Variations for Violin and Organ in A Minor	Joseph Rheinberger
8)	Chorale in E Major for Organ	César Franck

Ticket prices, etc.

⌒

To Fräulein Reinacher, teacher at the Ill School in Strasbourg

                   Strasbourg, Nikolausstaden 5

                   3 February 1921

Dear Fräulein Reinacher,

I was very moved by the donation made by your schoolchildren. These contributions, gathered together sou by sou, are accompanied by so many thoughts that they are especially sacred. I thank you from the bottom of my heart, and please express my deep gratitude to the children. I will tell the sick Negro children about the helpful children at Strasbourg's Ill School. Here is a photograph of my little Negro boys.

                   With my best wishes,

                   Albert Schweitzer

Please send me your address so that I can put you on the mailing list for later publications, which I will send out from Africa from time to time.

~

To Axel Boberg, organist at St. Peter's Church, Malmö

                   Strasbourg, Alsace, Nicolausquai 5

                   At present, Barcelona

                   6 March 1921

Dear Honored Conductor,

Here I am in Spain, playing the organ at the Spanish premiere of J. S. Bach's *St. Matthew Passion*. The performance and the reception of the work are equally good. It is an honest-to-goodness musical festival for the people, the Protestant passion in this entirely Catholic country. A Walcker organ as big as the one at St. Peter's, but not as good. How often do I think of all the friendliness you showed me in Malmö!

                   Best wishes,

                   Your

                   A. Schweitzer

~

To Prof. Dr. Gustav Adolf Anrich

> Heidelberg, c/o Frau Prof. Fischer
> Erwin Rohde Strasse 9
> 6 May 1921

Dear Compatriot,

It has been months since you inquired so sympathetically about my future plans. At the time I was wandering in darkness, but now it is getting somewhat lighter, which is why I am now able to give you a brief report during my visit in this city.

My invitation to deliver guest lectures at Uppsala last summer pulled me out of my stagnation.

But then my situation promptly went to the other extreme. I had gone to Sweden as a desperate, half-sick man (my surgical scar was still festering), but I became healthy and enterprising there. I managed to repay my debts easily, earning twenty-five thousand francs within four weeks of performances; this encouraged me to continue my activity, so I returned from Sweden.

Since then I have been working on my philosophical book, *Philosophy of Civilization*; both its volumes, which were partially done in Africa, will be completed this summer. There is talk of my being offered a professorship in a neutral country, but I think I will remain true to fulfilling my idea of medical help among the natives.

The way my idea has been received in Sweden, Denmark, and Switzerland makes me hopeful that it will prevail. Thus, the University of Lausanne asked me to give two lectures on this project and the ways of implementing it, and my lectures were followed very attentively. I doubt very much whether I can continue my work in Gabon. Since I advocate maintaining the international character of the Mission and humanitarian enterprises, I will most likely prefer seeking a new sphere of activities in Cameroon, where the League of Nations guarantees something of an international atmosphere, or perhaps I will work with Dr. Wilhelm in China. But all this is quite indefinite. I may be in your neighborhood this fall. Best wishes to you and your fellow theologians.

~

To Prof. Dr. Arnold Meyer, Dean of the Faculty of Protestant Theology, University of Zurich

> Gunsbach
> 10 July 1921

Dear Honored Dean,

I am deeply honored and deeply moved by the invitation from the
members of Zurich's Faculty of Protestant Theology who are considering me for a chair that would be within my field of interest. There
is no place I would rather teach than Zurich, and it would be wonderful teaching among all of you who have treated me in such a
friendly fashion. I am homesick for teaching, and I also long for a
structured life. On the other hand, I know that I have to do my duty
and continue the struggle for humanity in the colonies, difficult as it
may be in these times and as hard as the accompanying insecurity
may be for my wife and myself. Since last summer I have been able
to assume that my health has been restored after my two operations,
and this fact is crucial to my decisions. God has given me back my
health, as far as can be judged, and to me this means that I ought to
stick to my plans despite all difficulties hampering them these days.

I am well aware that, along with teaching, I could pursue my
speaking and writing. However, the verse "In the beginning was the
deed" is especially true of the medical mission. The misery I have
seen in Africa forces me to devote my energy in every possible way
to sending out physicians.

Thus, with a heavy heart, yet knowing that I am following the
truth, I must adhere to my course across a precarious ocean no matter
how tempting the harbor may look. Please understand. For the third
time in my life I am renouncing the teaching profession. . . . It has
never been harder for me to do so.

But now, my dear friends, please accept my heartfelt thanks for
thinking of me and allowing me to regard myself as being one of
you in spirit—virtually a member of Zurich's Protestant Faculty *in
partibus infidelium.*

> Best wishes,
> Your devoted
> Albert Schweitzer

To Dr. Ernst Kurth, Berne

Gunsbach

19 September 1921

Dear Friend,

I am delighted that things are going better for you. Just be patient. . . . Here are the notes on me [for an article on Schweitzer as a musician]: I am from an old Alsatian family of pastors and organists. As a boy [I was given] excellent organ lessons by Eugen Münch, the organist at St. Steven's in Mulhouse, Upper Alsace, who died prematurely. At eighteen [I began studying] with Widor,[1] a teacher at the Paris Conservatory and an organist at St. Sulpice. At his prompting [I] wrote my work on Bach, which was published first in French, then German (1908), then English.

I spent a long time as organist of the Bach choir at St. Wilhelm's in Strasbourg, the Paris Bach Society, and the great Catalan musical society Orféo Català. [I have] performed Bach and César Franck in Germany, Switzerland, Denmark, France, and Spain. Campaigned aginst superficial virtuosity and for a spiritualized playing. Campaigned for a depth of playing and for bringing out the intrinsic architecture of Bach's organ works. In this way [I have] influenced the current generation of organists.

[I have] advocated my ideas by collaborating with Widor on an American edition of Bach's organ works (Schirmer, New York), in which we went through every piece, offering suggestions for the phrasing, the dynamics, the change of keyboards, and the registration.[2] [This project] has also come out in French and German. Unfortunately, since it was printed and published in America, it is now unaffordable in Europe because of the unfavorable exchange rates.

This winter I will give concerts in Switzerland, Denmark, Sweden, and England in order to earn the funds for keeping my hospital open in the jungle. In Africa [I did] not get out of practice because the Paris Bach Society gave me a pedal piano [i.e., a piano with organ pedals]—a piano specifically built for the tropics. It is kept in a zinc-lined crate, which protects it against tropical humidity, and whenever the piano is used, it is rolled out on rails.

My efforts toward reforming organ construction: from the factory organ back to the organ of quality and distinction, from the unnecessarily complicated organ to the simple one, from the shrieking organ to the sonorous organ. The ideal organ unites the merits of both the French and the German organ. In this respect I have been a pioneer. My paper, "The Art of German and French Organ Building and

Playing" (Breitkopf und Härtel, Leipzig, 1906). At the 1909 Vienna International Music Congress I was elected chairman of the section for organ construction, which produced the "International Regulations for Organ Construction" published in German, French, and Italian.

I have always been enthusiastic about the old sonorous organ at the cathedral of Berne. I play mostly Bach and César Franck.

~

To the Reverend Martin Werner, Krauchthal, Switzerland
c/o Dr. Karcher, Basel
Eulerstrasse 33
4 October 1921

Dear Colleague,

My deepest thanks for your very dear lines.[1] I am always touched when someone tells me that I have become his guide in understanding Christianity. At the moment I am on a concert and lecture tour of Switzerland . . . at the end of my tether. Next Thursday, October 6, at 8:00 P.M. in a French church, I am giving a talk in German on my hospital. Can we get together afterward? On the seventh I will be in Lucerne, and then I will be back in Berne on the ninth for an afternoon organ recital. Next, on the tenth, I am going on to Neuchâtel for concerts in the French part of Switzerland. Can we get together either on the sixth or the ninth? Hadorn knows my address, so does Paul Haupt (university bookstore, Falkenplatz),[2] and so does Gilgien (music shop). Sunday afternoon I'll be practicing the organ in the cathedral. Recital at 5:30. Too bad you didn't speak to me after my lecture. Would have loved to see you. Had heard about you and your work from faculty members. Looking forward to getting to know your work. Glad you're going into teaching. Several positions will be open in Switzerland in the near future. You may have learned that I myself was invited to the University of Zurich as a systematic theologian, but I have to remain true to my work. Count on me, only [I must have] the morning with Mohr, needless to say! So try to get together with me. Letter in telegram style. Am tired, have to write a lot today. Give lecture in Aarau.

Yours,
A.S.

[My piece on] Pauline mysticism is finished. Illness and philosophical work interfered. Will be guest lecturer at Oxford in February.

~

To Pastor Lauterburg, Saanen

Lund

8 December 1921

Dear Pastor, Dear Mrs. Lauterburg,

My life was dreadful for several weeks. There was an organizational error in my Swedish tour. The planned schedule could not be adhered to because of geographic distances. No sooner did I arrive in Stockholm than I had to change and reorganize everything. Nights of writing letters, days of phoning, telegraphing, and all the while lecturing or giving concerts daily and traveling those huge distances by train. I felt utterly drained. Now the worst is over, but I am still very tired. How can I thank you for everything you have been for me? I cannot put it into words,[1] but it shines and burns in my heart. . . .

The day before yesterday and also yesterday I gave two lectures on St. Paul's mysticism here at Lund, the second most important university in Sweden, and in the evening I gave an Advent organ concert at the huge cathedral. Tomorrow this concert is [being] repeated at St. Peter's Church in Malmö, and then [I will] promptly hop the night train to Stockholm, where I'll play a recital the next day.

Christmas will be dismal for me, far from my wife and child. I spend my days on a quiet farm in the middle of a forest. Staying in Sweden until January 25. Then off to Oxford until mid-March. My Oxford address is c/o M. J. Naish, 90 Southern Rd. Then three more weeks in Sweden and back to Alsace for an Easter rest. Oh, these train trips!

~

To Baron Lagerfelt and Greta Lagerfelt, Duseborg, Sweden

Malung [Central Sweden]

5 January 1922

Dear Friends,

It is touching—so many letters from you! I have reread them several times, deeply moved. I have no sense that I, a tired, wretched man, can mean anything to other people. . . . I am simply obeying the biblical verse: "Unto whomsoever much is given, of him shall be much required" [Luke 12:48]. I believe that God has assigned me the task of establishing a philosophical Weltanschauung that *reconciles thought and religion*—something that will contribute to human progress. The

Weltanschauung of the Kingdom of God. However, this philosophy has power only if I live it. And as if to test me, the war came and made everything a lot more difficult for me.... Now it is done with.... Sweden settled it for me in 1920. And both of you have given me a great deal more than you realized ...[1] Everything became clear for me at Nybyholm during those days of June 20–23.... And ever since, both of you have been part of my life. And someday you will receive the book about my new Weltanschauung, "The Philosophy of Reverence for Life." ...

Dear Minister Gabrielson[2] was so kind. He spent one and a half hours helping me write. You will not find out how late at night it is. Give Caramba [the Lagerfelts' dog] a *tape amicale* [friendly pat]. Best wishes from my profoundly grateful heart. You have no idea how much you and my days at Mogard meant for my physical and spiritual recovery (despite the work I did).

> *De coeur,*
> Albert Schweitzer

A simple man in Dalarna gave me a present, a beautiful fur cap, so that I might have one too! His old cap, but very beautiful.

~

To Anna Schäffer, teacher, Mulhouse
Sweden
25 March 1922

[f]

Dear Mademoiselle Anna,

You must be wondering what's become of me ever since I had soup at your home on that radiant autumn day. I have been traveling, and I have given *thirty-five concerts*. After Switzerland I toured Sweden, as of November 17; I spent Christmas at the home of friends in a forest. In late January I traveled from Stockholm, via Berlin, Brussels, and Ostende, to Oxford, where I spent five weeks giving my philosophy lectures at the university; next, I spoke at the University of Cambridge and at scholarly societies in London, lectured at the Quakers' theological seminary in Birmingham,[1] and gave recitals.

But it takes iron nerves to endure this kind of life. Luckily, I had a secretary in Sweden and England who helped me with my correspondence and accompanied me on my travels; I don't know how I could have managed without him.

This evening I am relaxing with friends who have an estate on the

Baltic Sea, near Nörrköping. So now I have time to write to you. However, the dinner bell is ringing. Please give my best regards to your sister, to Mademoiselle Maisch, and so forth, and to anyone who inquires about me.

≈

To Prof. Wilibald Gurlitt, University of Freiburg im Breisgau
Gunsbach, near Colmar, Alsace
8 April 1922

Honored Colleague,

My heartfelt thanks for your very kind lines. You have no idea how much it means to me that someone with greater technical and historical knowledge than I have is tackling the problems of organ construction and helping truth to win out. You have no idea how much I suffer during my concert tours. . . . Factory organs are ubiquitously replacing the organs built by master craftsmen. The Swedes are tearing down splendid old works and putting up new ones with razor sounds and many, many playing aids!

Since I am going to Africa in the fall, I have to complete my philosophical work this summer, so I will be traveling as little as possible. But I will be visiting Freiburg to see the organ.[1] I will let you know whether I am not too exhausted and too absorbed to speak within the framework of the seminar on "Ideal Organ Construction."

Too tired (I have *190* letters to answer) to write in detail. I hope I can also find money for you. If I can help you get free subscriptions to foreign magazines, please give me the names.

Lest I forget: The best organ maker in Belgium is Paul de Maleingreau, a highly talented composer and a young organ teacher at the Brussels Conservatory. (Address: Brussels-Uccle, 26 rue Henry van Zuylen.) He is free of any national prejudices. If you send him the specifications concerning the organ and invite him to view it should he be in the Frieburg area, then he is sure to be greateful to you. Tell him that I am behind it. Write him in German, by all means. You will see that he is an ally in problems of organ building.

Hoping to meet you soon,
Albert Schweitzer

≈

To Werner Reinhart, bursar of the Collegium Musicum, Winterthur
Traveling, 10 May 1922
c/o Dr. J. Karcher, Basel
Eulerstrasse 33

My deepest thanks for all the kindness you have shown me. On Sunday, May 27, I will be back in Winterthur, albeit only for a few hours. I have been haunted by the memory of the beautiful organ, even though I have since viewed the most beautiful instruments in England and Sweden. I am playing for the church fund. I hope I can manage to see you despite my rehearsals.

~

To the Reverend Dr. Oskar Pfister, Zurich
On the train
27 September 1922

Dear Friend,

Here is the manuscript, on the day promised! [The piece in question was "From My Childhood and Youth," the first draft of which was suggested by Pfister, who recorded his conversations with Schweitzer in shorthand.] [I] am not sick with astonishment at making the deadline.

However, what I am sending you is not a revision of your manuscript but something entirely different.[1] You see, when I began revising your text, three things that I had not previously considered became clear. First of all, the information I dictated to you is only partially suitable for children. My university days go beyond the scope of childhood. Secondly, such intimate things should really appear as something that I myself am telling. Thirdly, for children, a moral conclusion would be necessary.

And so, tired as I was, I spent a day and a night writing down my experiences until my confirmation and, after that, just a brief glimpse of my plan to become a medical missionary, plus a moral. Thus, these pages would be a marvelous introduction to the excerpts from my jungle book.

When I read the text aloud to my father, he greatly enjoyed it. I hope you are satisfied too.

We may have to change the title of this little book. Make some suggestions. *Send me the galleys of both my memoirs and the excerpts from the book!!* Without fail. And send me back the manuscript of my memoirs. I want to save it for my child.

Worn out—but happy! For now the problem of the memoirs of my adolescence is solved. I am only embarrassed that I didn't realize from the very outset that the treatment has to be both autobiographical and ethical! So it is my fault that you wasted your time writing about me.

PART FOUR

1923 - 1930

~

To Prof. Dr. Adolf von Harnack, Berlin

Permanent address, Königsfeld

22 September 1923

I was delighted by your friendly words. You will receive *Civilization and Ethics* any day now.[1] In this book I wrestle with the problems of an ethical view of the world. . . .

At the moment I am entirely a doctor. Without a single free day I am at the Strasbourg clinics all day long to learn a lot more about surgery. I am overjoyed that I have mastered the cataract operation. In late November, after a variety of delays, I will return to my patients. However, I am grief-stricken because my wife is ill, and I have to leave her behind in Königsfeld. But I hope that she will recover completely.

I often think of the chaos that prevails here now. Sometimes I have to pull myself violently out of my bleak brooding and get to work. You probably have the same experience. . . . The horrible thing about it is that usually only the most inappropriate economic measures are taken. Coercion is applied when only absolute freedom would help. That is tragic.

Writer's cramp forces me to keep my letter brief.

~

To Noël-Alex Gillespie, a student, London

[1923]

[*f*]

Dear Mr. Gillespie,

I am looking for a young man who can accompany me to Africa for six months as a companion, secretary, and, above all, English tutor.

We should leave at the end of January, spend a month traveling about in British Cameroon, and then move on to Lambarene. There you would help me set up the household and organize the hospital.[1]

Since you are very young and this trip might be of interest to you, I wonder if your teachers would have any objections to your interrupting your studies for six months. . . . Think about it, ask them, and write to me at Gunsbach, near Munster, Alsace, during the next week.

In haste,

> Your truly,
> Albert Schweitzer

Naturally I will pay for your entire trip.

～

To Werner Reinhart, Winterthur

> Permanent address:
> Gunsbach by Munster, Alsace
> 1 January 1924

Dear Herr Reinhart,

I was pleased to get your October letter from the Indian Ocean. By now you must have received the second volume of my philosophy of civilization (*Civilization and Ethics*), to which the first was merely a kind of introduction. If ever you have the time, please write me what you think of this elementary justification of idealism. I do hope that you feel a rapport with this philosophy of reverence for life.

Departure for Africa: late January or early February. An encouraging improvement in my wife's health. Address still Gunsbach. Everything is sure to be forwarded from here.

My meeting with C. F. Andrews was excellent! Now both volumes of my philosophy of civilization have come out in English, from Black, Soho Square, London.

～

To Mrs. Rieder, London,

> Permanent address:
> Gunsbach by Munster, Alsace
> 13 January 1924[1]

[f]

Dear Mrs. Rieder,

I thank your son [Noël-Alex Gillespie] for his delightful letter and the lovely photograph. I am comforted by the thought that he will soon be looking after me. . . . We will land in Duala. There, we will leave a good portion of our luggage at the Protestant mission. Then we will go to Victoria—and Buea (the seat of the resident of British Cameroon), and from there we will forge on into the interior in order to find an area that would be suitable for eventually establishing a second hospital. This will take us four or five weeks. . . . The simplest solution would be . . . to carry banknotes, keeping them in a small leather pouch around the neck, under the shirt. That is what I do. Can your son take photographs? I would be very grateful to him if he could bring along his camera!

~

To Archbishop Nathan Söderblom, Uppsala

> Dakar, Senegal
> 1 March 1924

I have just set foot again on African soil. It is mainly because of you that I can do so, which is why I feel impelled to write you a note of thanks. I am embarking on my new work, weary but confident.

It was very hard for me to say good bye to my wife and child at the Strasbourg terminal, but we made an effort to be courageous. So far my trip has gone smoothly.

A young English student from Oxford is accompanying me for several months as an assistant and secretary and also to teach me English. I suffer greatly from not knowing English, and I will now try to learn it.

It will take us three weeks to reach Duala because our ship, a Dutch freighter, will be stopping at nearly every port. I have chosen this means of transportation because I want to be all alone with my companion, with no other passengers, so that I may rest and work more effectively.

From Duala I will take a longer trip into the interior of British

Cameroon. There, in the abandoned territory of the Basel Mission Society, I would like to locate a site for a possible second hospital, assuming I eventually find the wherewithal and the physicians to do so. From Duala we will go on to Cape Lopez and Lambarene.

From far away I keep abreast of your activities and your travels as much as I can. I am glad that you are home again and able to rest. Take care of your health! Had I known you were spending some time in Nauheim,[1] I would have visited you for a couple of hours.

My wife is doing a lot better, but we cannot stop worrying about her as yet. Rhena is a dear, quiet child. They are living on the edge of the Black Forest. Here is the exact address: Frau Albert Schweitzer, Königsfeld, Baden, Germany.

My very best to your dear wife, all your children, the Quentzel family, Professor Kolmodin, Dean Stave, organist Ullmann, and all the others.

Many good wishes from your devoted
Albert Schweitzer

Every year on April 22 I think a lot about Uppsala. That was the day I arrived there, at your place, in 1920!

Give my best to Bishop Billing, Jr., when you see him.

~

To Otto Heuschele, Waiblingen

Albert Schweitzer
On board SS *Orestes*
En route to Equatorial Africa
1 March 1924

Dear Herr Heuschele,

During the hubbub of packing for my second trip to Lambarene, I received your kind note (through dear friends) about my philosophy of civilization. I feel an urge to tell you how happy you've made me.[1] I believe that some of the things I have tried to formulate are amorphous, and that a large number of us are experiencing what I have experienced myself: the search for a comprehensive and elementary ethics, an elementary philosophy per se. Now, I am returning to the jungle with years of notes—some of them well advanced—for the third volume. The book is to develop gradually during the quiet evenings. But first comes an intermezzo: the completion of *The Mysticism of Paul the Apostle*, four-fifths of which has been ready for publication since 1911.

I hope that when I return to the whites I will someday have the opportunity to make your acquaintance. It would be a great pleasure for me.

With best wishes, from the sea, by the Senegal estuary,

Albert Schweitzer

7 March 1924: We are just landing in Sierra Leone (Freetown), where I am mailing the letter. So far the trip has gone well, but the difficult part lies ahead.

~

To Pastor Hans Baur, Basel

Dakar, Senegal
2 March 1924

Dear Friend,

Trip smooth so far—which cannot always be taken for granted.

Now, after sleeping a lot, I am halfway back to normal. I am using my first stopover to send you[1] my best wishes from a corner of the earth that is hotter than Baden Terminal in Basel.

Pay all my bills that you receive, [using the] hospital account. I cannot always notify you far in advance. Send me a note on such paid bills so that I can keep track. Never send me any originals of the bills. Always hold on to them.

My fondest wishes, in haste, with my very best to you and yours,

Albert Schweitzer

~

To the Congregation of Kork by Kehl
[From a report concerning a possible restoration of the organ in the Protestant church of Kork, Baden.]

Prof. Dr. Albert Schweitzer
On board the *Orestes*
Accra, in the harbor
Gold Coast, Africa
19 March 1924

(1) The material condition of the organ is to some degree excellent, in both material and artistic terms. The former beauty of the tone of the organ is still discernible in its current state of neglect.

(2) Hence, the organ does not have to be rebuilt but simply care-

fully restored and its unique beauty preserved. This is the best and cheapest route, but the most difficult and most laborious for the organ builder.

(3) The first manual can remain as is, so far as the wind chests and pipes are concerned, but the wind chests and pipes have to be thoroughly repaired. Damaged parts have to be replaced. We would have to jettison a few registers that are unsalvageable. However, I hope they can all be restored.

(4) The mechanics cannot be retained. Ideally, the old mechanics should be replaced with a new, noiseless one, but this would be too expensive. That is why the pneumatic action of the slider chest has to be built out, as was done with outstanding success at, say, the Protestant church of Ruprechtsau near Strasbourg, by the Fritz Härpfer firm in Bolchen, Lorraine. This allows us to keep the old wind chest, which gives the organ its beautiful tone, and it is also the cheapest possibility. . . .

(7) The pipes that are necessary for the correct size of the pedal are to be remade on the model of the old pipes.

(8) I do not feel it is necessary to add a new reed stop to the pedal.

(9) A good coupler between the first keyboard and the pedal!

(10) An electric bellows (ventilator). Make sure the ventilator is positioned and inserted in such a way that no buzzing can be heard in the church.

I would recommend the following organ builders who know something about restoration:

(A) Fritz Härpfer in Bolchen, Lorraine, who so masterfully restored the 1740 Silbermann organ at St. Thomas's, Strasbourg, and is now considered one of the foremost authorities in this field.

(B) Steinmayer in Oettingen (if I am not mistaken). Herr Härpfer is quite willing to stop off in Kork while en route to Strasbourg, view the material of the organ, with no obligation on the part of the congregation, and give you a free estimate of what the restoration would cost. He is acquainted with the organ, for he already saw it once.

It is my pleasure to give the Kork congregation a gratis assessment of a restoration of its valuable old organ. With my best wishes for the success of this project,

Albert Schweitzer

~

To Pastor Hans Baur, Basel

Lambarene
Easter Monday 1924, evening

Dear Friend,

Finally reached Lambarene on the Saturday before Easter. The ship that brought me is to carry this letter back down the river. Hence, only possible to write in telegram style. Call Karchers about my arrival.

My hospital is partly on the ground, completely overgrown—a Sleeping Beauty mood. Roof over operating room, pharmacy, and examination room has almost fist-sized holes! Likewise roof of my house. This morning I valiantly began to work on the roofs. Saturday afternoon, two hours after my arrival, I was already in my boat, hunting for plaited leaves to repair the roofs. I laboriously managed to collect a hundred! The natives do nothing but chop down trees; the wood commands high prices. Nor can I find any boards. This afternoon, with four Negroes who cut a road for me through the underbrush, [I] crawled around in the woods, looking for a building site.

You can now somehow let it be known in the religious press that I am in Lambarene. A short but useful text, not too many details. How often I think about you and yours.

Much affection,
Albert Schweitzer

~

To Clement Chesterman, M.D., Yakusu, Belgian Congo

[Lambarene, April–May 1924][1]

[*f*]

Dear Colleague,

My departure from Europe was delayed by Mrs. Schweitzer's illness; she is staying on in Europe with our little daughter. I arrived alone in Lambarene on Saturday before Easter, and on a table I found your letter as well as everything else contained in the envelope. However, I could not thank you immediately because my home and my hospital were in a wretched state.

Allow me now to tell you how much joy your message has brought me. Your paper on the theme of the rich man and poor Lazarus is very lively. If you could send me two or three copies of the journal in which it appeared, I would be very pleased. I am happy that my little book [*On the Edge of the Primeval Forest*] has brought us together. It is comforting and helpful to know people who do the same work.

Now I would like to ask you for a big favor. Please send me very precise details on the treatment of leprosy with injections of gynocard and morrhual. I am very deeply interested in this topic. And [please send me] details on your treatment with tryparsamid. I am delighted to hear that you have had great success in this area.

My best wishes to you, Mrs. Chesterman, and your staff.

~

To H. Kuhl, engineer, and H. Osterloff, architect, Strasbourg
[Lambarene]
20 July 1924

Dear Gentlemen and Helpers,

Well, sirs, now things are getting serious. The barracks, which is the workshop, has to be shipped to Africa.[1] So how are we going to tackle this?

(1) First, the route. Simply transfer the shipment to Seegmüller and make available to him all the material from the bill of lading and the customs declaration. According to my inquiries the customs office at the port of discharge, Port-Gentil, will require the following items to be specified along with their exact weight: the wrought iron, the screws, the tools, the boards, and so forth. No duty has to be paid, . but the customs officials want to know everything for their statistics.

(2) Packing. The bundles of iron should not be heavier than what five or six moderately strong men can lift without too great a strain. Likewise the packages of wooden parts and the crates containing the small items, the screws and the rest. Several small crates, 70 × 50 × 50 [centimeters] in size, would be preferable to a single big one. And strong crates, solidly reinforced with large straps and squares. The oil for the paint in solid, not overly large tin drums, which are to be well packed in crates.

The small iron parts likewise in crates rather than bundles. No matter how solid the bundles are, an awful lot of stuff gets lost. So all iron parts less than half a meter long in crates rather than bundles, even though this may be far more expensive. You have no idea how brutally and carelessly things are treated on a ship. . . .

(7) New purchases to be shipped with the barracks: Please buy me

twenty more pieces of corrugated iron approximately one meter wide and three meters long. (This will be for a storeroom for provisions.) Likewise, twenty more angle bars about three centimeters wide for every surface and three meters long, with a hole every forty centimeters on every surface. They are to be used as posts for fencing in the chicken yard, so they don't have to be strong.

(8) Don't forget to include all necessary tools (for drilling, riveting, and so forth. . . .

Gratefully yours,
Albert Schweitzer

P.S. Send the bills to the Reverend Woytt, Oberhausbergen.

~

To the Reverend Martin Werner, university instructor, Krauchthal

All Saints' Day
1924, evening

Dear Friend,

When the river steamer brought me the second physician[1] and your book [*Das Weltanschauungsproblem bei Karl Barth und Albert Schweitzer* (The Problem of a World View in Karl Barth and Albert Schweitzer)], I hastily devoured it at night (instead of writing letters for the outgoing mail) and was thoroughly moved by it.

Today, since I was able to take off from work at two in the afternoon because the second doctor is with me (and I love celebrating All Saints' Day and Reformation Day), I reread the book calmly, reaffirming my initial impression even more strongly: You have written something that had to be written, and you have done a marvelous job of writing it. In purely technical terms, the structure is elementary and makes a powerful impact. It reveals an artistic creativity that your earlier style never hinted at. This is more than lucidity, this is a fascinating presentation. Now I am no longer worried about your career. I was worried that you were blocking your career because of your commitment to me, but now I have no more anxieties on that score. Anyone who can understand and present things so effectively is bound to make his mark. All he needs is to be patient and remain himself. This is a great load off my mind.

Thank you from the bottom of my heart for everything that you as a thinker are doing for my ideas. You have the makings and the talent of an original thinker, and you are sacrificing the impulse to express your own ideas in order to advance mine. . . . You are doing something that I cannot do. I must live my ideas here, in difficult conditions, and you have taken over the job of allowing the logic of my ideas to unfold. How can I ever thank you!

The rain is pattering on my foliage roof as I write to you; the noise is thoroughly deafening. And where you are, the autumn mists are swirling and the autumn crocuses are blossoming in the meadows. My heart is terribly homesick for autumn, for mountains, for fresh air. Here, the worst season is now heading this way. Constant sultriness.

Now that the second physician is here, I hope I can regularly spend my evenings working on St. Paul's mysticism. I am looking forward to it so much. And someday we will be together in Krauchthal, walking across meadows and fields. . . . It's like a dream.

You must have seen my wife in Basel. How glad I am for her that she could experience this herself. She has so little from me; a day such as the one in Basel is a comfort to her amid all the difficult sacrifices she makes in order to allow me to remain true to my calling.

My best regards to your dear wife. Remain healthy and creative. Thank you for everything. . . . Good-bye until we meet again in Krauchthal.

My best to you,
Albert Schweitzer

∼

To the Reverend Hans Baur, Basel
Lambarene
2 December 1924

Nothing left of the huge, lovely canoes that could be seen here ten years ago; the big trees from which they are made have all been chopped down and sold. The natives make do with wretched little canoes, which are capsized by the slightest wind on the river or the lake. As a result, so many patients can't even be brought to me.

Things have reached such a pass here that the Mission station sends out canoes in order to bring Christians from the surrounding area for the church feasts; otherwise, they would be unable to come.

Please be cautious and write sparingly about my plans; stick to things that have already occurred because plans that are told to many people no longer belong to a person. He is then bound by them. In Africa, however, we must constantly alter our plans completely or table them.

To Emmy Martin, Kork near Kehl
[Lambarene]
Monday, 9 February 1925

Great news: On January 28 the motorboat finally arrived in good condition.[1] The people who know boats praise it. 3.5 horsepower. Room for five people with about six hundred kilograms of baggage or twelve people without baggage. It has already proved to be of great use. It runs very economically, so this is a good acquisition. You people will also enjoy it when you're here. The motor is so simple that even I can use it quite reasonably.

These last few days [have been] quite bad. Many white patients. This morning, while I was writing, five motorboats arrived almost in unison. One brought a sick Dutch woman from Cape Lopez; she is remaining here. The American is leaving tomorrow morning by motorboat and boarding a ship in Port-Gentil. Since he still has to be bandaged, he is being accompanied by Nessmann, who is greatly looking forward to this trip. He'll probably be gone for a week. Fräulein Mathilde [Kottmann][2] is healthy but very tired.

If Fräulein Haussknecht can arrange to come for the autumn, then she should do so. If things go on like this, we eventually won't be able to get along without two female assistants. I can give Fräulein Haussknecht four thousand francs a year for her sister, but first she ought to try a vacation here, for we have to see whether she can take the climate. Under no circumstances should she give up her career now. Africa must first be tested. I would like to write her all these things myself, but I do not have the time or the strength. So please pass this on to her.

To Baron Lagerfelt and Greta Lagerfelt, Duseborg, Sweden
[Lambarene]
Palm Sunday, 1925

We've been doing a lot of work; last night, in flickering lamplight, while a storm was raging outside, howling through the palm trees, [we] performed an emergency operation on a man who was brought to us in the darkness with a broken leg and congested lungs. But today we wanted to have Palm Sunday for ourselves. We—the three doctors and Fräulein Mathilde [Kottmann]—went boating with several rowers to a silent lake with many islands. We ate lunch sitting on tree roots on the bank. Now the two doctors have taken off with Fräulein Mathilde to circumnavigate one of the islands,[1] and I am sitting alone on a tree root, celebrating Palm Sunday, peering through palms at the blue sky, with insects humming all around me. This lake is almost like the lake of Nybyholm but very lonesome. Once there were villages here; now nature has again become everything.

I am thinking of the procession into Jerusalem. In the trees, the birds are singing alien melodies. Huge ants are wandering over my body. Oh, how silent everything is, how overwhelmingly silent. That powerful and tragic hosannah, utterly unrestrained by human din, is penetrating this hush, from time into timelessness. For this is timelessness. There will never be any history here because this lake belongs exclusively to the sunshine, the trees, the insects, the birds, the clouds reflected in the water.

Now I will stop writing and will think Palm Sunday thoughts about both of you, you dear, true, pious friends.

~

To Monsieur Garnier, administrator in the lower Ogowe region
Lambarene-Andende
Wednesday, 5 May 1925

[f]

Dear Monsieur Garnier,

In your letter, no. 388, of April 30, you asked me to visit Monsieur Isaac's lumberyard in N'Zobié, north of Lake Azingo, because, according to information from Monsieur A. Guérin, who is running the lumberyard during Monsieur Isaac's absence, a dysentery epidemic is raging there.

I left here on Sunday morning, May 3, and arrived at the lumberyard on Monday afternoon, May 4.[1] The lumberyard, which was set up in 1923, is located on a thoroughly logged, airy height overlooking a river with torrential water. Inland, some ten minutes from the camp, there are several clear-water springs. The camp is surrounded by a huge banana plantation. The huts, made of bark, are well built, roomy, at adequate intervals from one another, and, like the entire camp, very clean.

When I arrived there were 107 workers at the camp—most of them belonging to the Bendjabi, Issogo, or Massanago tribes—plus twenty-eight women and two children. I examined every worker. They look fine and are well nourished. Their diet consists of bananas, rice, palm oil, as well as meat and fish, depending on how good the hunting and fishing are.

I found seven injuries, medium-large to small, which Monsieur Guérin is treating with permanganate and iodoform. Judging by the scars, I concluded that there had been a half-dozen more injuries that have healed well thanks to the treatment. One case of pneumonia and one case of malaria.

So, aside from the dysentery epidemic, the state of health is quite satisfactory for workers in a Gabon lumberyard. Monsieur Guérin assures me that no worker has died here from the time the lumberyard was established in 1923 until the outbreak of this dysentery epidemic. The latter broke out on April 15, approximately. Thirty-one workers fell ill; sixteen of them died by April 27. Since then there have been no further deaths. The women and children have been spared.

Of the fifteen convalescents, I saw five at a trading post in Azingo and ten at the lumberyard. They seem to be recovering well and are not particularly emaciated. Monsieur Guérin had treated them with bismuth nitrate and bismuth. Each patient receives three injections of emetin. Those who still have blood in their stool are being sent to my hospital. The rest are quarantined in a separate hut and, along with other treatments, will be given Stovarsol as soon as I can get this medicine to Monsieur Guérin.

For my part, I will notify all the people in charge of lumberyards—to the extent that I can reach them—that they ought to keep a supply of Stovarsol because this is currently the simplest remedy, with a high success rate in the battle against dysentery.

~

To Siegfried Ochs, director of the philharmonic choir, Berlin
Lambarene
18 September 1925[1]

Dear Friend,

I was overjoyed by your acknowledgment of my interpretation of the sinfonia in the Christmas Oratorio. As it gradually dawned on me, I was virtually intoxicated because the usual sentimental rendition of this music went completely against my grain. It happened while I was on the way home from a rehearsal of this Christmas Oratorio: Sitting at the organ, I suffered despairingly through all the conductor's antics in this piece. Then I thought of the strength and force of Rubens's angels, and suddenly I saw the heavens open and I heard angels powerfully concertizing with wonderfully forceful strokes and an overwhelming sonority, and amid this music, the shepherds devoutly tooting on their poor shawms, the angels interrupting them with jubilant fiddling and ultimately sweeping them along. And there I stood outside my house, in the wet snow, and white clouds covering the stars overhead. Ah, to experience something like that again, to be so enraptured once again, once again.

~

To the Reverend Hans Baur, Basel
                              Port-Gentil
                              12 October 1925

Dear Friend and Helper in Need,

This is only a meager little business letter. I can't muster the strength for even the most vital correspondence.

1. In view of the price rises that will come with the new Gallic [French] taxes, I have ordered another shipment of medical supplies; it will cost thousands of Gallic francs. This has the following advantage: The physicians replacing me during my sojourn in Europe will find the most important medical supplies here, and they will not have to place orders, for which they may lack the proper experience. For ordering, too, must be learned.

2. Likewise, in consideration of the coming price rises, I have purchased here in Port-Gentil all the corrugated iron and all the nails and screws I will need to complete my hospital buildings.

Here in Africa I can somewhat judge the conditions and am able to cope with them. Furthermore, rice, for which I paid twenty-three hundred francs a ton, has gone up ten percent, so I saved five hundred francs at one stroke. This watching and calculating in regard to decisions involving huge sums are quite a strain on me.

Recently I also bought large amounts of lumber—boards and hardwood beams—at good prices.

~

To C. F. Andrews, a friend of Mahatma Gandhi, England
[Lambarene, 1926]

[e]¹

Something of the spirit of Jesus is always to be found in any true work of love, whether or not this is expressed in words. For myself, I would venture to say that I went to Africa in order to undertake a hazardous and difficult task, designated by the spirit of Jesus. My credo can be found at the end of my book, *Geschichte der Leben-Jesu-Forschung*. It says: "He commands. And to those who obey Him, whether they are wise or unwise, He will reveal himself in all the peace, the activity, the struggling and suffering that they experience in His fellowship, and they will experience who He is as an ineffable mystery."

By living and working here, I feel I am someone who is designated by Jesus and wishes to serve Jesus. It was not easy for me to give up my lectures at the University of Strasbourg and my career as a musician. I am naturally gifted in both areas, and so I leaned toward accepting the cogent arguments of my friends when they said that everyone should use his talents. However, through the spirit of Jesus I became certain that a man can be called to a specific place and to no other. He could be released from this obedience only if he knew that someone else could perform his task better.

This is the great mystery. The spirit of Jesus commands, and we must obey. I believe that this is the fundamental idea in the teachings of the apostle Paul. Jesus is the master of our lives, our Lord. We do not teach theories about Him—that is not the decisive test; rather, we teach the kind of obedience with which we serve Him.

When we got together in England, we had so little time and I was so exhausted that we could not discuss certain issues as we would have liked to. But if it is God's will, we shall meet again. I will try to stay on here for a few more months, although the two years that I wanted to spend here this time have already waned. But I cannot leave before these buildings are finished and my hospital starts functioning in a completely orderly way. I send my profound respect to Mahatma Gandhi. I am deeply moved by everything he undertakes and by the thoughts he imparts to others. I would very much like to make his acquaintance. Will it ever be possible for me to see him and also the poet Rabindranath Tagore, whom I have wanted to meet for such a long time?

≈

To Elie Allégret, director of the Mission Society, Paris
Lambarene
12 February 1926

[*f*]

Dear Monsieur Allégret,

The plantation I wrote about in my last letter is truly necessary for
my hospital—more so than I myself believed. For weeks now I have
been unable to buy bananas. I feed my patients rice. Nor do we have
any sweet bananas. Currently, in addition to my carpenter, I have
two workers who know something about carpentry, and I am starting
to prepare houses for my patients in the plantation so that I can have
enough beds for all my dysentery patients. If the auxiliary carpenters
stay on, I hope to complete a group of houses during the dry season
and transfer most of the patients to the new hospital grounds.... I
have asked my friends in Alsace to find a young carpenter and send
him to me, for at this time I have to devote myself completely to this
construction work, even though I have more important things to do.
Monsieur Monnier will introduce the young man to you when he is
found.

Otherwise, I have nothing crucial to write about. You know about
the dismal situation on the Ogowe from the missionaries' letter, and
about the anxieties concerning Ovan! How are we to feed the missions? Because of the famine, almost no caravans are coming.

My assistants are fine. Dr. [Victor] Nessman will be leaving us to
do his military service. He was an excellent colleague, thoroughly
committed, loved by Europeans and natives. What made him particularly valuable was his organizational talent.

≈

To Prof. Wilibald Gurlitt, University of Freiburg im Breisgau
Lambarene
23 February 1926

Dear Colleague,

I was delighted by your letter of 20 December 1925 informing me
that a conference on the art of the German organ will take place in
Freiburg on April 8–10. I will participate in spirit from far away. It

was exactly twenty years ago that my piece on the art of the German and the French organ[1] appeared with the warning shout: Back to the true organ! This warning shout was so unexpected that it brought me nothing but derision. However, my Alemannic obstinacy stuck to its guns. It was very bizarre being the voice in the wilderness. I did not lose my faith in the victory of truth; I only believed that it would be much slower in coming.

At the 1909 Congress of the International Society of Music in Vienna, we formed a section for organ construction. There, I felt understood for the first time. We worked the nights through to complete the Regulations for Organ Construction. Originally, no regulations were planned. It was only in the course of our discussions that we got the idea of establishing a few guidelines.[2] How many of those who sat around the table, so enthusiastic about the noble cause, have since gone to where everything is the most perfect organ sound! Those were gripping days. Our discussions were excerpted in the large report issued by the International Society of Music. However, the spirit that imbued us during those days of Pentecost cannot be rendered by any account. We were together all day long and until deep into the night. We even had our meals together to avoid losing any time for our discussions.

I estimate that there were about twenty-five of us, chiefly organ builders and "organ inspectors" (as the phrase went in those days) from what was then Austria and from England. Something very new for that time was posited: Not only was the organ player to be the "inspector" of the completed organ, but the organ had to be designed, discussed, and built in terms of a constant ideal cooperation between player and builder. This notion was an achievement in those days. Today, it is starting to be taken for granted. Now, a younger generation has taken the matter in hand and carried it further. These younger people have experimented with pipes and wind pressure and wind chest and studied the old organs scientifically, whereas we had to protect those old organs from being burned. And we, the earliest pioneers, are delighted that the younger people have gone beyond us to achieve all these goals. Nor does it bother us that some of these younger people are no longer aware that we dug the ditch through which the waters are now foaming.

Anyone who deals with organs is transported beyond all that is human and all-too-human and purified to feel the sheer delight in truth, and he venerates organs and the sound of organs as the great spiritual educators that teach us to experience a conviction of eternity.

In these terms I send my very best wishes from the jungle to you and all those who are meeting with you. I do not have to tell you how deeply I regret that I cannot be among you. May you all be united in the grand attitude that belongs to this great cause.

Best regards from the jungle,
Albert Schweitzer

P.S. The Breitkopf und Härtel publishing house is reissuing my maiden effort about organ building. I am not revising it. A brief afterword will explain in which direction progress has since been made. This text consists of only a few lines, but I would appreciate your reading the proofs in case anything has to be corrected. I will instruct Breitkopf accordingly.

Once I have time, I plan to begin reworking the regulations for organ construction, adding the new findings. I probably won't return to Europe until the end of summer. I have to move my hospital to a different site, somewhat farther upstream, because our space here is too cramped. So as you can see, I am still "building away." Instead of struggling with organ makers, I am now arguing with Negro carpenters about doing what is most expedient.

〜

To Berthel Schleicher, Lenggries

Lambarene
7 April 1926

Dear Fräulein Schleicher,

When the books from Beck publishers arrived in Lambarene, I naturally pounced first on Tim Klein's *English Pirates*, and I am sure you won't take it amiss. I have not yet fully emerged from the mind of a fifteen-year-old boy. But to my credit I can say that as soon as I devoured that book, I immediately reached for the Malwida letters, reading them all night long (to the detriment of the work that I was supposed to do the next day). Now I would like to congratulate you for your very tactful work.[1] You have, I believe, selected things of universal value, things that show the noble woman in her true light, a cultural phenomenon of the past. Will such a life ever be possible again? It requires not only an intellectual personality but also the social and intellectual qualities of the period. . . . In any case, these letters do a great deal to make Malwida comprehensible to us. Naturally, I was most interested in the passages in which she talks about Wagner, Nietzsche, and Romain Rolland.

Neitzsche's character was and had to remain completely alien to her. She felt a lot of compassion, and he needed kindness.... That was what kept them together, but they never understood each other. How strange the things that bring people together.

~

To August Albers, C. H. Beck publishing company, Munich
Lambarene
7 May 1926

In the darkness of the swiftly falling night, I can make out the still very distant rumble of the motorboat that is bringing Dr. Lauterburg back from a sick lady. I was terrified because a tornado was approaching in the sky. How sweet the motor sounds from afar. The atmosphere is so sultry that people can barely stand up. We are drenched in sweat. Not a breath of air.... Now the motorboat is arriving. Dr. Lauterburg shouts because no one has brought a lantern to the landing dock to show them the entrance.

Just what are you talking about? A reunion outside of Munich? I can only picture it as follows: you in your green tie picking me up at the train station and the two of us promptly stranded with a mug of beer at the pub, and you drinking to my health.

Best regards to Herr Spengler.[1] I think of him often. I understand so much of what he writes, and I admire the breadth and genius of his creativity.

Our baby chimpanzee (eight months old) was teething, which made it sick. It lay apathetically in its box. Fräulein Emma [Haussknecht],[2] its nurse, summoned the three doctors to daily consultations. Now the baby is bright-eyed and learning to eat all by itself with a spoon. If it gets angry, it bites. That is the great danger with chimpanzees and gorillas. Can we wean him away from that? Apes are so hard to train because one should never hit them. They never forget or forgive anyone for hitting them—even their dearest master.

~

To the Reverend Hans Baur, Basel

[Lambarene]

10 June 1926

Dear Helper in Need,

So overworked that I can't even think of gathering all your kind and unanswered letters to make sure I have not forgotten any of your requests. I'll take care of that later. But how often I think of you, every day! After all, it is thanks to you that I can now build serenely and without having to fear the instant ruin of the hospital.

As a matter of principle, I never comment on anything that others have published about me in a newspaper without my knowledge, and I never discuss my plans publicly until they are fully clear in my mind. I am timid and cautious in regard to the public and have done well in that regard. No one should act contrary to his innermost nature, so whenever you act on my behalf in regard to these trivialities, do so in terms of my character; otherwise, I will feel like the Liszt-Tausig version of a Bach fugue.

⌣

To the lumber dealers in the Ogowe Region

Lambarene Hospital

14 August 1926

[*f*]

Acting on behalf of the Health Service of Gabon, may I please ask you to check all your employees and your native personnel to determine if any of them have a skin rash with blisters. The blisters are filled with a gray and yellowish substance and are accompanied by fever and general malaise. If you happen to find such cases, I must ask you to isolate them from the others, lodge them in more distant huts, and inform me. Please do not send me these patients for the time being. Leave them in your lumberyard and, as precisely as you can, describe their present condition to me. If necessary, the hospital doctor will visit you. Please reply to my request as soon as possible.

⌣

To the Reverend Martin Werner, Krauchthal, Switzerland
Lambarene
22 August 1926
Address all letters to Gunsbach

Dear Friend,

If it weren't for the thought of all the good that one can do, then this life in Africa would be unendurable.

Moving my hospital has caused months of delay for my trip home, but I hope I can still manage to get home this year. I completely neglected to let you know that I am familiar with the commentaries of Drews and Raschke that you dealt with in your lecture. So much for the interpretation of the absurd. It is troubling to realize that this is where Drews ends up, for otherwise he has a very capable philosophical mind. Now you're on vacation, catching your breath for new projects.

Don't lose heart. *Create with a calm mind*—that has always been my solace. That is the way to accomplish something of permanent value.

~

To Robert Minder

Lambarene
3 September 1926

Dear Minder,

Despite my shyness, I will not let you prevent me from congratulating you on your excellent *Agrégation*.[1] You probably won't be getting that many congratulatory letters from the jungle anyway. I was delighted chiefly because of your health, for the tension caused by cramming all that knowledge into the brain is quite awful. After my comprehensive examinations, I felt like the trough of a fountain where laundry has been done and which can now be drained.

No great demands are being made on my intellect. I drive in the piles for pile houses, clear the jungle, direct excavations, supervise the laying of floors, try to figure out the best locations for laundry rooms and toilets, hunt for a satisfactory place for rain runoff, pick up crates at the river steamer. I am delighted that Lichtenberger[2] has such fond memories of me. Give him my best.

My assistants here are splendid, capable people. Everything functions without the slightest discord. A marvelous harmony rules all our activities. This is something quite unique.

Please send me your address when you're in "Kranopel,"[3] as we say in Gunsbach. I hope the climate does you good!

You have no idea how fond I am of you and what hopes I pin on you. But mature slowly. The great danger for the *Normaliens*[4] is their precociousness—you understand me.

My best to you.

> Your old
> Albert Schweitzer

~

To Prof. Dr. Karl Straube, cantor at St. Thomas's Church, Leipzig
> Lambarene, Equatorial Africa
> 31 October 1926
> Permanent address:
> Gunsbach, Alsace

Dear Herr Doctor,

I have just written to Professor [Julius] Smend, asking him to thank the committee of the New Bach Society for granting me membership in this body. Since you as secretary were most likely not uninvolved in bestowing this honor on me, may I ask you to accept this personal word of thanks.

Space and time, both of which, despite Kant, are realities, prevent me from sharing the work of the committee. But from a distance I follow everything that is done for Bach, and I am delighted. My best wishes for all your musical plans this winter. I hope to get to Europe in the course of the winter.

~

To the Reverend Dr. Oskar Pfister, Zurich
> 19 December 1926

Dear Friend,

What are you to think of me for answering your dear letter of July 24 only now and so briefly, with only a few lines, instead of delving, as I would like to do, into the problems that are hovering between us [concerning Schweitzer's concept of reverence for life]. But I have strength for only a few wretched lines.

As the most universal expression of the ethical, the only things I can still posit (despite its vagueness and coldness) is reverence for life. Life, of course, is the most universal and yet the most immediately determined phenomenon. Oh, what confusion was caused by the poet when he sententiously said, "Life is not the supreme good." I can apply this aphorism to myself, but I cannot apply it to someone else's life, for his life is precisely the one thing through which I relate to him. I must regard his life as his supreme good.

~

To Louise Pearce, Division of Medical Education, Rockefeller Foundation, New York

[Lambarene, 1926]

Dear Colleague,

It will soon be four years since we met in Basel and you received me in such a friendly way. Meanwhile, I have done a great deal of work here. My hospital is rebuilt. And since there is no longer enough space for the constantly increasing number of patients, I am about to move my hospital to a large site three kilometers upstream. We will complete our move in roughly six weeks. There are now three doctors here and three nurses. Now we are able to work in a truly scientific manner.

We constantly have to deal with sleeping sickness. Among the 150 patients that we hospitalize every day, we generally have some eight to ten cases of sleeping sickness, if not more. Major sleeping-sickness centers are located not far from here, some 140 kilometers away, but they are separated from us by waterfalls. We hope that we can work there too. Because of the waterfalls, people cannot reach us easily, so we have to get to them. I am writing to ask you whether the Rockefeller Institute can help us out with tryparsamide since we are now in a position to perform spinal taps in all cases of sleeping sickness. We have already obtained some tryparsamide, and it has been very successful, but we lack the wherewithal to acquire as much as I need. That is why my colleagues are approaching Mrs. Pearce with this request. You are in America, and if you can support our request, then please do so. Our work here was made difficult for a year because of famine and large-scale dysentery epidemics, as well as beriberi due to the natives' eating rice imported from Europe. Now things are better. I myself feel relatively fresh despite the long and difficult work here.

~

To C. E. B. [Lilian Marion] Russell
Lambarene
7 January 1927

[f]

Dear Mrs. Russell,

We were overjoyed by the news of your impending arrival! We all thank you![1] No need to bring along a collapsible house! By the time you arrive, our buildings will be completed, and you will have a lovely room for yourself. If you set sail on March 1, your fellow passenger on the *Asie* will be Dr. Mündler from the French part of Switzerland; he is coming to our hospital. That will be very nice.

In Port-Gentil you will find a representative of IHIM,[2] H. Halley, the agent of Chargeurs Réunis [United Shippers], who will be at your disposal for the landing and the customs process. If you need more help, please ask the director of SHO.[3] All these people have been notified. Please write down their names.

As for money, take along five thousand francs (that is the most that can be taken out of France). Beyond that, you would do best to deposit a certain amount in pounds sterling or Swiss francs (not French francs) with the hospital treasurer in Basel, Switzerland, the Reverend Hans Baur, Leonhardgraben 63. Then, in Lambarene, you can withdraw as much as you like in French francs through a commercial firm in Paris, and this firm will be promptly repaid in Paris by H. Baur. H. Baur has been informed. But you will need money only for the return trip. In Lambarene itself you will not spend a penny, given our simple life-style. Have the money that you are depositing with Reverend Baur transferred from *England* and not France, for any export of money from France is extremely difficult.

Now everything has been said. We are looking forward to your arrival. Our heartfelt thanks for coming to help us.

～

To Siegfried Ochs, director of the philharmonic choir, Berlin
Lambarene
10 February 1927

Dear Friend,

The hospital was moved on January 21.[1] What a hubbub! My two colleagues loaded the things and the people at the old hospital, and I received them at the new hospital [located several kilometers farther upstream].

And how overjoyed the people were when each one was allowed to pick out his own plank bed! And how quickly the fires started burning. During the transfer a white lady showed up to have her baby. She, too, was given a bed on the spot! So the move worked. In the evening I collapsed on my bed, blissfully tired. I do little if any writing. It is too tiring after my work in the awful sun and all the irritations of overseeing several groups of workers. My only relaxation is practicing on the organ. I do this passionately in every free moment. A whole series of preludes and fugues have been thoroughly reworked and are now more profound and better crafted. At times I think: What will it be like when you perform this on a good organ for Siegfried Ochs!

Oh, what you wrote about [Heinrich] Schütz is so true. His was a tremendous mind. What a creative force—and what a treatment of the vocal line. The Bruckner mass is no child's play even if you have the score on your stand. When I was a child, no aunt ever gave me any promise that she did not keep. I made sure of that. And I will likewise always keep my word with you.

At present I am building the large residence and the barracks for the cook, the boys, the washer, the water carrier, the gardener, and other domestics. Today, in the blazing sun, I again drove in piles for these pile dwellings, and I also supervised the digging of a well. [I] felt every clod that was turned over to see if it had a trace of dampness . . . still in vain. This is what the patriarchs went through in Canaan. I have no idea when I'll be coming home. All at once you'll say: Look who's here!

And now, good night. My best to your dear wife, to your sons. Perform beautiful things, keep the choir well disciplined, and remain as young and fresh in the Berlin cold as I in the Lambarene heat.

~

To the Reverend Martin Werner, Krauchthal, Switzerland, and the Reverend Julius Kaiser, Lucerne

Lambarene
20 February 1927

Dear Friends,

On a quiet Sunday evening (there are so few in Africa) I have again taken up your catechism, enjoying myself "as an expert" (if I may say so) and immersing myself in it critically. And now, before my eyes close, I would like to tell you both how delighted I am. Your project is up to date and courageous.[1] It has one big failing: You allowed that Albert Schweitzer (b. 1875) to talk, and to talk so much even though many things could have been expressed far better by the reformers. But, dear friends, that is something you have to settle between yourselves. Albert Schweitzer, as I know him, is completely disheartened and humbled about appearing as a guide for the young people who are to be led to God. May it turn out for the best and enjoy God's blessing. And now for my joy at the overall liveliness and structure! Creative delight and enthusiasm are behind it all! I object to one thing: the use of catchword summaries, as early as on page 14. This is lackluster for a child. I would much rather see a terse, lively expansion of the summaries. These sections interfere with the overall liveliness. Think [it] over for a new edition! Also: I would absolutely increase the number of biblical quotations so that they predominate. Your text is modern in the best sense of the word, but then you absolutely must have the biblical counterweight. Also, the biblical verses have to be in normal print and the nonbiblical pronouncements in small print, to maintain a purely visual distinction. This will not make your book any longer. You can easily print your nonbiblical quotations even smaller. After all, the readers are children, and their eyes can manage anything. The numbers you indicate [are] very good. I would rework pages 25 and 26 into a single text. I believe that this would make your ideas more effective. On page 28 I would add some statement or other from the Avesta about the spiritual meaning of the labor that transforms the wilderness into fertile land. You can see how closely I have been perusing your book. Might we someday sit down together and talk about it? How wonderful that would be.

~

To Kanzo Uchimura, Tokyo

Lambarene
3 March 1927
[printed on 5 June 1927 in *The Japanese Christian Intelligencer*]

Dear Mr. Uchimura,

Frau Martin, who manages my affairs in Europe,[1] has informed me about the huge donation that the men and women of your Bible house have made to my hospital at your behest. Please tell all of them how deeply moved I am. The hospital is now so big that I am quite concerned about maintaining it. How good it makes us feel to hear that people far, far away are so dearly and sympathetically helping us to carry this burden. I have no idea how I can thank all of you. On January 21, we moved into the new hospital, three kilometers upstream from the earlier one. The latter was too small from the very outset, but I did not dare build a new one. I was terrified of the great expense and the labor. Ultimately, however, I had no choice, for I was unable to isolate the contagious patients adequately from the others or properly lodge the mentally ill.

Within one year I have built an entire village of Quonset barracks on piles. There is enough room for 250 patients and the people accompanying them! The normal number is 150 patients, but at times many people come simultaneously or an epidemic breaks out!

How happy the patients now are because they can sleep under a rain-proof roof. Unfortunately, the hospital is still incomplete. I have been back on the equator for three years now, and it will be quite a while before I can return to my wife and child in Europe. Luckily, my health is good despite my constant fatigue. Once again my undying gratitude! The doctors and the nurses also send you their very best wishes.

~

To Dr. Fritz Trensz, Strasbourg
[Physician at the Lambarene hospital, 1926–1927]
Lambarene
12 March 1927[1]

Dear Trensz,

It has been oppressively hot for weeks now. The rain still refuses to come. The river has barely risen. N'Tschinda [Dr. Lauterburg] is doing his best to perform the hospital work by himself. How happy I am that Dr. Mündler will be arriving in two weeks. Luckily, not that much has happened so far. The formalities for taking over the construction site cannot be completed until a fence has been put up around the portions that have been built on. I had seen that rule in the regulations but hoped to get around it. I have been exempted from complying with a number of things, but apparently not this one. And so I am building this fence with Mademoiselle Mathilde Kottmann and the loyal black nurse, *qui a le privilège de travailler avec le grand docteur* [who has the privilege of working with the great doctor]. Dominik gathers the wood and the fence grows nicely.

~

To Prof. Dr. Oskar Kraus, Prague
[Upon receiving an honorary doctorate from the University of Prague]
Lambarene

23 March 1927

Dear Friend,

And now I have found many friends in Prague and even honors that I would never have dreamed of—and all because you have spoken up for me—for me, a man whose views run counter to your ideal of thought[1] in an extremely crucial aspect. I repeatedly think of the sacrifice you are making by speaking up for me. This adds something to my feelings for you—something that cannot be put into words. Thank you. Enclosed are my thanks for the faculty and for the chancellor and the senate. Please check to make sure the texts are correct. If there is anything you object to, please send them back to me so I can revise them. Also, please let me know whether I should send a word of thanks to the president of the [Czechoslovakian] republic [Tomáš G. Masaryk]. I am having a hard time writing. An abrasion on my right hand has grown into a painful abscess because it was cauterized by the whitewash I was using for the rooms of the new house. I am doing better now, but the bandage is making it hard for me to write. I also have to write a lot of letters to Cape Lopez because there are customs problems regarding the baggage of the new physician, Dr. Mündler. All his trunks and crates are at the customs office, and I am paying an incredible storage fee day after day. Ah, African red tape. But these things are far more grueling here than any work.

⌐⌐

To the administration of St. Jacob's Church, Hamburg
Return address: c/o Frau Professor Annie Fischer, Hamburg
on the train, Sweden

24 November 1927

I am now able to tell you when I will be passing through Hamburg. I will arrive in Hamburg, en route from Lübeck, on Saturday, December 3. Since I will probably be staying only a short time, I would like to start examining the organ immediately on Saturday. [Schweitzer had been asked by the church to provide an opinion on restoring the valuable Arp-Schnitger organ.] Would you therefore please make sure that I find the organ open and that I can get inside the organ as well.

One more question: For years now friends and music lovers in Hamburg have been after me to perform Bach on a Hamburg organ. I have never been able to do so because my stays in Hamburg have always been too brief or else I have been too busy. However, since I will be in Hamburg on Sunday, December 4, and the church will be heated anyway, I thought of playing Bach music on the St. Jacob's organ as a kind of Advent service for music lovers—if this is all right with you. The performance could take place either in the afternoon or toward evening—whichever time is more convenient for the church. Free admission for everyone, and a collection at the end, say, for the homeless or for Christmas for the homeless. Naturally, the church congregation would be invited to this celebration.

~

To Alice Ehlers, U.S.A.

[before 1928]

Dear Mrs. Ehlers,

Have you been cursing me? Heaven knows what the good Basel musicians [who regarded the harpsichord as Bach's favorite instrument] have been lamenting about with you! My position is the same as it has always been: The harpsichord is a historically interesting instrument, and we should properly cultivate it nowadays,[1] but it was never Bach's *ideal*; rather, he wanted an instrument on which he could play "cantabile," and that was why he kept returning to the clavichord. The ultimate version of the clavichord is the piano with its twofold resolution, which permits both singing and emphasis.

That is the truth. Fortunately, it allows a great deal of space for the harpsichord; but this truth must occasionally be spoken whenever someone utters the false doctrine that the harpsichord was Bach's ideal. I assume that you fully agree with me on this point. Believe me, it has not been easy for me to go into detail about the harpsichord issue in several cities, but a lot of fantasies about this matter have been articulated. We all have to serve the truth.

Faithfully and sadly yours,
Albert Schweitzer

~

To Hans Stalder, M.D., Bordeaux
                                Strasbourg
                                20 July 1928

Dear Dr.,

You are celebrating your birthday in Bordeaux. Please allow me to
congratulate you. After all, you will be devoting this new year of your
life to my work.[1] May it be a beautiful year for you in every way.
Rest assured that I care for you not only as my assistant but also as
a person, and that I am deeply interested in everything concerning
you. You will not recognize yourself after returning home from Africa,
where, by working independently and experiencing the grandeur of
primal nature, you will receive something that Europe can never give
you. The wonderful thing about Africa is that one feels absolutely
necessary there every single day. In Europe one can always be replaced
by somebody else. In Africa one is irreplaceable among poor people,
and you will cherish these people.

   So enjoy your trip—the wonderful nights on deck when the ship
glides along under the tropical sky.

                                Much affection,
                                A. Schweitzer

~

To August Albers, C. H. Beck publishing company, Munich
                                Königsfeld
                                8 August 1928

Dear Friend,

   1. I have written to the head of Beck. Am generally in agreement with the business aspect.

   2. Regarding the Goethe Prize[1] [the city of Frankfurt had
awarded Albert Schweitzer the Goethe Prize on 28 August 1928,
Goethe's birthday], please send Dr. Landmann, the mayor of
Frankfurt: (a) both volumes of my philosophy of civilization; (b)
Wasser und Urwald; (c) *Jugenderinnerungen*; (d) *Christentum und
Weltreligionen*; and please bill me for these books.

   3. I will truly enjoy the celebration on the twenty-eighth only if
you as my friend and chronicler attend. Now listen: Take some
time off, buy a round-trip sleeping-car ticket, and charge it to my
prize. You ought to accept this from me. Don't argue. Order your
ticket immediately.

The celebration is to take place on the twenty-eighth, at twelve noon, in the Goethe House. We will arrive on the twenty-seventh and stay with Dr. Eugen Jacobi, Schaumainkai 67, not far from the railroad station, right across the main bridge. We'll get you an invitation, which you can pick up from us. In the evening I'll be playing the organ.

Do be a good fellow and come.

Best,
Albert Schweitzer

[From the text of Schweitzer's speech upon receiving the Goethe Prize of the city of Frankfurt on 28 August 1928]

My own destiny is such that I experience the destinies of our age and the concerns about humanity with an acuteness that goes to the very nerve center of my existence. Before us, Goethe worried about and worked for his time. Conditions have become more chaotic than even he could foresee with his clear vision. Our strength has to be greater than the conditions themselves if we are to become human beings in this situation, human beings who understand the times and manage to cope with them. We have to wrestle with ourselves and with everyone else so that, in an age of confused and nonhumanitarian ideals, we may remain true to the great humanitarian ideals of the eighteenth century by carrying them over into the thoughts of our time and seeking to realize them.

To Erwin Jacobi

29 August 1928

Dear Herr Jacobi,

I don't know whether you read newspapers in your new position. In case you don't, let me inform you that I have received the Frankfurt Goethe Prize and that, on the day of the ceremony, I stayed in the home of your parents, together with my wife and child. I was delighted when your mother told me that you like your new job. As a man who will someday bear great responsibilities, you cannot see enough and learn enough while you are still learning today. I am confident that during these important months your mind will gather all that is necessary.

~

To Max Drischner, composer and cathedral preceptor at the Niko-
laikirche, Brieg, Silesia
1928–29

Let me confess: I proceeded to play your pieces, delighting in their
marvelously natural form and inventiveness.[1] Quite simply: The chorale prelude ["Wie schön leuchtet der Morgenstern" (How beautifully
the morning star shines)] is wondrous in its style and its inventiveness.
So lively and so perfect in its form. This is who you are! And you must
remain true to yourself! I am so happy that you are yourself in your
compositions, even though you create in the spirit of the classics of
the organ! So, many, many thanks for the great joy you have given me.

~

To Prof. Dr. Edmund Husserl, Freiburg im Breisgau
Königsfeld, Baden
14 September 1928

Dear Professor Husserl,

Here in Königsfeld I am with Professor Bixler of Smith College,
U.S.A., with whom I have a philosphical and musical rapport.[1] Professor Bixler will be spending the winter in Freiburg in order to
attend your lectures and make your acquaintance. He has asked me
for a letter of recommendation, and even though it is unnecessary, I
am doing so in order to take this opportunity to send you my heartfelt
greetings. I hope I get a chance to see you this winter.

My best, in haste,
Your very devoted
Albert Schweitzer

~

To Dr. Hans Stalder, physician at the Lambarene hospital
Nuremberg-Augsburg
on the train
11 December 1928

Dear Dr. Stalder,

Now you'll soon be feeling like an African! I am sending you these
greetings from the train that is taking me home from Prague. Factual

instructions for physicians (about dealing with the administration, bills for the mission, and so forth) are contained in my letter to Dr. Hediger, and I have asked him to convey the information to you.

I am so glad that you are there and, like Fräulein Mathilde [Kott-mann], that you are cultivating the lovely spirit that should prevail in a hospital. I am worried about Fräulein Mathilde's health. Watch over her carefully. Once I'm in Strasbourg, I will try to obtain a tropicalized violin.

I have been working very hard—giving a lecture or a recital almost daily since September 25. But it is a joy to work on gathering funds for the hospital. Now you know the wonderful sun of the rainy season and the glorious cloud formations. One is always homesick for them.

With kind thoughts,

Your grateful
Albert Schweitzer

~

To Prof. Dr. Adolf von Harnack, Berlin
[Reply to Harnack's letter of 7 March 1929, informing Albert Schweitzer that he had been elected an honorary member of the Prussian Academy of Sciences]

[March 1929]

Excellency,

I was bowled over by your card—how is it possible that I have been deemed worthy of such an honor? It just won't sink in. But I am delighted, absolutely delighted. Since I have every reason to assume that you are behind this honor, I must thank you in particular.

You cannot imagine what you have done for me. I am quite especially delighted because in a sense I am replacing Bode.[1] I would never have so much as dared to think that I might someday have some link to the Academy of Sciences—I, the woeful man who has to work simultaneously in different areas. And now I am to be an honorary member of this society. I thank all of you from the bottom of my heart.

Today I am writing to Privy Councilor Planck to express my gratitude to the academy. I spend my nights working on St. Paul. It will be a lot more comprehensive than it once seemed. The title: *St. Paul's Mysticism in Its Relationship to Early Christianity and Hellenized Christianity.* The large size of this work is due precisely to my references to earlier and later developments. But I felt this was necessary.

If it is at all possible for me to visit Berlin prior to my departure for Africa, I will do so. But first St. Paul has to be completed.

>With my best,
>Your deeply devoted
>Albert Schweitzer

~

To Hans Pfitzner

2 May 1929

Dear Maestro,

In a few days you will be sixty years old. Please allow me, among so many others who love and admire you, to express my most heartfelt wishes. I consistently follow everything concerning you and your work. You are far closer to me than you realize. Your cantata, *Von deutscher Seele* [Of the German soul], has been one of my greatest spiritual and musical experiences. We all thank you for remaining yourself and serving art purely instead of making concessions to the times. That gives your work its wonderful solemnity. Created neither out of the time nor for the time, it has a timeless significance.

What difficulties you have gone through and what anxieties you have endured! I have often thought about you!

May your glorious creativity keep allowing you to give us many of the beautiful things that we hope to receive from you.

I am writing to you during a train trip. Hence the wobbly penmanship.

>With my very best wishes,
>Albert Schweitzer

With warmest memories and with deep respect and gratitude for all the depth and beauty you have given us.

>Emmy Martin

~

To Marc Lauterburg, M.D., Lambarene
[Schweitzer's fellow physician at Lambarene for many years]
>[Strasbourg]
>1 October 1929

I have received your letter of 29 August [19]29, and I thank you *from the bottom of my heart* for agreeing, if it is at all possible, to stay on until my arrival in late December. I don't have to tell you what this would mean to me. You know the situation I'm in and what your perseverance would mean to me. I am greatly saddened by your worries about your wife, and I thank her for remaining despite her anything-but-splendid state of health. I know what sacrifices she is making. The new man, Dölken, is a very kind person. Introduce him to everything. It would help me greatly if you broke him in.

I am in the midst of packing in Strasbourg. My head is burning so badly that I can't even write properly, but you understand all this.

~

To Margit Jacobi, Frankfurt am Main

Near Capo Blanco, south of the
Canary Islands (see atlas)
Wednesday, 11 December 1929[1]

We can no longer imagine that we have come from winter and storms. I myself am utterly preoccupied with the final chapter of St. Paul, which is to be completed during this voyage. I began this final chapter on the very first day out. During the stormy days I lay either on or under the dining room table where I was writing. Oh, this writing on the dancing ship. Now it is sailing almost smoothly, but writing is always tiring. I wonder if I'll complete the chapter on this trip.

My wife is not doing splendidly. She has trouble adjusting to the climate at sea level after the high altitude of Königsfeld. I am constantly afflicted by anxieties that I do not express. At times I am astonished that I can still work.

~

To the Reverend Hans Baur, Basel

near Dakar
13 December 1929

Dear Helper in Need,

You have probably read the newspaper stories about the heavy storms along the Atlantic coast and the victims they have claimed, and you have probably been worrying about us. We have escaped relatively safe and sound. As we were leaving Gironde, the barometer suddenly plunged to "storm," and then it all began, for four days.

Near Gibraltar the barometer climbed to "Fair Weather," and since then a stiff northeaster has been driving us southward on an agitated sea and under a clear sun.... Thank you for coming to Muhlbach. Replacing the organ that my grandfather built meant so much to me. And you could see the way I realize my ideal of a village organ— everything geared to simplicity and beautiful sonority. I feel like someone who, in a perverted generation, remains loyal to the truth.

I am starting to hear the rattling of the hoists that are lifting the cargo on deck so it can be unloaded. After that we have to flee the ship because it will be loading coal, which suffocates us.

~

To Hans Martin

[1929]

Dear Hans,

Now you have your *Abitur* [high school diploma]. How happy I was when I got mine! You'll feel happy too.[1] Congratulations, and enjoy your rest. As for the university: During the first two terms, a few specialized courses, which you will conscientiously attend and work for, really cramming. Start on your major right away. Along with that, general lectures, especially the history of philosophy, Roman literary history, and so forth. Later on you won't get a chance to broaden your education, so use the first two years. Do not avoid the friendships that are offered. Friendships from university days are a treasure throughout life.

Get used to keeping track of your expenditures and getting by on a specific monthly sum. I will be giving you 20 (twenty) marks every month of the semester (May, June, July, October, November, December, January, February) for concerts, theater, and so forth. Ask your mother to lay it out for me. Use the money only for these purposes and possible excursions (but not sports nonsense!).

Buy the books you need. One works a lot better if one owns the books outright. Do not avoid the dry courses, for they, too, are necessary. Keep a complete and solid course notebook, but leave each left page blank, so that you can subsequently add things from books while reviewing the lectures. You will then have an easy time with exams.

If you follow my advice, you will have a fine life as a student. Increase your knowledge of Latin.

Best wishes,

Your old

A. Schweitzer

~

[From Helene Schweitzer's letter (about her return voyage to Lambarene) to the friends and benefactors of the hospital]

Lambarene

10 January 1930[1]

Who can describe the feelings that were stirred up when, toward evening on December 23, the shout rang out: "The lights of Port-Gentil!" Twelve long years had passed since I last saw that coast, as it sank behind us on the horizon in October 1917.

Now the lights flashed on, then more and more of them, and when our ship anchored in the bay near 10:00 P.M., the row of lights stretched a long way toward the dark tip of the peninsula.

We spent the night on board and did not go ashore until the next day after our masses of luggage were unloaded.

We enjoyed the hospitality of our old prewar acquaintance, Herr Baumgartner, who, together with his darling wife, so touchingly looks after us—and indeed all the helpers of our project as they pass through; we cannot thank him enough for his kindness.

We will be traveling all though the night, stopping only once, at the crack of dawn, at a Negro village in order to load wood for the engine. It is like a dream to be once again gliding calmly and silently up the river without suffering the din and agitation of the big ship or the soaring square of Port-Gentil. Here on the river things have developed in a contrary direction: The shores lie still and dead; nature seems to have returned to a virginal state. Many villages that I once knew have disappeared. Countless oil palms and an occasional mango tree reveal that human settlements used to be located nearby. Now, white herons build their nests here and there along the banks, and are so untimid that they barely fly up when our ship sails by. A passion for hunting is aroused in one of our fellow passengers. He already wants to aim a gun at these noble birds. I can scarcely hold him back from this barbarity.

The Ogowe flows so quietly that one can barely tell how strong its current is. However, we usually hug the shore to avoid struggling against the full strength of the river. Since this is the rainy season and the water is deep, we can easily travel like this with no danger of running aground on sand.

And today is Christmas Eve. I have experienced all sorts of Yuletides, I have celebrated Christmas Eve under a fir tree, a pine tree, a palm tree, and a juniper tree, but this one is unique in that it is Chritmas only in our thoughts and memories.

On St. Stephen's Day, Thursday, December 26, at two o'clock, we arrived at our steamer's landing place in Lambarene. How greatly this landing place has changed! New houses, new roads—even a hotel has opened here. I can hardly recognize the few buildings of the trading companies from earlier times.

It will be night by the time we get to the hospital. All we can distinguish in the torchlight is a tangle of figures with joyfully excited faces turning toward us. We cannot survey the huge complex until tomorrow, but the large, airy dining room is a joy: It welcomes us and we gather—fourteen strong!—for dinner, a bit of friendly socializing, and then evening services in conclusion. The next morning a short tour of the hospital and the adjacent parts of the plantation.

What repeatedly overwhelms me is the thought of how much has been accomplished in a relatively brief period and also the practical layout of the buildings, which aims chiefly at allowing as little sunshine as possible to hit the walls and letting in as much air as possible everywhere. And the principle of creating endurably cool residential areas in this agonizingly hot land has been heeded not only for the whites but also for the blacks, both sick and healthy. We often hear our employees—the cook, the boys, or others—express their joy at these airy, healthy homes.

~

To Baron Lagerfelt and Greta Lagerfelt, Duseborg, Sweden
Lambarene
Palm Sunday, 1930

Today, with Helene, we sailed out to the Palm Sunday place in the quiet lake, from where I wrote to you years ago. Perhaps you mentally looked for me there.

I sat in the shade of a huge lakeside tree, at the site of a former village, where now a dense grove of oil palms is growing skyward. Sometimes I am so deeply moved by the thought that I have found and can utter the philosophical expression for the ethics of Jesus' love in my doctrine of reverence for life, so that people can be led on the road to Jesus through true and profound thought.

Once again I stood on the road from Bethpage to Jerusalem, shouting my hosannah at the King of Peace on His donkey . . . and I thought of you people, who are mentally celebrating Palm Sunday with us.

In the morning, before we left, I preached to the blacks at the hospital; the subject of my sermon was Jesus' entrance into Jerusalem.

I now preach every Sunday morning, not at the Mission station but at the hospital.

The moon is shining softly through the palms, its beams touching the water.

～

To August Albers, C. H. Beck publishing company, Munich
on the river
Sunday, 27 April 1930

Dear Friend,

We spent the night [in Cape Lopez] in the musty home of a European—a house eaten by gnats and other vermin. We had to get up at the crack of dawn and gather our belongings in the dark, for the boat [to Lambarene] was scheduled to leave with the first ray of dawn. That was a bad time. But now it's all forgotten. The sun is inundating everything with marvelous light. Ah, if only you could be here! We are still passing through the lowland with raffia palms, screw pines, and papyrus, no high forest. It feels as if we are traveling about in a huge hothouse. And wonderfully mild air plays around us. I am writing on the edge of the ship, sitting under a sunshade.

A huge expanse of land, which will remain useless as long as the world exists, because nothing can ever be grown in this swampy lowland, which is constantly flooded. But what does "useless" mean? This sumptuous wilderness is an end in itself. Above us, a radiant white and blue sky that looks as if it had been painted in watercolors— a sky such as you people have never seen. We are now gliding through a narrow canal from one arm of the river to the other. We have already passed several rafts drawn by motorboats; the *Ingo* and other ships in the harbor are waiting for them. Outside the house where we spent the night, fifteen thousand tons of lumber are tied up in landing floats, ready to be shipped; the wood belongs to the company that owns this boat, which has been gracious and merciful enough to take us along. Otherwise we would have been trapped in Cape Lopez for a long time. The ship is carrying sixty barrels of cement and iron ties for narrow-gauge railroads (German reparations deliveries), which are to transport lumber from the lumberyards. Oh, these water palms! Each more sumptuous than the next! Unfortunately, our ship, which was built for the ocean rather than a river, has too deep a draft. There is no guarantee that we will make it to Lambarene without spending a few nights on sand. In any event, we cannot travel by night, so we will be spending the night more or less decently in a trading post that is famous for its mosquitoes.

All day long we fear the night. Even worse than the mosquitoes are tiny gnats which no mosquito net can ward off. You toss about in a hot bed with burning arms and a burning head. I'd love to see your face after a night like that. In Lambarene, where all the grass around the houses is kept mowed, there are no such gnats, or practically none. Because of these little gnats I am writing you with a thick head as if we had been swilling the best Munich beer all night long.

Thank you for all the kindness you constantly show us. My *St. Paul*[1] must have come out by now. I haven't managed to do any writing yet. First I have to revise my self-presentation for England and also the second volume of *Zwischen Wasser und Urwald*.[2] Then on to the note for my philosophy of civilization, [volume] III. This has to be a tremendously simple fugue! Oh, if only I could start on it tomorrow. Whole sections are already stirring quite vividly in my mind.

~

To Dr. Paul Siebeck, J. C. B. Mohr publishing company, Tübingen
Lambarene
9 May 1930

Dear Dr. Siebeck,

The mail just brought the first copy of St. Paul [*The Mysticism of Paul the Apostle*], and I want to tell you right away how happy I am that this book has been born. And many, many thanks for everything you have done to make my work easier. It is still a mystery to me how I could write the final chapter *so clearly* in the dining room of the ship, amid the dreadful heat, the racket made by the stewards, and the screeching tangle of gramophones. But I had been carrying the text inside myself for a long time. All I had to do was cast it in sentences.

(The nurse who is in charge of the household has just come and handed me tomorrow's menu! We're so far from St. Paul. But I have to keep my mind "open" to everything.)

At present there are many blacks with severe bronchitis at the hospital. Isn't that ironical under the equator?

To Lotte Schall, Königsfeld

Lambarene

Sunday, 13 July 1930[1]

Dear Lotte,

I belatedly received your letter asking whether it is cowardly of you not to defend me when you hear people saying nasty things about me. You can hold your tongue. It's not cowardly. You simply ignore it because it's ridiculous. Once I'm back in Königsfeld, you can tell me what accusations are leveled against me. Until then, hold your peace.

This is a quiet Sunday afternoon. There was hustle and bustle this morning, but now it's quiet.

I wrote that at 3:00 P.M. Then I was summoned to one of our surgical patients, whose condition had worsened (the case was desperate from the very outset); right after that they brought in a man who had been wounded by a rifle shot, and he soon died. I had to prepare the deposition for the judicial proceedings. . . . And then came nightfall. That was my quiet Sunday afternoon.

Just imagine: I have a forest of some two thousand palms around the hospital, all of them oil palms! And how they all shimmer in the moonlight. But I am nevertheless homesick for the Donis Forest [Königsfeld], where, one evening last year, I spent a moment getting a breath of fresh air.

To the family of Adolf von Harnack, Berlin

Lambarene

19 July 1930

Upon reading the newspapers that came here, I was grief-stricken to learn about the death of Adolf von Harnack, and in these lines I would like to express my profound condolences to the family. Ever since 1899 when I went to Berlin to attend his lectures, and where he was kind enough to invite me to his home, I was devoted to him with love and admiration, and I was delighted that he remained fit. At the end of last fall when I had to return to Africa, I spent a day and a half in Berlin, actually for the sole purpose of seeing him. In these last few weeks I was also delighted to receive two letters from him about theological problems, and I answered both. Now he is no longer among us. May the things he has given German theology and thereby the Christian world remain forever....

~

To Dr. Kaphahn, Regierungsrat [government councilor], Dresden
[Lambarene]
15 October 1930

Dear Herr Regierungsrat,

On 26 July 1930 you were kind enough to write to me about negotiations for my taking the position of regular associate professor for the New Testament at the University of Leipzig. I would like to thank the ministry and the faculty for honoring me by thinking of me for this position, but, alas, I cannot consider your offer. [The Lambarene hospital] is such an urgent task that I must ignore my personal desire to return to scholarship and art. My decision is especially difficult in regard to the prospects offered me by Leipzig because this position would have delighted me in every respect.

Thus I have no choice but to express my profound regrets and my deeply felt gratitude to the ministry. I have already written to the Theological Faculty.

Please convey my most respectful compliments to His Excellency, the Minister of Education.

With my very best wishes, I remain,
Yours very sincerely,
Albert Schweitzer

P.S. I am sending you this letter via Strasbourg, where I am dispatching all my letters in a large registered collective envelope, since letters are in great jeopardy because of their valuable stamps and therefore often go astray.

~

To Eugen Jacobi, engineer and doctor in political science, Frankfurt am Main
Lambarene
26 October 1930

Dear Friend,

Whenever I immerse myself in the dismal news from Europe, I think of all the spiritual and professional anxieties that this must be causing you, dear friend. Will the sky clear up when we meet again on the station platform and resume our classical dispute about carrying the baggage? . . . I hope so with all my heart. . . .

With loving thoughts,

Albert Schweitzer

~

To Dr. Paul Siebeck, J. C. B. Mohr publishing company, Tübingen

Lambarene

27 October 1930

Dear Dr. Siebeck,

I was unprepared for the cornucopia of good news that was brought by your letter of 13 September 1930! Why, this is marvelous! Now for the individual questions.

1. *The Mysticism of Paul the Apostle.* You did the right thing reprinting it so soon. In the future, please proceed in the same way.

2. Reverend Leyrer: In proofreading he is as reliable as he is tough. Don't be put off by the latter trait. Before you print another set of proofs, please give him a chance to find all the typographical errors.

3. I am delighted that the postcard has been successful.

4. The new edition of *The Quest of the Historical Jesus.* If I can maintain my health and my strength, I will use a visit in Europe *to shorten* this book (that is, the chapters that are no longer topical) and bring it up to date. But this is a long way off. I am therefore in favor of your plan to print another two thousand copies. Before tackling a revision of my book, I want to rework my history of research on St. Paul, my Bach, and complete the third volume of my philosophy of civilization.

~

To Josselin de Jong, Driebergen, Holland

Lambarene

28 November 1930

Yes, indeed, the term "reverence for life" has a lot more substance than its mere wording seems to indicate. But that is as it should be— the thought greater than the verbal façade.

Reverence for life is the Christian love—universal and necessary to be thought about—that deals with reality.

≈

To Baron Lagerfelt and Greta Lagerfelt, Duseborg, Sweden
Lambarene
23 December 1930

B. [Emma Haussknecht] has just been ringing the evening bell at nine o'clock, and, as usual, all the dogs are showing up to sit around the bell tower and howl throughout the ringing. And the sound is solemn under the palms, amid the noise of the cicadas!

I am so relieved that Helene is really doing better. I would ask for little else to make my happiness complete. My one desire for Helene to be in decent health is always on my mind.

Much misery in the hospital. A European got his foot caught in the propeller shaft of the motorboat, and it shattered his foot. We are unable to bring down his high fever even though we cleaned his dreadful injury and drained the pus from the ankle. The entire house for the white patients is overcrowded.

At present it is terribly, terribly hot here. Christmas Day is mid-summer's day, after all. But my room is so well ventilated that I can work here evenings without being drenched in sweat.

Best wishes for the year 1931! To both of you.

With best regards,

A. Schweitzer

I would be delighted if the AS [Albert Schweitzer] Committee [for the Lambarene hospital] were to convene in Stockholm.

PART FIVE

———— ❧ ————

1931 - 1937

~

To Emmy Martin, Gunsbach
Lambarene
14 January 1931

Well, it was a beautiful birthday. In the morning, outside my room, they sang: "Harre meine Seele" [Tarry, my soul] and "Ach, bleib mit deiner Gnade" [Ah, tarry with your grace].[1]

Late at night I more or less completed my self-presentation, which will now be titled *Out of My Life and Thought* because I talk about books and my thoughts.[2] Naturally, I'll be spending weeks revising and cutting it, but I'm not worried. The work doesn't have to be continuous, whereas working all the way through to the end requires a coherent effort. And nowadays Dr. Meyländer and the *Doctoresse*[3] have enabled me to stick to my work, often for entire afternoons. I've also been burning the midnight oil. Now I am truly somewhat tired, but I hope my fatigue will soon pass. Mentally, I am not quite free. This labor was weighing me down. The parts I have to trim are the chapters summing up the contents of books.

~

To the Reverend Klein, Diemeringen, Alsace
Lambarene
18 March 1931

Dear Klein,

So listen and learn. The Mission and the hospital are unhappy because all the grindstones of red sandstone that are bought here are of a wretched quality. I therefore suggested asking you if you could go directly to the source, a good place, and get us *eight* top-quality grindstones with square holes: They should be eight to nine centimeters thick and forty-five to fifty centimeters in diameter. If I am not mistaken, I once met a grindstone manufacturer through you. You would be doing the Mission and me a *huge* favor, and I would be overjoyed to have grindstones that remind me of your area. So: *eight* pieces, two per crate, a solid crate with iron bands! Not more than two, otherwise [the] crate will be too heavy for a canoe. Make sure the overseas packing is first-rate! Thick boards. Send the whole shipment to Monsieur Paul G. Leenhardt, 15 rue Fougate, Marseilles, with a letter indicating that these four crates of grindstones are to be added to the shipments for the Protestant Mission in N'Gomo, Gabon. Forgive me for burdening you with such things. My best to all of you.

> Sincerely,
> Albert Schweitzer

I'm writing letters in the last minute before the mail goes off. Hence no personal news.

~

From Albert Schweitzer's circular letter to the friends and patrons of the Lambarene Hospital, Whitsuntide 1931

God bless you!

> Lambarene
> Sunday before Palm Sunday, 1931

Dr. Otto Schnabel came to Lambarene, together with Fräulein Emma [Haussknecht] and Fräulein Bertha [Künzli], in order to view the place where his daughter spent two years as a physician and to take her home for some well-deserved relaxation. They left together on the evening of September 17. The female doctor [Anna Schnabel] who had performed such great services and reaped so much love was escorted to the canoe by black hospital patients holding torches and calling "good-bye" to her long after the canoe had vanished in the darkness.

Then, for a number of months, there were no arrivals and no departures, until 19 March [1931] when Dr. Meyländer had to leave for home. This time he had been able to come for only nine months, but during this period he performed enormous services from the hospital thanks to his knowledge and energy. He did us all a lot of good with his constant kindness and good cheer.

For the time being Dr. Schmitz and I will be performing the medical duties by ourselves. But we soon hope to have a third physician.

I am always deeply moved whenever I look at the large portrait of Dr. [Erich] Dölken,[1] who died in 1929 during his voyage to Lambarene. His picture hangs in the consulting room. From his frame he peers into the room as if he were participating in our work.

Dr. Meyländer took a great deal of work off my hands, and I used those months for the construction work together with Herr Zuber, who was kind enough to remain longer than he originally planned. First we got going on the new barracks for the mental patients because the old one was being used for the dysentery cases. The new barracks was finished in April. It contains six airy cells plus day rooms for natives as well as one room for Europeans. The building for the mentally ill was constructed with the funds donated by the Guildhouse parish in memory of its deceased member Mr. Ambrose Pomeroy-Cragg. When the building was done, we attached the same memorial plaque that is to be found at the church of the Guildhouse parish.

Dominik [native worker], who entered my employ in 1924, has been back with us for six months after spending two years as foreman in various lumberyards. For the moment, however, he is not employed inside the hospital; instead, he is involved in the construction work.

It is our constant joy to have a black staff that is truly devoted to the hospital and doing a labor of love.

The Mission station, which can be reached only by water, is too far from the hospital to allow the patients and their companions to attend services there. We therefore have prayers at the hospital every Sunday. If I am prevented from preaching, then I am replaced by Fräulein Haussknecht. The services are held outdoors. I often have to raise my voice to be heard over the racket of the hundred weaverbirds in the nearby palm trees.

I preach under the overhanging roof of a ward, amid the worshipers who have taken their seats underneath; the rest sit under the overhanging roof of the opposite building. Next to me stand two translators, each of whom renders my every sentence into one or two languages because members of different tribes come together in the hospital. For the prayer, which is likewise translated sentence by sentence into three or four languages, there are quite a number of people who fold their hands for the first time.

It is my hope that the lumber workers from distant areas may take home something of Jesus' Gospel and make it known there. For the second time areas that our missionaries have not yet reached have dispatched requests to send evangelists there so that the inhabitants can hear more of the "stories" that they have been told about by people who were in the hospital.

May our European friends see from these lines that we are joyfully at work doing a great deal of good with the funds that they send to the hospital for these suffering people who otherwise would not be helped. With deep gratitude, we remember those whose goodness enables us to work here, and we ask them to keep helping this necessary work.

~

To Dr. Felix Meiner, publisher, Leipzig
[Regarding the publication of Schweitzer's autobiography, *Out of My Life and Thought*]

[Lambarene]
5 June 1931

Please allow me to use the titling system that I use in all my books to orient the reader. The chapter title is at the top of the left-hand page of the open book, and the title of the subsection is at the top of the right-hand page. Check the indications for typesetting and the proof sheets of my St. Paul.

The text I am sending you has been revised so thoroughly that nothing else can be changed. The proofreading should therefore be limited to correcting typographical errors and perhaps revising an occasional word or two. You can have the typesetting done by machine.

My proofreading will be taken over by Karl Leyrer, a city pastor, Bismarckstrasse 57, Stuttgart. He will give the final go-ahead. Please go along with whatever he says. He has proofread all my works (even in manuscript form). My wife will also read the proofs. The Reverend Leyrer and my wife (Königsfeld, Baden) will each receive *two* copies of all the corrections, revisions, and post-revisions. So please get in touch with Herr Leyrer, who is one of my dearest friends and helpers.

In advertising the work, please avoid anything noisy since this would not be in keeping with either the spirit of the book or me. My book will find its audience, and you will be delighted with it. Its meaning lies in the way it takes a position on the spiritual issues of our time by focusing on one man's experiences. It has turned into a kind of confession.

I neglected to ask you: Please send two copies of every set of proofs (including revisions, post-revisions, and final proofs) to my address in

Gunsbach, Alsace; they will be forwarded to me here, allowing me to follow the printing of the book. I apologize for causing you these expenses, but on the other hand, I believe that since the manuscript is absolutely clean, you will save a great deal in proofreading costs, so you can allow me these few extras.

Well, I think I have touched on all the essentials. I have put a great deal of myself into this book—something that was very difficult for me to do; and so I wish it bon voyage.

~

[From the memorial talk for Archbishop Söderblom]
at services in Lambarene
delivered on 26 July 1931

Yesterday we received the news that the Protestant archbishop of Sweden, Nathan Söderblom, had passed away. You were unacquainted with this name. You did not even know that there are also Protestant archbishops. You know nothing about the land of Sweden, where the winters are so cold that you could not live there. But the archbishop knew about you, and although he was unknown to you, you have good reason to commemorate his death now, at the end of divine services. This hospital is now standing here and patients are being cared for here because this archbishop contributed to it.

Had it not been for the dear archbishop, who was concerned about you, then I do not know whether the hospital would ever have been rebuilt. That is why today, when so many people are mourning his death, we remember him here, too, with profound gratitude. You have lost a father whom you did not know. God has summoned him to His kingdom.

~

To Greta Lagerfelt, Duseborg, Sweden
Lambarene
4 August 1931

So the good archbishop [Söderblom] is dead. I am grateful to you and Mrs. Martin for notifying me promptly and enabling me, at least in spirit, to join the mourners at the Cathedral of Uppsala. The cable arrived on Saturday, July 25. On Sunday, at the end of services, I gave a short memorial talk on the archbishop, and I am enclosing the text with this letter. How often I thought about the archbishop as I went through the hospital, remembering that when I was in Sweden in 1920, I wondered if I would ever manage to get the hospital going again. I don't know whether I could have built it without him. Now I am very glad that I again wrote all this to him a little while ago. He knew how thankful I was to him. His death is a great loss to Protestantism. He alone, standing between the British and the German world, managed to accomplish what neither an Englishman nor a German could do. Today we again—or rather finally—have a pan-Protestantism, and this is a grand historic fact. But what will become of the work if he is not leading it? We need him more than ever now.

~

To Minoru Nomura, M.D., Fukuoka, Japan, Yakataburu Hospital
                            Lambarene
                            6 August 1931

Dear Colleague,

Your dear letter has reached me by a circuitous route. As far as I know, my *On the Edge of the Primeval Forest* has not yet come out in Japanese. I am delighted that you care so much about my book that you would like to take the trouble of translating it and also trying to get a publisher interested. I agree in principle, and I am deeply grateful to you, only I do not have my book affairs in my head or at hand, because I cannot put the necessary strain on my memory and would therefore only bungle the entire matter.

I am having this letter forwarded to you by Mrs. Emmy Martin, Gunsbach, who is in charge of my business affairs, and I am asking her to contact you about this matter. She is acquainted with my Japanese business affairs and my Japanese friends, and she also knows which publisher has issued other books of mine in Japanese.

Ah, so you were recommended to me by my dear Uchimura. We have corresponded with each other. I am very sorry that I have not met him personally. I should have gone to Japan long ago, but I simply cannot find the time. I need my vacation in Europe in order to complete my works. I hope that someday I will have the pleasure of shaking your hand. Best wishes for your health. And many, many thanks for your kindness in getting in touch with me.

                            Sincerely yours,
                            Albert Schweitzer

To the Reverend Hans Baur, Basel

Lambarene

16 September 1931

Now that banks are collapsing throughout Europe, I am deeply worried about the hospital accounts. You are my only hope. Keep your eyes open and take our money out if there is even the slightest risk. If need be, purchase a large safe and keep the money there in banknotes. The interest is so low anyway that it is negligible compared with the safety factor. So do the right thing if necessary. I am relying on you entirely. How I regret that I cannot be in Europe now in order to assume the full responsibility.

To Superintendent D. E. Rölffs, Osnabrück

[1931]

I am very interested (too much so, no doubt) about my religious feelings, but everything is summed up in the concluding words of *The Quest of the Historical Jesus*: Jesus the Lord! Peace in Christ! Jesus has simply kept me prisoner since my childhood. However, I do not see my work in maintaining religion as an enthusiasm that is given to some and not given to others; rather, I feel I have to blaze a trail from thought to religion. It is my conviction that thinking leads to all profound truths of religion and that people become religious once they start thinking. The ethics of reverence for life is nothing but Jesus' great commandment to love—a commandment that is reached by thinking; religion and thinking meet in the mysticism of belonging to God through love.

To Prof. Dr. Oskar Kraus, Prague
Lambarene
7 November 1931

Dear Friend,

Many, many thanks for your dear letter of 3 November 1931. I didn't
mention President Masaryk simply because I didn't want to sound as
if I were name-dropping! Yes, dear friend, and I'll be damned if I
recognize any *objectively valid* quality distinctions in life. Every life
is sacred! And "sacred" means that there is nothing else, just as no
other speed can be added to the speed of the ether. Value judgments
are made out of subjective necessity, but they have no validity beyond
that. The proposition that every life is sacred is absolute. In this respect
I will always remain a heretic. It is a question of principle, one that
reaches deep into the foundation of my outlook on life. I pity you for
having such a person as your friend, but I am looking forward to
your history of the value theory.

I am now totally involved with Goethe because I am supposed to
deliver the ceremonial address in Frankfurt for the centennial of his
death. Your article on pessimism and optimism is excellent.

~

To Prof. Donald Francis Tovey, Edinburgh
Lambarene
23 November 1931

Dear Tovey,

Once again I have to tell you how lovely your edition of *The Art of
the Fugue* is. How often I reach for it in the evening in order to
browse through those wonderful notes. It never stops pleasing me
that you dedicated this work to me. It is so wonderful that your name
and mine are joined together in the shadow of the great name of
Bach![1]

Miss Deneke[2] is doing marvelously in Lambarene and performing
great services for me.

With best regards to you and your dear wife.

Albert Schweitzer

~

To Emma Haussknecht, Schweitzer's supervising colleague in Lambarene

[On the ship] *Brazza*
12 January 1932

Despite the pitching of the ship, I have written enough letters for everybody to receive one, including all the people in Port-Gentil and Libreville.

Outlining the Goethe speech by holding the paper on my lap is not so tiring. I am always anxious about you.

God preserve you.

Yours,
A. Schweitzer

⌒

To Emma Haussknecht

Speichergasse 2, [Strasbourg]
16 February 1932

Thank you for all the dear letters you have sent me. This is truly a whole book! How often have I worried about you—and how kind of you to go into such detail about everything. Here I'm in a whirlwind. Trips to Königsfeld, Paris, Basel, Mulhouse. . . .

A good amount of money is coming in for the work thanks to the many letters we have written! They have made quite an impact. I visited your sister's grave last Sunday afternoon in Colmar in splendid winter sunshine.

I am delighted that you are holding prayer meetings [at the hospital]. I don't know how to thank you.

⌒

To the staff of colleagues in Lambarene
[After Schweitzer's speech at the Goethe Centennial of the City of Frankfurt,[1] 22 March 1932]

Gunsbach
30 March 1932

To Everyone: Dear Helpers,

The Goethe speech has cost us 250 letters: negotiations concerning all details with Frankfurt, people asking us for seats at the opera house where the celebration took place, requests for me to deliver Goethe lectures in all sorts of cities. Those were horrible days, but everything worked out. Thousands of requests for seats had to be turned down. The opera house can hold only sixteen hundred. I was unusually fresh for the speech. I spoke quite freely on the stage of the opera, one and a quarter hours! In the evening I had to repeat the address for the radio, and records were also made of it. I hope I get one. The mayor was so happy about my lecture that he instantly engaged me to deliver the Goethe address on Goethe's two hundredth birthday in 1949.

And right after Frankfurt, the correspondence for the concerts. First, beginning in mid-April I'll be giving a series of charity recitals in Germany, starting with Stuttgart. At the end of April I'm off to Holland where I'll be playing in almost all the major cities; I've set aside part of the receipts for the Dutch unemployed. Next, England; [honorary] doctorate in Oxford on June 14. Then, Scotland; doctorate in Edinburgh.

And back in early July. Then more charity recitals in Germany (Munich, and so forth) . . . and finally . . . in Gunsbach, quiet work on my philosophy of civilization. Tonight I'm traveling to Strasbourg to attend Dr. Trensz's wedding; he was with us in Lambarene. Also meeting Dr. Nessmann. In Frankfurt I saw Herr Steiner and his dear wife, the sister of N'Tschinda [Dr. Lauterburg]; she used to be in Lambarene. In Gunsbach our group is made up of my wife, Rhena, Frau Martin, Hans [Martin], Fräulein Mathilde [Kottmann], and Aunt Canada [Mrs. Russell]. Although all these ladies are writing letters, there is no possibility of our coping with the dreadful amount of correspondence. . . . Some days there are as many as forty letters, not counting the recital letters.

~

To the helpers and physicians in Lambarene
(c/o Emma Haussknecht)

Bussum by Amsterdam
24 May 1932

To Everyone:

The worst part of the Dutch tour is behind me! Last week I played five concerts on five consecutive days, but everything went well. Now the concerts no longer come back-to-back, although I still have a few left. My Dutch tour will wind up on June 6, then I'm off to London, Oxford, Manchester, Glasgow, Edinburgh. From there directly to Munich, where I'm speaking at the university on July 7 and then giving a recital two days later. Next, probably more concerts in Ulm, Heidelberg, and so forth, and then toward mid-July home to quiet work in Gunsbach. I'm looking forward to it.

The concerts are well attended. In Amsterdam over two thousand people showed up. Unfortunately, I have no time to visit my Dutch friends. I have to focus constantly on playing and speaking, and all the correspondence for organizing the concerts. You have learned from Mr. and Mrs. van der Elst that I saw their parents. I recognized Mr. van der Elst, Sr., without an introduction: He and his son look amazingly alike.

At one of the Dutch churches (in Arnhem), Aunt Canada [Mrs. L. M. Russell] suddenly showed up, and she has been participating in the tour for ten days now. Our group is made up of the following people: Emmy Hopf[1] and a young Württemberg organist to pull the stops; Ida Zürcher, who plays the pieces for me so that I can hear them in the church; Aunt Canada, who pops up during rehearsals and vanishes afterward in some hotel; and Frau Martin.

How happy I am for you all that the heat spell is over. In spirit I experienced the final weak tornadoes with you and the arrival of the fresh breeze.

~

To Romain Rolland

Danham Massey Hall, Altrincham
tel. 309
19 June 1932

[f]

Dear Friend,

If you are not too tired or too busy, please have a look at this letter from the young Earl of Stanford, who shares our anxieties about the future of mankind and is fighting for the future of the spirit, which can save us. You will be happy to make his acquaintance.

Very sincerely yours,
Albert Schweitzer

~

To Martin Buber

                              3 December 1932

Dear Martin Buber,

I so greatly cherish your books. Alas, fatigue and a dreadful workload
prevent me from writing to you as I would wish. But I want you to
know that I have not forgotten you,[1] that I follow all your work with
interest, and that I would so much like to have a conversation with
you someday. Will this ever be granted to me? How often I envy you
for your calm and peaceful creativity! I am inflicted with disquiet
and all sorts of things; I then have to struggle in order to concentrate
on my work. Often I just don't have the strength. . . .

   The Hidden Light[2] is splendid. How much life there is in the rab-
binate. I feel so strongly about it. Jeremiah and Isaiah and Ezekiel[3]
are splendidly translated, but I find *Zwiesprache*[4] particularly valuable
because you give of your own self and I find so much that we have
in common. . . . I especially thank you for this wonderful simplicity
and for your deeply personal thoughts.

   In February I am returning to Africa. I hope that by then I can
complete the rough draft of *Mysticism of the Reverence for Life*.

                    Sincerely and devotedly yours,
                    Albert Schweitzer

                         ～

To the Philharmonic Chorus, Berlin; conductor: Otto Klemperer
[For the celebration of the fiftieth birthday of the Chorus with the
performance of Johann Sebastian Bach's Mass in B Minor]

                         5 December 1932

Siegfreid Ochs [former conductor of the Chorus] was one of the first
to recognize the importance of the phrasing and accents in Bach and
to act accordingly. He took for granted something that was not self-
evident before him; namely, that Bach's tone line can assert itself in
the strings only if all the instrumentalists employ the same phrasing
and emphasis. That was why he carefully entered all the necessary
information into the parts before placing them on the music stands.
Siegfried Ochs kept surprising us anew with the vivid and lively
rendering of the orchestral part.

   Siegfried Ochs was so thorough in clearing away the purportedly
classical ideal of performing Bach, and he did it as only a fiery personality like him could. He made short shrift of a conviction that was

widespread even among the most capable musicians; namely, that Bach had to be underplayed and undersung in a rigid tempo and in a style that was called as objective as possible. Ochs had an awareness of the elementary life that asserts itself in this perfect form. And he sought to do justice to both life and form in the same manner. Grand architecture in tremendously animated lines: That was his ideal of performance. Now many people may not have always agreed with his tempi (which were extremely vivace) and his dynamics (which were extremely lush), much less his tendency toward virtuosity; nevertheless, his rendering was an experience. For Bach's music, as he performed it, always emerged before the listener in its tremendous construction and its wealth of details. This interpreter, who always aimed at the most cunning effects, also had an innate knack for utter simplicity. This always struck me as the secret of his musicianship.

Siegfried Ochs's great achievements in regard to Bach were ultimately due not only to his musical sensitivity and ability but also to the fact that Bach was a great spiritual experience for him. Siegfried Ochs had something of Bach's profound meditativeness. He had an introspectiveness that drew him to the creator of the passions and cantatas. Those of us who were lucky enough to be more intimate with him learned that the great conductor was a deep person who lived in the works of the maestro of St. Thomas not just as a musician but with all his soul. The piety inscribed in the texts meant something to him. And this profound emotional response to the spirituality of Bach's works was revealed in his renderings. It was transmitted to the other musicians in rehearsals and to listeners who had ears to hear with in performances.

The Berlin Philharmonic Chorus gave us such perfect Bach performances under Siegfried Ochs, and now, under Otto Klemperer, it is celebrating its jubilee with the B Minor Mass; may the choir keep carrying out its mission of bringing us closer to Bach in the spirit of its great and unforgettable conductor.

~

To Arthur Honegger, composer

Permanent address Gunsbach
19 December 1932

[f]

Dear Monsieur,

Please don't think ill of me. . . . Last spring you were kind enough to send me your beautiful scores: *Cris du monde* [oratorio, 1931], *Horace victorieux, Musique pour Phèdre*, and *Symphonie pour Orchestre*....[1]

I was silent. At the time I was giving organ recitals in Holland, England, and Switzerland, and after returning home I had to get over my fatigue.... I am overworked, and as a result my correspondence is suffering. Let me tell you how happy I am to be in possession of your scores and how grateful I am to you. All my best wishes for all your creative labors. We are looking forward to further beautiful works from you. Please also give my best regard to Madame Honegger.

~

To Eugen Jacobi, engineer and doctor of political science, Frankfurt am Main

> on the steamship *Brazza*
> 23 March 1933
> Below Gibraltar

Dear Friend,

You were supposed to hear from me long ago, but you know that my friends must take a backseat in my correspondence. I have to thank you for so many things. It was so kind of you to allow your wife to help us with the packing in Strasbourg. She works so quietly and quickly that one could not wish for better help, especially since she is now so well versed in so many matters concerning Speichergasse [the location of the Strasbourg depot for Lambarene] and Lambarene. And then you so kindly wanted to get together with me once more. We are now looking forward to meeting again. I often think of the two of you and everything that you are going through in this difficult time. May everything be somewhat brighter when we meet again. I will be thinking of you frequently!

From the bottom of my heart,

> Your old
> Albert Schweitzer

~

From a circular letter to patrons and friends of the hospital

> Lambarene
> Friday, 28 April 1933[1]

The following physicians remained in Lambarene [during Schweitzer's trip to Europe in 1932]: Dr. Pieter van der Elst and Dr. Barend

Bonnema, both Dutch, with their wives. Mrs. van der Elst worked in the dispensary, Mrs. Bonnema in the operating room.

Fräulein Emma Haussknecht (from Alsace) ran the material side of the hospital. She took care of purchases, correspondence, and book-keeping, maintained the boats and the buildings, employed the able-bodied inpatients, acquired the food necessary for the patients and their companions, and oversaw the care of the plantings and the herds. In this way the doctors, being relieved of all secondary matters, could devote their full time and energy to the sick.

There was work galore. In 1931 the number of patients was already rising steadily. In 1932 the hospital had an average of 250 to 300 black inpatients, whereas when I had done the construction in 1930 and 1931, I had counted on a daily average of 200 inpatients, although I anticipated space for 300.

Part of the reason for the flood of sick people was that the hospital was becoming more and more widely known; however, a major factor was that Dr. van der Elst was doing such an excellent job in surgery. Under his aegis this section of the hospital work expanded more than ever. Hosts of sick people traveled as far as three hundred miles for operations.

[Tuesday]

How marvelously surprised I was to happen upon a path above the hospital and see that it had been planted with rather large breadfruit saplings, nearly all of which are thriving splendidly. Some seventy of these little trees, which are usually hard to obtain, were given to us by the Mission station at Lambarene-Andende. Now we have about one hundred breadfruit trees, and the ones that were planted in 1926 are already starting to bear. Unfortunately, the breadfruit season lasts only a few short weeks, and the fruit cannot be stored.

There are now so many fruit-bearing oil palms, mango trees, and banana and papaya shrubs in the plantation that the patients and their companions can pick as much as they like.

Shortly before my arrival, a group of people from the interior, after coming here for surgery, left for home on a steamer sailing up the N'Gounié; the skipper was charitable enough to take them along at our request. One of these patients included an old man who had regained his eyesight when Dr. Bonnema removed his cataract. He was so overjoyed at his good fortune that he solemnly danced around in the hospital.

Tschambi, who is mentally ill and has been in the hospital since 1926, was well enough for months to go about freely. But last night he suddenly began to talk confusedly and dangerously. Luckily, his attendant, Mendume, heard him and had the presence of mind to instantly clean out his cell (in which he had stored dangerous tools and empty bottles that could be used as missiles) so that, after curfew, Tschambi returned to his cell as usual and was locked in without putting up any resistance. Mendume has received a nice gift for being so quick-witted.

For the subject of my first sermon, which I gave last Sunday at the hospital once again, I chose a verse from chapter five of Thessalonians: "In every thing give thanks: for that is the will of God in Christ Jesus concerning you."[2] I told the patients and their companions about the crisis in Europe and explained to them how grateful they ought to be to God and the people in Europe who are making sacrifices for our hospital in the spirit of love so that despite the extremely difficult conditions we still have the wherewithal to maintain this charitable work. My statements made a deep impact on them, but nevertheless, unlike my helpers who were participating in the service and myself, the Africans were unable to grasp what it means for us to continue our work in this difficult time and what sacrifices our friends in Europe are making.

The prayer with which the service closed included our gratitude for such grace from God and such kindness from other human beings.

~

To the Reverend Hans Baur, Basel
Lambarene
11 July 1933

Dear Friend and Helper,

I am suffering from being torn between hospital work and philosophy. Oh, how I wish I could be here just once without being occupied with a book. However, my book is advancing.[1] The simple plan is slowly crystallizing. As I write this, a large canoe is moving by down below with singing paddlers. The rhino that lives near the hospital is very angry now because it has a cub. It attacks the boats at night, and one woman has been seriously hurt. You can imagine what I think of German Protestantism, which is now becoming a fellow traveler [of the Nazi regime]. Indeed, all current events are so depressing now. Ah, my spirits are very low when I work on my philosophy. People are turning away from all humanitarian ideals.

How far we have strayed from the eighteenth century. . . . But we mustn't lose heart.

With tender thoughts about you and yours,

Your old and grateful
Schweitzer

~

To Dr. Maud Royden, instructor and preacher, Guildhouse parish, Kensington

Lambarene
27 December 1933[1]

Dear Maud Royden,

I am enclosing the new Lambarene report, which is to be used for the English bulletin. Mrs. Russell was kind enough to translate it and type it. Thus, I am sending you a copy simultaneously with one to Miss Bronner.

You can see from the report that I had to erect a second building for the mentally ill; first of all, because the first building was no longer large enough, and secondly, because we have so many noisy mental patients who agitate the others and cause them sleepless days and nights. This was of great concern to me. All at once, close to the end of the dry season, I decided to construct the building.

How delighted all the quiet mental patients were, Tschambi and the others, when they heard that they would be free of the noise and disturbance from which they suffer so dreadfully. The new building is at a good distance from the others and separated by banana shrubs and coffee hedges, which muffle the noise. The new cells—there are six—are larger and airier than in the first building, which was why it was harder to make them so solid that the inmates could not break out.

Today, a new mental patient arrived. Tschambi is doing well at the moment. He is working with Mrs. Russell again. Another mental patient has improved so greatly that he can get water for the incarcerated mental patients and tend to their other needs as well. He is worried about a mental patient who never speaks.

With best greetings to you, your helpers, and all friends at Guildhouse,

Albert Schweitzer

~

From a circular letter to the patrons and friends of the hospital
[Lambarene]
February 1934

It is always a wonderful moment when a skipper who has agreed to take our surgical patients back upstream to the interior docks his steamer or motorboat here. Each of the home-bound travelers takes along provisions for several days (cassava, bananas, and dried fish); a specific sum in small coins in order to buy food during the trek and to present the agreed-upon gifts to the people ferrying him across rivers; letters of recommendation (in a metal box) to the officials through whose districts he travels. For this trip home most of the patients have saved some rice from the hospital food ration, and they carry it in bottles.

The boat is off. Brown hands wave farewell. May these dear people have a safe journey after leaving the boat.

Only a person who has lived in equatorial jungle lowlands can appreciate how refreshing the glass of cool water is that is brought down to the doctors and nurses in the hospital at 10:00 A.M. and 4:00 P.M. [from the new icebox]. How much more smoothly the work goes when your tormenting thirst is slaked for a while; this was never the case with the drinking water, with its temperature hovering between 75 and 80 degrees Fahrenheit.

Thus we gratefully appreciate everything that helps maintain our physical performance. However, we find our real strength to work every day by recalling the grace that we experience in serving the mercifulness of Jesus among the poorest of the poor. And whenever we thank God, who has assigned us this splendid work, we also thank the dear people whose gifts to our project enable us to carry it out.

~

To Prof. Dr. Benedetto Croce, Naples
Gunsbach, Alsace
26 May 1934

Dear Benedetto Croce,

I am delighted by what you have sent me, and I am thrilled that you feel so positive and so kindly about my autobiography. Oh, how I had to struggle with myself to write it. It is indeed a dangerous undertaking. . . . You know what harmony exists between us. We both wish to work at maintaining individual culture that preserves its bond with the past.

I hope that someday I will have the pleasure of getting together with you. If ever you come to Central Europe, do please try to meet me. I will be in Lausanne from June 1 to July 14,[1] Pension Haeussler, 12 avenue Victor Ruffy, and in Gunsbach (not far from Colmar) from July 15 to October 10.

≈

To Elly Heuss-Knapp, Berlin

12 January 1935

Last night, upon arriving in Lausanne, I found your dear article in *Die Hilfe*.[1] You are spoiling me! How beautiful the story of the cripple who was carried up the stairs! I was deeply moved by what you wrote about me. . . .

I am delighted by the overall high level of *Die Hilfe*. It is very important for the Naumann legacy to be preserved in this way.

I was also thrilled by the review of my book on Indian thinkers[2] and by the fact that the reviewer picked one of the big raisins out of the cake. That's what raisins are for.

My best regards to both of you [Theodor and Elly Heuss].

Albert Schweitzer

≈

To Prof. Martin Buber

[Lausanne]
15 January 1935

Dear Martin Buber,

Ever since we met in Königsfeld, I have thought about you frequently and, as you know, with great love. But I was so busy and so awfully tired (you can tell by my handwriting) that I did not exist for acquaintances and friends. I had to sit still. Then in the fall I had to lecture at Oxford and Edinburgh. And now you have sent me such dear wishes on my sixtieth birthday! I thank you from the bottom of my heart. I was especially delighted to hear from you. Around this time you will be receiving my new opus, about the philosophy of the Indian thinkers, from the Beck publishing house. It is an attempt at understanding the evolution of Indian thought and the role that ethics plays in it. I hope I have the pleasure of seeing you during my next trip to Europe. On February 5 I am sailing back to Africa. My best to you and your wife. My wife also sends her best. And be assured that I often think of you with love and respect.

~

To Louise Hindermann, Gunsbach
                              Madeira
                              10 February 1935

This is my first trip to Africa on a ship that's stopping in Madeira. I am quite saddened by the thought of the Müller family[1] who sought treatment here—uselessly, alas—for the consumption they were stricken with. How deeply moved I was in my childhood at the thought of their living in the mild air of this distant island. No one in Gunsbach today knows about that drama—ah, everything is so quickly forgotten. But you Hindermanns still remember the family and feel gratitude, as we do. That is why I am sending you these lines from Madeira, knowing that you will understand the memories I live with here.[2]

   The voyage was very stormy. The day before yesterday we had hail—and today mild, mild air. The vineyards rise in terraces. Best regards to all the Hindermanns. I hope that the dear sick child is doing well. *Auf Wiedersehen.*

                              Your old
                              Albert Schweitzer

~

To the Reverend Hans Baur, Basel
                              on the Gold Coast
                              on the steamer *Amérique*
                              18 February 1935

Dear Friend,

Now we are back in the tropics where there are no storms and not even stiff winds. Not a single wave ruffles the sea. The steamer is sailing as if it were cruising on Lake Geneva. The sky is misty and melts into the sea on the horizon. The sun does not even come out at noon. Astern, the coast is moving as a forested strip along the horizon. We are stopping in Sassandra this afternoon and taking aboard the Kroo people to do the loading for the final leg of the voyage. I am completing the manuscript for the publication of my Oxford lectures,[1] which is why I am absorbed in the "value philosophy" of Jamesian pragmatism (which gets mightily on my nerves) and the recent—indeed, the most recent—philosophy in general. What systematizing and theorizing! But there's an interesting religious strain that is noticeable in everything. I am also sleeping my fill, something I haven't done in years.

≈

To Dr. Victor Nessmann, Strasbourg
[Physician at the Lambarene Hospital, 1924–25]
Lambarene
4 April 1935

Dear Colleague,

Everything is fine here. Schatzmann is back and helping me build. It makes us feel ten years younger. We are adding three rooms to the consulting room by enlarging the building in a downstream direction. Next comes the TB building and the replacement of all wooden columns with concrete columns in the old buildings. On one of those days three strangulated hernias came here within half an hour! This morning we operated on five hernias.
    With loving thoughts of you, Madame, and the good children,
                                        Albert Schweitzer

≈

To Margit Jacobi, Frankfurt am Main
Lambarene
6 July 1935

As I have already written to you, I have your counterpart: A gentleman with inexplicable fever has been in our hospital for eighty days now, and I am greatly worried. I cannot send him to Europe since he is totally penniless. But he is doing better now. If ever you two were to meet in the quiet mountain village [Gunsbach], you could be the best of friends. Last night [we] received an accident victim for surgery: a rolling tree trunk, a shattered foot. He survived the operation. Tomorrow afternoon, Sunday, once the letters are dispatched, we (that is, those of us who are not on duty) are going for a picnic on the sandbank.

I am happy that things are looking up for you, so make plans for a convalescence in the mountain village [Gunsbach].

But now for my business correspondence. . . .

A puff of fresh air from the South Pole is now passing through the palms to me.

May God grant that you keep improving nicely! Good-bye.

My very best,

> Your old
> Albert Schweitzer

~

To Dean Richard Kik, Ulm
[Head of the Ulm Group for the Lambarene Hospital]
> Lambarene
> [July 1935]

My deepest gratitude for everything. The medicines are wonderful. Today I can write only very briefly. My eyes are tired and need to be spared, but my heartfelt thanks are expressed to you without words or signs. I have to be in England and Scotland from late October to around Christmas. . . . My Edinburgh lectures will also deal with the latest German philosophy, which is why I spend my evenings going through the appropriate works. The swift reading is very hard on my eyes.

Best regards to all my "Ulm" friends.

~

To Hilde Martin, organist, Königsfeld
> on the steamer *Amérique*
> near Dakar
> 3 September 1935

Dear Hilde,

Well, I am getting closer to Europe. And now let me ask you for a big favor. I am supposed to draw up the program for the Bach Society recital in London (October 28). I will be playing choral preludes: "In dich hab ich gehoffet, Herr" (Peters V 33), "Wer nur den lieben Gott lässt walten" (Peters V 54), "Lobt Gott, ihr Christen" (Peters V 40), and "Helft mir Gottes Güte preisen" (Peters V 21).

Now pay attention: For these chorales I need the choral movement in the key of the choral preludes, by Bach, if there is one by Bach; if not, then by any old master. Please make three copies of each choral movement with the words of the first verse. Plus, on a separate sheet of paper, just once, the remaining lines of the song. If the texts are too long, then [just write down] a collection of five stanzas. Send all this to my address in Gunsbach. From there it will be forwarded to me once I am in Lausanne. But do it soon and write legibly. I am already behind in regard to England. In case you don't have everything, then send me whatever you have for now. "Wer nur den lieben Gott" is, I believe, among my score packages (choral voice) in Königsfeld.

One more thing: What is that melody that belongs to the fughetta "In dich hab ich gehoffet, Herr" (Peters VI 34!!)? Can you find me a choral movement for it? How beautiful the fantasia, which is not a fughetta.

~

To the staff in Lambarene

London
25 October 1935

The crossing was good. I spent a lovely day with Dr. Goldschmidt in Paris. A friend lent me his automobile for the day so that I could take care of all my errands, so we spent many hours in the car. At Place de la Concorde we thought of Monsieur de Lucca when all the cars drove around in a circle. We also drove out to see my uncle in St. Cloud and Widor in Chantilly. This morning he brought me to the train (we went to the opera last night). [I] had a good crossing and am now in foggy London. . . . Mrs. Russell already has the many letters that need to be answered. My wife came directly, but she's freezing in the badly heated rooms.

The letter is being mailed tonight—perhaps it will still reach the ship.

Best regards from me and my wife,
Albert Schweitzer

~

To Dr. Walter Reinhart, Winterthur

Langnau

3 May 1936

Dear Dr. Reinhart,

Since it is better for everything to go through you, I am hereby informing you of the times when I would like to practice on the organ in Winterthur. Please be so kind as to let me know if this schedule will be convenient (you have my travel addresses). Please telephone Herr Karl Matthaei and ask him whether he has slated any rehearsals for these times, then please be so kind as to open the church and the organ on Tuesday, May 12, at 2:15 [P.M.] and send someone who can show me how to switch on the bellows motor. I apologize for causing you extra work. My deepest gratitude for this.

Best wishes,

Your devoted

Albert Schweitzer

On the day of the recital itself I will probably stop rehearsing before seven (if everything goes well) and rest at the home of Reverend Zollinger, who lives near the church.

I would like to ask for the following rehearsal times at the Winterthur organ:

Tuesday, May 12. I will be arriving from Zurich at 2:03 P.M. and would like to go directly to the organ and practice from 2:15 to 7:00 P.M.

Wednesday. I will likewise be arriving at 2:03 P.M. and would like to rehearse again from 2:15 to 7:00 P.M.

~

[Schweitzer's outline for the program]

(The poster text is also to be used for newspaper advertisements):

≈

Town church of Winterthur
Wednesday, 13 May 1936
Start: 8:15 P.M.; Finish: 9:45 P.M.
Religious concert
Organ: Albert Schweitzer
Choir: The mixed Winterthur choir
under the direction of Herr Walter Reinhart
Program

1. Prelude and Fugue in
   F Minor   J. S. Bach
2. Choral Preludes for Organ and Chorales for Choir:
   A) Kyrie, Gott Vater in Ewigkeit;
   B) Christe, aller Welt Trost;
   C) Kyrie, Gott,
   Heiliger Geist   J. S. Bach
3) Andante in D Minor   J. S. Bach
4) Choral Preludes for Organ and Chorales for Choir:
   A) Vater unser im Himmelreich
   B) Jesu, meine Freude
   C) Komm, Gott Schöpfer,
   Heiliger Geist   J. S. Bach
5) Prelude and Fugue in
   C Major   J. S. Bach
6) Cantabile from the Sixth
   Organ Symphony   Charles-Marie Widor
7) Chorale for Organ in
   B Minor   César Franck

≈

To Margit Jacobi, Frankfurt am Main
[in Europe, 1936?]

Dear Friend,

I have not been writing, for I am horribly tired and horribly depressed by everything that has been happening here. How shall I find the strength and pleasure to work on philosophy here? I am thinking so much about everything that is weighing down on you [the Jacobi family was Jewish].

Now let me ask you: Have you recovered enough to come and convalesce in the village [Gunsbach] in early July if nothing unexpected happens? The trees outside the window facing the meadows are always asking about you. Can you travel alone or should Fräulein Mathilde [Kottmann] pick you up? I hope that something comes of this plan.

Best wishes,
Your old
A.S.

Don't worry about Erwin.[1] Everything will be all right there!

~

To Rabindranath Tagore

Gunsbach
15 August 1936

[f]

Dear Rabindranath Tagore,

As you know from our mutual friend C. F. Andrews, I have authored a book on Indian thinkers. It was written in German and is now coming out in various languages, including English.[1] I believe that Mr. Andrews has already given you parts of the English translation. He told me that they were of interest to you. I have had the publisher (Hodder and Stoughton, London) send you a copy of the book. Its title is *Indian Thought and Its Development*. Our mutual friend Winternitz of Prague had seen the manuscript. If you read the book, you will note that I have tried to make Indian thought and its depth and grandeur understandable to the European public, which is very ignorant in this area and still believes that Indian thought is identical with the philosophy of Arthur Schopenhauer.

As a true European I have presented Indian thought by analyzing it according to what we call the critical-historical method. I do not think that you will agree with my analysis or with everything I say about you, but I do believe that you will feel the profound understanding of the grandeur of Indian thought in this book and my rapport with it. Let me also tell you on this occasion about my great esteem for you and your thinking.

I am spending several months in Europe, giving lectures and recitals. At the end of the year I will return to my hospital in Lambarene, Africa.

~

To Waldemar Ahlen, organist, Stockholm
                                     Gunsbach
                              11 October 1936

Dear Friend,

Thank you for everything that you are doing for my hospital with
your art. I hope that the organ does not suffer from the renovation
of the church! When shall I be visiting Sweden again?

Last December I did sixteen recordings of Bach organ works for
the Columbia Gramophone Society at a London church. This October
I have to do another twenty-five, likewise by Bach, on a (wonderful)
restored Silbermann organ in Strasbourg [Church of St. Aurelia] for
the same company, plus César Franck's first two chorales.[1]

Best wishes,

                         Your old and grateful
                         Schweitzer

Do you know a young organist named B. Andreas Herserud, Lin-
digö I? He has written me that he is trying to play Bach according
to my principles of simplicity and clarity, which greatly pleases me.

~

To Edouard Nies-Berger, Los Angeles
                              [Gunsbach]
                              6 November 1936[1]

Dear Mr. Nies-Berger,

I am taking the liberty of recommending to you Dr. Gerhard Herz,
who is emigrating to the U.S.A. He previously lived In Düsseldorf
and is an excellent musicologist. He has [written] a very interesting
book on the history of the Bach movement—that is, what Bach's
disciples did to propagate the master's works during the late eighteenth
and early nineteenth centuries. This book was published by Haupt
and is widely recognized.[2]

Because of his [Jewish] background, Dr. Herz has no future in
Germany and is therefore moving to the U.S.A., where he has family.
I know him personally as a capable and kind person, and I am
therefore venturing to ask you to help him, as far as you can, to make
contact with musicians and music journals. If you can do him this
favor, I would be as grateful to you as if you had done it for me.

Do you ever think of Strasbourg? Recently they did a very good performance of Schumann's *Paradies und Peri*. I am still playing in the St. Thomas recitals. In January I am returning to Africa. My mailing address is still Gunsbach, Alsace. From here, everything is forwarded to me in Africa.

I am giving this letter to Dr. Herz so that he may pass it on to you when he is in your area.

⁓

To the Youth Group of the Reformed Church in the United States
Gunsbach, Alsace, France
[during the 1930s]
Copy for Emmy Martin

Dear Young Friends,

Upon returning from Africa I found your letter, which informs me that for several weeks now you have been dealing with my ideas and my work in Africa. Since we live in this fellowship of thought, I am delighted to send you my best wishes. What you find in my works is an attempt, a feeble attempt, to think the thoughts of Jesus, who is the master of us all—think them in the spirit of our time and turn some of them into a reality. We all have to serve Jesus and achieve fellowship with God through Jesus, through love. Some people, very few, are destined to serve Him in their entirety. These people have the easiest time of it. Others are destined to serve Him in ordinary dealings with other human beings, virtually as a small sideline to a main vocation, or to fulfill an ordinary but difficult obligation toward their near and dear. This is a lot harder. Others are destined to serve Jesus by renouncing and suffering. This is the hardest life of all. I myself know many, many people who through ordinary activities or in renunciation and suffering serve Jesus with far more difficulty than I in my way, which draws attention. On the other hand, many people never get to serve Jesus because they keep casting about for some great and visible way of serving Him, and they thereby overlook the modest service that He has designated for them.

Therefore, my dear, young, faraway friends, keep your eyes open, and you will find the ordinary service that He has designated. Ah, God needs all of you so that the sun of His love may shine in this world. You must feel in your hearts that you are the neighbor of all human beings with whom you have dealings, and you must see if someone needs to have some loving service performed for him in a simple way. And do not forget that those who need our love the most are the members of our family and household. With them we are often lacking in conduct and action in the spirit of Jesus. May each of you recognize what sort of help Jesus needs from you and may you perform even ordinary service with joy. May we all find in Him the peace that is greater than all reason.

With my best wishes,

Albert Schweitzer

~

To Margit Jacobi, Frankfurt am Main
on the train
between Lausanne and Basel
20 January 1937

I spent two days in Strasbourg listening to the sample recordings for Gramophone in St. Aurelia. Mr. Legge, the representative of the London Gramophone Society, had come to Strasbourg for that purpose. He found the records wonderful, a lot more beautiful than the London ones! And he said that I ought to make a lot more records in the future. Some of these records will come out in early summer— in Germany too. When you visit Erwin [Jacobi], please bring him records from me as a greeting. We are still traveling along Lake Neuchâtel, which is being agitated by a foehn.

I am taking lovely memories of the village on my trip to Lambarene. Ah, how rich one is if one has beautiful memories. I will always hear the sound of the village bells, with which I have been intimate since childhood. And how lovely it is that you, too, are acquainted with these bells and remember them.

Now the lake has come to an end. It was lovely writing to you without being hindered by work. This is my last letter to you from Europe. Please write me promptly when you visit Erwin and send me his address.

God protect you. I hope you have taken along some joie de vivre and optimism from the village [Gunsbach]. I am leaving Strasbourg on Tuesday (evening). The ship is sailing on Friday evening, the twenty-ninth. Don't write me in Bordeaux. I cannot enjoy letters amid the hustle and bustle of boarding ship. I know that you're thinking about me. And in my thoughts, I walk into the room that faces the bare trees of the garden.

AS

~

To the president of Harvard University

[Gunsbach, 1937]

Dear Mr. President,

My dear student, Dr. Herbert Spiegelberg, whom I regard as an expert in philosophy[1] and also greatly esteem as a human being, is planning to emigrate to America in a little while since he has no future at German universities because of his background. If you can do anything at all for him, then please help him out. You may rest assured that he deserves it and that you would be making me very happy.

I still regret that I cannot attend the celebration of your university because of my urgent work and because I have to be ready for my return trip to Africa. But I do hope I can come later on.

To Prof. Arthur Stoll, Sandoz, Basel

Lambarene

[May 1937]

Dear Professor Stoll,

I am now back to work at the hospital. The heat is dreadful at this time. You have to muster all your energy to accomplish anything. Today there are some 300 patients in the hospital. During a few days recently there were only 250. What a great joy. But it did not last. My work this afternoon consisted of reviewing the pharmacy stocks. I've drawn up a list of the serviceable medicines we need [from] Sandoz; it is enclosed. I believe that your Paris branch can send them to us by parcel post, which is why I have written it in French. Or else you can send them to us from St. Louis. For our local customs office (if we cannot be present at the customs processing in Port-Gentil), it is easiest if the items come from France. We have endless use for the Calcium Sandoz ten percent ampules. The local water is severely lacking in calcium, and so are the bananas and the cassavas.

Thus we now always promptly use Calcium Sandoz Intraveineuse to treat the undernourished people, and the results are excellent. If any woman who comes to deliver a baby is undernourished, she is given Calcium Sandoz intravenously, and the babies demonstrate the success of the mothers' treatment. All these people are poorly nourished and are also afflicted with anemia because of chronic malaria. So please take care of the enclosed order and send the bill to H. Fritz Dinner, Gotthardstrasse 29, Basel; he processes our payments in Switzerland. My heartfelt thanks in advance.

I still fondly remember the lovely hours I spent with you and your near and dear, but I was in such a hurry back then. I hope that some day I can relax in your home.

~

To Monsieur Caval, administrator in the upper Ogowe district, Sindara

Dr. Albert Schweitzer Hospital
3 May 1937

[f]

Thank you for allowing the blacks from the interior who come to my hospital for surgery to ride the motorboat that you use for the mail. We (my colleagues and I) are very grateful to you.

If by any chance there are sick people who want to come to my hospital for an operation and there happens to be a vessel (a boat of the Chargeurs Réunis or the SHO)[1] from Sindara that requires payment, please allow these patients to sail. The captains know that I will pay their passage.

And if you have any sort of expenses for these men that you cannot cover with the budget of your subdivision, please let me know the total. I will send it to you immediately. And if your motorboat has any free space when it goes upstream and you allow cured patients to come along, you would be doing us a great service. Let me thank you in advance.

We are so busy that I cannot foresee any one of us going to Sindara very soon. If you come down to Lambarene, we would be very happy to see you.

With best wishes from the doctors in my hospital and from me,

Sincerely,
Albert Schweitzer

~

From Albert Schweitzer's circular letter to the patrons and friends of the Lambarene hospital

Lambarene
May 1937

Greetings in the spirit of the Lord!
We arrived in Lambarene on February 18 at 11:00 P.M. Fräulein

Emma [Haussknecht], the physician Fräulein Anna Wildikann, and several nurses were waiting for us on the landing dock for the steamer. From far away we saw the lanterns swinging to welcome us.

Boarding two motorboats, we sailed through the mild moonlight toward the hospital, which is located several miles from the steamboat dock and not on the large branch of the river, but on a side branch that is nevertheless 550 yards wide.

After shaking many black hands, I fell asleep amid the noise of the African crickets, a sound I have been familiar with for years.

The next morning the baggage had to be removed from the steamer. A trading post was friendly enough to lend us a small steamer. Luckily, the feared tornado never came. By sunset all the crates were in the Quonset barracks that I built several years ago for storing and unpacking the luggage.

The following Sunday I once again held services at the hospital. During my absence I had been replaced by Fräulein Emma [Haussknecht].

As I ascertained during my first tour of the wards, the hospital is really overcrowded. This is true not only because a large influx of patients has been coming from the interior during the past few months but also because the healed patients cannot be sent home as they ought to be. Normally the brief dry period runs from mid-December to the second half of January, but this year it lasted until late February, and because of the low water level, the steamers cannot sail up the N'Gounié, the large southern branch of the Ogowe. Unfortunately, the major routes to the interior start from the final navigation point of this branch. Thus the hospital has to shelter and feed quite a number of people because we cannot send them home until the rain starts and the waters rise.

~

To Monsieur Simon, SFA (SHO) Lumberyard, Azingo, Ogowe District

> Albert Schweitzer Hospital
> 3 June 1937

[f]

Dear Monsieur Simon,

Your boy, Antoine N'Zamba, is probably in a tertiary stage of sleeping sickness. We no longer handle sleeping sickness; the government physician is responsible for your camp—which has the great advantage that the patients can be observed regularly after receiving treatment.

I therefore ask you to transport this poor boy to the government doctor. Please do so as quickly as possible.

What a sad case!

With my best wishes,

Sincerely yours,
Albert Schweitzer

~

To Emma Haussknecht, Dakar

Lambarene
20 June 1937

Late in the night before mail pickup: very tired. These lines are meant as a friendly greeting in Dakar. I'm delighted that you're coming and that I'll have time to break you in calmly. We're preparing everything in Port-Gentil for your arrival. Don't forget to go to the commissioner first thing in the morning and ask him to return the deposit to you. He first has to get it from the shippers,[1] which will take time. And the steamer won't wait.

Keep nothing but your hand baggage when you go ashore. Incidentally, old Baumgartner will tell you what to do. Wait for the ship on his pinnace. He usually comes when the ship arrives near 10:00 P.M.; he'll come aboard. But you won't go ashore until the next morning.

Have a good trip and have a good rest. *Auf Wiedersehen*,

Best,
Albert Schweitzer

~

To Prof. Dr. Oskar Kraus, Prague

Lambarene
26 June 1937

Dear Friend,

Here I am back at my old job in the dreadful heat. Ah, you often have to summon your last ounce of strength to do what has to be done. Every evening, to which I add a good portion of the night, I work on my philosophy book. Regardless of the length of the book, I am trying to present an overview of the development of human thinking in terms of the affirmation of the world and life and the problem of ethics. At the moment I am completing the chapter on Chinese thinkers.[1] It has been haunting me for years and requires a lot of work, but I do not regret it. There are wonderful minds in Chinese philosophy, not only during the classical period but also in the renaissance of the Sung Dynasty, all the way to the eighteenth century. And these two great directions, running side by side until today: Taoist mysticism with its rejection of knowledge of the world and the ethical naturalism of Kung Tse and Meng Tse. And how these two directions attract one another; the syntheses that have been attempted! But over everything the deep, natural ethics that has been disadvantaged in our European thinking. Well, I've been enjoying it. Granted, the book is getting much too thick, but I'm not thinking about that, at least for the moment. Now I am writing *for myself* the great romance of the development of human thinking.

Best wishes and best regards to you and your daughter,

Your old
Albert Schweitzer

Until now it was terribly hot, but for several days here, thirty miles south of the equator, cooler drifts of air have been announcing winter in the southern hemisphere. It is now high summer forty miles north of here, which is twelve miles north of the equator.

~

To Dr. Maud Royden, Guildhouse Parish, Kensington
[1937]

[e]

I had the good fortune to stumble upon a spring that never runs dry. To keep the walls from collapsing, I had to line them with thick concrete blocks, which Fräulein Haussknecht and I managed to accomplish. The well has an excellent pump, which draws the water from a depth of twenty feet. The pump began its work several weeks ago, and it is a joy to see the happiness of the blacks who come here for water every day. The pump is never still for even five minutes and is very expensive for the hospital. It will be used for five months of the year during the dry season. In the rainy season the inpatients get water from the large cement reservoirs that are built into the hill and gather the rainwater from our roofs.

An inscription, notched in the cement on the wall, will commemorate Dorothy Mannering, and thus her name will be visibly linked with this well of pure water in Equatorial Africa—something that is so precious for all the people who enjoy it.

~

To Ernst Klatscher, Prague

[1937]

Dear Friend,

I don't know whether I have answered your letter of 7 May 1937 in regard to the translation of *Decline and Restoration of Civilization*, but in any event I am writing to you again. I am delighted that the book will be coming out in Czech. I especially love this book. It is a program for our era.

Perhaps I made the mistake of overabridging the book (the original manuscript was twice as long), but then again, this shortness may be an asset. In any case, let us leave the text as is. Tell Mrs. Dortalova how much joy she has given me, and take care of all the business matters—contracts and so forth—as best you can. Also settle the question of the translation fee. Ah, how much work you are saving me! I am enclosing a note for Mrs. Dortalova. Please get it to her. Ah, how much I cherish you all in Prague! When will I be with you again?

~

To Hans Martin

Lambarene
26 September 1937

Dear Hans,

My deepest gratitude for your August letter from Gunsbach. How lovely that you were there after all.

Everything is going smoothly here. I already knew how wells are dug, but now I also know how their walls are built. It is an art.

I am still polishing the [chapters on the] Chinese.[1] They are marvelous fellows. I am enjoying this quiet, silent work! Since my arrival I have never been further than half an hour away from the hospital.

With loving thoughts,

Albert Schweitzer

~

To Monsieur Simon or his representative
Re: The worker Simba, SFA (SHO) Lumberyard, Azingo

Dr. A. Schweitzer Hospital

Lambarene

25 October 1937

[*f*]

Dear Monsieur,

On 28 August 1937 a man named Simba, age twenty-five, was sent
to us from your Azingo lumberyard because of symptoms of mental
disturbance: hospital file P 2574.

He suffers from a persecution mania. We have been observing and
treating him for two months. There are periods when he can circulate
freely, albeit under observation, of course, but he is incapable of
submitting to the discipline of a lumberyard and will always cause
difficulties. We suggest that you cancel his contract on the basis of
the information you receive from us. Until further notice we will
keep him in the hospital, for he would be at risk in village life. Please
let us know when the contract is canceled. From then on I will keep
him in the hospital at my expense until he is able to return to his
village. Please also ask the lumberyard to send him his belongings!

You can send me this man's papers and whatever he needs to obtain
his savings.[1] I will keep them for him.

~

To Lincoln Memorial University, U.S.A.

Lambarene

15 November 1937

For this university, which was founded at the personal request of
Abraham Lincoln, I wish that the spirit of that great and noble man
may inspire the students and arouse their enthusiasm for the ideal of
the truest and deepest humanity. It is only by reviving the spirit of
humanity as embodied in Lincoln that mankind can find its way out
of its present material and spiritual predicament. Even as a boy I was
deeply impressed by Lincoln's personality.

~

To Prof. Albert Fraenkel, Heidelberg
Lambarene
7 December 1937

Dear Professor Fraenkel,

How often I think of you as the father of strophanthus therapy, to which we owe some great successes.[1] I have not yet received your monograph. After consulting with the government botanist in this area, I can tell you that two varieties of strophanthus occur here in the Ogowe District. The more prevalent one is *Strophanthus thollonii*, which grows massively along the shores of the Ogowe, but it is not rich in strophanthin. The other variety, *Strophanthus gratus*, which is a lot richer, grows exclusively in the jungle, especially in the area of N'Djolé (ninety miles northeast of here). I am enclosing a fruit of *Strophanthus thollonni*.

When the nurse, Fräulein Mathilde [Kottmann], was standing on the veranda holding the fruit, the blacks screamed in horror: "That's very poisonous!" I, too, cannot imagine that the arrow tips smeared with a paste made from these seeds can do very much, but the blacks claim otherwise. However, they very often rely purely on tradition. . . .

I will send you a better photograph of the plant as soon as I have your monograph.

When I was in England and Scotland, I was so overextended with recitals and philosophical lectures that I could not go anywhere during my last two sojourns in Europe. I would rather complete my philosophy book than travel. At the moment I am working on the history of Chinese philosophy, the first draft of which goes back to 1920. . . . But I hope we can meet again. I have thought about you from time to time. There are four physicians here and eleven European nurses. On the average, the hospital has 270 to 300 native patients. The main activity is surgery.

To Prof. Dr. Albert Fraenkel, Heidelberg
Second letter

Lambarene
8 December 1937

Dear Herr Fraenkel,

I took the strophanthus seeds down to the hospital and questioned the hunters. They told me that they dry the seeds, grind them, make a thick paste with water, and apply it as densely as possible to the arrow tips. Then, if they shoot birds or monkeys, they have to wait under a tree. After a while the animal grows weak. The monkey vomits, and then it drops from the tree. It doesn't usually work with larger animals (wild boars and the like) unless several arrows hit the mark. One man from the interior claims that they even use this arrow venom when hunting elephants. They all agree that it is very poisonous, and one or another of them has heard about its use on human beings. But they refuse to talk about it.

If you can send us recent literature about the strophanthin treatment, you would be doing us a big favor.

PART SIX

———— ❦ ————

1938 - 1939

To the chiefs of Galoa villages near the hospital
[Lambarene]
Sunday, 9 January 1938

[f]

Throughout the night of January 8–9, tom-toms were beaten in the villages until five in the morning. The inhabitants thus prevented the hospital patients from finding relief in sleep and the physicians and nurses from gaining the strength to serve the sick. I am sad to see that the Galoa people, who are so well served by my hospital, are heedless of the injustice they are doing to the hospital with that nocturnal racket. A few of the patients are extremely sick and are at death's door. . . . In Europe and elsewhere there are laws prohibiting noise in a hospital area. I, for my part, would not complain about the use of a tom-tom, but at issue is the sleep of many poor patients! I am therefore asking the villages not to beat tom-toms after the hospital bell announces curfew (about nine o'clock). Should the tom-toms continue into the night, I will be forced to lodge a complaint with the district commissioner. It would sadden me if I had to get into a dispute with a populace with whom I have been living peacefully for twenty-five years now, but I have to protect my hospital.

To Monsieur Moussa, Kaussa à Kango, subdivision of Libreville
Lambarene
[1938]

[*f*]

My dear Moussa,

Poor Baballi, who underwent a successful operation at the hospital, died of pulmonary tuberculosis today, 30 October 1938. He must have been harboring the illness for a long time. We are very sad because we loved him very much.

Baballi had given one hundred francs to Pahouin Mainghe Bakalle of the village of Akanobor, subdivision Kango, to be passed on to you after his death, but I think it would be better to send you the money directly. I will therefore mail it to the chief administrator of the subdivision of Kango, asking him to remit it to you. Baballi's other belongings will be brought to you by his companion, Abdou of Kango. I believe that would be the best arrangement. We are very sad that Baballi, who recovered from his hernia, died of tuberculosis.

With best wishes,

Your devoted
Albert Schweitzer

~

To Baron Lagerfelt and Greta Lagerfelt, Duseborg, Sweden
Lambarene
Palm Sunday
10 April 1938

Today is Palm Sunday. But this time we are not boating to the small, silent lake. We are all simply too tired to undertake anything. And in this dreadful time our spirits are far too low for us to celebrate. We don't have the energy to get out of our daily grind, so this time the letter will be written at my desk and not in the thick of the jungle. I sit at my desk all day long when I am not being summoned to the hospital, and I try to write the most urgent letters. This is very strenuous because it is horribly hot and sultry.

However, even though I am working like this, my thoughts are in Jerusalem, your high-built city. And what happened there—the entrance of the Lord—is, for me, the prelude to something that has to come someday: the beginning of the Kingdom of God. I feel alienated from the whole new trend of ideas because all these people no longer carry within them the idea of the Kingdom of God. They fail to see the distant goal, without which one goes astray, but that is why we must carry this yearning and assurance all the more solidly....

We must be the people who preserve true thought for a time to come. How well I now understand the prophets who, in the time of the coming and the destruction of Jerusalem, thought about and looked forward to the subsequent future, transcending the present.... That is how Palm Sunday should be. I know that your Palm Sunday thoughts are crossing lands and seas to reach me in Lambarene, just as mine go out to you.

From the bottom of my heart,

Albert Schweitzer

~

To Paul Haupt, publisher, Bonn

23 June 1938

Dear Herr Haupt,

Now for some news that will come as a surprise—a pleasant one, I hope. I have a new book for you! Its title is *African Stories*, and it is roughly the same length as *On the Edge of the Primeval Forest*. It's a loose sequence of serious and humorous stories from Africa. Only a few of them are about the hospital. The manuscript is just being typed. I'll be sending you a copy in two weeks, ready to go. You can then decide whether or not you want it. Meiner has the publishing rights for Germany and all other countries except Switzerland and France. You can have the rights for Switzerland *directly from me*. Please write me whether you want the book.

~

To Dr. Herbert Spiegelberg [emigrated to the United States]

Lambarene

25 July 1938

Dear Herbert,

I wonder how you're doing. You managed to make it at the last moment.[1] Now it will be getting much harder to find refuge.

But don't lose heart! Keep your head! You have such a good mind that you are bound to make your way over there.

In the evenings I sit at my desk. My study of Chinese philosophy has come a long way. On the side I have amused myself by writing African stories, a mixture of serious and humorous ones. When will we see each other again? Give me a permanent address in the U.S.A. where I can write to you, and from where things can be forwarded to you.

With my best wishes and loving thoughts,

Your old

Albert Schweitzer

I hope you see Rhena in New York. And if I can help you with any recommendations, simply ask me. I'll be more than happy. You can get Rhena's address anytime from my American publisher, Henry Holt & Co. (257 Fourth Avenue, New York).

≈

To Léon Morel, missionary, and Georgette Morel
[during the Morel family's trip to Europe]

Lambarene

28 August 1938

[f]

Dear Friends,

Here you've given us a present to celebrate the twenty-fifth anniversary of the hospital! I thank you with all my heart; it is so touching of you to think of my work.[1] And what great favors you have always done for us. It was a joy for me that the missionaries thus took part in the twenty-fifth anniversary of the hospital, and I thought that the day would pass unnoticed. In June I thought about the [missionary] conference that took place back then in Samkita![2] And about our correspondence concerning the orderly whom you were trying to find for me and who did not come. His name was N'Zeng, if I'm not mistaken. How long ago all that was. Today, I have twelve black orderlies! And we even have a Galoa nurse; her name is Antoinette, and she's Protestant.

We were worried about some nurses who were very ill and had to be sent home. This has never happened to us before, but we have to survive everything. I myself am in decent shape given the work I'm obliged to do. Every morning I'm out by 6:45, putting the workers to work. I'm constantly trying to improve the hospital. The well that Mademoiselle Emma [Haussknecht] and I dug and walled in last year has been copiously supplying water throughout the dry season for the entire hospital and the household. It's incredible!

To Dr. Victor Nessmann, Strasbourg

Lambarene
20 November 1938

[f]

Dear Colleague,

I am sending you Monsieur Pouzin from Port-Gentil, where he runs his father's lumberyard. In 1936 he saw a Parisian specialist in radiotherapy (he'll be giving you a letter from the physician) about a wart on the inner part of his sole. The wart vanished, but a lesion opened in the same spot in September 1938. In October, Monsieur Pouzin came to us with this bad lesion. It is the size of a two-franc piece, and all around it the foot is swollen, red, and sensitive to pressure. Since Monsieur Pouzin has made up his mind to go home, and we are thoroughly puzzled by this case, we prefer not to operate. Monsieur Pouzin would like to be treated by a specialist in Strasbourg. I am sending him to you and asking you to do your best for him. If the case requires it, please take Monsieur Pouzin to Monsieur Leriche or some other authority in Strasbourg.

To Margit Jacobi, Frankfurt am Main

7 December 1938

One more thing, which goes without saying: If your situation requires my help [because of her Jewish background], you can fully count on me in any way, including materially. There was really no need to write this, but sometimes it's good to say things that go without saying.

To Dr. Ladislaus Goldschmidt, Lambarene

Gunsbach
3 February 1939

Dear Doctor,

Yesterday, in Bordeaux, I sent an airmail letter to the hospital, and today I have received your dear airmail letter of 17 January 1939, just as I am unpacking. I was tired and depressed (tired because I kept taking care of letters from the big sack during my train ride from Bordeaux to Strasbourg—even at night; depressed because of the distressing political situation). Thus, your dear and very detailed letter was truly invigorating for me.

How splendid that Bayer's quinine preparation has proved itself so well. Your comments on the failure of Digitalie Naturelle strikes me as highly important. So let's stick to Novurit and drop Novasurol and Salyrgan. Sleeping sickness is supposedly making great advances in the Upper Volta territories on the Ivory Coast.... It's good that you diagnosed lues II [syphilis]. I hope the man doesn't bring us too much publicity.

The European situation is very confusing.... I had to answer your letter promptly and quickly since [my reply] has to go off tomorrow in order to reach the avion [plane]. But I had to tell you immediately that you've done me a world of good.

How relieved I am knowing you're there.

~

To M. Fillit, N'Gomo

Lambarene
[1939]

[f]

Re: Nzog Nzaré, instructor in Port-Gentil
The instructor at the Mission school in Port-Gentil has just arrived, brought here in his family's pinnace. He is suffering from a very extensive, very painful periostitis of the left tibia, accompanied by fever. We instantly took the necessary steps. I am writing to you promptly to tell you that the patient will be immobilized for at least two weeks. We hope that this periostitis is not concealing an osteomyelitis, which would be far more serious and last longer. For the moment, we cannot say anything definite.

~

To Jeanette Siefert, Colmar

Lambarene
[April 1939]

[Because of the possibility of war, Albert Schweitzer, after a brief stay in Alsace, returned to Lambarene to continue running his hospital.[1]]

I am writing to you from down in the consulting room, for I insist on again spending almost the entire day down here. The construction work is over and done with. . . . In Colmar I couldn't talk about going away. In case of war, what would become of the people here if *mesures contre les étrangers* [measures against foreigners] were taken! So I have to be here; it's my duty toward the people helping me. I make sure that I do not overwork. . . . We have to believe that a different time will come eventually and that we will then see what we have to do.

With loving thoughts,

Your old
Albert Schweitzer

~

To Fritz Dinner, Basel

Lambarene
Palm Sunday, 2 April 1939[1]

Dear Friend,

We're having an agitated Palm Sunday. The two nurses are leaving today, operations have to be performed, and twenty new patients from the interior have just been dropped off here by a motorboat. . . . A motorboat is now heading across the water, carrying the luggage of the two departing nurses. What a time we had getting the people together on a Sunday to stow the crates into the boat! Now I'm sitting at my desk for a moment, but I have to go down right away to see how the operation is going (Dr. Goldschmidt is performing it). Also, we are all waiting to hear the tooting of the steamer bringing the mail, and we don't know whether it'll arrive at twelve or four or midnight.

Otherwise everything is fine here. I feel fairly well rested from the six weeks I spent at sea [round trip between Lambarene and Bordeaux]. I'm also able to work on my philosophy book in the evenings. I've gotten back into the material quite nicely.

> Your devoted
> Albert Schweitzer

~

To Lotte Gerhold-Schall, Königsfeld

> Lambarene
> 21 July 1939

Dear Lotte,

I am writing to you to express my best wishes for your son.[1] I was very happy for you. How I wish the boy could have been born in a better time than this so that he might have enjoyed a quiet youth such as I was blessed with. Alas, this is impossible for the present generation. But may he remain healthy, become capable, and have a good heart . . . and grow spiritually. The most important thing is still what becomes of a person spiritually. Please transmit my congratulations to your husband. Rhena was deeply impressed when she got to know my work here.[2] This is my third [consecutive] year on the equator . . . but I'm enduring it nicely. I often wonder how I manage to stay on my feet with all this work, this fatigue, and my many anxieties. But I would love to go strolling with you again through the Donis Forest in Königsfeld. Will we ever do it again? I hope you're in beautiful Königsfeld now. Ah, how lovely when the train climbs over Triberg [in the Black Forest], and you smell the fragrant fresh air! Think of me when you go there.

   With ever-loving thoughts,

> Albert Schweitzer

Best regards to your husband.

PART   SEVEN

————— ∞ —————

1941 - 1946

~

[From 1940 to 1945, Albert Schweitzer's letters to people in English-speaking countries were usually sent in English translations, most of which are still extant and are reprinted here as is.]

~

To Edward H. Hume, M.D., Christian Medical Council for Overseas Work, New York

Lambarene
9 January 1941

[e]

Dear Friend,

I have received your welcome letter of the 30 September 1940. The address is correct. There are now American boats which come directly to Matadi, Belgian Congo. For there the letters and postal packages arrive here in the Gabon.

Certainly you were anxious about us, but the hospital continues to function; we have sufficient food and enjoy good health, although [we are] a little fatigued.

It is nearly four years that I am once more on the Equator. But I have conserved my energy. We have a great deal of work here at the Hospital.

How may I thank the Christian Medical Council for the offer to send us what is needed here, from the U.S.A.[1] I am deeply thankful for it. Kindly convey my sincere gratitude to Mr. Allen O. Whipple, M.D. And to Mr. O. H. I. Lerrigo, M.D. I am availing myself of your kindly offer.

It is quite impossible at the present time for us to receive anything from Europe. It is therefore in the nature of a miracle for me, the help offered by friends in the U.S.A.

Unfortunately it is not only medicaments and instruments which are needed, but also articles for the household. I take therefore the courage to ask you, if you would kindly ask a Commercial Firm to furnish us [with] these necessities. Also please choose someone of experience for superintending these purchases and dispatchings.

I do not know what would happen to me now if I hadn't friends in the U.S.A. to maintain the work which can no longer be maintained in Europe! I shall never be able to thank you sufficiently. I never thought, the day when you were at Gunsbach, that I should be obliged to ask of you such great help. But if it is not possible to send me the articles for the household, please let me know. I should not wish to cause any trouble.

We are on an average about thirty persons at table, including our white patients. Naturally, we eat also a large quantity of the local fruits, sweet potatoes, bananas, and ignames [yams]. Unfortunately the sweet potatoes, which replace potatoes, are only available four months of the year; and do not keep.

During the eight months of the rainy weather it is hardly possible to grow anything other than salads [lettuce], beans, and leeks. But during the dry weather we gather enough tomatoes to enable us to make preserves of tomato sauce, which is very useful to us for seasoning rice.

It is striking how Europeans lose appetite in the damp heat. This is one of my sorrows [worries] concerning my helpers. Therefore I try to find anything for animating the appetite. Potatoes cannot grow here, the climate being too hot and too damp. But sweet potatoes are an excellent substitute during a short time in the year. Sometimes we get some potatoes from Cameroon, where they are planted. But is it rather seldom.

These indications [that] I give you may help you to understand our ways to live here.

Now the question [of] how to pay for all this. Mr. Everett Skillings at Middlebury College in Middlebury, Vermont,[2] received contributions for my hospital. I ignore [that is, do not know] the amount of these gifts. If the sum is not sufficient (and I am afraid it will not be sufficient) in consequence reduce the order of the supplies I ask for. My order comprises the most necessary supplies for the next two years. So if Mr. Skillings has not a sum sufficient to pay them, reduce the order. I ask, please to reduce it. But if you reduce [it], please do not diminish the five kilos of quinine. We want them absolutely.... I would even have asked for six kilos if it would be less expensive.

I am sending you a list of articles for the electric lighting which we need.

We are as a rule, in the habit of using petrol lamps for lighting here. But for the operating theater, the consulting rooms, and the dispensary, we need better lighting, the petrol is also very expensive here. We have a small generating set which can furnish the current for the lighting, which we intended installing before the outbreak of war. We would still like to install the electricity for better lighting, in case we are obliged to operate or to tend to the sick at night, also to be able to economize petrol. We would be very glad to have electric lighting in our operating and consulting rooms. That would be a great help for us. But I am afraid this is a great deal of bother I am causing you.

I hope that you and Mrs. Hume are in good health. Please pay my respects to Mrs. Hume.

One day I hope we will meet again at Gunsbach.

～

To Dr. F. G. Cawston, Britannia Buildings, Durban, South Africa
                    Lambarene
                    27 November 1941

Dear Dr. Cawston,

I am deeply grateful for your letters of October 17 and October 30. You have done me a great service by giving your guarantee to Bayer Pharma, Johannesburg, for the four small bottles of Novocain. Bayer Pharma has now allowed me to transmit payment of the four pounds through Banque Belge d'Afrique in Brazzaville, which makes things much easier for me. I have not yet received the package, but I hope it will arrive soon. In the future I will try to order directly from Bayer Pharma in Johannesburg [to avoid] bothering you.

Meanwhile, the lovely metal catheters have arrived. How kind of you to send them to us. They are finer and lovelier than the ones we have, but we are still happy to have the latter. Let me suggest that we hold on to them until the end of the war and then send them back to you. In any case, our deepest thanks for all your kindness.

～

To Prof. Dr. Bixler, president of Colby College
                    [Lambarene, February 1942]

I absolutely have to tell you how moved I am that so many kind
people in the United States are helping me with their gifts so that I
can keep my hospital going in these difficult times. I sense how much
you yourself are doing to interest such people in my work. I am
certain that you spend a lot of time writing letters on my behalf. I
know from experience how much work such things require. That is
why I would like you to know how grateful I am to you.

The medicines have not yet arrived. I am worried about all the
dangers that may threaten them en route. How splendid it will be
when they arrive. All of us—doctors and nurses—are looking forward
to them. We always have a lot of work in the hospital. Naturally, we
are all rather weary from our long sojourns in this climate, but we
are healthy. I have already told you that we have enough to eat. We
do our work as best we can. When shall we meet again? My wife,[1]
along with me, sends you, your wife, and your children her best
regards. Again, thank you so much for everything.

~

To Gardner Evans, organist, Chicago
                    Lambarene, Gabon
                    French Equatorial Africa
                    10 August 1942

                                                [e]

Dear Mr. Evans,

I [have] just received your letter of June 29, which I [am] answer[ing]
at once.

Bach's compositions for organ never aim at any mere virtuosoship.[1]
They all have been composed for the church. They lose their true
character when played too quickly. They lose then even their effect,
as the hearer can no more follow the tone-line and imagine the
structure of the composition, but hears only a chaos of sound. We
know that the organist Hesse from Breslau, who surrendered [that
is, handed down to] us the old tradition [of] how to play Bach's organ
works, played all fugues (even the great Fugue in G Minor) in a very
moderate tempo. . . . Widor and Guilmant, who heard Hesse and also
old organists in Germany who had known him, have assured me [of
this]. Bach himself could not think of playing his organ works quickly.

I have myself in Alsace . . . played organs of Silbermann of the eighteenth century on which the pressing-down of the keys was a real effort. Another impediment is the fact that the keys in these old organs go down twice as deep as in modern ones. An old great organ, on which all difficulties of the old mechanisms can be experienced, is in Leeuwerden in the north of Holland; but what wonderful sound it has.

[The final paragraph of this English-language letter has been lost; the translation is based on the German version:]

The main thing in performing Bach's works is to present them as clearly and vividly as possible to the listener. Whenever I have played Bach in Europe, audiences were intially surprised by my slow tempi. But I stuck to my guns, and the people got more and more used to them and then took them for granted. My teacher Widor played Bach in a very moderate tempo.

~

To Roy Finch, Civilian Public Service, Camp Coleville, California
Lambarene
28 August 1943

Dear Mr. Finch,

Through Prof. Everett Skillings I have just received your friendly lines of December 1942 and the news of the valuable gift that was sent to my hospital by the Choral Club of the camp. I am deeply moved by the fact that this gift is the result of a sacrifice. My deepest thanks also for the gift from the sale of fish. I was very interested in the lovely program of the recital for my hospital. Your gift will be turned into medicines that I have ordered from the United States. Special thanks are due to you for the words you have devoted to my work and my ideas. Currently, we have a great deal to do in the hospital.

At the moment my main job is surgery since my colleague, who is in charge of the operating room, has left for several months for a vacation in the southern African mountains. I myself am fairly able to endure the very hot and muggy climate here, and I hope I can keep working until the end of the war without having to go on vacation in a different climate. The work here is very strenuous because there is so much to do aside from medical duties. You have to make sure that the critically ill and the lepers are properly fed and receive soup and fruit.

I have been here steadily since 1937 except for twelve days in early

1939 when I took a quick trip to Europe to settle some affairs and make purchases.

Could you give the chorus members and their conductor my warmest regards and tell them once again how deeply grateful I am. Special thanks to Mr. Everett for talking about my musical impact. Every evening, if I am not too tired, I practice on my pedal piano.

May God grant us all a speedy peace and may humanity emerge into the light from its terrible darkness.

My wife and I send you our best.

~

To Dr. Maud Royden, Nestlewood, Baylays Hill, Sevenoaks, Kent
Lambarene
25 October 1943

[f]

Dear Maud Royden,

I was very touched by your taking the trouble to write to me and sending me news about yourself and dear Hudson Shaw.[1] I received your lines in perfect health. In June I sent my young colleague on vacation that he might relax a bit; throughout these months I have been doing all the work in the hospital on my own, helped only by Dr. Wildikann[2] who is a remarkable worker. The division of labor is as follows: She takes care of the women and children and I the men, urology, and surgery. I'm very happy to be doing operations again, to which I devote two and sometimes three mornings a week. There is so much to do here in surgery, especially in regard to hernias and elephantiasis tumors. Luckily, we still have material for operations. I spend two hours a day overseeing the workers in the garden and the plantation and directing the two carpenters who are still busy maintaining and repairing the many hospital buildings. I am touched by the great kindness that our friends in Great Britain continue to show toward my work, and I frequently recall the hours I spent at Guildhouse. At present my wife is spending a brief holiday at the seashore. It is a blessing that I can endure the infamous jungle climate so well.

With kindest thoughts,

Your devoted and grateful
Albert Schweitzer

~

To the Reverend E. S. Fuminaga, director of the Manoa Mission, Honolulu

[1943]

Dear Reverend Fuminaga,

Professor Skillings has forwarded the kind letter that you sent with a gift from your Sunday school in late 1942. Please tell the children how deeply grateful I am for your great sacrifice. Their gift will be used for the many sick black children in my hospital. They will receive medicine and blankets to protect them against the great dampness of the nights here. They are very grateful for your help. Most of the children suffer from large ulcerations on their feet. Our medical staff consists of three physicians and four nurses. Naturally, we are exhausted by the great amount of work and the hot, muggy climate, but we nevertheless have the energy to do our work. The kindness we experience from so many people gives us new courage every day.

With loving regards to the children and to you and your assistants.

Your devoted
Albert Schweitzer

To the Reverend F. E. Raymond, Forestville, California
Lambarene
7 March 1944

Cher Monsieur Raymond,

Thank you for your very kind lines of 17 November 1943, which I received today. Please convey my thanks to your church for wanting to help my work in these difficult times. My hospital owes so much to our American friends. If we are still able to perform the most urgent operations regularly, it is because we received catgut from the United States in 1943. I was very interested to read that you, too, were once involved in missionary work. How hard it must be to give it up for reasons of health. There are three of us doctors and four nurses at my hospital. The only possible way to send gifts to my hospital is through Prof. Everett Skillings, Middlebury College, Vermont. He collects the donations for me and forwards them through the Foreign Missions Committee unless he uses them to buy medicines in the U.S.A. for my hospital.

Once again, my warmest thanks.

With best wishes to you and your church,

Albert Schweitzer

~

To David Rosolio, Tel Aviv

Lambarene
25 November 1944

[*f*]

Dear Monsieur Rosolio,

Thank you for your friendly lines of September '44. It is very kind of you to be so interested in me. Let me give you some information that may be useful for your article. . . .

I spent many nights [in my early Strasbourg days] corresponding about the building of organs for which my advice was sought. Even in Africa I still correspond about this subject. The first organ that was restored under my supervision was the Silbermann organ at St. Thomas's Church in Strasbourg at the beginning of the century. The work was artistically carried out by the Alsatian organ builder Fritz Härpfer, who subsequently implemented further restorations of this nature.

On my concert tours I have gotten to know the most interesting organs in Europe. I have also frequently taken special trips solely to view organs that interested me. When I went to Africa in 1913, the Parish Bach Society gave me a pedal piano constructed for tropical countries by the Gaveau firm in Paris. This piano has held out well, allowing me to practice my organ-playing technique. Upon arriving in Europe I instantly feel at home with organs. I perform chiefly the organ works of Bach, César Franck, and Widor as well as Mendelssohn-Bartholdy. I consider Mendelssohn, as Widor did, the creator of the modern style in organ music. His two final organ sonatas [V and VI] are masterpieces, which I study and always play with renewed interest. If I am not too tired I joyfully study the organ every evening on my pedal piano.

I greatly admire the monumental organs in Holland. The old English organs are very beautiful. Some of my favorite organs are to be found in Swiss cathedrals. In Alsace there are several lovely medium-sized organs that were built according to my principles. At the Muhlbach church where my grandfather [Pastor Schillinger],[1] a connoisseur of organ construction, presided, I installed a model organ for a small village; it was based on the organ built under his supervision and then destroyed during World War I. . . .

Please say hello to Monsieur Ravina and extend my good wishes to him for the success of his encyclopedia.

~

To Emil Mettler, London

[Lambarene]
January–February 1945

[e]

On the day of my 70th [birthday], in the evening, and at the stated hour by the BBC,[1] we had gathered in the room of one of the hospital patients, a European who had brought with him a most excellent wireless set, so that he should not feel too lonely at the hospital.

Picture the scene[2]: the whole staff, my wife and myself and all the European patients gathered together in front of the radio, [which] was already lit, although the loudspeaker, to begin with, gave out only scratching and spitting noises.

The heat was terrible! Sweat dripped from our faces and hands. Through the open window, which is covered with a mosquito net, we could see the palm trees lightly swaying in the wind and heard the concert of crickets chirping in the grass. From afar, beyond the river, where a small village is situated, came the sound of the tom-toms. Suddenly, the loudspeaker stops scratching, and we hear a tribute from the BBC, then a voice introducing the organ pieces, then the organ record itself, and a voice saying: "Dr. Schweitzer himself is listening at this very moment in Lambarene." I was deeply moved.

Luckily, there was no storm in the air, consequently no atmospherics, so that reception was clear. A European at Lambarene who owns a powerful radio set told me the following day that he had never heard any transmission of music from so far, so perfectly clear.

And suddenly there is silence again. We hear once more the branches of palm trees slowly swaying in the wind and the chirping of crickets. We remain seated for a while before leaving the room. The stars twinkle through the palm trees in front of the house.

After supper the wireless station at Brazzaville transmitted a special program. They had also taken note of my [birthday] and expressed in sympathetic words their thanks for the services I had rendered to the country, but, unfortunately, these came through very indistinct owing to a tornado which swept some parts of the country.

Thank you for sending me the little volume of sermons on *The Will of God* by our friend Leslie Weatherhead. . . .

Greetings to our friends. May God preserve them from all dangers.

I think every day of those who endure so much suffering in London. When will the end come to all this misfortune?

Even if Peace comes soon, I would first have to replace all the hospital staff and initiate the newcomers before there would be any likelihood of my being able to go on furlough.

We have some anxieties about a food shortage. The harvest of manioc and bananas has failed. Luckily, I was able to procure some rice from the interior. About Gunsbach and my house where you stayed with me, I know nothing.

With best thoughts from my wife and myself, I remain as ever

Cordially yours,
Albert Schweitzer

~

To the General Council of Congregational Churches, U.S.A.
[Lambarene]
23 January 1945

[e]

[Your] telegram arrived just in time for my birthday. Your kind wishes for my seventy years have given me great pleasure. I am deeply moved that you have thought of proving [that is, showing] me such friendliness. Alas, for what I have to do and for a long time, it might be good for the hospital if I could go on directing it, I ought to be thirty and not seventy years old. But it is a great privilege that at seventy I am still able to do the necessary [work]. Every day I realize with profound gratitude toward God the grace that at my age I can still do my work in the African jungle.

By the great gift, which the telegram announces and to which you have so generously contributed, I am stirred with emotion, and I thank you from the depth of my heart. This magnificent present will find good use. It will help to nourish the many single sick in my hospital who have come from afar and don't possess anything and who are a constant sorrow [that is, concern] for me. The natives of the virgin forest here are nearly all very poor. I have not only to give them food but also to put a blanket and a mosquito net at their disposal. And very often they have to stay here for weeks, even for months. I feel so sorry if I have to send away a patient who has not quite fully recovered, in order to economize the food which I am obliged to give him! Your wonderful gift frees me of much sorrow [that is, anxiety] of that kind. This is a glorious feeling for me, to whom deliverance [from] such [anxiety] gives back fresh courage.

What makes it so difficult to work in this country is the terribly hot and moist climate. Here in the lower parts of the [jungle] it is worse. Farther in the interior, in regions [at high] altitudes, it is better. I have the splendid privilege, for which I thank God every day, that I can stand this climate fairly well, but some of my coworkers suffer much from it. One of our nurse[s] has been so exhausted by it that she had to be sent to Cameroon in August 1944 to restore her health and is recovering only very slowly. But in general, we keep steadfast and [maintain] the necessary energy to do our work. We are two [male] doctors, one lady doctor, and four nurses. My wife too takes her part in the work. We are all longing for the return of peace. But when it comes, we shall still have to wait for those from Europe who come to take our places. My wife and I shall probably be the last to return. While I write this, late in the night, a tornado has broken out and brought some refreshment of the air.

It has meant much to me that in this difficult time, the friends [in] the U.S.A. have [provided] such generous help to my hospital. Without it I don't know how it could have been kept running. How delighted we were in 1943 when several cases of medicines from the U.S.A. arrived safely! And now, for the second time, a number of cases have crossed the ocean and are waiting in an African port, from where we hope they will soon be transported to the mouth of the Ogowe and up the river to Lambarene. You will know that the Mission station of Lambarene [was] founded by American missionaries in 1874. It is thus of the same age as I. With Dr. Nassau, one of the first in Lambarene, I was still exchanging letters in 1913 and 1914. Amongst the very old Christians, the memory of the first American missionaries is still alive. So it seems wonderfully providential that in the hardship of our time, the American churches [give] their help to the Lambarene hospital. Once more, deepest thanks for your kindness!

Mrs. Schweitzer and I are sending you and the members of the General Council our kindest regards.

~

To Erwin Rueben Jacobi, Palestine

27 January 1945

[*f*]

Dear Friend,

I am very touched that you have remembered my seventieth birthday. My deepest thanks for your telegram. As I held it in my hand, I envisioned how we would have celebrated this day in Alsace, surrounded by friends, if the times were normal. And your dear mother would have been with us. Will we ever learn anything about her? Madame Siegfried Ochs[1] was also transported to an unknown place. How often I think about your mother who did so much for us. I've heard from Mademoiselle Mathilde Kottmann, rue des Greniers in Strasbourg; her letter is dated December 6 and arrived here on the twenty-sixth. She is well. I can picture your mother in an apron, helping Madame Martin pack the things for Lambarene. Madame Martin is in Gunsbach; we have no word from her.

My wife and I send you and your wife our best regards. When will I see you again?

Cordially,
Albert Schweitzer

〜

To George K. Bell, Bishop of Chichester, the British Council (Dr. Schweitzer's Hospital Fund)

Lambarene
23 March 1945

[f]

Monsignor,

I am writing to tell you how touched I was by the sympathetic way you and other members of the Council spoke about me and my work in a letter addressed to the editor of *The Times* on the occasion of my seventieth birthday [published on 14 January 1945].[1] I was greatly surprised by this way of remembering my birthday. Thank you from the bottom of my heart. How many good things I have received from my friends in Great Britain since the start of my work.

I have to thank God that I can still stand at my age and that I can still do my job. I can withstand this debilitating climate remarkably well.

We see much misery every day. On each of these days I think of the dangers that threaten London and its surroundings daily. Shall we see an end to these horrors soon? And even when peace comes, I will have to spend a few more months in Lambarene, sending my present coworkers home and receiving and breaking in new ones.

Best wishes from my wife and myself,

Your deeply devoted
Albert Schweitzer

∽

To the Reverend Dr. George Seaver, Dublin
[In March 1945, Helene Schweitzer, in Lambarene, sent information
to Dr. George Seaver,[1] Albert Schweitzer's biographer in Dublin. She
had returned to Lambarene in August 1941 after a difficult journey
via Portugal, Portuguese Angola, and the Belgian Congo to help her
husband in this difficult period. In her letter to George Seaver, she
now reports:]

[e]

I would be delighted to answer your questions, especially because it
gives me a chance to express my gratitude to your country; for it
provided very effective assistance for my journey. I also received
exceedingly friendly and active help from the Red Cross in Geneva.

Since I knew a British visa was necessary, I asked the Red Cross
to get me the address of the London agency to which I would have
to apply. The reason I gave for my trip was that I was the eldest of
the nurses in Lambarene and could make myself useful there because
no young nurses were available. The Red Cross informed me that an
envoy was just about to leave for London, and he would submit my
application, but I might have to wait a long time for a response. It
really did take a long time. But then I received a wonderful surprise:
a telegram and then a letter that did not contain the address I had
requested; instead, I was told I could leave immediately. Furthermore,
the appropriate offices in London had indicated that my journey
should be facilitated as much as possible!

My next step was to obtain permission to leave France. During
earlier discussions of this problem, I had been told that if I could get
the permit indicating my admission to the colony, I would have little
or no difficulty getting a passport. However, when I unexpectedly did
obtain this permit, it took seven weeks to gather the necessary papers
and passes for leaving Bordeaux and then, subsequently, another four
weeks to get out of Lisbon. Indeed, I received my final passport exactly
half an hour before the ship was to leave the harbor!

My voyage on a neutral (Portuguese) steamer took place without
any incidents, in broad daylight and in a radiant nocturnal illumi-
nation; and my reception in Angola was quite consistent with the
friendly assurances I had received from the authorities in London. I
was also relieved of another worry. I had somewhat anxiously steeled
myself for a long, slow three-month trip through the jungle of an

unknown region; but to my great relief, it turned into a week of motoring along new roads and finally a ride down the familiar river to the hospital, where I arrived on 2 August 1941.

Upon arriving, I learned that I was the first and, to my knowledge, the only person who had succeeded in coming here legally from France since 1940. Once again, and with profound gratitude, I would like to express how deeply obliged I feel for the wonderful assistance that I have so often received in my life; it was mostly perfect strangers whose undeserved friendliness helped me to endure everything, which would otherwise have been so difficult.

[About Albert Schweitzer:] Forty-three years have gone by since we first became friends and started working together. We met with a sense of responsibility for all the good things that we had received in our lives and with the awareness that we would have to pay for them by helping others. It has been the pride and joy of my life to follow him in all his activities and to be at his side; and I only regret that lack of strength prevented me from keeping up with him. But even he, no matter how strong and rugged he may be despite his hard and ceaseless work, needs a complete vacation, which he has not had during the nine years he has been out here. May the end of this disastrous war come soon and with it a possibility of humane living conditions for all mankind!

~

[This text by Albert Schweitzer, dated "Third Advent Sunday, 1945," appeared in a circular letter to the patrons and friends of the hospital. It described several months during 1944–45 when it was extremely difficult to send letters to most European countries.]

[1945]

Although we are not always kept informed, we are nevertheless haunted and oppressed by the terrible things that keep happening. We are worried about so many people who are close to us and endangered by the events. We are virtually overcome with shame that we have enough to eat here while millions of people far away are starving. We are horrified by the news of what is happening in the prison camps, about the mistreatment of the Jews, and about the sufferings of deported populations. We are shaken by the plight of the Dutch, about which we are now only gradually finding out.

We know that all of us have to pull ourselves together every day and get to work despite our constant dejection. We simply cannot fathom the fact that our calling is to help compassionately while others are condemned to suffer or have to perform an activity that causes suffering and death. The fact that we are blessed in this way gives us new strength for our work every day and makes this work precious.

The news that the war in Europe was over reached us on the afternoon of Monday, May 7. After lunch I was at my desk, completing urgent letters that were to be brought to the ocean-bound steamer at two o'clock. All at once a white patient who had brought along his radio popped up in front of my window. He shouted that according to German bulletins transmitted by the radio station in Leopoldville, Belgian Congo, a European armistice was about to be concluded at sea and on land. But I had to remain at my desk in order to finish the letters, which had to go off very soon. After that I had to go down to the hospital where the cardiac cases and other patients were to be treated at 2:00 P.M. During the afternoon the bell was rung and the gathered hospital inhabitants were told that the war was over. Later on, despite my great fatigue, I had to drag myself to the plantations to check the work.

It was not until evening that it hit me, and I tried to imagine what the end of hostilities in Europe means and what the many people must feel as they experience the first night in years without fear of imminent bombings. While the palm trees softly rustled in the darkness, I went to the shelf, took down the small book of sayings of Lao Tse, the great Chinese philosopher of the sixth century B.C., and read his poignant words about war and victory.

> *Weapons are tools of disaster, not tools for the noble person. He uses them only when he has no other choice. . . . Calm and peace are supreme for him.*
>
> *He wins, but it brings him no pleasure. If anyone felt pleasure at winning, he would be feeling pleasure in murder. . . .*
>
> *At a victory celebration, the statesman should take his place according to the custom of funerals. The killing of large numbers of people should be mourned with tears of pity. That is why the man who has won in battle should act as if he were attending a memorial service.*

Since autumn 1945 we have been in a difficult situation regarding food for our many patients. Our shortage of bananas and manioc was ultimately caused by the rain that fell during the dry season in the summer of 1944, preventing the natives from burning the felled forest and, to a large extent, doing the necessary plantings. This lack of plantings is being felt now when they would normally be bearing fruit. My fears for the war years have now come true after the war.

Luckily, a very capable district commissioner farther inland, in the Tschibanga region, has, since 1942, been prodding the population to grow rice in the suitable areas. This rice is trucked to Lambarene along the new road, and I buy as much of it as I can, given the inevitable inflation since early 1945. Thus, since October when the villages could no longer supply us with bananas and manioc, I have been able to provide rice for our inpatients and employees. If the district commissioner had not introduced rice growing in his area and if contributions from the friends of the hospital had not provided me with the wherewithal to purchase a significant amount of rice, then I would have been forced to shut the hospital down in October, just as the schools at the Mission stations have been closed because no food is available for the children. However, I am still not certain that my rice will hold out until enough bananas and manioc become available again.

Since the end of the war, prices here have been climbing swiftly and steadily, whereas until then inflation remained within relatively moderate bounds. Thrifty as we may be, I have to assume that the cost of running the hospital will soon quadruple!

Thus, the future existence of the hospital will be highly problematical. We doubt whether it can even survive since we cannot as yet estimate the impoverishment that is spreading everywhere.

But we trust that the friends of our hospital will remain loyal to it even in the coming difficult circumstances. We can assure them of one thing: This work is necessary, and in the future it will be more necessary than ever. We who know how much physical misery exists here and what the hospital means for the many people involved dare to ask our friends: "Help the hospital and keep it open for them."

≈

To Erwin Rueben Jacobi, Tel Aviv

Lambarene

12 June 1945

[f]

Dear Friend,

You can well imagine that your letter announcing your mother's demise has shaken me deeply. I had kept hoping that she could survive. . . . [1] You know how close I was to your parents, your sister, and yourself. I so greatly enjoyed getting to know your father better and better. Whenever he came to Strasbourg and occasionally took his meals with us on Speichergasse, we could sense that he was relaxing. That was where I really got to know him. After her first operation, your mother rested in Gunsbach. She was still rather weak. I saw her there for only a few days since I had to go out of town. She enjoyed the peace and quiet of the valley and the house, but she sensed that she was not completely cured. How much kindness she showed all of us who were working for Lambarene, and how many things she did for us! I have conveyed the news of her demise to Madame Martin and Mademoiselle Mathilde [Kottmann] in Alsace. . . . Both of them, and also Mademoiselle Emma [Haussknecht], were deeply attached to her. My wife has asked me to express her profound sympathies in your great grief. . . . It still has not fully hit me that I will never see your mother again. . . . You can always be certain of my deep friendship for you. . . . You are the only member left of that family to whom I was so attached. The time I admired your mother most was when she was so courageous during her early period in Frankfurt when she was concerned about your father's health. . . . My best wishes to you, your wife, your child.

Yours truly,

Albert Schweitzer

~

To Mathilde Kottmann, Strasbourg
Lambarene
2 July 1945

[*f*]

This morning I wanted to write to you in peace and quiet while waiting for the mail, but I've just discovered that one of the recent surgical patients is showing the first symptoms of tetanus! So I have to spend the entire morning down below, preparing all the solutions to begin treatment. . . . I'm jotting down these lines for you before breakfast. Mademoiselle Emma [Haussknecht] is down in the garden, planting cabbages before breakfast. . . . You can see that we are completely absorbed in our work. I have learned that planes and boats will be even rarer than we thought. Here, all the people who hoped to go back to France in early May are very worried, as are the Borellis and the Galleys.¹ I myself was very skeptical from the start, but let's change the subject and not get discouraged.

The main thing is that we know you're going to come, and we'll hold out until you're finally here. And then we'll dump all the work on you. Yesterday I ran into Monsieur Wehrli, and he sends you his regards. He now runs the hotel[2] instead of the Juvins, who are waiting to go home. This is a thoroughly gray morning, a typical morning in the rainy season. . . . There goes the breakfast bell. After wolfing down my breakfast, I'm going to switch on the icebox, and then I'll be busy all morning with the poor man with tetanus.

From the bottom of my heart until we meet again,

Your devoted
Albert Schweitzer

≈

To Edouard Nies-Berger, organist with the New York Philharmonic Orchestra, New York

Lambarene
6 October 1945

[f]

Dear Monsieur Nies-Berger,

I'm deeply touched by all your efforts on behalf of my work. Many recitals have been given for me, and with fine material results. Harlem, Brooklyn, Coatesville! You are a loyal friend of my work. I don't know how to thank you. I am worried about the future of my project! Many friends who used to help me in Europe are ruined for a long time. The letters I receive from Holland are heart-wrenching. . . . There is total misery. In Alsace, entire countrysides have been destroyed. . . . Every day I tell myself how much I owe all of you in the U.S.A. for continuing to support my work. It's providential.

I was very interested in what you wrote me about Bruno Walter. Give him my best. I am writing to Reverend Harding and the Sunday school children. The letter is enclosed in a separate envelope. I hope that your wife is resting nicely in Arizona. As for me, my life is a bit less tiring since the arrival of Mademoiselle Mathilde [Kottmann] (who has been on the hospital staff since 1924. I sometimes manage to get to bed a bit earlier. Thank you again for everything.

My wife and I wish both of you the very best.

Albert Schweitzer

I still haven't received your composition on the Resurrection. I've read the analysis of the piece in the program you sent me.

≈

To John Ritzenthaler, New York

Lambarene

1 November 1945

Dear Compatriot,

Whenever I spent a holiday in Gunsbach, I often preached from the pulpit of my grandfather Schillinger. Now the Muhlbach pastor is Herr Klein, who was my student when I taught theology at the university in Strasbourg. Muhlbach did not suffer in the war.

We now have something of a famine here. It was caused by the far-too-meager yield of the crops planted in the summer of 1944. We have almost no bananas and almost no manioc. Since I have been acquainted with the countryside for a long time, I could see the disaster brewing. And last spring when a trading post in Lambarene happened ("happened" is the right word) to be carrying rice from the interior, I stocked up on it. I paid for this wholesale purchase with the American donations that I received for my seventieth birthday. The kind gift from the Unitarian Service Committee was a major factor in this purchase. How grateful I am to the members.

The chance to buy rice was unique and unexpected! And we have been living on this rice since July. If it were not for this supply, I would be unable to feed the sick and would be forced to send them home! The situation will gradually improve as of next spring when the crops that were sown last summer will start to yield. Such famines occur here every ten years or so. What would have become of us if this had happened during the war years!

My best regards to Mr. Broocks, Dr. Joy,[1] Dr. Fletscher, and our other Boston friends.... Please tell them that their donation, transformed into rice, was a great boon.

My wife and I send you, your wife, and your children our best wishes. Special regards to John, my young medical colleague. I'm delighted that he doesn't have to go off to war now.

~

To Madame Nessmann, Strasbourg

16 November 1945

Dear Madame Nessmann,

Thnk you from the bottom of my heart for sending me the three photographs of our colleague. How lovely of you to go to all this trouble. We were very interested in the two more recent photographs.

However, we are also framing the other one, which was taken during his sojourn here, and we will place it in the large consulting room. Our warmest thanks for everything you have reported to us about his activities in Perigord and his tragic end. You have told me many things I did not know. . . . [1] I was also very interested in what you wrote me about the children and how loving they are with you.

~

To the Reverend Dr. George Seaver, Dublin
[1946][1]

[e]

My ability to sleep soundly enables me to carry out such things and get by without taking off a single day. But if only I could have a free day to finally sleep my fill, a day to concentrate entirely on completing my book, doing my music, and playing my organ at leisure, strolling, dreaming, and reading for sheer relaxation! When will such a day come? Will it ever come? But for now, I thank God, who has given me the health and strength to live this life, in such an onerous climate and with so many demands constantly being made on me from all sides. I am sustained by the knowledge that I am granted the privilege of devoting myself to suffering people, and also by the thought of noble-minded friends who enable me to continue my work.

~

To Prof. Dr. Max Planck, Berlin
Lambarene
20 January 1946

Dear Herr Planck,

As the "senior" Goethe Prize laureate,[1] I welcomed every new laureate with a friendly note until the war. And now that I can resume this tradition after such dreadful years, you happen to be the one whom I am congratulating. I am deeply moved. The fact that you have been chosen signifies for me that the prize is again being awarded in the spirit of Goethe. I regret that I cannot attend the ceremony. But I have so often thought about you during these years and anxiously wondered what had become of you! And now the horror is behind us, and I can look forward to seeing you again. How wonderful it will be! If only we could get together just once in the stillness of Gunsbach. Gunsbach and my house are still standing. I myself have spent these years constantly trying not to collapse in this awful climate and in my work. We have managed to keep the hospital going and functioning through my connections in England and the U.S.A. and because we were able to resume contact with southern Africa in late 1940. But the difficult thing was to stick it out and remain somewhat able-bodied through all my years in this muggy tropical climate! I have succeeded.

~

To Guido Valcarenghi, Buenos Aires
                              Lambarene
                              French Equatorial Africa
                              12 April 1946

[f]

Dear Monsieur Valcarenghi,

I received your kind letter of 28 February 1946 in which you asked me about the possibility of a Spanish translation of my book on Bach. I am quite touched that you are interested in this work, and I will do what I can to honor your request. The situation is as follows. The rights to this book on Bach belong to Breitkopf und Härtel, Leipzig, who asked me to write it in French, then in German. Since then my publisher has licensed the English-language rights for England and America to Black, Soho Square, London. I feel that the simplest solution would be for me to discuss a Spanish translation directly with Breitkopf in Leipzig as soon as we can correspond with Germany, which is not yet the case. But I believe that this will soon be possible. I will ask him to grant you the rights with the easiest terms, and I will inform you of his reply. Please let me know by airmail if this is all right with you or if you would rather deal directly with Breitkopf. I'm on very good terms with the house, and I believe I could obtain the best terms for you.

~

To the members of the Nederlandsche Bachvereeniging [Dutch Bach
Association] on their twenty-fifth anniversary, Naarden, Holland
Lambarene
30 July 1946

I deeply regret that I cannot join you when you celebrate your anniversary September 13 and the following days. For various reasons
it is impossible for me to go to Europe now.

It was so kind of you to name me *Eere-Voorzitter* [Honorary Chair-
man] together with Prof. G. van der Leeuw. I thank you from the
bottom of my heart.

You paid me this honor because you knew that I have always been
deeply interested in your Bachvereeniging. I heard about it when it
was only just starting.

Then, during frequent visits to your country, I had opportunities
to see the deep understanding of your musical circles for Bach's art;
I also saw how extensively the Bachvereeniging cultivated and implemented the interest in the maestro of St. Thomas.

On the days of your festivities I will be with you in spirit, sharing
your delight that after the difficult years you and your nation have
endured you may now again experience days on which spirits are
uplifted in beautiful celebrations.

Bach's art is being appreciated more and more, and the number of
people to whom it is important is steadily increasing. I see these signs
as auspicious for the development of a future spiritual life.

The great esteem for Bach shows that the people of our time still
have a sense of simple, upright, perfect, and genuine values and true
depth, and that spiritual energies are still operative in our world,
which is ruled by so many external and foolish ideals. Spirituality is
needed by our time and ourselves.

Bach is a spiritual educator through the spirit of the religious texts
that he so movingly set to music, and through the spirit of his music
per se.

Wherever his music has an impact on people, it influences them
spiritually. Bach is a precious gift to our time, one of the lights that
shine through the darkness in which mankind today must seek the
road to a deeper spirituality.

May all of you who celebrate this Bach festival in Naarden delight
in the splendid gift and return spiritually enriched to your everyday
lives.

~

To Hermann Hesse

Lambarene
4 December 1946

Dear Hermann Hesse,

I have just learned from a Swiss newspaper that you are being awarded the Goethe Prize. As the senior Goethe Prize laureate and as an admirer of your creations, I would like to tell you how delighted I am by the news and I would like to express my heartiest congratulations. I feel a bond with you in the ideal of humanity. Both of us remained loyal to this ideal in an age when it lost prestige. This creates a togetherness that I have vividly experienced during the past few years.

I hope that when I go to Europe I will have a chance to get together with you somewhere—perhaps during a Goethe ceremony in Frankfurt.

I still don't know when I can get away from here. For various reasons my presence is required here for the time being. I have to thoroughly initiate the physicians who have come here to replace me. Although I am tired, I still manage to keep going.

To my great shame I must admit that I know you live somewhere in Ticino, but I can't remember where, and I have no reference book available to look it up. So I am sending you these lines through my niece, Frau Dr. S. Oswald, Mühlebachstrasse 77, Zurich.

As I write this, at night, the flashes of a distant tornado are illuminating the palm tree meadow outside my room. Wait, there's one more thing I have to shamefully admit: There are no flower gardens to celebrate here. All the available land around the house belongs to the palms and the orange and tangerine trees. Growing flowers is impossible because of the freely grazing hospital goats.

When I have to work as a mason and put up walls with unhewn stones, I gaze at the stones in my hand, trying to decide how to hammer them. At such moments I, as a Ticinese, sometimes feel that they come apart in the appropriate way.

My very best to you and your wife,

Your devoted
Albert Schweitzer

PART EIGHT

---∞---

1947 - 1953

~

To Charles Michel, Strasbourg-Mainau
Lambarene
13 January 1947

Dear Friend,

If you now tried, in your horribly icy weather, to picture how I am spending the last evening of my seventy-second year, you wouldn't have a clue, even though you are not unintelligent. You see, I am taking the Alsatian lists of donations that you have sent me in such nice penmanship and am neatly putting them together in a "fascicle" (as office jargon put it in the good old days). And I am doing the same thing with your letters as far as I can track them down and dig them up in this chaos of unanswered mail. Both fascicles will then go into a file (a green cardboard folder) that will be labeled: (1) List of gifts from Alscace; (2) Letters from Charles Michel![1] If only I could spend the final working hours of this year of my life more effectively!

And now I have to say *merci.* My deepest thanks for your dear letter of 8 December 1946 and the enclosed lists. Yes, you two did the right thing, you and your conspirator Goetzelt. Thank you for your initiative. And his three drawings are lovely. He did fine interpretations of the photographs. The choice of homilies is fine, and the delicate issue of language is also nicely resolved.[2] The final result is magnificent. How lovely and how good for me that I have such dear people as you two, who are intent on propagating my work and are so effective and perceptive about it. *Ci-joint* [herewith] a note for Herr Goetzelt. I am also writing to Herr Hoepffner (whose father and I were friends).

I am writing to you (it will soon be eleven o'clock) in an oppressively sultry atmosphere. Not a single puff of air is coming through the wire meshes. The kerosene lamp is only increasing the heat. It acts like a slow-burning oven. To prevent the sweat from dripping on the paper, I keep having to wipe it off my forehead; it really runs hot (as Schiller says in "The Song of the Bell").

Again I thank you from the bottom of my heart. With best regards for you and yours,

Your old
Albert Schweitzer

P.S. 17 January 1947. The page of signatures has arrived. Warmest thanks to everyone!

~

To Dr. Fritz Buri, Täuffelen, Canton Berne
14 October 1947[1]

Dear Friend,

I hope you have received the letter that I wrote to you some time ago. So many letters that leave here get lost because of the all-too-interesting stamps. I have just reread your study, *Albert Schweitzer and Our Time*. I was fascinated by your spiritual portrait of me. I find you have drawn certain lines more sharply than I realized in my own soul-searching, and I feel that you are right. Let me tell you again that the structure of your work is very natural, which makes it very effective. Ah, I would never have dreamt that the ethics of reverence for life would be defended so valiantly and be so widely recognized! I often come across the phrase "reverence for life" in a book or magazine, and the author doesn't even realize that this expression is new and was coined by me. So this term is already circulating.

With best wishes to you and your wife,

Albert Schweitzer

~

To Elsa Reger

[Lambarene]
December 1947

Dear Frau Reger,

I have received your friendly note of 15 October 1947 in which you[1] inform me that I have been named an honorary member of the Max Reger Institute. Allow me to tell you how delighted I am that your high-minded foundation has created an institute to properly take care of Reger's art and how honored I feel that I may belong to this organization as an honorary member. Thank you from the bottom of my heart.

However, I have not earned this honor for anything I have done for Reger's oeuvre; my artistic career was, alas, too brief for me to do anything special on behalf of Reger's works for the organ. This was taken care of by others, especially Straube, and far more effectively than I could have managed, for people only wanted to hear me perform Bach. All I did for Reger was to admire him as a great creative artist and to express my admiration. As a composer for the organ, he was quite special. His works do not derive from anyone, not even Bach, contrary to what is usually assumed and to what he himself thought. Rather then deriving from Bach, he is connected to him through what they have in common: their way of thinking in grand, autonomous, and antithetical musical lines. He is a born contrapuntist and a brilliant one, and he would have become what he is even if Bach had not been his forerunner.

All of Reger's works for the organ were with me during my first stay in Africa. I took them along in order to focus on them in peace and quiet. I had heard some of them over and over when they were performed excellently by my Basel friend Adolf Hamm, the cathedral organist, who unfortunately died young (he was one of Straube's best students). From the very start the deepest impact was made on me by Reger's powerful choral fantasies. One doesn't know what to admire most: the poetic content of the choral or the structure and its wonderful style. And what magic emanates from the simpler choral preludes. . . . As for Reger's chamber music, their strongest impact was made on me when they were performed by my dear friend Wendling and his quartet. What life pulsates in these creations, what a wealth of themes and motifs! Reger's chamber music was a grand experience for me.

The significance of his work will only be appreciated in the future. I have had many opportunities to see that other countries are not yet really acquainted, much less familiar, with him. The fault is to be found largely in the two wars and the interwar period, which set up barriers to becoming acquainted and familiar with him—barriers that would otherwise not have existed when it was time for Reger's art to go out into the world. But the day when he will be revealed to the music world as what he is can only be delayed but not blocked. Thus, I have not earned the honor that has been paid to me. However, I believe I am qualified to become an honorary member because of my veneration for Reger's art. What I feel constitutes the special essence of his art is the simplicity of the outlook that produced it. Reger was a modern artist in an unmodern person. He was not obsessed with gaining prestige, recognition. He created because he had to create, and his creative urge was entirely devoted to music with no secondary goals. He is similar to Bach not just in his art but also in his entirely unencumbered creativity. Reger's works possess the magic of the chastity that was also the aura of the organist of St. Thomas's.

But, alas, I will not be granted the privilege of joining you, the keeper of his legacy, and his other admirers to celebrate the day when he would have turned seventy-five and to delight in his works at the Reger festival. I will still be far away. But I will be with you in spirit. Once again, my deep thanks!

≈

To Frau Planck, Göttingen

[Lambarene, 1947]

Dear Frau Professsor,

The demise of your dear husband has affected me deeply. A man who did great things and was a great person has left us. I venerated him, and it was a great joy for me to be in contact with him, although I did not have the opportunity of getting together with him.

His letters were so elevating, and he will eventually be given his due for his achievements as a thinker. He was not only a brilliant scientist but also a profound thinker, and as such, he expressed convictions that are important spiritual matters. But what difficult things he had to endure in his old age! And in these difficult things, he proved to be an upright man on whom many eyes were focused. He represented the eternal ethical values of civilization against those people who tried to encroach upon and devalue them. In a horrible time he thus provided comfort and strength for many people who did not wish to go along with the general aberration. He therefore achieved as much on a spiritual level as on a grand, scientific level. In a period when so many scholars and scientists turned out to be small, he showed his noblest humanity and calm fearlessness. How grateful we are to him. How precious his memory is to us.

≈

To Paul Haupt, publisher, Berne

Lambarene

7 February 1948

Let me thank you from the bottom of my heart for all your interest in my works and all your love for me. It is good that you show so much devotion in taking care of my affairs. After all, I have neither the time nor the strength nor the concentration to do so myself.

One legal matter: Herr Lind,[1] as far as I remember, has indicated to me that his income on the work is to go to the hospital. I wrote him back, telling him that I was touched by his plan but asking him to think it over in case he needed [the money] for himself. What has he worked out with you?

This is no simple issue. Actually, the occupation authorities have the right to lay claim for reparations to anything a German earns in other countries. The question is whether it is legally permitted for him to donate his fees to the hospital or whether they will be confiscated. On the other hand, everyone has the right to work for free. Please think the matter over. If I were you, I would not write to Lind about this legal point. It makes no sense to stir up a hornets' nest. Let things alone for now until we can deal with them personally. Oh, how complicated the world is today!

～

To Professor Albert Einstein, Institute for Advanced Studies, Princeton, New Jersey

Lambarene

30 April 1948

Dear Friend,

I have often written you in my thoughts, for, at a distance, I have been following your life and work and your position on events of our time. However, I am hindered by writer's cramp, which I inherited from my mother, so that numerous mentally drafted letters remain unwritten. But now that I, compelled by circumstances, have to miss the opportunity of getting together with you in Princeton, I have no choice but to write to you and tell you how sorry I am. In an issue of *Life* that has just come into my hands, I see pictures of your institute, and they simply increase my regrets about what I have to give up. The photo of you and Dr. Oppenheimer is poignant, and whenever

I see a picture of you, it evokes the memory of the lovely hours I spent with you in Berlin. . . .

Dr. Oppenheimer must have told you why I cannot come. I am no longer a free person: In everything I do, I have to consider my hospital and make sure I do whatever is necessary for its survival. Today, every enterprise is so thoroughly encumbered by all sorts of rules and currency matters and the like that it requires tight reins every step of the way. That is why I cannot travel far from Lambarene or for any length of time that would prevent my being here when needed. At the moment I have no doctors who are fully familiar with procedures here. The two doctors assisting me are about to end their two-year period and will be replaced by two new ones, whom I have to break in. And as for all the administrative work, I have no one who could take over the necessary decisions and responsibilities. An example: When a devaluation of the franc was in the offing (despite official assurances to the contrary), I had to run the risk of investing all available funds in rice, petroleum, textiles, and anything that could be purchased at the trading posts in order to replace the diminishing paper money with tangible goods while there was still time. By so doing I was in danger of running out of the wherewithal to settle outstanding bills and to pay the (large) black hospital staff. No one else could risk placing the hospital in such cash-flow difficulties by exhausting our treasury, which was in bad straits anyway. I took the chance and saved thousands [of francs] by going through with the purchases, which exceeded our funds. In this way I saved the hospital from a financial crisis, which would have come if we had waited until the devaluation and then been forced to buy at the rising prices. This is just one example among many. Who would ever have thought that I, a decent theologian, would turn into a gambler and speculator in order to keep the hospital afloat. But the hospital is worth my becoming a slave.

Nevertheless, I have not abandoned hope of doing other work. There is one thing I absolutely stick to no matter what: Every night, even if only for three-quarters of an hour, I practice at the pedal piano not only to remain fit as an organist but also to improve.

I constantly carry around my [work on] philosophy. Many chapters of the third volume of my philosophy of civilization are already finished, and the others are so far advanced in my mind that they can be set down on paper. But first I have to put much secondary work (including masonry) behind me so that I can write somewhat peacefully and regularly. At the moment I am eating my way through the pudding wall that surrounds never-never-land. It may be a modest never-never-land, but it is enough for my wishes. All I want is to have the morning and the night hours for myself and devote my afternoons to hospital work. And while these wishes may be coming true only modestly, I am nonetheless managing to give definitive shape to the third volume [of the philosophy of civilization, and ethics]. The whole question is whether I can have capable people here who are able to take over as much of my work (especially dull-minded subsidiary work) as possible. The third volume is planned as a symphony of ideas. Never in my life have I thought and felt as musically as during these past few years. The third volume has chapters on mysticism and religion in connection with ethics.

For now, we have three doctors, including myself, and seven white nurses, including one American. Without the material help from our friends in the United States, the hospital could not be kept afloat, no matter how carefully we husbanded our resources. My special field is urology. Furthermore, as head pharmacist I have to work out all orders and keep the large dispensary neat. At the moment I have to treat a lot of leprosy cases. We are using the new American medicines, Promin and Diasom, and they truly achieve results that previous medicines did not. At present we are treating some fifty lepers. Leprosy is very widespread here. I am enclosing a layout of the hospital. A Swiss engineer who stayed here on the way through drew it and gave me a number of copies. I built most of these houses over the years with an old black carpenter and did most of the masonry myself. There are no capable craftsmen in the new generation of natives. The members of the older generation went through a proper apprenticeship and training with Catholic and Protestant craft missionaries. The natives in the new generation do their learning at so-called industrial schools. They consider themselves too good to become real craftsmen. In general, what will become of the native population in all the colonial territories if the tendency of today's generation is to emancipate itself from farming and craft! Seen from up close and from the inside, the colonial problems look very different from the way they do when seen from far away and on the outside.

Well, I have let myself go on and am forcing you to read several pages of my scribbling, but it was a great joy to get together with you mentally in these nocturnal hours at my desk. When will we have a chance to really get together? Will the day ever come?

I read in *Der Aufbau* [a German-Jewish newspaper in New York], which is sent here regularly, that you have received a prize that involves a flight around the world. I hope you can play hooky—to use our good old student lingo.

Please give my best regards to Dr. Oppenheimer. I would have been delighted to make his acquaintance. How is your violin?

My very best,

Your devoted
Albert Schweitzer

The hand that suffers from writer's cramp endured valiantly to-night. My wife is currently in Europe, living in the Black Forest and in Switzerland. She is in relatively good health. My daughter lives in Switzerland with her husband and four children.

~

To Dr. Max Rehm

[Königsfeld]
18 March 1949

Dear Herr Rehm,

Alas, as you have already learned, nothing can be done about the [Stuttgart] contract. Naturally, I remember your father very well. Indeed, I can still clearly picture his face.

What memories of St. Nicholas's you evoke in me![1] What a lovely time that was in the old Strasbourg! If ever you hear that I am in Stuttgart, please come and see me. My deepest thanks for your kind thoughts.

With best wishes for you and your wife,

Sincerely,
Albert Schweitzer

~

To the Reverend Dr. Rudolf Grabs, Fernbreitenbach over Berka, Eisenach District

Königsfeld, Baden
19 March 1949

Dear Friend,

Many thanks for your kind letter of 3 February 1949. It was very moving. I spoke to the publisher Biederstein about granting permission for quotations for the collection, and I got him to agree and to get in touch with Meiner and arrange everything. Basically, the publishers do not like the idea because a number of small collections have come out. I will take care of things with Mohr in Tübingen, so everything

The Munster Valley countryside around Gunsbach.
Below right: the Albert Schweitzer House.

The house Schweitzer was born in, Kaysersberg, Upper Alsace.

In Gunsbach: the church and the Albert Schweitzer House (right).

The meadows behind the Schweitzer House (left) with a view of the mountain slopes.

*St. Nicholas's Church, Strasbourg, where
Schweitzer served as preacher.*

As an instructor at the Theological Faculty of the University of Strasbourg, 1912.

Helene and Albert Schweitzer, 1912.

View of the lateral branch of the Ogowe, where Albert Schweitzer first set up his hospital. The roofs of the first huts are at bottom.

Schweitzer's first lodging in Lambarene (1913–17).

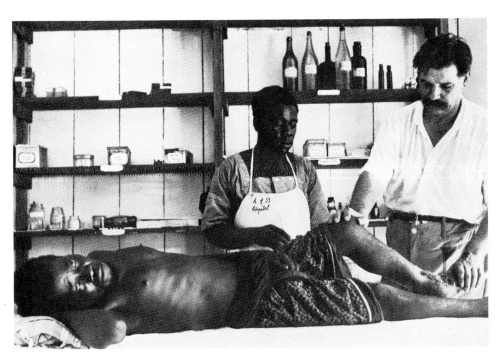

A foot abscess is treated.

Crates for the second trip, 1924. In the basement of the School of St. Thomas, Strasbourg, with students.

In a motorboat on the Ogowe: The final letters are written en route to the mail boat.

Outside the reconstructed old hospital, 1925.

The hospital as seen from the Ogowe.

At the organ of the Grote Kerk, Deventer, Holland, 1928.

With his Strasbourg teacher, the Old Testament scholar Karl Budde, in Frankfurt am Main, 1929.

*In the courtyard of the newly built hospital (1927)
in Lambarene.*

Outside the consulting room.

Lambarene, circa 1932.

With the cantor of the School of St. Thomas, Prof. Karl Straube (center), and Fritz Münch (left) at a recital by the St. Thomas Choir at St. Wilhelm's, Strasbourg, 1935, with Schweitzer at the organ. (See letter of 9 May 1950.)

During the address at the church service in the hospital, Schweitzer flanked by two interpreters, 1940.

Receiving the Nobel Peace Prize in Oslo, 1954.
Helene Schweitzer is in the middle.

With Pablo Casals at the organ in Gunsbach.

Going through a manuscript with Robert Minder,
Paris, 1959.

A conversation with Father Dominique Pire, Nobel
Peace laureate, Gunsbach, 1959.

Preparing the framework for a concrete wall, 1956.

Construction work, 1956.

Practicing a J. S. Bach composition on the pedal piano, Lambarene, 1956.

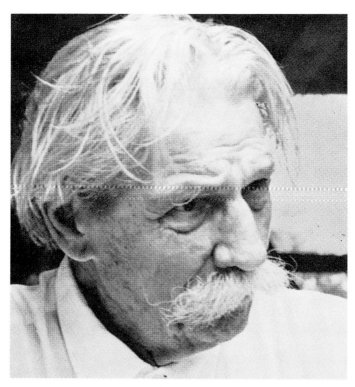

After 1960.

Children in the inner courtyard of the hospital.

will be in order. One bit of advice: Do not make the collection too long. A relatively short one will make a stronger impact.

In regard to the large biography, do as you like.[1] I'm sure you'll do the right thing. A bit of advice here too: Make it brief, if only to keep the price as low as possible, for this makes a great difference today.

Recently (upon returning from Lambarene), I stood at the grave of my friend Baur [in Basel]. One more thing: Address all your letters to Königsfeld. That's the simplest way. If I'm gone, they are forwarded to me. And always type them for the sake of my overly strained eyes.

And now, God be with you, dear friend. With loving thoughts to you and yours. When shall I have the pleasure of shaking your hand and thanking you?

Best,
Albert Schweitzer

~

To Margarethe Klinckerfuss, Stuttgart
> Permanent address:
> Gunsbach, Alsace
> 19 March 1949

Dear Margarethe Klinckerfuss,

What a splendid surprise—your interesting and dear book,[1] written in seclusion! I have sinfully neglected my own work in order to browse through your book and obtain some loving information about artists who are spiritually close to me. To think that you were with Schleich, whom I greatly admire![2] You have no idea what local anesthesia means for a tropical physician. And your work also evokes the Bach Festival in Tübingen. How the part surfaces. . . . I hope you are recovering nicely from the consequences of your serious accident. Again, my deepest thanks for your dear book.

~

To Jean Baptiste Kempf, tailor, Gunsbach
[Schweitzer's schoolmate]

[New York]
1 July 1949

Dear Jean Baptiste,

In Europe I was unable to thank you for doing such a lovely job of restoring my gray and black suits, so let me thank you from here. But you almost did something terrible to me.[1] The local customs officers are very strict, and when they saw the two suits, they said, "Monsieur, these are new. You'll have to pay duty on them." They wouldn't believe that [they] were old. I refused to pay, so they brought over a high-level officer who gaped at me and shrugged. Then a "super-level officer" was summoned. After listening to the story, he said, "Yeah, yeah, we know all about those new clothes that are supposed to be old. . . . And who's the tailor who turned your old clothes into new ones?"

I said, "Sir, he is Jean Baptiste Kempf in Gunsbach."

"Aha!" he snorted. "Why didn't you say so right away! Jean Baptiste Kempf is an old master tailor! If he gets his hands on some old clothes, you can be sure they'll eventually look like new!" Then he told the customs men, "Okay, don't harass Monsieur Schweitzer. He's right. Put the chalk cross on the trunk and *laissez-le aller* [let him through]." Next, he looked at the tie that Germaine had fixed for me, and his eyes seemed to say: "I wouldn't mind having one myself." He left after saluting and saying, "*Amusez-vous en Amérique* [Have a good time in America]." He was a really high customs official. So you see, the whole thing turned out all right.

My best wishes to you and your wife, and take care of your heart.

Your old
Albert Schweitzer

～

To Mathilde Kottmann, temporarily in Bordeaux

A. Schweitzer, 2 July 1949
c/o Dr. Emory Ross
156 Fifth Avenue, New York 10
[on the train]

Well, the voyage went smoothly. The ship was entering New York harbor and had another hour and a half to go; I had just completed my texts of the French and German Goethe lecture[1] when who should come aboard but Monsieur Ross (who had arrived with the passport inspectors) and some forty photographers and an equal number of journalists. I had to go on deck and be photographed for almost an hour and then spend over an hour answering questions from the journalists (and I was so tired because I had worked until late at night).

But I'm doing better than I expected. The lecture has turned out well. I've had to make myself available to individual journalists for three or four hours a day. It's already night.

Sunday morning. Last night the editor of *Life* came to see me. He is coming along to Aspen to hear the [Goethe] lecture. He wants to write a new and, this time, detailed article for *Life,* and he has read my books. I had to spend an hour and a half answering his questions.

For the past hour we've been traveling through a plain filled with grain and tobacco. Nothing but isolated farms. The houses look strangely small. We'll be in Chicago in another three hours, with a one-hour stopover. There E. [Edith] Lenel will be coming to the train. I hope to be back in Gunsbach on July 30. I believe I did the right thing in agreeing to give this speech and coming to America.

~

To Lotte Gerhold-Schall, Königsfeld

Sunday, 3 July 1949
[en route from New York to Aspen, Colorado]

I'm sitting in a direct train, New York–San Francisco, which I will leave in Denver. I will then be driven to Aspen, Colorado, eight thousand feet high, to lecture on the sixth and the eighth, and then, coming down from the heights, travel on to Chicago where I am to be awarded an honorary doctorate on the eleventh. For ten hours now we have been rolling at sixty-five miles an hour, crossing an immense plain in wonderful weather. It is enchanting.

The train ride from New York to Aspen takes about fifty hours. I manage to write during stretches when the car doesn't bounce too badly. In Chicago I mailed a letter to M. [Mathilde Kottmann] who is sending a new nurse from Bordeaux. Now it's your turn. It's questionable whether you'll be able to read the carbon copy of the trip from Europe to America. New York was lovely but tiring. I had to receive or pay visits all day long. My friend Ross,[1] in whose home we took all our meals, kept inviting five or six people to every lunch and dinner. This meant conversing at the table. It is hard to endure all this until July 22, the day I sail back to Europe. And I won't even have peace and quiet on the boat because the other passengers keep making demands on me.

From Chicago I'll head back to New York where I will be inspecting organs and visiting pharmaceutical factories every morning from the fourteenth to the eighteenth, and receiving visitors in my friend Ross's apartment every afternoon from two to seven. Postcards will notify friends and acquaintances that I will be in during those five afternoons. On the night of the eighteenth it's off to Boston where I will see organs and friends; from there [I'll go] to Harvard University nearby where I will likewise see organs and friends. On the twenty-first it's back to New York where I will then set sail on the twenty-second. I'll be in Le Havre on the twenty-ninth and in Gunsbach on the thirty-first.

~

To Emma Haussknecht, Lambarene

[Paris]

29 September 1949

Dear Emma,

I'm at the Hôtel Malherbe, 11 rue de Vaugirard (near the Luxembourg) in Paris after two days of visits and shopping here. I have visited my old piano teacher Philipp (eighty-seven years old) who has been living in America since the start of the war (he's Jewish) and has come to Paris for the holidays; the playwright Cesbron (a rising star) who will soon be mounting a play (I believe I wrote you about it), *Docteur il est minuit* [Doctor, it's midnight]. It takes place at my hospital in Lambarene in 1914, just before the outbreak of World War I.[1]

People who know the play, including one of the most important actresses in Paris, are deeply moved by the spirit that imbues it and by the dramatic situation. I haven't read it, I only know the overall plot. Monday I played to invited guests in the dark church of St. Aurelia [in Strasbourg]. That was the beginning of my farewell to Europe. Now I am doing nothing but preparing for my trip. Tonight I am leaving for Strasbourg. Tomorrow I'll be absorbed in checking the already packed crates with Mademoiselle Mathilde [Kottmann].

I'll be leaving Gunsbach around the twenty-fourth in order to have enough time in Bordeaux. The ship is sailing on the twenty-eighth of October. Monsieur and Madame Kopp (I recently saw her in Strasbourg) are traveling on the same boat. Dr. Israel has written me that he will be in Europe or leaving for Europe in early 1950. I don't know when the lady doctor will be sailing, but I foresee that I may be the only doctor in Lambarene for several months. This is destiny's response to what I said during the war—namely, my arrogant statement that the hospital will stay open and function even if Mademoiselle Emma Haussknecht and I are the only ones to remain.

~

To Wilhelm Furtwängler, Clarens, Vaud
Lambarene
6 December 1949

Dear Herr Furtwängler,

Yes, it's been a long time since we got together in the beautiful Strasbourg days and at the home of dear Curtius. But I've occasionally thought about you, and you have probably thought about me. I believe I last saw you in Zurich, around 1936, in the audience of my lecture on the essence of civilization. You were wearing a light-colored suit. I thought about you often and, I believe, sympathetically during your difficult years. I also heard about you from a nurse who, while en route to Lambarene in 1943, had stopped off in Lisbon where you were concertizing with your orchestra. You and I have one thing in common: the privilege of starting something and seeing it through. You have an easier time of it than I because you can devote yourself to a single activity; I am involved in several at once. Everyone has to follow his path.

Now for the subject of your letter of 21 November 1949. I would love to do what you have asked me to do, but it is impossible. At the moment I am working here as a physician in difficult circumstances. Any time I have left—if my correspondence ever allows me—is devoted to two things: completing works that I would like to finish before my demise and practicing daily on the pedal piano so that I may feel at home on organs in Europe. . . . I know you will understand. I hope I have the pleasure of seeing you once more somewhere, sometime. I follow your works from a distance with keen sympathy, and I dream of hearing you and your orchestra again. Please give your orchestra my best regards. At present I am indispensable here. Please say hello to Ansermet[1] and the other gentlemen who are joining you in the planned cultural work.

~

To Mayor Krauss and the Town Council, Königsfeld
Lambarene
16 February 1950

Dear Mr. Mayor, Dear Members of the Town Council,

The copy of your letter of 31 December 1949 arrived here in late January. Although I have not yet received the document (ocean-going mail is slow), I do not wish to delay my response any longer. As you may well assume, being made an honorary citizen of Königsfeld has both surprised and delighted me. I can still vividly recall how friendly Mayor Weiler and Herr Hammer of the Moravian Brethren were in welcoming me when I spoke to them about my desire to build a house in Königsfeld. What lovely times my wife, my daughter, and I spent up there! Last winter, despite my great fatigue and responsibilities, I greatly enjoyed spending several weeks there and, after such a long absence, meeting old acquaintances again and listen to the rustling of the wind in the fir trees. I would gladly have spent the spring and summer there.

And now you have let me know that you understand how much I like Königsfeld, and you have not only naturalized me, an outsider, you have also given me the right to be one of you. My wife also expresses her deep thanks. It will now be a very special pleasure for me to drive from the train station up to Königsfeld, through the woods, along the beautiful road whose windings I am so familiar with. I do not know when it will come about. For the moment I am firmly entrenched here. I have to break in two new, young physicians, which will take a great deal of time because medical work here is thoroughly different from the work in Europe. I also have to organize the hospital in such a way that it will keep going even when I am no longer among the living. Nevertheless, I am looking forward to the time when I can again breathe mountain air up in Königsfeld and see my friends there without being as weighed down with work and fatigue as I was during my stay exactly one year ago.

Sometimes I think about all the problems now confronting you, with providing food and shelter for refugees. I gained some insight into this dilemma last winter. I hope you manage to solve it in the best way and make Königsfeld a home for the homeless.

I am writing to you by lamplight while the crickets are making their noise outside. A tornado was brewing in the sky, but it went away. Here, too, we have not been having our normal rainfall for several years. I understand that Central Europe this winter, like the two previous ones, it not quite normal in this respect. Well, now I've started rambling. Once again my deepest thanks for the honor you have shown me and the joy you have given me.

With best wishes from my wife and myself,

Albert Schweitzer

~

To Richard Kik, Ulm
[Chairman of the Friends of Albert Schweitzer]
Lambarene
21 February 1950

Dear Friend,

Mademoiselle Mathilde has also written to me about the forty-three lectures you have given on me.[1] I am quite embarrassed that you (and your bike) are going to such trouble for me, but I feel that it is beneficial to spreading the idea of reverence for life, and this comforts me, for otherwise I could not accept it. How right the American was when he said: "Dr. Schweitzer is a billionaire in friendship"—and you are one of the highest figures in these sums.

Now the second young physician, Dr. Naegele from Alsace, is working with me. The other one, who came in late January, is Dr. Percy, a Hungarian. I am pinning great hopes on them.

My deepest thanks for everything you are doing for me.

With my fondest thoughts about you and yours,

Albert Schweitzer

~

To Hans Georg Siebeck, J. C. B. Mohr publishing company, Tübingen
[11 March 1950]

Dear Herr Siebeck,

First I have to tell you how delighted I am that a new edition of my books is being considered and that you want to accept the challenge.

Ah, how many inquiries I have gotten about when my books will be available again. . . . After receiving your letter I turned back to my scholarly history of the life of Jesus. Upon rereading my book, I had the impression that it is a historical document: a document about how Jesus' life was treated in the late nineteenth and early twentieth centuries in the great period of German theology, the period when German theology was grappling with the truth. And my book should be preserved as such. It depicts the struggle to know and understand the life of Jesus from the start of that struggle until 1913, shortly before the beginning of the world war when a new era commenced. As I wrote, I took the entire critical literature into account. The reader of my book will witness that entire theological age. I was deeply moved upon rereading all the names, of which even the greatest have virtually faded by now. So please reprint my book as is. This will also be the cheapest solution. Someday someone else can report on the research on the life of Jesus since that period and then encounter other problems. I will not respond because he will not be reporting on great, bold scholarship such as was available to me. So publish the book as is.[1] I believe there is no other book that recreates the era of those earlier theologians as mine does, building a bridge from this period to that one. I'll write you a brief foreword justifying the republication of the book in its old shape.

You are not just any publisher for me but the publisher who first published me at the suggestion of my dear teacher Holtzmann in Strasbourg. I will never forget this. I gratefully remember your dear grandfather, whom I knew well; he did much for theology and philosophy and was very kind to me, a young whippersnapper. I still recall the way he once came to Strasbourg at the beginning of the summer holidays and talked Windelband into sacrificing his vacation in order to write a history of Greek philosophy (which proved to be a masterpiece). And I once got together with your dear father in Tübingen just after he came back from autumn vacation: I (as a physician) noticed his strange excitement, which others could take as natural vivacity. Thus I feel tied to your publishing house through long years of friendship.

Unfortunately, we can no longer tend your uncle's grave in Gunsbach.[2] His remains, together with those of other Germans who died in combat, have been transferred to a lovely military graveyard in the valley. There was nothing we could do.

I am writing to you from my desk in the consulting room, surrounded by the hustle and bustle of the hospital. Since I have two new young doctors with me, I am busy from dawn until dusk, trying to squeeze out a little time for correspondence as best I can.

My fondest wishes to you, your dear mother, your family, and your colleagues as far as I still know them.

~

To Dr. Heinrich Beck, publisher, Munich
                              Lambarene
                              3 May 1950

Dear Dr. Beck,

My deepest thanks for your letter of April 12 and the royalty statement. You have done me a great service. I am delighted that you have also published my Goethe speech.[1] It adds to the others. It renders Goethe's personality as I have come to see it over the years. His spiritual simplicity and his great spiritual nobility are what I have come to feel more strongly . . . things that are beyond all appearances. I was captivated by the great earnestness that was part of him since his youth and also in his *Sturm und Drang* period. I wanted to bring that out by resurrecting him for my audience. It was only during the past few years that I truly came to understand the Faust problem and the reason he wore himself out working on this material.

I would have loved to go through the expanded version of *On the Edge of the Primeval Forest,* but I had no time. I've revised the French version, rewriting and simplifying a few things. Should you plan a new edition of the book, I would be very grateful if you allowed me to establish the definitive text.[2] The second part, 1924–1927, was taken from printed letters to friends, which were simply jotted and scrawled. It would therefore be worthwhile to revise the material and offer the text as it should be. I would chiefly be doing some cuts, especially in the medical portions.

Thank you for putting me in touch with Haupt.[3] I feel that a bit of your friendliness toward him has been shown toward me too. After all, he once issued a number of my works at his publishing house, and he has done a great deal for me.

~

To Prof. Dr. Karl Straube, Leipzig
                              Lambarene
                              9 May 1950

Dear Professor,

From time to time I have recieved news about you from Frau Lotte
Gerhold. Since I am indispensable here at the moment and cannot
even dream about going to Europe for Bach festivals, I have to forgo
the opportunity of seeing you during this period. But I must tell you
that I have thought about you quite often—you who have devoted
your life first to Reger and then to Bach. I can still recall how I first
learned about your Reger interpretations. That was in 1899 in Berlin,
and then later I heard you perform Reger in Strasbourg. How right
you were to devote yourself to that creative spirit. Someday he will
have the recognition he deserves. Today people have turned back to
a long-lost era, producing organs on which Reger cannot be played.

   And then you served Bach, the immortal, at St. Thomas's, the site
of his creativity. I deeply regretted that you more or less gave up the
organ in order to devote yourself fully to the School of St. Thomas,
but you knew best what had to be done. It was a great delight to
meet you in Strasbourg when we joined forces at St. Wilhelm's—
you with the St. Thomas Choir, I at the organ. And the three of us
were photographed together there, you, Münch, and I—a picture that
is a fond memory for me. During the war I sometimes wondered
how you were, then I received my first news about you. If I understand
Lotte Gerhold correctly, you are ill, but I hope you will soon recover.

   I have penned this note at night simply to tell you that, like so
many other musicians during these Bach weeks, I am thinking about
you, the man who has done so much for the Master, and to send you
my best wishes and salutations.

   Please remember me to your dear wife.
                              Yours truly,
                              Albert Schweitzer

                              ~

To Dr. Anna Wildikann, Jerusalem [she had spent seven years as a
physician in Lambarene]
                              Lambarene
                              16 May 1950

My deepest thanks for sending me this mosquito repellent. I'm also
going to try it out against *fourrous*. Since the second half of February

I've had two young physicians with me: Dr. Percy (whom you know) and Dr. Naegele (an Alsatian with a German father), who is about to be naturalized as *citoyen français* [a French citizen]. Both men are outstandingly capable and are striving to work in my spirit and my traditions. The two of them have a sound knowledge of surgery and considerable experience, and to make sure they will be trained here to become capable surgeons, I am having Dr. Groh, a surgeon from Saarbrücken, Saarland, come out for eight months. This was made possible by the kindness of Governor General Cornut-Gentille.

However, the 140 lepers require a lot of work ... and great expenditures. But the results are truly fine. I haven't been writing much, but I hope I can do so in a while. Best regards to all my Jerusalem acquaintances. The commemoration of the founding of the university must be beautiful.

> Best,
> Albert Schweitzer

~

To Gustav Woytt, Strasbourg

> Lambarene
> 23 July 1950[1]

Dear Gustav,

Here's the preface.[2] Do me a favor and turn it into elegant French by collaborating, if possible, with Canivez[3] or whatever his name is, and send me the text in French so that I can see it before it goes to the printer. You're doing me a big favor because I'm so busy here and so tired that it would be a great strain on me to do the French text. The draft of the preface, to which I am adhering in every detail, was prepared on April 30. I completed the final draft today, Sunday, 23 July 1950, at my table in the *salle de consultation* [consulting room], where I am on duty Sunday afternoon.

I am doing well and manage to get things done when I lead an orderly life, but if I can't, it really takes its toll on me. I accompanied my wife to Port-Gentil on July 4 in order to see her off on the boat on July 8, and when I returned, I was quite exhausted because I had been forced to accept invitations, pay visits, and engage in conversation. I had to make up my mind to decline the governor's invitation, as one of the oldest Gabonais, to join the centennial celebration for the founding of Libreville. The *déplacement* [traveling] and the *devoirs mondains* [social duties] wouldn't have been too good for me. But here in this orderly existence, in which I am completely autonomous, I can frolic about. I am even overseeing some masonry work, though I regret that I can lend a hand only moderately if at all when heavy rocks have to be moved.

Now, today, I can get to the preface for the new edition of the history of research on the life of Jesus. And next, all my leisure will be devoted to completing *The Kingdom of God and Primitive Christianity*[4] so that I can be done with it by the time I start thinking about going to Europe. Enjoy your vacation. I picture you people lying on the sand in Trebur. I almost envy you.

My best to the three of you,

Albert Schweitzer

Write me your opinion of *Il est minuit docteur*.[5] I couldn't hear it here because the broadcast couldn't travel this far. My best regards to Chavez.

≈

To Madre Maria, Eremo Francescano, Campello, Umbria
[Mother superior of a community of French nuns]
Lambarene
27 July 1950[1]

[f]

Dear and Venerated Mother,

I was deeply moved by the letter you wrote to me on my seventy-fifth birthday, I celebrated that day during one of the most difficult periods of my life. Of my two physicians, one had left several weeks before, and the other was about to depart; and their replacements, who were scheduled to arrive by the end of autumn, were unable to come.

Thank you for the news about yourself and the sisters.

St. Francis of Assisi made a deep impact on me, and I have dealt extensively with the history of the order that he founded. He was a force in the development of Christian piety. When I came to formulate the idea of reverence for life as the fundamental idea of ethics, I felt I was enunciating, as a philosophical and religious idea, something intrinsic to St. Francis but in a new revelation of his thinking. Yes, dear Mother, it's comforting to know that one's mind communes with the minds of other human beings who, together with us, seek the truth of truths, the most spiritual truth, which gives us the strength to live. And now, in my meditations, I will often think about you and your companions and about what we have in common. I will never have the time or strength to come to you as a pilgrim, alas, but I will frequently be with you in thought as if I had crossed your threshold.

I was delighted to learn that you meditate with music before your daily work and that you love Bach. I commune with myself in the evenings, after the day's labor, by playing on my pedal piano that the Parish Bach Society gave me as its organist in 1913. Just before writing to you I played the prelude to the Advent chorale "Veni Redemptor Gentium."

I am also the physician for the Catholic mission station located right across the river from us. Recently, two nuns were hospitalized here for many weeks—one for typhus, the other for an intestinal illness. When they left, both of them could resume their work. The ringing of the mission bells reaches us across the river. We, too, have a bell among the hospital palm trees. It announces the Angelus, and on Sundays it calls people to services.

I have a great deal to do not only medically but in regard to everything that contributes to the hospital work. Now, during the dry season, we have to repair the houses, overhaul the roads that were washed out by the torrential rains accompanying the tornadoes, and take care of the garden and the plantation. During the next few days I'll be a mason and a carpenter. I hope I won't get too tired so that I can work in the evenings and give definitive form to *The Kingdom of God and Primitive Christianity*. Once I have that behind me, I can tackle the third volume of *The Philosophy of Reverence for Life*.

As I am writing to you, the Dutch nurse, Ali [Silver], is coming to bottle-feed a poor three-week-old antelope that natives found in the jungle. Its name is Theodore, and it will be my roommate for a year. After that it will live in an enclosure in front of the house together with other antelopes that we have taken in and brought up in the same way.

When I was preaching at St. Nicholas's Church in Strasbourg, I would conclude the service by quoting a verse from Philippians: "The peace of God, which passeth all understanding, shall keep your hearts and minds through Christ Jesus." Let me take my leave of you and your companions by quoting that verse, which I consider one of the pearls in the Gospels and in which I have often found peace in affliction and strength in weariness. May we all be blessed by the peace of God, which takes possession of our hearts. When these words of the apostle Paul are before me, my thoughts will go to you. Let us unite in these words as long as God grants us the grace of serving Him on this earth. . . .

Albert Schweitzer

~

To the Reverend Robert Hirt, Hohweiler, Alsace
Lambarene
10 October 1950

Dear Friend,

I have learned that on Sunday, November 12, you will be celebrating
the fiftieth anniversary of your arrival in Hohweiler. How I wish I
could join you, probably as one of the few of our fellow students from
back then. Instead, let this note express my congratulations and speak
to you.[1]

We have gone in very different directions. You were designated to
lead a parish through decades. I was designated to go out into the
world. Your lot was lovely. I can feel it, for I carry a yearning for a
vicarage in my heart. For a long time I nursed the hope of returning
home from Lambarene in my later years and spending my twilight
years as pastor of a small Alsatian parish. Now I see that I have to
keep working here even in my old age.

Knowing you, I realize that you have always striven to become
what a pastor should be for your congregation. With my father I saw
what it means when the minister and the parish are bound together
through many years, and I saw how this bond can become a blessing
for both.

As the offspring of Alsatian ministers, you had the example of your
family members who preceded you as pastors and, like them, you
followed the ideal of quiet and loyal service. In regard to the good
you have thus done, you, too, can see only as much of the outcome
as is granted us human beings to see during our earthly days. But
anything that is done in loyalty is not in vain, and during the coming
times some members of your flock will gratefully recall what you
have given them. That was what I had the opportunity to ascertain
in my grandfather's congregation.

There were three of us who belonged together in a special way at
the seminary, at the university, and in life: Ney, you, and I. The
friendship binding us has always remained the same. With deep
emotion I remember the day when we met again in Strasbourg after
the first war. Your memory has also retained that day. Now our other
friend is no longer among the living.

But we still have that privilege. We are even blessed in that we
can still work. Both of us value work as something precious and are
grateful to God from the depths of our hearts.

I will be with you in thought on the day that you and your parish celebrate your jubilee. I will hear in my heart the words spoken from the pulpit, and I will share in the joy as all of you step out into the autumnal landscape. . . .

Dear friend, both of us have been exceedingly blessed in our lives. Each of us, in his worries, his efforts, his experiences, has been allowed to receive the goodness of God. May we, as blessed people, become blessings for others and continue as blessings as long as God allows us to wander down here.

My warmest wishes to you and your congregation,

Albert Schweitzer

~

To Erica Anderson, New York

Lambarene

13 November 1950

Dear Mrs. Anderson,

My deepest thanks for your kind letter and your friendly offer to shoot a documentary about my life and my hospital, thereby creating a source of steady financial support for the hospital.[1] I can fully appreciate the value of your high-minded offer and yet, much to my regret, I cannot go along with your plan. The main reason is that a film about my life and my hospital would be a difficult, almost impossible project. There is no plot, after all, but only a sequence of tableaux. And how hard it would be for a film to capture the activities in the hospital. It is an action that offers nothing for the eye.

Therefore, take my advice and drop your risky plan of shooting a film here. You would only have problems and frustrations. It is difficult for me to write this, but I have no choice. Here, you could sometimes wait ten days just to shoot for fifteen minutes! Such is the jungle climate in Equatorial Africa.

~

To Prof. Dr. Josselin de Jong, The Hague

Lambarene

4 January 1951

It is a great deal of work keeping abreast of all the new medicines. At times I think that at my age I should stop making the effort. On the other hand, there is something wonderful about witnessing incredible progress in therapy.

I have been straining mightily to give definitive form to works I have begun. This takes place at night. At the moment I am occupied with my latest theological work, *The Kingdom of God and Primitive Christianity*,[1] which I wrote during 1945–49 and which I would like to shorten as much as I can so that the book won't be too thick.

Twenty-five years ago I proclaimed that the world was unknowable and that it was impossible to base a philosophy on knowledge of the world. Now, because of the direction taken by science, professional philosophy has been forced to adopt my viewpoint. When my book appeared, the professional philosophers never would have imagined that they would have to do so someday. Thus, they now have to deal with the ethics of reverence for life.

～

To the directors of C. F. Peters, music publishing house, Leipzig
Lambarene
[1951]

Gentlemen,

The wonderful facsimile edition of the Brandenburg Concertos is lying on my table in Lambarene. When Bach completed his final draft of this wonderful score, he could not have dreamed that someday it would go out into the entire world and even wind up in the jungle. Thank you from the bottom of my heart for this invaluable gift. You cannot imagine what it means to me. During the days of the Bach commemoration everyone who venerates the Master and knows how he achieved recognition remembered the Peters publishing house, for it was Peters that first paved the way for him by publishing his organ works. I myself always use that edition for practicing and playing, and I am delighted that you offer organists nothing but the notes instead of patronizing them with a text about fingering, phrasing, registering, and performing. Your edition leaves organists alone with Bach. Often, when practicing at my pedal piano, I imagine what it must have been like for organists during the mid-nineteenth century when they finally had all of Bach's organ works before them and were able to gain a notion of his oeuvre. Today's generation cannot appreciate this, whereas we knew organists for whom the Peters edition of Bach's organ works was the grand experience.

I would have loved to attend the Bach festivals in Leipzig, but I couldn't get away from here. I had to content myself with having my name appear next to the names of those who made these festivals possible. I have been delighted to hear what these festivals were like and what sublime experiences they offered to the listeners. For several days Bach made us rich in our poor times. During that period I frequently thought about Straube, Bach's loyal servant who did not live to enjoy these celebrations.

Once again, thank you for everything: for the exceedingly precious gift that the Peters publishing house has sent me and for what it has achieved in blazing a trail for Bach. I hope that someday I will have chance to thank you personally.

Pleace accept my best wishes for you and your colleagues and my fondest hopes for the future prosperity of your publishing house.

~

To Dr. Minoru Nomura, Tokyo
[Chairman of the Japanese Association for the Lambarene Hospital and Schweitzer's Work]

Lambarene
[1951]

Dear Friend,

I am deeply impressed by everything you are doing for me, and I wonder how you manage to find time for that and also your work at the clinic. For, alas, from my own experience, I am all too well acquainted with the problem of doing something else along with working in a medical institution. My gratitude for what you are accomplishing for me also expresses my admiration for your ability to do so along with your medical activities.[1] I am leaving everything up to you, for I am not familiar with the conditions you work in.

I am delighted that you are now bringing out a whole series of my works.[2] As I wrote to the translator, I am touched that you regard my thoughts as valuable for the spiritual conviction that mankind ought to develop. I hope you are right. I knew that the idea of reverence for life would eventually make its way, but I never would have dreamed that I would live to see the beginnings of its influence. I owe these developments to people who advocate that idea in various parts of the world.

At the moment my life is complicated because I am trying to finish some works that have been in progress for years now, and I would like to complete them before my departure from this world. I am working more at night then a man of my age should, but I have no choice.

Best wishes from your grateful and devoted

Albert Schweitzer

~

To Jack Eisendraht

Lambarene

[1951]

Dear Herr Eisendraht,

After drudging all day in terrible heat, I am so tired and so handicapped by my writer's cramp that I cannot write to you as I would
like. Thank you so much for your very kind donation. It is helping
me feed the 240 lepers who are being treated here with the new
American medicines.

I have just killed a mosquito that was buzzing around me in the
lamplight. In Europe I wouldn't kill it even if it were bothering me,
but here, where mosquitoes spread the most dangerous form of malaria, I take the liberty of killing them, although I don't like doing
it. The important thing is for all of us to properly mull over the
question of when damaging and killing are permissible.

Most people are not yet truly acquainted with this issue. They still
approve of thoughtless damage and killing and enjoy the sport of
killing (hunting, fishing, with no professional need to pursue them).
Some people who came up the river to my hospital shot, purely as a
sport, at all the creatures they saw: the pelican (which still has to feed
its three chicks), the caiman, which sleeps on a branch looming into
the water, and the monkey peering at a boat.

I try to make all such people think about their actions. Much will
be achieved once people become reflective and wisely realize that they
should damage and kill only when necessary. That is the essence. The
rationalization of individual cases is a different matter. Someone
brought me four poor pelicans whose wings had been so badly slashed
by unfeeling people that they cannot fly. It will take two or three
months before their wings heal and they can fly freely. I have hired
a fisherman to catch the necessary fish to feed them. I always pity the
poor fish to the depths of my soul, but I have to choose between
killing the fish or the four pelicans who would surely starve to death.
I do not know whether I am doing the right thing in deciding one
way instead of the other.

~

To Prof. Dr. Albert Einstein, Princeton

Lambarene
28 February 1951

Dear Friend,

Let me call you that, for it expresses my feelings about you and the hopes and anxieties we share about the future of mankind. I know how kindly you spoke about me on the occasion of my seventy-fifth birthday, and I would like to tell you how good it made me feel. I was so sorry that I could find no opportunity to meet with you during the three weeks I spent in the United States during the summer of 1949. I am not giving up hope that we can get together eventually.

    With my best wishes for your health and your work,

Your devoted
Albert Schweitzer

To Friends in Israel

Lambarene
8 March 1951

Dear Friends in Israel,

In regard to the inquiry you have sent me through Engineer [Erwin R.] Jacobi, Tel Aviv, I must unfortunately reply that at the moment, much as I desire it myself, it is absolutely impossible for me to visit you and also realize my long-nurtured dream of seeing the Holy Land. The Lambarene hospital needs me so badly that I cannot make any definite plans in this dangerous period; I have to be available here and give up all plans if conditions become even more precarious. I'm still quite hale and hearty, but I have to take better care of myself than before. My top priority is to complete these works in progress as best I can *in the necessary quiet and concentration*: a well-advanced theological work, the third volume of my philosophy of civilization, a book on organ construction (since today's organ construction is on the wrong track). In Lambarene I can make strides only by working at night (excessive night work that I should not demand of myself); in the daytime I am absorbed by all the work required at the hospital. However, my writing needs total concentration, so if I do leave Lambarene for a while, it can only be for working quietly in Gunsbach.

    My motto is: Set thy house in order. I have to put the affairs and organization of my hospital in such good running order that it can keep going after my death; I have to try to give definitive shape to my unfinished writings. I can write only in complete concentration and by remaining in one place. . . . Those are my plans for the coming months. I cannot travel during this period. This is a heavy loss for me, extremely heavy since it means giving up my trip to Palestine, which would mean so much to me because of the land and the people I would see there. But I have no choice. And as for what will happen once I have completed the bulk of my writing, I dare not picture it except in dreamlike hopes. And in those hopes my trip to Palestine moves like a cosmic nebula trying to become a sun. My deepest thanks for the kind invitation.

Best wishes to all of you, those I know and those I don't yet know.
Cordially,
Albert Schweitzer

~

To Pastor James H. Sink, Immanuel Union Church, Staten Island, New York

Lambarene
8 April 1951

[f]

Please let me tell you how happy we are about the help that your congregation has given us in this very difficult period. I spoke about it to Fräulein Emma [Haussknecht]; both of us were touched by your promise to help us every year. The number of our patients is constantly rising. For four years now we have been getting a growing number of lepers, whom we are treating with the new American medicines (Promin and Diasom). At the moment we have two hundred lepers! Feeding all these people is enormously expensive; furthermore, it is often difficult to obtain food for all these sick people in the jungle. The plantations of the surrounding villages that supply bananas and manioc for the hospital are frequently devastated by elephants. I always have to have reserves of several tons of rice so that we don't run out of food in case the villages fail to deliver enough bananas and manioc. The treatment of leprosy with the new American medicines is far more successful than what we could attain in the past. I have been treating leprosy since 1913 and am happy to see the results that we are achieving today. The day before yesterday a group of twelve lepers arrived here: they are from the interior and traveled 250 miles to get to us.

~

To Dr. Fritz Buri, university instructor, Basel, and Prof. Dr. Martin Werner, Berne

Lambarene
15 April 1951

Dear Friends,

Through Frau Martin you have received the first few chapters of *The Kingdom of God and Primitive Christianity*[1] for your revision.

Please treat this matter with total secrecy. Talk to no one about it! I absolutely must count on you in this respect, for I absolutely dislike working on a book that the public is already discussing.

I share this reluctance with H. S. Chamberlain. We once had a long talk about it in Bayreuth. So please honor my request. The texts that you are getting were written mostly at night. Please use a very soft pencil (which can easily be erased) and write your comments between the lines. If your comments are long, then please put them on a separate sheet of paper that can then be glued to the edge of the appropriate page. Be very critical, for I was exhausted when I wrote, and a number of reference works were not available to me; I may therefore have made some mistakes. The quotations are placed in such a way that the bibliographical page numbers are penciled in over the typed figures. This means that I corrected them while going through the typescript. After giving it a great deal of thought, I decided to supply only an incomplete overview of the prophetic and late-Jewish expectations regarding the Kingdom of God and the Kingdom of Jesus. I tormented myself to keep the book as short as possible, and I hope that you are satisfied with these chapters. The depiction of the prophetic and late-Jewish expectations enables me to treat them as a totality in regard to Jesus and Paul rather than piecemeal. This greatly simplifies the presentation in these two chapters. The chapter on Paul is also being rewritten and is working out. The more I see of what is happening in today's Christianity, the more convinced I am that I was right in daring to tackle this theological work, although it has totally upset all my plans for what is known as my "twilight years." I am forced to exert myself almost beyond my own strength; but it had to be.

~

To Pastor James H. Sink, Immanuel Union Church, Staten Island, New York

[1951]

[f]

I have read with great interest your ideas on preaching the Gospel. How right you are to insist that the preacher should preach not only on what Jesus asks us to do but also on how to do it. I always loved my father's simple and practical sermons, and I have done my best to preach in his spirit. And I have always asked my students to preach in such a way that the faithful can take home from church something to use during the week. Feeling and judging as you do, I was very interested to read what you have written on loving those who are so hard to love. We have the great duty to help the faithful understand what Jesus asks of them in daily life and to help them achieve it.

～

To Dr. Leo Wohleb, president of South Baden, Freiburg im Breisgau

11 June 1951

Confidential

Dear Mr. President,

I am delighted to accept the [Hebel] Prize,[1] but I cannot accept the accompanying sum of money because I cannot permit myself to get anything out of Germany for my Lambarene hospital as long as so much suffering and so many refugees still exist in Germany. I refuse to budge in this matter. You must therefore allow me to hand the check back to you and ask you to employ the money as you see fit. I think you might use it to help old and indigent writers and artists and also refugees. I would really like that. You could probably focus on refugees in Freiburg or Wiesbaden. That would be your decision since you are familiar with the conditions. Please just go along with my suggestion: Instead of accepting the money attached to the prize, I am turning it over for its best use for the needy. You can do so immediately because I will be sending the check back to you as soon as I arrive in Königsfeld.

Please be so kind as to do as I ask you. And when I have the pleasure of seeing you, please tell me which people have been helped by the prize.

My very best wishes,
Albert Schweitzer

And once again: I am overjoyed at receiving the Hebel Prize—I almost used an Alemannic phrase, "a *Mordsfreid*"[wild joy], thereby expressing my Alemannic spirit.

~

To Jawaharlal Nehru, Prime Minister, Delhi
5 August 1951

[*f*]

Dear Mr. Nehru,

I was very moved by your friendliness and your good wishes for 1951. Please forgive me for responding so late with my good wishes. Neither of us really has an easy life; we each carry a heavy burden of worries and responsibilities. I often think of all the difficulties that you have to brave as head of the Indian government—difficulties that are significantly increased by the fearful state of the world. How much energy you must have to muster to take the path that you have mapped out for yourself. I, too, have a difficult life, but unlike yourself, I do not have to lead a nation and watch over its destiny. All I have is a hospital. Nevertheless, running it is quite a task. I ought to be a lot younger to perform all the work that comes upon me.

At night I try to provide the definitive shape for two books in which I am presenting my philosophical and religious thoughts.[1] The war prevented me from concentrating on them as much as I wanted to. But I must consider myself lucky that I can still accomplish something.

I have had to give up my long-nurtured plan of visiting India. How interesting it would have been to make the personal acquaintance of the Indian thinkers of our time. I am overburdened by my obligations, and I ought to be younger for traveling. However, I am striving as well as I can to keep abreast of the issues and personalities of your country and also to follow your activities. My wife and I have not forgotten the hours you spent with us in Lausanne.[2] Now I live in Africa almost permanently. My visits to Europe are rare and brief. I spend them in my Alsatian village where I feel at home and where I have my old friends. What a privilege to spend one's old age in the village where one passed one's youth and to rediscover the memories rooted there. I do not believe, dear Mr. Nehru, that we will ever meet again, but we think about each other and we understand each other, for we each have to carry out a task that absorbs us and that constitutes our destiny.

~

To August Heisler, M.D., Königsfeld
[Summer 1951]

I was acquainted with you before I first met you. My teacher and friend, Prof. Arnold Kahn in Strasbourg, brought you and your colleague Schall to my attention when your food table came out. Then my first medical discussions with you were significant for me. What I learned from you was not something completely new; I had already made a few observations that overlapped with yours. But the area covered by your observations was a lot more comprehensive than mine. It was extremely rewarding for me to get to know them. I was also prompted to be more attentive to the things I encountered within the precincts of my experiences. Thus, you have given me what many others have similarly received from you. As a result, today you have to put up with our celebrating you as someone who has acquired some valuable insights for us and who has educated us to observe.[1] As an educator, you prove yourself in your moderation. You never one-sidedly underestimated the achievements of medical science as it has developed. You advocate only the right of all-around observation, which completes the treasure trove of knowledge making up the science of medicine. You make us realize that if all of us who stand at a patient's bedside wish to practice our profession correctly, we have to be able to do our bit toward increasing medical knowledge. Let me also thank you for encouraging us to attend properly to the spiritual part in the behavior of patients and in our behavior toward them.

After all, we cannot pay enough attention to the fact that medicine is not only a science but also an art in which our existence has an effect on that of the patient.

~

To Wieland and Wolfgang Wagner, Bayreuth
[Gunsbach]
11 August 1951

Dear Wieland Wagner, Dear Wolfgang Wagner,

When I found out in Lambarene that the Bayreuth Festival was going to resume, I was overjoyed, for Bayreuth represents some of the loveliest memories of my life. I first went there to attend the new performances of *The Ring* in 1896, and I returned a number of times. I got to know Frau Cosima [Wagner],[1] and I was close friends with

Siegfried Wagner for many long years. I saw both of you as children when I visited Bayreuth after the first war (it must have been around 1923). . . .

When I learned that the two of you were to be entrusted with the resumption of the Festival, I knew you wouldn't have an easy time of it. How I would have loved to come, but I was held back by work I had to complete during my brief stay in Europe and by a huge number of purchases I had to make for my hospital. I'm simply no longer a free man. Now as for the anxieties that impelled you to send me the telegram, please don't take them so hard. I am kept up to date by friends who attended the performances and who possess sound judgment, and I am familiar enough with the problems of staging those tremendous works: For two decades I watched your dear father, a man of outstanding expertise, tussling with them. I still have vivid memories of the marvelously simple production of *The Ring* in 1896, a staging that goes back to the premiere, and the *Parsifal* that went back to the 1880s. However, [one] cannot simply reproduce them. The modern listener brings along different viewing demands on the basis of watching plays and films. The point is to reconcile old and new in the proper way. The listeners have no clear idea of the problem. They make inconsistent demands. If your father were running Bayreuth under today's conditions, he, too, would be controversial.

And if I may, as his friend and in his spirit, advise you in your current situation: Let people discuss things with their lips and pens. Do not respond. Do not try in any way to join the discussions, affect them, or justify yourself. Simply continue on your way, toward future festivals; strive to be true to and preserve the spirit of Bayreuth as your father did, and let the Bayreuth tradition take shape in our era, using the experiences of the experts who are loyal to Bayreuth. It was partly this latter approach that enabled your father to achieve such great things. In every respect go your way in the spirit in which your father would go his way in his calm, fine, quiet manner. You will then be on the right track. Respond to criticism with accomplishments. And listen not only to the critiques but also to that which is with them and near them and is stronger than they: the satisfaction in so many hearts that Bayreuth exists again under the aegis of the descendants of the great *Meister*. This is not proclaimed in grand words and blazing lines, but it is here. You should and must be aware of the love for and confidence in you that many people feel, just as I do. This is the spiritual capital that you possess for your undertaking. The latter permits you to give any critique its due and to devote yourself to the great task that you have been assigned, to dedicate yourself in the proper spirit, proper joy, proper sense of responsibility.

Bayreuth is important not only to the German nation but to the entire civilized world. We witnessed this in previous decades, and new generations will have the same experience.

Bayreuth is not just music, it is a process of experiencing profound emotion and sublimity through the ideas about human existence that were given shape in Richard Wagner's dramas.

Preserving this heritage in a pure form for the world, having Bayreuth continue to exist as the Bayreuth that it became—that is the great and difficult task that has fallen to you. The people who criticize the new productions are not doing so simply for the sake of criticizing; they venerate Bayreuth and want to make sure that it fulfills its calling. And when I mentally shake your hand with the great sympathy that I feel for your enterprise, then many other people are doing the same thing, albeit tacitly. If ever I am allowed to attend the Bayreuth Festival during a future visit to Europe, then I will be realizing one of my deepest wishes for the time that is still granted to me. And when I then walk through the streets of Bayreuth, I will imagine running into your father and hearing his "Hello there!" as heartily as it came from his lips.

Please give my best regards to the conductors who are appearing at Bayreuth. And please convey my best wishes to your mother. I can imagine what the renewed existence of the Festival means to her.

Yours truly,
Albert Schweitzer

As I am writing this, one of my musical friends, who has come here directly from Bayreuth, is playing the grand piano in the next room, reminiscing about the performance.

~

To Christoph Martin
[Emmy Martin's grandson]

[1951]

Dear Christoph,

As a friend of your grandfather and grandmother, and your parents, I am writing to you from far away to express my heartiest congratulations on your birthday.[1] May you find the right path in life, that is, the right spirit that produces the right kind of behavior. May you acquire a true education, and may your thoughts attain the noble and profound humanity that prepares us to find the right way and to take it. May the spirit of Jesus become your light along the way and help you to find peace in everything you encounter—the peace that is higher than all reason.

⁓

To Lotte Gerhold-Schall, Königsfeld

on the train, in Denmark
27 October 1951

All my holiday plans were turned topsy-turvy because I was trying to complete the last three volumes—the chorale compositions—of the American Bach edition with the translator, who was in Gunsbach.[1] The manuscript of comments on the individual chorales was finished years ago, but giving it a definitive shape and cutting it took longer than I thought. I'm still not done, so I'll have to finish up on the boat. Then came the Frankfurt celebration[2] [Peace Prize of the German Book Industry] and the speech I had to give. It took me ten days to write it. Then an unexpected trip to Paris. And finally: the recordings from late September until October 12.[3] As you have probably learned from Helene, they specifically sent the recording apparatus (installed in a car) from America with a sound engineer who specializes in recordings of organ music. Originally, only a few pieces were to be recorded on the Gunsbach organ as souvenirs for my friends, but then the sound engineer told me that I should record all the pieces on the organ. (I had already given up the plan to make more records than I had made in Switzerland during July because I was afraid it would take too long and be too exhausting.) But I could manage to have myself recorded playing my organ in Gunsbach.

So I recorded for two weeks: Widor's Sixth Symphony, Franck's First and Third Chorales, Mendelssohn's final organ sonata, and various pieces by Bach. Then, on the fourteenth, I was off to Zurich and then Strasbourg–London–Rotterdam–Hamburg–Copenhagen–Sweden–Hamburg–Strasbourg.

I plan to return to Strasbourg on November 3 for my final travel preparations, but around the fifth I'll probably be spending a day or two in Königsfeld. Next, I have to go to Switzerland to place orders for medicines and then to Paris for another day or two. On November 19, departure from Strasbourg for Bordeaux.

⁓

To Emmy Martin, Gunsbach
[After setting sail from Conakry, West Africa. Schweitzer had agreed
to play the organ in the church in the port of Conakry during a
stopover of several hours while traveling to Lambarene]
                    1 December 1951

This time, Conakry (they're on the dock now) was a mad rush. We
arrived at seven o'clock. I was hoping to head straight for the organ.
But the abbé wasn't there to pull the stops, and the organ key wasn't
there either, even though I had asked them in my letter to prepare everything so that I could rehearse right after the arrival of the
ship. . . .

And the *audition* [recital] was scheduled for nine-thirty! I barely
had time to register the pieces in a makeshift way—and the church
was already filling up. Well, the whole thing went quite nicely after
all. The bishop thanked me very sweetly; many young people had
come from the interior, including Robert Jung's son [from Strasbourg],
whom I had baptized.

After a brief visit with the governor, I drove back to the ship to
spend some time with Maigret, Robert Jung's son, and other people.
Unfortunately, I couldn't invite them to lunch since the ship was
sailing at twelve-fifteen. So everything turned out beautifully after
all. The heat in Dakar and Conakry was worse than any I had ever
experienced in those places.

≈

Message for the celebration of de Brazza's hundredth birthday
                    [Lambarene]
                    15 February 1952[1]

                                                        [ʃ]

This message comes from Lambarene, where de Brazza's colonial
career began. While writing these words I can see the foot of the hill
on which the buildings of my hospital are located, and I can see the
branch of the Ogowe by which the young explorer reached Lambarene, the village of King Renoké, at sunset on 12 November 1875. He
was to find the king to be a friend; he put at the explorer's disposal
his pirogues, his rowers, his knowledge of the countryside, and his
influence on the chiefs, and enabled de Brazza to go upriver and

discover countries that would form the nucleus of the colonial empire that he was to found.

Between 12 November 1875, the date of his arrival in Lambarene, and 14 September 1905, when he passed away in Dakar, de Brazza accomplished something that will inspire admiration for as long as mankind retains the knowledge of the events of our era.

For far too long interest has focused solely on his accomplishments. Only gradually have people also grown aware of the extraordinary personality of the man behind them. I feel that only today do we see him in his true greatness.

His qualities as an explorer, an organizer, administrator, and diplomat, great as they were, would not have been enough to make him the leader that he was. They constituted the instruments at his disposal. These instruments were fully utilized only because of the human qualities that were his.

Had it not been for his human personality, which impressed the chiefs, starting with Renoké of Lambarene, and gained their trust, he would never have been able to travel from Ogowe to the very heart of Africa and convince those tribes to place themselves under the protection of the country he represented.

Without the moral ideal that inspired him and obliged him to regard the rule that he was establishing as a means of performing a basically civilizing work, he would not have become the colonizer whom we admire.

De Brazza proved that he was a new kind of colonizer when he arrived in Africa and instantly launched the struggle for the abolition of slavery. Throughout all the successive enterprises of his career, his supreme goal was always to create a condition consistent with reason, emotion, and ethics.

In celebrating the centennial of his birth, we are paying tribute not only to the empire builder but also to the man. He stands before us as the representative of true civilization, of the humanity that is the basic component of true civilization. Ever since the beginning of our century we have believed we could emancipate ourselves from that humanity; but we have failed to realize that we are setting out on the road to chaos.

The centennial of de Brazza's birth is particularly important because it draws our attention to his personality. It confronts us with a man who was profoundly and nobly human in his thought, his attitude, his actions. History entrusted him with a message for our time. Let us heed the truth that he has to teach us. Let us be impressed and edified.

Albert Schweitzer

~

To *Svenska Morgonbladet,* Stockholm

Lambarene

24 February 1952

Dear Sirs,

In a wire that I received on 27 December 1951, you asked me to respond by telegram to the questions concerning what mankind needs most for 1952. I promptly wired you that I could not provide an answer in the form requested and that I would, instead, reply in a letter. The telegram style did not strike me as feasible.

It is only today, on the last Sunday in February, that I am able to answer your questions.

I will leave it entirely up to you to give your audience reasons for these belated reflections for the new year.

If you consider it unfeasible to run my text in *Svenska Morgonbladet,* then that, too, is your prerogative. Do as you think best.

WHAT MANKIND NEEDS MOST AT THIS TIME

All of us together, as far as we are capable of thinking properly, feel that it is peace that has always been necessary to mankind, and now more than ever before. After all, henceforth, any war fought with the dreadful modern weapons would wreak inconceivable destruction and annihilation. And since it would be far more of a world war than the two on which we look back, it would bring such misery to mankind that we dare not imagine the manner of human survival.

Since, for us, so much depends on preserving peace, which is seriously threatened, our time needs that which serves to prevent war. There is no lack of effort toward this end. Rulers and parliaments keep issuing declarations that they do not want war. Associations for understanding between nations try to gain prestige for the viewpoint that agreement must be reached on the controversial issues and to begin negotiations that would seem to lead to that goal.

All efforts along these lines have their importance. If they succeed in preventing war, then it will be felt throughout the world as an immeasurable good fortune that people ultimately did not dare believe in.

But it is not enough to try to avoid the now threatening war. These efforts must be joined by far more extensive and comprehensive efforts to bring about a real state of peace. The situation of mankind in our time implies that we must deal with the problem of peace in a manner entirely different from that of the generations before us. They could resign themselves to a simultaneity, an alternation, a tangle of war and peace as well as they could. But now that war has developed into the horrible thing that it is today, we must admit to ourselves that the issue is no longer just a possible avoidance of war. If we are not to perish, a permanent state of peace must be created. Our efforts must aim at bringing a peace that is no longer menaced by war.

The political lack of peace together with its inherent danger is not a separate issue, it is merely the terrible manifestation of the ubiquitous lack of peace. The reason for this lack of peace is that we take it for granted and consider it reasonable that the course of things should be determined by power that opposes power. We are resigned to the circumstance that in any area the resolution of existing problems is the result of struggles waged by powers and influences against one another. We accept the fact that all agreements putting an end to this kind of struggle are only temporarily valid. No permanent under-standing comes about but only a provisional covering of antitheses.

The conditions of our time no longer permit us to pin our hopes on the natural course of things. They compel us to picture a human condition that is brought about by the spirit of peace, something that corresponds to the Christian idea of the Kingdom of God.

Through Christianity, the idea of a kingdom of peace has been known to mankind for centuries. People did not believe they could make it come true. It was viewed as something purely religious that could not be applied to reality, but actually it *is* something that should and must be realized.

This insight is urged upon us by the times in which we live. If mankind is not to perish, then we have no choice but to place our hope in the spirit, which is different from the spirit of the world.

The conviction of peace, inspired by the fear of horrible wars, is only a shadow of the true conviction. The latter exists only when we yearn for the cessation of the lack of peace, to which we are subjugated in all things by the spirit of the world.

This can happen only with the emergence of a new spirit that animates us. This spirit cannot be proclaimed in the world or put an end to war if it does not first settle within us and begin its work.

Anyone who seriously begins to obey that spirit will experience something of Jesus' blessing of the peacemakers. Granted, in his striv-ing to serve peace, he will not be successful in everything. He will be misunderstood and smirked at. He may even encounter distrust as if he had ulterior motives for his peace efforts. But none of these things

are worth considering compared with what he brings about. He will
be certain that he is acting in accordance with the truth and that he
can achieve what is necessary. With faith and confidence we may
challenge mankind to devote itself to the spirit of peace. Anyone who
earnestly does so will not be disappointed; instead, he will partake of
a joy he did not know.

We have no idea how many people will follow the call of our time
to quietly pave the way for peace, but one thing is certain: We have
to make a start toward what has to happen.

If at first it is only a few in every place and a few thousand in
every nation, then this is already an announcement of the spirit of
peace, a proclamation that cannot remain hidden.

We must never give up our faith in the spirit or the hope we pin
on it.

The yearning for peace is great in the hearts of mankind today.
For them, a revelation of the spirit of peace will be an experience
with unforeseeable consequences. It is only through the miracle of
awakening the spirit of peace in mankind that it can be kept from
perishing.

May it be granted to us that the efforts toward avoiding war are
successful and that in the time that is thereby given us we can make
the spirit of peace so powerful that it will start to become the Kingdom
of God in ourselves and in the world.

Albert Schweitzer
Lambarene, 1 March 1952

～

To Queen Elisabeth of Belgium, Lacken Castle, Belgium
on board the Foucauld
near the mouth of the Niger
8 July 1952

[f]

Madame,

Your Majesty must have been surprised to receive long-playing records
sent by Mr. Hill of New York.[1] Alas, I should have warned you that
these were sample recordings of my performances last autumn on the
Gunsbach organ: they were made by Mr. Hill for Columbia [Records].
Mr. Hill had made several of these sample records and offered to give
me one or the other series, so I asked him to send a series to Your
Majesty. However, during that period I was so overwhelmed with
work that I was unable to take care of even my most urgent corre-

spondence. It is only now, as the *Foucauld* sails along the African coast, that I can again pick up my pen, and I am losing no time in amending my mistake by apologizing to you profusely.

I set sail on July 5. During August and September I will be in Gunsbach at the disposal of Mr. Hill and the machines he has brought from America. In October I will be obliged to travel. Paris (where I will pay the fifty visits that I should have paid before my election to the Académie Française), London, Rotterdam, Hamburg, Copenhagen, Stockholm. I'll be returning to Lambarene in mid-November.

Last year when I had to go to London, I was hoping I could pass through Belgium and pay you my respects between trains, but nothing came of it. When all was said and done, I did not have enough time for that detour. If it is possible for Your Majesty to pass through Gunsbach this year, then my organ and I would be profoundly happy and we would strain to do our best. I have prepared Franck's second chorale for Columbia; I have always been moved by the depth of this music, which I came to appreciate when it was published several months after the maestro's death.

~

To Emma Haussknecht, Lambarene
                    on the *Foucauld*
                    [1952]

Because of my correspondence, my fatigue, and my premature departure, I did not get a chance to talk to you about the work that has to be done, but I will now do so in writing.

Don't forget to put in large reserves of sand as soon as the sandbanks are out. Check our stocks of cement and usable lime.

With Dr. Percy, check the boats in the boatyard and also see whether the motors can be turned on and are well lubricated and wrapped up and covered. This [is] very important because the two motors are very expensive.

See if we have a spare transmission belt [for the icebox]. If not, send me the exact dimensions—width, thickness, length—so that I can order a spare belt through Ittel and bring it along. I want to start my shopping as soon as I arrive.

I am writing to Dr. Percy to label the sacks sent by SHO[1] and stow them away. You unpacked them. He is to contact you. The alcohol has to be labeled profusely to prevent any mixups.

~

To [West German] President Theodor Heuss, Bonn
Gunsbach, Alsace
15 August 1952

Dear Friend,

Upon arriving in Bordeaux, I heard that your dear wife [Elly Heuss-Knapp] had passed away.[1] You can imagine how shaken and saddened I was. After all, she was part of all my lovely memories of the old Strasbourg, and we got along so well from the very first day we met. When our old Strasbourg was a thing of the past, each of us followed the other's career. I was so happy that she joined you on your path through life together, and ultimately she found a position in which she could utilize all her desire and talent for making a difference. I witnessed this from very far away, and I was delighted from the bottom of my heart. It has been almost a year since I saw her, but again there was something to admire: the way she bore her suffering, so quietly, so courageously. I often thought about her with deep sympathy, knowing as a doctor what she was forced to endure. Ah, if one knows what suffering her disease causes, one does not truly dare to mourn her demise; one is almost relieved that her suffering has come to an end. Let me tell you how deeply I share your grief. Frau Luise Bresslau-Hoff has told[2] me so much about her. She was still filled with what she had witnessed.

I have no idea when it will be possible for me to visit you. This brief stay in Europe is crammed with work, And I must make sure that I remain very quiet for the moment, living without traveling, since I have to go easy with my heart. During that difficult last sojourn in Lambarene, my heart was terribly strained. I won't be undertaking anything until early October; instead, I'll be working quietly in Gunsbach. There is only one thing I hope I can do: go to Frankfurt on August 28.

With my fondest thoughts,

Albert Schweitzer

~

To Dr. Emeric Percy, Hôpital Dr. Schweitzer, Lambarene
Gunsbach
26 September 1952

Dear Doctor,

Many, many thanks for your kind and long letter of September 13, which I received on the twentieth. You are forgiven in advance for not writing earlier since you are doing an amazing amount of work in various areas. My stay in Europe is terribly difficult because of all the demands being made on me. In this respect it is harder on me than my previous visit, but in regard to my anxieties about Lambarene, I am far better off than last year! And I owe this to you.

At the moment I am working on my speech for the Academy on October 20: *Le problème de l'éthique dans l'évolution de la pensée humaine* [The problem of ethics in the evolution of human thought].[1] It is hard to sum up what the treatment of this subject requires. I try to keep my mornings free to make headway with this work. Unfortunately, I don't always succeed.

In regard to the electric engine, you fully convinced me in Lambarene. I thank you, and I will follow your advice. It is nice that you could help out poor Reckenmann. Bringing down his blood pressure like that is quite an accomplishment. If only he had come to us for treatment earlier. I have already learned that the motor can be started from the top. We are all very grateful to you for that. How lovely that you are also taking care of the water pipe stands. When I return, we'll talk about the question of the pipe for the house for white patients.

Best,
Albert Schweitzer

To Ali Silver, Lambarene

at night, in the train
from Stockholm to Malmö
15 November 1952

Dear Ali,

It was lovely seeing the old acquaintances again in Stockholm. Those days were taken up with visits and chains of invitations. I didn't have fifteen minutes to myself on either day and, as in Paris, I had to keep improvising unexpected speeches that were thrust upon me.

When the queen presented the medal to me, it all went very simply. I entered her salon at twelve o'clock on the dot, accompanied by three members of the board of the Red Cross. She handed me the [Prince Carl] Medal with some friendly words.

And I had a lovely surprise: Right after my arrival on the evening of the thirteenth, I was taken into a room chock-full of people. Without a word of explanation I was placed in a chair in the aisle between the chairs. The lights instantly went out . . . and suddenly I was in Lambarene. The film of the Swedish Mission began. It is very simple and good. When the antelopes stuck out their heads to eat, there was movement in the room. But the climax came when Pierrette [the cat] licked my arm, peering up coquettishly while I wrote. Her acting is marvelously natural.

Now I'm heading south, ever south, until I'll be with you people again. . . .[1]

Best,
A.S.

~

To Friederike Maria Zweig

Lambarene
28 December 1952

Dear Frau Zweig,

By the time I heard about your seventieth birthday, it was too late to congratulate you punctually. So I am doing it belatedly. I sometimes think about you. Occasionally I picture you standing before me in Gunsbach. I was deeply moved by your biography of our departed friend[1] [Stefan Zweig]. How right of you to put up this monument in which you stand before us with him. Many of my friends are grateful to you from the bottom of their hearts. I am sending you my best wishes on your seventieth birthday. I hope that someday it will be granted to me to see you again. I spent some time in Gunsbach during late summer and autumn, now I'm back in Lambarene.

I am writing about your birthday to Frau Martin who is still doing the work in Gunsbach. She, too, has fond memories of you. Unfortunately, my wife could not come along to Lambarene. She can no longer endure the heat.

My very best to you,
Albert Schweitzer

~

To Thornton Wilder

Lambarene
17 March 1953

Cher ami,

If you are in Europe and working, then you should not miss this chance to visit Gunsbach. It doesn't matter that you don't know Frau Martin. Within ten minutes you will feel as if you've been friends for a long time. And since I can't be in Gunsbach, it is comforting to know that others can spend time there in my place. I am so sorry that you have to work on your new book in hotel rooms and among hotel guests and that whenever you stroll outdoors you keep running into people instead of remaining alone with nature. In Gunsbach you will have that rapport with nature, so go to Gunsbach in my stead and live there in tranquility, working as I would do if I could be there. You won't be intruding. Frau Martin will go about her work without paying you much heed. That is how we act with visitors and guests. I hope that my explanations are as clear as Kant's *Critique of Pure Reason* or the structure of a Bach fugue. So:—off to Gunsbach, *vers la vie simple et la vie du travail* [toward the simple life and the life of work].

My fondest wishes,

Albert Schweitzer

From Gunsbach you can take several outings to Colmar and see the Isenheim altar of Grünewald (Master Nithardt). How lovely the spring is in Gunsbach....

~

To Jacques Feschotte, Paris

Lambarene
18 March 1953[1]

[f]

I have just finished the chapter on the ornaments for the introduction to the Schirmer edition of Bach's chorales. I believe I have cleared up the issue of Bach's trills. If you understand enough German, I'll have Frau Martin send you a typescript as soon as I have one.

~

To the directors of the Schirmer publishing house, New York

Dr. Albert Schweitzer
Lambarene, Gabon
French Equatorial Africa
18 March 1953

Gentlemen,

We can finally go ahead with the edition of the three volumes of Bach's choral compositions.[1] Please accept my profuse apologies for this terrible delay, but I was so overworked that I could make no headway with this project, despite my desires. And then came my election to the Académie Française,[2] which gave my 1952 sojourn in Europe an entirely different form from what I would have liked. I had to write my acceptance speech and remain in Paris, paying and receiving official visits. This was not foreseen in my schedule. Then there was something else that caused a delay: the issue of the performance of Bach's embellishments, especially the trills. I already dealt with this question when I wrote my book on Bach, and I have been haunted by it ever since. There was no telling where Bach wanted a short trill or a long one, to realize the full value of the trilled note.

I simply could not find it in my heart not to provide organists with clear indications about the performance of Bach's ornaments in our edition, rather than supplying unclear instructions and pretending they were clear. I was ashamed to be giving them stones instead of bread, so I reimmersed myself in the problem and kept drilling away where I had first started drilling in my book on Bach. It had become clear to me by 1950 that Philipp Emanuel Bach's work on keyboard music has no reliable information about his father's ornaments. This means that the solution can be found only by directly studying Bach's ornaments. I therefore began this research and had gotten quite far by 1951. I saw the road and then reached my destination. I now believe I have found the authentic rules for performing Bach's trills— rules that fit all cases, whereby nothing is left unclear and everything is simple. Now I can, in all good conscience, do the edition with Mr. Nies-Berger. So please forgive me for taking more time than planned. I believe it was worth it.

I will now give Mr. Nies-Berger instructions concerning the problems of the edition, and I will ask him to discuss this with you and obtain the opinions of experts.

Best wishes,
Albert Schweitzer

To Madre Maria, Mother Superior of the Franciscan Convent, Eremo
Francescano, Campello, Umbria

[1953]

[*f*]

Another verse by the Apostle Paul that is a light on my road: "Love
forgives everything, it believes everything, it hopes for everything, it
endures everything." What comfort and what encouragement this
sentence brings to our daily lives. It helps us overcome the grief that
other people cause us. It allows us not to condemn them or lose hope
in them.

Since I last wrote to you in 1950, I have had three years of overwork,
three years of great anxieties. With the 250 lepers, my hospital has
doubled in size, which, in turn, means a doubling of work and also
of anxieties, especially material ones. It is very difficult to continue
such an enormous enterprise in times of economic instability. However, I do keep finding the wherewithal. People are so good to
me. . . . The altar picture [which Schweitzer had received from the
Franciscan convent] is very dear to me, and I am keeping it safe and
sound. The altar is pure simplicity, corresponding to the Gospels, to
the altar of Christ with His disciples. I would be happy to have another
sign of life from you. My best regards to all the sisters. May God's
peace be with all of you!

~

To Dr. Felix Meiner, publisher, Hamburg
                                    Lambarene
                                    8 April 1953

Dear Friend,

Let me join the people congratulating you on your seventieth birthday.
Considering the amount of work that lies ahead for you, I feel it
would be better if this were only your fiftieth birthday. But since it
is your seventieth, we would like to share your joy that you are still
so marvelously fit, and we would like to express our wishes that you
may remain hale and hearty for a long time.

If some future person should write the history of German book
publishing in the twentieth century, he will have to report on the
extraordinary destinies that challenged its existence during the first
half of the century. At the same time he will have to point out that
it never lost its courage in its plight; instead, it mustered the energy
to stand its ground and achieve amazing things.

Among the names of those who were hardest hit and who worked their way up again most courageously, your name, dear friend, will be one of the first. The things that you have dared to try and that you have accomplished are almost incomprehensible for those of us who have witnessed them. We also know the conviction in which you found the strength to start all over again despite your twofold ruin because of the dreadful events. This conviction was your high opinion of your profession. You wanted to place valuable books back in the hands of the present generation so that it would continue partaking of traditional culture and intellect. This will make many of today's young people grateful to you, as was the earlier generation when your Philosophical Library offered them the possibility of become familiar with the works of the great thinkers in a manner that had never existed before.

Thus, I myself was already grateful to you before I even met you. When I tell you about the importance that your Philosophical Library had, I know I am expressing something that many people in the previous generation thought and are still thinking. We are delighted that your idealism and courage as a publisher aim at making it possible for today's generation to have the same opportunity that was granted to us.

I have to extend my very personal thanks to you for forcing me to write *Out of My Life and Thought*. Without you, I would never have dreamed of it. I was fully preoccupied with other works, but you employed a publisher's diplomacy in 1929 to get me to supply a self-presentation for your series *Philosophy of the Present in Self-Presentations*. If you had not had my dear friend Oskar Kraus as your crony, you probably wouldn't have succeeded. I found the whole business unpleasant because, being fifty-four at the time, I felt I was still too young to write about my life.

In fact, an old pastor stopped me on the street in Strasbourg and took me to task: "What's this I hear, Albert! You're already writing about your life? That's a sign of arrogance. A person should do something like that only when he's past seventy. I just wanted to tell you that. Don't be offended." Having spoken his piece, he left. Nor did I disagree with him. But Herr Felix Meiner, with his publishing logic, simply had a different opinion. Once he received my brief self-presentation, it grew of its own accord into *Out of My Life and Thought*.

Without your publishing obstinacy, dear friend, I would never have penned that document of the life and thought of a now vanished time. At seventy I would not have managed to write these memoirs. The conditions of 1945 and the subsequent years have permitted no meditation about the past—not to mention that I would never have found the time to write about it.

But now, enough about publishing. You are also a human being and valuable to me as such. In the heat and stillness of the tropical night, let me tell you, dear friend, that I have liked you personally since the first hour I spent with you and that our friendship of many years means a great deal to me. I am looking forward to the day when I can see you again in Hamburg, and I plan to spend some proper time with you.

Tomorrow morning an African in his canoe will carry this letter downstream to Lambarene and deliver it to the post office. That afternoon, in the airplane that will fly low over my hospital and stir up the palm fronds, my letter will begin its long journey north.

With warmest wishes,

Albert Schweitzer

To Schirmer Publishers, New York
Lambarene
11 June 1953

Dear Mr. Schirmer,

(1) I have definitively made up my mind not to include any discussion of the embellishments in the score [of the edition of Bach's choral preludes]. The table of embellishments that I am adding to every volume solves the problem in the simplest way. The few cases requiring some reflections on performing several complicated trill figures will best be treated in the text pertaining to the appropriate choral composition. It is a lot better if the performer is confronted with the Bach score as such, without any additions.

(2) So all that Mr. Nies-Berger has to do for the score is add the appropriate verses for the given song and find the best place for them. It would be best if he did that with the technical people in your publishing house. Naturally, I would be delighted to receive a printing sample of two or three chorale beginnings so that I can get some idea of the overall appearance and also possibly express my opinion.

(3) The omission of the indications for performing embellishments in the score will make the publication much simpler.

(4) I have always felt that all three volumes should be issued at the same time. However, after due consideration I now feel that

volume six should come out right after its completion. The advantage would be that this edition, which people have been awaiting for some time, would appear with no delay. It will take a while to complete the seventh and eighth volumes, and I am not in favor of rushing something like this through. I also have a special reason for publishing volume six right after completion. Various musicians have concentrated on the problem of performing Bach's embellishments and published studies on that subject, and I have presented my theory to them by sending them a copy of my chapter on that issue. It is an old principle of mine to publish nothing without first obtaining the opinions of experts. These scholars generally agree that Bach distinguishes between two kinds of trills: the pralltriller (inverted mordent), which breaks off the note, emphasizing it; and the trill that dissolves the whole note, as can be concluded from an unbiased study of Bach's ornaments. All I had to do was observe these things and then have them confirmed by examples in Friedemann's keyboard booklet.

For the next few months, I will be staying in Lambarene, where I consider myself indispensable. I also want to remain here to work on the edition of the choral compositions in peace and quiet. Packing, traveling, arriving, unpacking, setting up in Gunsbach, receiving visitors . . . all these things would jolt me out of my work schedule, as was the case last year when I also had to pen my acceptance speech for the Académie Française and spend a long and very exhausting time in Paris. For the coming months I will belong only to my hospital and Schirmer Music Publishers.

I pity you, dear Herr Schirmer, for having to read my handwriting, but I cannot concentrate properly when I hear the clatter of the typewriter and hunt and peck the keys; I am therefore letting my pen move across the paper calmly and silently.

With best wishes to you and your colleagues,

Albert Schweitzer

Please forward the enclosed letter to H. Nies-Berger right away. I have to send most of my huge correspondence by airmail. This is a large expense, so I try to save on air postage as much as possible.

~

To Suzanne Oswald, Schweitzer's niece, Zurich
Lambarene
5 November 1953

Just as I was starting this letter at 1000 A.M., four visitors dropped by—if that term can be used on the equator. I invited them to lunch, and until then they can wander around the hospital and the plantation. So now I'm finally sitting at my desk.

Now the Nobel Peace Prize has come on top of everything else.[1] Journalists sent by press agencies are landing in special planes. Telegrams from press agencies in Paris, London, and New York arrive with questions that I am supposed to answer by cable. It's touching but strenuous. I've been devoting whole days to all this. It was Dr. Guy Schweitzer who heard the news (on the radio) last Friday evening at eleven and came to tell me.

Dozens of telegrams are pouring in from people whom I hadn't expected to hear them. A very warm cable from Vincent Auriol [president of France].

[Schweitzer received the Nobel Peace Prize in Oslo on 4 November 1954 and gave a speech: "The Problem of Peace in the World Today."]

~

To Gunnar Jahn, Nobel Prize Committee, and to August Schou, Oslo
Lambarene
30 November 1953

[f]

Thank you for your letter of November 23. It is very kind of you not to take it amiss that I cannot come on December 10. That date would be totally impossible for me. You suggest October [1954]. That would be fine. I intend to remain in Europe until November 15, so I can arrange to come to Oslo during October.

As the recipient of the Nobel Peace Prize, I am tempted, as I have written you, to talk about the problem of peace in our time. I know that this is a very thorny issue, but perhaps it would be worthwhile trying to treat it in a thorough manner by seeking to envision how to get humanity today to truly want peace and how we could try to bring peace about. If you have no objections to my tackling such a vast and topical issue, I will do so. As is my habit, I will begin drafting the text several months ahead of time. But if this subject seems inappropriate for some reason or other, then please say so quite frankly. I will then abandon it and write about the idea of reverence for life as a foundation for the idea of peace.

~

To Dag Hammarskjöld, secretary general of the United Nations, New York

Lambarene
19 December 1953[1]

[f]

Dear Mr. Hammarskjöld,

When you were elected secretary general of the United Nations, I read in a British magazine that you sympathize with my idea and that your motto is "Service." I wanted to write you at that time, not to congratulate you on being elected, for you should not be congratulated for taking over one of the most difficult positions; I simply wanted to send you my best wishes. But since I am always drowning in work and fatigue, my letter to you was not written, which was the fate of many other letters. Mentally, however, I did send you my good wishes.

Perhaps someday I will have an opportunity to visit you in Sweden. I always go to Sweden whenever I am in Europe, especially to see my friends Lagerfelt in Gammalhil. Baroness Lagerfelt, my Swedish translator, has been seriously ill for many months and is almost totally blind.

I am also supposed to go to America, but I don't know when my work and my fatigue will permit me to do so. In any case, I would be very happy to make your acquaintance.

~

To Max Tau, Oslo

Lambarene
23 December 1953

From a compilation of press statements that you[1] took the trouble to put together, I have learned that many important men in Norway are speaking out on my behalf. And the only response from the jungle of Lambarene is silence.

And then came October 31 and the Peace Prize. You really mucked up my life! Journalists descended on me like locusts (they had to be put up here) and forced me, a poor wretch, to give them information, interviews, and answers to lists of questions. I had to talk into a steel tape machine. I had to wire articles of two hundred to three hundred words to newspapers . . . I had to write them down at night, contenting myself with three or four hours of sleep. And at the same time I had gravely ill patients, white and black, who were causing me no end of anxiety. A white man died. . . . Telegram from the New York publisher about the manuscript I haven't delivered[2] . . . that's all I needed! So at night I have to attend to the revisions and final draft of the last portion of the manuscript. . . .

I have recovered only very slowly from everything I endured in the first two weeks of November. Hundreds of letters are waiting to be answered, but they must all take a backseat to the work I have to do. Before the heavy rainy season starts in February, a good portion of the lepers' village has to be completed. The seriously ill lepers cannot endure the rainy season in the decaying bamboo huts.

From my speech to the assembly on December 10 you learned that I am using the major part of the prize to buy cement, hardwood beams, and corrugated iron for my buildings. What great material services the prize is performing for me!

As you probably know, I will be going to Oslo in the second half of October [to receive the Nobel Peace Prize]. I am looking forward to it and doing my best to have a few free days and visit you as a rational creature that has had enough sleep. I hope to arrive in Europe during the summer.

With fondest thoughts of you and your wife,

Albert Schweitzer

PART NINE

1954 - 1965

To the Albert Schweitzer School in Berlin–Neukölln
[On the occasion of its dedication on January 14]
14 February 1954

[To the pupils:]

I am deeply touched that it was you who suggested that the school bear my name! Now we are linked by the loveliest bond in existence: a joint desire for goodness. I hope that many warm and beautiful friendships develop among you. I had such friendships at school, at the Gymnasium [secondary school] in Mulhouse, Alsace. Those were friendships for life. That is why I hope that you cherish friendship. It is a precious good.

And maintain the right spiritual relationship to your teachers. Respect them as the people who are not only teaching you knowledge but also trying to educate you for a proper life. Do not make their work difficult through pranks and misbehavior, through inattentiveness and negligence; let them educate you with joy. You have no idea what a mental strain it is to teach and how hard it is if the right spirit does not prevail in a classroom. I may say these things to you because you have chosen me as your patron.

To Richard Kik, Heidenheim

Lambarene
14 February 1954

I must tell you how delighted I am that you have so nicely solved the problem of the reports as a circular letter.[1] I am too tired and unconcentrated to write an appropriate report. I would have to start with 1945, mentioning and expressing my appreciation for all those who have worked for, left, or joined my project since the beginning of the second war. Otherwise, I could not start the report. And this would require a labor that I simply could not perform without neglecting my urgent daily work.

I am straining myself as much as I can, but I have a clear sense that I cannot overdo it; otherwise something irreparable might happen. I dig in my heels and simply leave aside whatever I cannot take care of at the moment, and I tolerate any spoken or unspoken reproaches that are leveled at me. I know that hardly anyone else could take the work more seriously or conscientiously than I who have become a prisoner of work in my old age.

And so: Your fourth circular letter is wonderful. In regard to the excerpts that have to be made, you can take the lead. You never become sidetracked, you simply take the rational path, illuminated by the muses, keeping apart the things that have to be included and those that do not. This is a rare virtue, as I, alas, know from experience.

Shipments of bandage material. What lovely words on the packet of birthday letters: "accompanied by five bandage material shipments." These shipments will be something valuable for us. How lovely that our funds permit this. But think it over: Perhaps three shipments would be enough for now so that we can leave enough money in our treasury to order medicines (new ones, valuable ones) from Germany and also help poor people in Germany, especially those who have been expelled [from ethnic German territories] and those who have lost everything.

I always have to think about these poor people who are so often embittered. So give it some thought. I have sent a very friendly letter to the Hartmann firm,[2] but I haven't mentioned the possible reduction to three crates because I want to leave it up to you. I am trying to find my bearings among the new pharmaceutical products in Germany. I would also like to order medical books.

With fond thoughts,

Albert Schweitzer

≈

To Hyoei Ishiwara, Japan

Lambarene
25 April 1954

Dear Mr. Hyoei Ishiwara,

My warmest thanks for your kind and detailed letter and for the photograph of you in the midst of your students. It is so good to know what the people one feels attached to look like. I am already familiar with you as the pupil of Kanzo Uchimura, as his successor in his enterprise for spreading the Gospel, and as a translator who devotes himself to my works. What a chore it must have been to translate *Decline and Restoration*! How can I ever thank you enough. I was very interested to hear what you told me about your life.

Yes, spreading the simple Gospel of Jesus is beautiful. I had a profound veneration for Uchimura. How sorry I was that I could not visit Japan to see him! But I had neither the time nor the wherewithal to take that trip. I have been tied to Lambarene since 1913. It is true serfdom, but I endure it. It is part of my life. I was very interested in the copy of your *Biblical Magazine* in which you write about Uchimura and myself. At night I am still working on a theological book that is to be my theological testament. It is as good as done, and I only want to provide its final shape [*The Mystery of the Kingdom of God*]. However, other work keeps interfering. In late May I am going to Europe for four and a half months, but I will not be able to work there as much as I would like because I have to travel (Norway, Denmark, Sweden, England, Switzerland) . . . for the sake of my hospital. Thus I have to be very modest in my demands for time to do quiet and concentrated work. I believe it is the same for you, even though you have no hospital to run and you aren't haunted by anxieties about its survival.

Please give my best regards to your wife and your students.

Once again, my deepest thanks for your understanding and your love.

To Edouard Smiths

Lambarene
21 May 1954

I cannot retire! I must serve the hospital as long as I live. It needs me. But I hope that when the village [for the lepers] is done, I can again find time at my desk. At the moment I am working on music. Later on I will complete a theological work. The manuscript that required so much effort during the past three weeks was a report I was asked to do on the hospital.

Everything in my hospital is equally necessary. When I receive donations, the money helps me feed the many patients. My great concern is feeding them, having the wherewithal to feed them. The current staff is just large enough for the workload. Each member has to do a great deal.

I don't know how many letters we receive. I can only answer some of them, and writing so much at night has seriously overtaxed my eyes (and my hand).

But I want to answer as many letters as I can. I suffer when I can't. I must not reject any human being. I feel duty-bound to make myself as available as I can to everyone who wants me.

~

To Abbé Pierre, Paris

[June 1954]

[f]

Dear Abbé Pierre,

I am writing to you in pencil on a launch on the river. I have been following your activities longer than you realize, and I feel a great liking for you.... I am writing *after thinking about it for four days.* Please take my remarks as a token of deep affection, as words from an older man to a younger one.

The task to which you are called consists of getting French people to deal with the question: "Who is my neighbor; what can I do for him?"[1] You are in your element. This is a river that makes the earth fertile.

Dear Abbé Pierre, the task to which you are called is unequivocal. Your activities are getting people in France close to the problem of "Who is my neighbor" and helping them to see, showing them, how they should care about the people whom God sends their way. It is your task to gather this host of people who feel urged by their consciences to help their neighbors not only by participating in specific works but *through personal action.*

In his last sermon at the temple in Jerusalem, our Lord Jesus Christ, according to Matthew 25, asked us to carry out this action for all people who are obviously in trouble: the hungry, the naked, the imprisoned, the thirsty. At the Last Judgment we will be measured by the sum of our responsibility and judged by our active service!

You are transmitting this call in our time, in our situation. You have the inestimable advantage of *preaching in deeds!* The ideas issue from the intrinsic reality of your activities. *Words are only a musical accompaniment here!* Preserve this special privilege for yourself! Take in everyone who feels called upon to care about his neighbor. Divide the labor that falls to their lot either individually or collectively. Arouse in them the spirit of loyalty and simplicity. You are only at the beginning of your mission. The start was easy. You have kindled enthusiasm. Now you have to keep this enthusiasm alive, guide it, transform it. Dear Abbé Pierre, you will encounter the difficulties that inevitably follow a birth. Stand your ground.

The world expects highly effective ideas. It demands a labor that is performed in the spirit of the Gospel and that is also in proper order and achieves its goal. It expects the spirit to transform the given reality. What you owe the world is this: to move all good will to an enthusiastic, personal, and sensible commitment. Therein lies the great problem. Whatever you do toward this end will arouse people of good will throughout the world and encourage them to lend a hand in other countries.

You are assigned the task of gaining acceptance *on this level*, which has been designated for you. Therein lies your task. May God grant you wisdom and strength to make the Gospel shine in the darkness of this world.

If ever I go to Paris, I would love to shake hands with you. I have been planning to do so for a long time.

With my fondest wishes,

Albert Schweitzer

To a handicapped woman (Rhineland)
[Lambarene]

You have been given a hard life of endurance. God wants to help you endure properly, endure in stillness, so that people may feel in you the strength that helps you transcend unhappiness, so that they may learn through you the endurance that falls to their lot. We must all endure and learn endurance. When I was a preacher in Strasbourg, I had a poor confirmee who had crippled feet and was sick. I would visit him every Sunday afternoon. He had managed to find peace of mind and, without realizing it, he preached to the preacher who visited him in order to comfort and encourage him. Don't tell yourself that no one likes you. No, people are concerned about you.... And when they see that you are struggling for peace of mind, then you are the giving one. It is the spiritual person who is important and not the physical one. The Apostle Paul had the falling sickness, epilepsy. He knew that some people despised him for it, but he also knew that many people received comfort from him, the poor man, because God's strength and God's peace were revealed in him. And the same is true of you.

You are suffering as a physical person, but the spiritual person can work his way through the suffering to peace of mind and guide others to peace of mind. Do not quarrel with God, do not quarrel with man; leave all incomprehensible things alone, seek only one thing: the growth of the spiritual person, so that you may achieve peace of mind, which is higher than all reason, and so that you may give people something of the spirit of peace.[1] I am writing this as someone who has been allowed to do a great deal of work in life but who also has many problems and pains because the work and the anxiety that burden him are too great. I have experience in struggling for stillness in God. That is why I can talk to you about it. Believing in God means wanting to live in the spirit of God, for God reveals himself to us through the spirit. And keep your Sunday as a holiday of the soul. Sit quietly in a corner of the church and reflect. Listen to the sermon and preach to yourself. And read the New Testament to see what Jesus has to say to us. The spirit of God was in Him.

With fondest thoughts,

Albert Schweitzer

To Gerrit Osterwijk, Gossel, Holland
Bordeaux
12 June 1954

Dear Mr. Osterwijk,

I have taken a long time to express my thanks to you for the wonderful Rembrandt Bible [you have given me] on my seventy-ninth birthday. I know that it was you and other friends who went to so much trouble to get me this present. I have written to Mr. Burger who was in charge of the whole thing, and now I would also like to express my thoughts to you who have been so dedicated in everything regarding my work and myself. I really love Rembrandt because his religious art is related to Bach's and because Rembrandt helps us see the Bible's contents pictorially.

I am looking forward to the Dutch medicines. Send them along on the Dutch ship but pack them in crates that contain nothing else. That is, in separate crates. And prepare a separate customs declaration for them with a French translation. You don't have to translate the names of the medicines, just the general text: *Produits pharmaceutiques de Hollande. Don pour l'hôpital du Docteur Albert Schweitzer à Lam-*

baréné [Pharmaceutical products of Holland. Gift for the Dr. Albert Schweitzer Hospital, Lambarene]. Indicate the weight of each kind of medicine and the price in Dutch florins. If this declaration is properly set up, then I won't have to pay any duties on the medicines.

~

To Pastor Erich Meyer, Frankfurt am Main
[Gunsbach, 1954]

Dear Friend,

Now pay attention! I have returned from Africa so exhausted that I cannot get rid of my great exhaustion. I have even been asking myself whether a trip to Frankfurt would be compatible with taking care of myself, which I must do. However, I will risk it after all if I feel all right around August 27. But it is not certain. . . . Hence my condition: No one is to know that I am coming! It will then be a nice reunion. You will find out that afternoon or evening whether I can possibly travel to Frankfurt.

~

To Prof. Ernst Beutler, Frankfurt am Main
December 1954

Dear Friend,

When we first met, I saw you primarily as the man who had become the great Goethe expert by brooding over Goethe problems. But when I became familiar with the results of your scholarship in the successive volumes of your Goethe edition, I understood the meaning of your research and marveled at its success and its scope. You have shed light on many things that were in darkness.[1] You have brought Goethe and his time closer to us in every respect. For this we are profoundly grateful. Your achievement brought you closer to me. From then on I was attached to you through admiration and gratitude.

I sought your company, and you were friendly and receptive.

Since the muses endowed us at birth with the precious gift of naturalness, we soon modulated from the polite key to the intimate key. I inspired this as the older man and the musician.

The automobile drive during which we had our first great discussion has remained unforgettable for both of us.

And so I owe Goethe one of the most beautiful and valuable friendships of my life.

I was deeply moved when you hung my portrait in your office at the Goethe House—the portrait that was painted on the day I became thirty years old, and that I then gave to the Goethe House. Thus, I am with you as a young man day by day, watching all your deeds and thoughts.[2]

May we be granted the privilege of occasionally getting together in person.

May you remain healthy and capable until well into old age, and may you carry out all your plans in peace and quiet.

We are already way down south now, and as I write I keep peering through the open porthole, gazing at the wooded shore as our ship sails along the African coast, on the blue sea. This radiantly sunny voyage, during which we can see the nearby coast for days on end, is something wonderful. Several days from now the ship will then glide across the equator. A few hours later it will anchor at Cape Lopez, where I will disembark. Then I will have to go through customs with my vast imports. Once that is out of the way, I'll have a two-day voyage up the tremendous jungle river to Lambarene, where my African life will resume with all the beautiful and difficult things that it involves.

With fondest greetings and wishes,

Albert Schweitzer

~

To Albert Einstein, Princeton, New Jersey
Lambarene
20 February 1955

Dear Albert Einstein,

Thank you from the bottom of my heart for your dear letter of 6 December 1954, which took a long time to travel from America to Africa. I was deeply moved by the donation of medicines in memory of a deceased woman who is fondly remembered in Princeton and whom I knew when she was a student in Switzerland. I have written a letter of thanks to the responsible parties. Please tell those of them whom you know that this donation means something very special to me. I am also sending a letter of thanks to the Squibb Company, which contributed to the donation.

Here is a line of thanks from Dr. Cenateen, who took the lovely picture of you and the two boys with the packages of medicines in the background. I'm very fond of it.

During the past few years I have sometimes written to you mentally, but I have never managed to do so physically. I have much business correspondence for the hospital, I've been weary for long months, and I suffer from such a serious writer's cramp (inherited from my mother) that many personal letters that I would like to write never get on paper unless something special happens.

We are mentally in touch even without corresponding, for we both feel the horror of our dreadful time and are mutually afraid for the future of mankind. When we met in Berlin, we could never have dreamed that such a bond would ever exist between us. . . . It is strange how often our two names are mentioned together publicly. I find it lovely that we have the identical first name.

In regard to new experiments with the modern atomic bombs, I am at a loss to understand why the U.N. cannot make up its mind to discuss the matter. I receive letters asking you and me and others to speak up and demand that the U.N. do so, but we have spoken up often enough. We cannot tell the U.N. what to do. It is an autonomous body and must find within itself the incentive and the sense of responsibility to try to stave off an imminent disaster. From a distance I cannot judge what prevents it from pulling itself together and doing so. Even if its efforts were futile, the attempt would have been made, and it would expose the points of resistance.

During the second half of 1954 I spent some time in Europe. My main task was to write my speech for Oslo on the problem of peace.[1] By thus studying the history of the idea of peace, I was amazed to discover that Kant's essay on everlasting peace deals purely with the legal and not the ethical aspect of the problem. However, for Erasmus of Rotterdam, the ethical aspect is at the center of discussion. The more one studies Erasmus, the more one appreciates him despite his failings. After all, he is one of the most important pioneers of a civilization based on humanitarianism.

Now I am back in my many-faceted African work. For many weeks I will have to spend most of my time completing the village for the 250 leprosy patients being treated in my hospital. I have to do a lot of excavating to level out the construction site of the village, which is to be built on a hill near the hospital. It has to be on a hill because mosquitoes spread malaria in the valley. The terracing work is taking almost more time and money than building the residential barracks with corrugated iron roofs and hardwood rafters (because of termites). I have to supervise the work myself because the sixty still able-bodied lepers who have to build the village obey only me as the supreme chieftain of the hospital. There is no way of coping with this attitude. I have two capable doctors with me. I have nine white nurses (Alsatian, Swiss, Dutch). If the construction work advances nicely, then a few weeks from now, alongside the hospital work, I hope I can find time to complete writings that have been waiting for a long while. Like you in Princeton, I try to live as quietly as possible in the jungle, but I cannot manage to do so because Lambarene has now become a landing point for airplanes. My sole relaxation is practicing the organ on my pedal piano. At the moment I am working on César Franck's last organ works. I assume that you relax with your violin. Well, this has turned into a long letter. My hand with the writing cramp has held out decently.

In conclusion let me thank you warmly for your lines about me in the book for my eightieth birthday.[2] They were the first thing I read when I got hold of the book and opened it up. I was deeply moved by your text. I could see that you appreciate my work on Bach. I cannot grasp or understand the possibility that I have exerted an influence in our time. It haunts me like a secret on the final stretch of my life. . . .

With fond thoughts,

Albert Schweitzer

~

To the Dean of the Albert Ludwig University, Freiburg im Breisgau
Lambarene
2 March 1955

Magnificence,

Your letter of 3 January 1955 did not arrive here until late February because it came by regular mail. The university would like to name the House of German-French Encounters the Albert Schweitzer House. I am deeply moved by the affection and the great honor thus shown to me, and I would like to thank the university warmly. I remember the beautiful day of the dedication last August. It is one of the most beautiful memories of my visit to Europe. And now this memory is joined by the news that the house is to bear my name. I don't know how to thank the university and the authorities.

With my most cordial regards to the honorable members of the senate and to your magnificence, I remain,

Truly yours,
Albert Schweitzer

~

To Prof. Dr. Robert Minder, Paris
[Chairman of the French Association for Schweitzer's Work][1]
Lambarene
10 March 1955

Mon cher,

Several days ago a recently arrived trunk addressed to Mademoiselle Mathilde [Kottmann] was opened; it contained several copies of a volume titled *Homage to Albert Schweitzer on His Eightieth Birthday*.[2] Now I can't for the life of me remember whether I knew anything about the plan for this publication. It was, as I have learned from the preface, [Mademoiselle] Sorel-Nitzberg who came up with the idea.

Whom am I to thank for the lovely volume, which is extremely valuable to me as a document by French friends? First of all you, no doubt! Thank you for providing me with this genuine and special joy. How many letters did it cost you? How many visits? How much agitation? How much annoyance at people who did not deliver manuscripts as promised? Oh, I'm familiar with the misery of people who prepare a festschrift! So be a good fellow and tell me who your fellow sufferers were! You have really gotten fine people to write, and a number of the pieces are truly interesting; for example, I didn't know about my prestige at the Theological Faculty of Strasbourg, which is clear from the truly interesting and solid contributions from Hauter and Hering. That was a surprise. And you managed to get Bishop Weber to write something. That is really unbelievable! And Honegger, Leriche, Jean Rostand: figures whom you have brought to me from afar. What nice pieces by [Fritz] Münch, Morel, Robert Weiss. I didn't know Romain Rolland's notes about my visits with him. . . . I can still see him standing in front of the ship in the December sun. A festschrift filled with life and warmth. I thank you from the bottom of my heart.

I am going to write to everyone who contributed. But one question: Are the expenses covered? How did you manage? Would not Mademoiselle Oliven [bookstore and publishing house] suffer a loss? Write me about it honestly.

For the time being there is no chance of my working at my desk. I have been completely immersed in correspondence now that I've been able to spend time at my desk again (for the past two weeks). What a different man I'd be if I could be writing again. . . . until late at night! Yes, I'm working again until around midnight.

My love to you and yours,

Your grateful
Albert Schweitzer

~

To Alsatian Parishes
A word of thanks for contributions
                    Lambarene
                    [March 1955]
                                        [*f*]

A number of Alastian parishes have made large contributions to my
hospital on the occasion of my eightieth birthday. I would have loved
to write to each individual parish to describe how deeply moved I
am by this kindness shown to my work and to express my thanks.
However, my enormous workload does not permit me to write as
much as I would care to. I am therefore asking these parishes to allow
me to tell them collectively what these gifts from my homeland mean
to me and how helpful they are to my hospital.

Since my return we have been working with renewed vigor to
complete the village for the lepers. During the last few days of February we finished the major excavations that are requisite for creating
a suitable construction site on a hill near the hospital. Now all we
have left is to build on the completed final quarter of the construction
site.

~

To Prof. Dr. B. W. Downs, university vice chancellor, Cambridge,
England
                    Lambarene
                    14 March 1955

Dear Mr. Vice Chancellor,

First of all, let me tell you how touched I am by the great honor you
have shown me by deciding to award me an honorary doctorate of
law. It was through Cambridge University that I began to be known
in England. That was before World War I. In 1910, Prof. J. C. Burkitt
of Cambridge initiated, and wrote a preface for, the English-language
publication of my work on the problem of the historical Jesus, *The
Quest of the Historical Jesus.* In 1912 he got his pupil, Mr. Montgomery,
to translate my work on the scholars who dealt with St. Paul, *Paul
and His Interpreters,* and he likewise got it published in England. In
1931 he got my work on St. Paul translated by Mr. Montgomery and
published with a preface by him [Burkitt]. After the first war, between

1920 and 1930, I paid several visits to Cambridge where I had many friends. I gave lectures on philosophy and played organ recitals.

And now Cambridge University is arousing all my memories of it by asking me to come on June 9 to receive the degree of Doctor of Law *honoris causa*. You have made a profound impact on me. Alas, I cannot leave Lambarene on that date, as I have already informed you by telegraph, But I believe I can arrange to come on a date that you will propose in the future.

May I ask you, Mr. Vice Chancellor, to convey my joy and profound gratitude to the University of Cambridge. With my very best wishes, I remain,

Very truly yours,
Albert Schweitzer

[The document of the honorary doctorate in law awarded by the University of Cambridge to Schweitzer contains the following lines: *"Quare verecunde quidem nec sine observantia salutemus militem hunc Christi fidelem, caritatis Christianae exemplum et nobis et posteris in saecula futurum. Duco ad vos Albertum Schweitzer, Ordini insigniter Meritorum honoris causa ascriptum."*]

~

To Prof. Dr. Albert Salomon, Amsterdam
                          [Lambarene]

Dear Professor Salomon,

It is good that there is a Bühler Höhe and a Magdalena Monnier. I have finally been able to come to your book. Neither I nor the nurse who helps me with my correspondence recalls receiving the book in Gunsbach or in Lambarene . . . which we cannot understand. You may imagine that if ever I had gotten it, I would have written to you forthwith, since you delve into the ethics of the reverence for life and say such valuable things about the ethical behavior of a physician.

And you read *Civilization and Ethics* in a concentration camp and meditated on it. A number of people have told me similar things. French POWs got to know the book in German prison camps. But how did it get into the camps? It was not compatible with the ideas prevailing under Hitler. . . . I have reread your remarks about reverence for life several times. They are quite consistent with this notion.

Now I find you as a representative of this truth through which our civilization can once again partake of humanitarianism. And you do so in such a simple and convincing way. How wonderful that your wife and I have already met in the area of music. Ah, what a lovely friendship that was with Siegfried Ochs!.... How much you grant the physician in your book!

~

To Nikos Kazantzakis

29 June 1955

I was deeply moved when reading your epilogue to the Pierhal biography[1] [with comments on St. Francis of Assisi].... Yes, around 1894, during my student days, I was absolutely shaken when I got to know St. Francis. Since childhood I had taken the same road and reached the same spirit, but I have never been able to speak or write about him and me together. I never refer to him. I am very reluctant to do so. He is a famous saint, I am an ordinary man. He possessed an intimacy of speech that is his alone. None of us should try to imitate that speech; no one should adopt it for himself. It was *granted only to him. The rest of us must speak in ordinary words.*

And now I thank you for the great love for me that you have expressed in this epilogue. Ever since I learned about you, I have known that we belong together, which is also evident to our mutual friends. We must get together at some point. I am going to Europe again this year—a necessity, alas. As of August 8 I'll be in Gunsbach where I have to complete an article on Bach's music. Later on, probably during the second half of October, I'm going to Bonn and also Paris. I also have to go to England. Is there any way we could get together? It would be best if you could come to Gunsbach. There we could see one another in peace and quiet.

~

To Marie-Marthe Lagendijk, nurse, Lambarene Hospital
                          [between Libreville and Duala,
                          at the start of a trip to Europe]
                          17 July 1955

Dear Maria,

I only managed to come to myself on the river [Ogowe]. In Port-Gentil I took care of a lot of urgent mail. Everything went smoothly—

I'm relaxed about leaving because I know that such a lovely spirit prevails among you people. And you have helped to create this spirit.
My best to you.

Albert Schweitzer

≈

To Frau Katja Mann, Kilchberg near Zurich
Gunsbach, Alsace
15 August 1955

Dear Frau Katja Mann,

I still cannot grasp the fact that Thomas Mann is no longer among the living. I can still see him before me, at his desk, delighting in his work, when we two contemporaries finally got to meet. I had been following his life and also his work ever since he attained a position in the cultural world through his first major book, when he was still young. Later on he had to fight for civilization against noncivilization. I can never forget those early days of the Hitler period when I was in Lambarene, wondering what was to become of our civilization, and I came across an article by him about what truly constitutes civilization. I was deeply impressed because he entered the arena and clearly and courageously expressed what our time needed. From afar I empathized with him about what it must be like to lose one's homeland and faith in one's nation. I had the same experience with Stefan Zweig, whom I knew well. . . .

After the time of struggle he found something like a new homeland in Switzerland and was able to carry out some of his plans in peace and concentration. Now his pen is at rest.

In the words I wrote about him for his eightieth birthday, I mentioned that we were both looking forward to meeting again. No sooner had I returned home to Gunsbach from Africa than I learned that he had passed away.

≈

To Ali Silver, Lambarene
[Gunsbach]
31 August 1955

Dear Ali,

Many thanks for your dear lines of August 21. Emma [Haussknecht] will tell you about my trip to Frankfurt and the Albert Schweitzer

Settlement,[1] which has twenty-five hundred apartments with room for over eight thousand people. They are asking my advice about so many things concerning this project! They wanted to plant nothing but ornamental trees in the large, open areas. So I said: I also want fruit trees. The children should not be unacquainted with the pleasure of picking and eating unripe fruit.

The architects then instantly noted that fruit trees also have to be planted.

How lovely that the hospital is running smoothly.

A.S.

~

To Helen Preen, Maikammer, Palatine
[Lambarene, 1955]

You are right to commit yourself on behalf of all living creatures, but do not count too strongly on new laws! What we need is to hope for a new spirit so that human responsibility toward all living creatures becomes something that is taken for granted! Here, as in all things, we have to rely on the spirit! Certainly, the laws for protecting animals have to be expanded, and it is up to animal protection societies to offer precise suggestions. But it would be very difficult to pass valid and truly useful laws. Believe me, I have dealt with this problem. We who have the true knowledge must be undaunted in our efforts, in word and example, to steer people toward this knowledge.

~

To Prof. Sigurbjörn Einarsson, Reykjavik, Iceland
Gunsbach
8 December 1955

Thank you so much for going to the trouble of studying my life so precisely in order to write such a thorough biography of me.[1] I would never have dreamed that you would go into such detail. Alas, I cannot read what you have written, but I sense that you did it lovingly. On December 16 I am sailing from Bordeaux to Lambarene.

~

To Howard Rice, University Library, Princeton, New Jersey, United States

[Lambarene, 1956]

[e]

Dear Mr. Rice,

I have heard from various quarters about the exhibition of my books at the library of Princeton University. But I was still reluctant to believe that what I heard was true. How could it happen that Princeton University (which I am very fond of because Albert Einstein enjoyed its hospitality) could be so interested in me as to collect my writings and try to complete the bibliography? Who launched this project? I am now in possession of several articles about this exhibition, so many interesting photographs of which have arrived in Gunsbach. Above all, I now have the name of the man who brought about and organized this exhibition and completed the bibliography. I am happy because I know to whom I can communicate my emotions about this honor and to whom I can express my profound gratitude. Dear Mr. Rice, I am deeply touched by all you have done for me. I know how much effort such work requires. Compiling a bibliography is much harder than writing books—or at least, so I imagine. And it is my fault, because I took no notes that might have facilitated the work. I have always been so busy that I have never written to my publishers as I should. To make matters worse, I have never kept my correspondence with them. Robert Amadou's *Essai d'une bibliographie* [Attempt at a bibliography][1] has taught me a great deal I did not know about my literary works, and if I had been able to visit this Princeton exhibition, I would have learned even more.

To Bishop Dr. Karel Reichel (Czechoslovakia)[1]

Lambarene

1 March 1956

Reverend Father,

As I write this, there is a lot of noise outside my room. Now, at 5:30 P.M., supper ingredients are being distributed to the inpatients who have done the work. They receive bananas and salt to prepare their meal. For fat, they obtain oil from palm nuts in the plantation. There they can also find seasonal fruit through most of the year....

Please let the congregation know that I was deeply touched by their prayers for my work and myself on New Year's night. And how lovely the slogan about peace and silence that was communicated to me.

~

To Prof. Dr. Kurt Leese, Hamburg
2 May 1956

I believe I have already told you that Sartre is my cousin. We are on good terms with those who know both of us. It is interesting that his attitude toward goodness is different from that of Goetz: Sartre does good for its own sake. We do not talk about philosophy; both of us aspire to the humanitarian ideal but along different roads (all this is strictly *entre nous*). Spiritually, in terms of my outlook on the world, I adhere to the religious idea, which for me is *Philosophia naturalis perennis,* the eternal philosophy of nature, so that I have become utterly unsympathetic toward existential philosophy, [which] is not natural philosophy.

~

To Arthur Piechler, cathedral organist, Augsburg
Lambarene
11 May 1956

Dear Friend,

Your dear letter of 19 April 1956 arrived during the past few days. Thank you so much for all the news. I have the plan of the organ. The canon will be mailed in a separate envelope from Königsfeld. How wonderful that Knappertsbusch is conducting the concerto for organ and orchestra. Give him my best. I hope you play the concerto yourself.[1] [I've] studied and restudied the plan of the organ. It's on my table. I feel it's solid. I have a deep love for the Augsburg organ. How wonderful its sound was, how warm, how transparent! And how beautiful it sounds in the church.

~

To Horst Marx-Reinhard and Manfred Caroselli, high school seniors, Wiesbaden

[Lambarene]
27 July 1956

Dear High School Seniors,

Your letter arrived today, and I read it tonight after a hard day. I am writing to you at night. I cannot write as long a letter as I would care to, I can only pen a few lines.

Maintain your ideal of humanity in your hearts and let it guide you in your relations with other human beings and with society. Do not simply talk about today's conditions, do not lose courage. The time demands not discussion from us but spiritual work, which emanates almost automatically from our conduct and our hearts. I am very weary as I write, but I hope you understand me. Enjoy the weeks following your graduation. They are some of the loveliest weeks that can be granted to you.

~

To Paul Gloess, Paris

[Lambarene]
19 November 1956

[*f*]

Thank you for praying for me. I was touched when reading about it in your letter. The unity of Christians will emerge not in the realm of ideologies but only in the realm of the spirit. The spirit is the essential thing. If all churches strive to live in the spirit of Christ, then they will all be fundamentally one. That is what I expect of the future. The spirit is one. It can be the same in the various ideologies. They are worth as much as the spirit imbuing them. All of us, the faithful and the churches, are assigned the task of letting ourselves be ruled by the spirit of Christ.

~

To the director of Breitkopf und Härtel, music publishing house,
Leipzig

Lambarene
8 December 1956

I am delighted to learn from your letter that my Bach book still enjoys
some prestige. Had Widor not asked me to write a book on Bach
because France had no really solid book about him, I would never
have felt prompted to do so. Much to my surprise, qualified critics in
Germany showed interest in the work and demanded a German
translation. They included Hugo Riemann and Fritz Lubrich. One
advantage of my book was that it delved into the problem of performing Bach, which no one had really dealt with before. In this
respect I benefited from my years as organ accompanist for Ernst
Münch's Bach performances at St. Wilhelm's Church in Strasbourg.

You talked to me about my interest in restoring the organ at St.
Blasius's in Mulhouse, but I don't know whether the people there
will heed my advice and build the organ as simply as Bach specified
in his report.[1] If they did, they would have something very lovely and
unique in the world: an organ designed by the young Bach.

~

To Minoru Nomura, M.D., Tokyo

Lambarene
2 January 1957

Dear Friend,

I am deeply moved that people would like me to come to Japan. Had
the second war not come, I would probably have turned up in your
country, but it was not meant to be. It is nice that you people value
me even though I couldn't make the acquaintance of your nation.
The spiritual bonds are the main thing, after all.[1]

I have had a lot of work and a lot of worry, but luckily I have
found good and likable physicians: a Dutchwoman, a Dutchman, a
doctor from Israel. I also have good nurses. Tomorrow Miss Maria
Lagendijk is going on vacation. Several weeks ago Tony van Leer[2]
returned from vacation. Ali [Silver] is still here.

~

To Friedrich Eichler, Munich

[Lambarene]
25 February 1957

Let me heartily thank you as an eighty-two-year-old for your edition of the thoughts of Marcus Aurelius, which you sent me for my eightieth birthday. How right you are to let this man express himself again in our time. The great merit of your publication is not just the good selection but also the insight you offer into the life and letters of Marcus Aurelius. To my knowledge you are the first person to do so. I particularly like your book because I view stoicism as the recurrent philosophy that issues from nature (and not from definitions) and because I have a spiritual rapport with late stoicism. Epictetus and Marcus Aurelius have a message for all eras.

To Prince Rainier III of Monaco, Monte Carlo

Lambarene
26 February 1957

[f]

I often think about Your Highness when the diesel motor hums and illuminates the operating room, which has been provided with the most modern furniture and equipment thanks to your generosity.

For more than a year now I have been in Lambarene, absorbed in making my hospital run as smoothly as possible, and I haven't had a day of rest, not even a real Sunday. I have ten excellent nurses—Alsatian, Swiss, Dutch—around me, and I am assisted by three young physicians who are knowledgeable and dedicated.

To Norman Cousins, New York

Lambarene
12 April 1957

[e]

Dear Friend,

I have just received a letter from Radio Oslo—everything is ready [for the broadcast of Schweitzer's speech against nuclear testing].[1]

The letter says that Radio Oslo will contact other radio stations and tell them that the president of the Parliamentary Nobel Prize Committee has, on my behalf, asked the Norwegian radio for its support so that as many stations as possible can broadcast my speech on the effects of atomic testing.

Norwegian Radio views it as a special mission to go along with Dr. Schweitzer's request and to get in touch with countless radio stations in Europe and other continents.

The text of the speech will be made public to the press on 24 April.

That is the content of the message that Norwegian Radio is sending to other stations. It will also send this message to North and South America, Japan, Australia, Africa. What Norwegian Radio is doing to assure a wide audience for this speech is wonderful.[2]

Originally, they scheduled the broadcast for 12 May. But I wired them that this was too far off. They then shifted a few things around, making it possible to air the broadcast on 23 April. I have warmly thanked them for all their efforts. I hope that you too are satisfied.

～

To Fritz Dinner and Frau Dinner, Basel
Lambarene
28 April 1957

Dear Friends,

You will be amazed to hear me speaking on the radio about the problem of atomic testing. I have been urged to do so, and I could not refuse because, as the Nobel Peace laureate, I was able to call upon the Parliamentary Nobel Committee and thereby also Norwegian Radio. This allows me to talk from an entirely neutral place and in such a way that my speech can reach the widest possible audience. In the course of three weeks Radio Oslo has gotten in touch with numerous radio stations around the world—a great task requiring a great deal of work. But the project has succeeded so well that for once someone will be talking quite objectively to mankind about the atomic problem that is threatening its very existence. I have intentionally limited myself to the issue of stopping the atomic tests. That is the most urgent problem. And one always has to make the right start. In this way I have already succeeded in making it clear to people that at last there is a ubiquitous public that is aware of the danger involved in nuclear weapons and that is demanding to be heard.

Previously there was no such public opinion. But it has cost me much work and letters and telegrams to make my broadcast on April 23 and to get many radio stations—in Asia and America as well—to air the text of my speech. One of the first stations was the Japanese one. Now I have to make up all the work that I neglected between mid-February and April 23. I hope you both are well.

I am writing to you from the consulting room, surrounded by the tangle of buzzing voices.

My love to you and yours.

Albert Schweitzer

~

To Lotte Gerhold-Schall, Königsfeld
Lambarene
6 June 1957

Dear Lotte,

Now Helene has gone to her rest . . . [1] and has not had to endure the suffering that could have been inflicted on her by a steadily collapsing chest. She herself, as I believe I have written to you, wanted to fly to Europe. She could no longer endure the heat. Helene really looked forward to returning home. She was cheerful. During the final period she was calm and silent here. You know how I have experienced all this and how deeply it has shaken me. I will never forget how loving you always were to her.

Yours,
Albert Schweitzer

~

To Rudolf Kastner, Vienna
Lambarene
July 1957[1]

I have always been interested in the unification of the Christian churches. Each has its special feature, each its justification. What should unite them is the spirit of Christ. If they are guided and spurred on by this striving, then they are spiritually united, which means more for them and the world than a unification based on agreements that will always remain a patchwork.

~

To Eduard Spranger, Tübingen

Lambarene
[1957]

Dear Professor Spranger,

I have always been greatly interested in your work and your influence. After all, as a thinker you are naturally close to life and absorbed in the problem of civilization.[1] It is generally said that you are continuing Dilthey's—unfinished—life's work, and this is truly the case except that you are closer to the present reality than he was. I first got to know him at the turn of the century, in the home of Ernst Curtius in Berlin. I was deeply impressed by his research outside the path of the usual historical investigations of modern thought.

Because I have been living far away since 1913, we have never managed to meet personally. I will do my best to make up for this during a coming visit to Europe and also to celebrate a reunion with Tübingen, a place that I revere. For that is where the historical investigation of Christianity actually had its decisive start. My acceptance speech for the Académie Française on the problem of ethics in the development of human thought will go out to you by ordinary mail.[2] Since I was allowed only the traditional thirty-five minutes, I could not treat this subject as thoroughly as I would have liked. I had to limit myself to a rough sketch.

~

To Prof. Dr. Gerhard Rosenkrantz, chancellor of the University of Tübingen, Tübingen

Gunsbach, Alsace
(until Monday evening,
18 November 1957)
Address: Hotel Basler Hof
Aeschenvorstadt, Basel

Magnificence,

Your letter of November 8 was a great and lovely surprise from the Evangelical Theological Faculty of Tübingen. It has a special meaning for me. After all, throughout my theological works I have always been influenced by Ferdinand Christian Baur.

I thus have been conceited enough to think of myself as a Tübingen native who was born elsewhere. This was further helped by the fact that my maternal grandfather, who bore the Swabian name of Schillinger, left Württemburg as an infant in 1801 and immigrated to Strasbourg, where he became an Alsatian pastor devoted to theological and philosophical scholarship.

This secret conceit of mine has now been sealed by the Evangelical Theological Faculty of Tübingen, which is awarding me an honorary doctorate. Please pass on my warmest thanks for bestowing this honor and this joy on me.

In two weeks I have to go to Bordeaux and sail to Africa. Meanwhile, I have to make and pack a great number of purchases. I have no idea how I shall manage to complete this and other work during these few days. Under these circumstances, it is impossible for me to travel to Tübingen. I would be very happy if representatives of the faculty could manage to come to Gunsbach to award me the degree.[1] In your letter, Magnificence, you have indicated this possibility. I would be delighted to accept it.

With my very best wishes, I remain,

Truly yours,
Albert Schweitzer

~

To Bertrand Russell, London

Lambarene
31 December 1957

[f]

Dear Mr. Russell,

On the final evening of 1957 my thoughts go out to you to tell you how greatly I appreciate what you have done during this year to smooth the way for the idea of peace.[1] I have thoroughly informed myself about everything that you have undertaken. I consider it very important that with the help of your American friends you have succeeded in organizing a meeting of the repesentatives of Eastern and Western nations to discuss the state of the world.

Your open letter to Eisenhower and to Khrushchev expressed the reflections of people who are dealing with the issues of our future. Please let me congratulate you for committing your authority in this way. I was in Europe during September, October, and November. There was no possibility of my visiting England. I could not do so because of the work I had to do during those weeks and because of my fatigue. I did not even find time to spend a few days in Paris, as I usually do during my sojourns in Europe.

I have not forgotten that in 1955, during my stay in London, you took the trouble to say hello to me in the restaurant of my good friend Mettler. I was deeply touched.

For 1958 I send you my best wishes for yourself and for everything that you will be undertaking to achieve victory for the cause of peace.

~

To Frau Brandenburg, Wernigerode, East Germany
[Lambarene]
3 March 1958

We believe that the souls of those who leave us enter the kingdom of peace and light and are with God. We may find comfort in that.
Albert Schweitzer

~

To Prof. Frédéric Joliot-Curie, Paris
2 April 1958

[*f*]

The European nations plan to accept NATO's offer of nuclear arms *without consulting their parliaments*. They want to confront their populations with a *fait accompli*. This is the danger we must address without losing any time. . . .

I find everything you write interesting. I would be very grateful if you could send your publications to me in Lambarene. How can we tackle the problem of the direct conversion of solar energy into chemical energy? As an old friend of Max Planck and Einstein, I am interested with my modest faculties in everything happening in the realm of science. Unfortunately, my hospital keeps growing larger and causing me great anxiety. Luckily, I have fine doctors and fine nurses, but I am forced to remain in Lambarene for many long months.

~

To Prof. Dr. Werner Heisenberg, Göttingen
[Lambarene]
4 April 1958

Dear Professor Heisenberg,

Let me offer you my heartiest congratulations from far away for the success of your great project. I know just barely enough about science to understand what you are after and to grasp the meaning of your solution. I would be delighted if you could send me the text of the paper you are reading at the Max Planck celebration. I corresponded with Planck about philosophical matters.

I sometimes think about our meeting at the organ in Lindau. . . .[1] When shall we meet again? During the fall of 1957 I spent several extremely tiring weeks in Europe.

With my best wishes to you and your courageous colleagues in Göttingen.[2]

~

To Lucie Ahreiner (c/o Frau Pastor Eva Reutenauer, Evangelical Congregation, Forbach, Moselle)
Lambarene
1 May 1958

[*f*]

Dear Child,

These lines are meant to tell you that I think about you every day and hope that your condition allows you to lead a tolerable life. I know you are surrounded by people who are devoted to you, and I am profoundly grateful to them.

This autumn (but keep the news to yourself), I hope to spend several days in Europe, and one of my first trips will be to see you.

With my best thoughts,
Your devoted
Albert Schweitzer

~

To Johann Hoostad, Oslo

8 June 1958

I prefer your investigations of the person who can be considered great
to those of Carlyle. In my opinion, great men are the great endurers,
the unknown great people who have overcome within themselves fear
and pain and horror and rebellion against fate. Active great people
always do so in only relative terms. The most important among them
are those who create ideas that spell spiritual progress for humanity.
But these people are great only as long as they themselves do not
believe or know ... or imagine that they are great, but rather see
themselves as loyal and blessed servants.

So if the younger generation votes for me as a great man, it can
judge in its own way, but I cannot let it obtain for me. I can see
myself only as a servant who therefore tries even more loyally to make
the most of the talents entrusted to him. There is no greatness without
humbleness, which also remains aware of the imperfection of all that
is human.

I have always considered it an obligating privilege to realize that
ethics must be much more and have deeper roots than has been
previously assumed. To see the ethics of reverence for life gaining
recognition keeps me upright and joyful in the hard life that I lead
in my old age. But all this is a gift that I have received without
deserving it. I must not see myself in any way as a great man because
I have not yet been tested in suffering.

~

To André Malraux, Office of the President of the Council
Lambarene
30 June 1958

[f]

Dear Mr. Minister,

I was deeply moved by your letter of June 23, and I thank you with
all my heart. I have certainly encountered any number of obstacles
in my work, and some were rather hard to overcome. Thus, if I had
further obstacles to overcome in this final epoch of my life, I would
simply turn to you. Thank you for the great sympathy that you have
shown me. I lead a very difficult life. My hospital has become too
large. I have at my side four doctors and twelve European nurses.
Luckily, almost everywhere in the world I have faithful friends who

give me the wherewithal to continue my work. I truly consider myself privileged to have such support in my enterprise, and I am also privileged in being capable of performing my work and in seeing the idea of the reverence for life starting to find acceptance. I don't know when I can come to France and have the opportunity of making your acquaintance. It will probably be toward the end of next year. Thank you again for your kindness.

~

To Gerrit Osterwijk, Gossel, Holland
[Dutch Association for the Lambarene Hospital]
Lambarene
13 July 1958

Dear Mr. Osterwijk,

Dr. van der Kreerk is now leaving us. After her long and very full sojourn here, she has the right to relax in Europe. Miss Albertine van Beek-Vollenhoven has also arrived in Holland. What good services both of them performed for us here! Miss J. Bouma is very capable and also very likable as a person.

Miss Ali Silver and Miss Tony van Leer, who have been in the hospital for such a long time, are doing excellent work based on their vast experience. Really, Holland has been playing a great and lovely part in my project for many years.

~

To Prof. Dr. Hermann Mai, dean of the medical faculty, Münster
Lambarene
28 July 1958

Dear Friend,

So you've pressured the faculty, which is at your mercy, to award an honorary doctorate to me, an old jungle doctor, as if he were a star in the heavens of medical science—and you've managed to get your way. Not bad at all! ... You must have good fetishes. I am deeply moved by your love for me, and I admit I'm delighted to have a relationship with the University of Münster. Let's hope I can manage to get there. But first I hope to see you in Lambarene. ...

I have the advantage of having kind foreign publishers to put out my pamphlet, *Peace or Atomic War,*[1] in several countries and several languages. They have been kind enough to put themselves at my disposal, and other publishers have followed suit. As a result, the pamphlet is now coming out in almost all European countries as well as in the United States, Japan, South America, South Africa, Australia, Canada, and elsewhere.

So, until we meet again in Lambarene, with fondest thoughts about you and yours,

Gratefully yours,
Albert Schweitzer

～

To Carl J. Burckhardt, La Bâtie, Vinzel, Switzerland
Lambarene
14 August 1958

Dear Herr Burckhardt,

You are quite right to remark that we have seen too little of each other. I feel as you do, but we are both concerned about each other.[1] How intensively I kept up with you when you went to Danzig [as high commissioner of the League of Nations]. My old age is filled with disquiet and worry. My hospital keeps growing.... And now I've joined the fight against nuclear weapons.

And so, in my old age, I am rowing a rocking boat across a stormy sea instead of sitting under my fig tree, which would be consistent with the Bible.... Unfortunately, I cannot come to Europe this year. My hospital cannot do without me. I am the least free of the free, and I have to resign myself to this fate.

My best to you until we meet again,

Albert Schweitzer

I have browsed through your correspondence with Hugo von Hofmannsthal, which your publisher sent me. It is important to me to become more intimate with Hugo v. H. through his letters. My deepest thanks.

～

To the Reverend Timothy Yilsun Rhee, Seoul, Korea
Lambarene
23 August 1958

Dear Dr. Rhee,

My warmest thanks for the [Korean] translation of my three speeches, *Peace or Atomic War?* You have given me great pleasure. I am trying to get these speeches circulated as widely as possible because I want to advance the argument that atomic weapons are contrary to international law. International law admits only weapons that have a limitable, local effect—that is, only those that destroy or injure the combatants they are aimed at, but not distant nonparticipants. I have developed this idea in these three speeches, and I hope that they are understood and that they help us to persuade the countries that own nuclear weapons to renounce them.

I get news about you through Frau Martin, which enables me to keep up with your work at home.[1] I greatly value your interest in my ideas and my hospital. Unfortunately, I cannot write to you as much as I would like because I have more work than I can handle and am very tired. I am also suffering from eye strain. Still, I hope that you can visit Lambarene, but you have to arrange to come when I am here. I may possibly go to Europe in late summer of 1959. Please work out everything with Frau Martin. I will pay for your trip. You have to allow me to do that. Once again, thank you for everything.

≈

To Pablo Casals, Prades

Lambarene
3 October 1958

Dear Friend,

I am sitting at my desk in the big consulting room, but before getting down to work I want to write you a note to tell you how impressed I am by your plan to play for the U.N. [General] Assembly on October 24, to give a speech attacking the nuclear arms race, and on that day to ask orchestras throughout the world to perform the "Hymn to Joy" with the chorus from Beethoven's Ninth. You are right to move the fight against [atomic] weapons to an artistic level. It will have an impact on people if a maestro like you deals with this issue, and it will create grand and noble publicity for this cause! But first you will have to deal with the censors who will want to make you give up the best passages in your speech. . . . Be a skillful Daniel [that is, David] against this Goliath. You cannot imagine how encouraging it is for me to have you join us in our campaign. I have the prosaic task of organizing it. We have been highly successful in getting the United States and England to stop their atomic testing. This happened sooner than I expected. The governments realized that in the long run they could not resist the public opinion that has been developing against the continuation of these disastrous tests. President Eisenhower was honest enough to actually come right out and admit the dangers of continuing [the tests], and he accepted the consequences.

Now we have to take up the struggle for the abolition of all atomic and nuclear weapons. If we are to succeed, we have to influence public opinion throughout the world. And in this struggle we have to use the most elementary and most obvious argument; namely, that international law prohibits weapons with an unlimitable effect, which cause unlimited damage to people outside the battle zone. This is the case with atomic and nuclear weapons. Their impact is so unlimited that nuclear tests in peacetime constitute a terrible danger even for remote populations. The argument that these weapons are contrary to international law contains everything that we can reproach them with. It has the advantage of being a *legal argument*. Thus, throughout the fight against atomic and nuclear arms, the watchword in every nation has to be that these weapons are against international law. If the battle is fought along these lines, it will achieve the desired result.

No government can deny that these weapons violate international law ... and international law cannot be swept aside! This concept absolutely has to be spread. You, too, in your conversations should try to get it abroad. Because of what we are currently experiencing, people are inspired to accept the idea of the prohibition of atomic weapons. Now a dispute over a tiny island off the coast of China could actually "degenerate into an atomic war at any moment."

An inconceivable madness has become reality, and it will be the same in all future struggles if we fail to get rid of those weapons.

I am not coming to Europe this year. My work won't permit it. I hope that your wife and you are in good health. Now I have to get to work.

━━

To Rev. Prof. Georges Marchal, Paris
Lambarene
5 October 1958

[*f*]

Dear Friend,

Thank you for your kind letter of September 26. What efforts you are going to for my sake! You are giving lectures for me in Europe and America.... I don't know how to thank you.

The Mysticism of Paul the Apostle[1] is now being translated into French! You did the right thing by printing certain portions in a smaller typeface. Did you know that I was one of the first people to use this technique for insertions? You will find this in my books. This technique was invented by my teacher, the philosopher Windelband [in Strasbourg]. He employed this technique in his writings on Greek philosophy. Being an organist, I was interested in this playing on two keyboards. Windelband also inspired my habit of placing key words on the sides; they help the reader to orient himself in the book. I applied this technique in my book on St. Paul [1930]. Can you get the publisher to follow this in the French edition?

In the fight against atomic weapons, we have to argue that they violate international law because their effect cannot be limited. They wreak the most dreadful havoc for great distances and also harm "nonparticipants," as stated by the way international law defines prohibited weapons. Nuclear arms must be abolished at any cost. The politicians have to be confronted by worldwide public opinion that says no to them. My friends and I are working on creating this public opinion: I, by spending my nights writing letters.

With my best wishes,

Your very grateful
Albert Schweitzer

~

To Dr. Joseph Lefftz, Strasbourg

Lambarene
13 October 1958

Dear Fellow Alsatian,

These lines are meant to tell you that I am one of the people who are overjoyed that your seventieth birthday is being celebrated with a volume based on numerous studies of the customs of our forebears. No one but you could have given us this work.[1] As I child I saw some of these things in Gunsbach and the villages of the Munster Valley as well as Pfaffenhofen, at the home of my paternal grandparents. One of my childhood memories is the sale of the beautiful pewter tableware that lay on our table and was also used in the kitchen. It was probably around 1880. I wasn't attending school yet. Dealers were going through all the villages, buying all the pewter at good prices. We were having a pewter boom. For the money they received, people could buy other good tableware. But I was thrown into utter confusion. How come we suddenly no longer had the lovely familiar pewterware? Why was I no longer eating from my pewter plate? Why were my parents so happy about the great transaction? It took a long time for me to get over my grief over the pewter tableware. Even today I can still see our two big beautiful soup tureens.

You first came to the Strasbourg Library in 1914. One year earlier I had been a steady customer there and was friendly with many of the librarians. . . . However, upon my return I heard about you and your studies of Alsatian cultural history.

Now you are seventy years old. May you keep sending us many interesting studies on our homeland.

~

To Dragan M. Jeremic (director of the Serbian Book Association, Srpska Knjizevna Zadruga), Belgrade
[Portions of Schweitzer's *On the Edge of the Primeval Forest* and *More from the Primeval Forest* had been published in Serbo-Croatian.]
Lambarene
15 October 1958

The two autobiographical works, *Memoirs of Childhood and Youth* and *Out of My Life and Thought*, are very dear to my heart, for they present the philosophy of humanitarianism in a popular way. The idea of spiritual solidarity with the world through reverence for life is the goal of everything I write and do. It is only by developing this spiritual civilization that the nations can behave differently toward one another. We all have to work together toward this new civilization, no matter what nation we belong to. Through these efforts we will move from the road of darkness to the road of life.

~

To the Rev. Dr. Ulrich Neuenschwander, Olten
Lambarene
19 November 1958

Dear Friend,

If you are acquainted with my life, you will be indulgent toward me.[1] I have made so many decisions without managing to obtain the proper documentation, and I always try to be of service. I am constantly asked to help people receive awards and other accomplishments. How many letters I write in these matters until late at night, straining myself to the utmost. . . .

And then people do unbelievable things. Newspapers claim that I have advocated this person or such and such a cause. Next, so many letters take me to task. In my life, being helpful is a knotty problem. But sometimes one is compensated by success when helping someone in a difficult situation. One then becomes relaxed and cheerful. My deepest thanks for your information.

Devotedly yours,
Albert Schweitzer

~

To Pastor O. Bauer, Meerane, German Democratic Republic
4 December 1958

Dear Pastor Bauer,

Regarding words and deeds in missionary work, I would simply like to say that it is very important for the blacks to feel that the missionary is making an effort to live and work in the spirit of the Gospel with his given talents. . . . After all, he is among the Blacks in everyday life, where Christianity is put to a great test, where he has to lead people to Jesus by means of his deeds and find the key to their hearts, where he has to struggle to show that he has something of the spirit of Jesus and must communicate it.

I have a fine rapport with the missionaries, including the Catholic ones, just as the representatives of the two churches are on good terms here—which adds to the prestige of Christianity.

~

To Keith Osborn, Detroit
Lambarene
7 December 1958

Dear Mr. Osborn,

I have regarded it as the true mission of my life to advance the humanitarian ideal in our spiritual life. This ideal is the fundament of true, profound civilization. I also think that young people should become familiar with it. I did not have it at school even though my schooling was very good; instead, I encountered it in Jesus' Beatitudes in the Sermon on the Mount. Even children should reflect on them-selves and their relationship to other beings and come to realize that reverence for life is the basic principle of goodness. Children should not just take over goodness as a tradition that they are taught, they should reflect and discover it within themselves as something intrinsic to them, that is theirs for a lifetime. Many teachers have told me that children are deeply impressed by the idea of the reverence of life because they possess it as experience and not just as something they are taught.

If mankind is not to be wiped out by wars with dreadful weapons, we have to develop an ethical civilization dominated by the idea of reverence for life—a civilization that can lead the nations beyond short-sighted, bellicose nationalism and enable them to coexist in peace.

~

To Prof. Fritz Behn, Munich

Lambarene
16 December 1958

Dear Friend,

The picture of your statue [of me][1] has been on my desk ever since I received it. How wonderful that it was sculpted in sandstone from the Vosges! I couldn't imagine it otherwise. I am so deeply touched. And how wonderful that you sculpted it yourself.

Now for erecting it. Frau Martin writes me that you are planning to erect the statue in Gunsbach this spring! Let's mull it over together. Don't consult anyone else. I am not in favor of having the statue erected in my lifetime. That would be pretentious. A statue should not be erected until a hundred years after a person's death. In our case, we can negotiate the date a bit downward. Two questions: Where is it to be kept until after my death? In your area or in Alsace (say, in the basement of my home)? Secondly, where is it to stand in Gunsbach after my death? On the square outside the church, in the schoolyard (where I played as a boy and looked down into the street, through the shade of the trees)? That is, within the village? Or on my rock! For I was there, immersed in thought. That is my spiritual home, that is where I would like to remain on and on in stone and have people visit me there.

That is where I am entirely at home, and I wish to remain in that creative solitude in stone, listening to the rushing of the river and the bells of the church where I preached, watching the playing of the clouds, experiencing the changes of seasons. . . .

I hope you are well and working productively.

Warmly,
Albert Schweitzer

Also discuss the financial aspect of this matter only with me. All expenditures on French soil are my business from the very start.

~

To Martin Niemöller

[Lambarene, 1958]

Dear Herr Niemöller,

I have benefactors for my work in Germany too, but I do not allow any help for my hospital to be organized.[1] I dare not risk taking charity away from the [ethnic German] expellees who need it so badly. I became somewhat acquainted with the refugee problem while staying in Königsfeld, and I know that the refugees, especially recent ones, need not only public but also private help, which is not adequately forthcoming in terms of means and people.

I made these observations during my last visit to Europe. That is why a well-known person like myself must make doubly sure not to take any help away from the refugees. So, first the refugees! But many, many thanks for your kind inquiry. One more thing: Where was your submarine in November 1917? Wasn't it near the harbor of Dakar? The ship on which my wife and I were being taken to Europe as prisoners was anchored with an entire convoy in the harbor of Dakar and did not dare venture out because a German submarine was lurking there. Some time ago, in an article about you, I read that your U-boat was in those waters during that period. I would be interested to know whether you were really out to get me, for which, of course, I would forgive you in advance, as a Christian. In any case, we are now shoulder to shoulder in the fight for the elimination of atomic bombs. I ought to participate by letter in the Paris demonstration in which you are taking part. . . . However, it is an old rule of mine not to participate in foreign demonstrations or petitions, for that would take up so much time that I could not manage it. My only choice is to refrain altogether. I am delighted that you joined the march in England. It made a great impact throughout the world. In regard to atomic matters, I have the great privilege, as a Nobel peace laureate, of being able to use Radio Oslo, which then mobilizes countless radio stations throughout the world. As a result, I have to hold back from participating in other demonstrations.

My best to your wife. I was so happy to meet her in Nierstein. I hope I can get together with you again. I fondly recall our meeting in Munster. If I am not mistaken, it was Professor Smend who introduced us. I enjoy the memory of that day in Munster.

≈

To Dr. Heinrich Beck, Munich
                    Lambarene
                    24 January 1959

Dear Herr Beck,

Many, many thanks for your kind letter of 12 January 1959. How
wonderful your philosophy of letters is: "I cannot expect any letters
from you unless I am to perform some service for you!" Ah, if only
all the people I know could follow this philosophy. But my main
publisher observes it, and that is enormously helpful.[1]

America and England have finally decided to abandon their idea
of halting nuclear tests for only one year at a time and, instead, will
work out an agreement to ban them outright. They have finally
realized that the public consensus that has gradually evolved would
not allow them to continue their tests. The horse that was to keep
drawing their wagon has been unharnessed. They had to yield,
which is not to their credit. It is their fault that an increasing number of tests continued for two years, causing an inconceivable pollu-
tion of air, soil, and ocean. The effects will intensify for twenty
years. . . .

Thank you for putting out [my pamphlet] *Peace or Atomic War* so
quickly and making it so well known. It has, if I am not mistaken,
appeared in fifteen languages, even Korean. I believe I have already
written you about that.

≈

To André Wetzel, M.D., Munster, Alsace
                    Lambarene
                    14 February 1959

Dear Friend,

I am now fully devoted to the hospital again. From dawn until dusk
I sit at my desk in the large consulting room, participating in the
entire hustle and bustle. It's like old times. I am also taking care of
some of my correspondence at this desk. The bad thing is the visitors
who drop by day after day, whether traveling from America to India
or from South Africa to Europe. I converse with them, and then they
are taken through the hospital by a nurse and come back to have a
drink and say good-bye. That takes up two hours of the day, and it's
hard to do good work if you have to converse in between. However,

one must bow to the inevitable. Still, it's interesting to get so much direct news from all over the world.

Are you people working well at the Munster Historical Association? If you publish anything interesting, please send it to me.

With my very best to you and your wife,

Albert Schweitzer

~

To Omar E. Hartzler, missionary, New Haven, Connecticut
25 February 1959

Dear Mr. Hartzler,

I am certain that you have done the right thing in following your call to help our black brothers. They need this from us, and I am sending you my best wishes for your career as missionary. My idea of reverence for life is not meant to guide the African in striving for his own and his nation's freedom. It is meant to get him to deal with more than himself in the spiritual world, where he is occupied with his soul and with the possibility of relating to other people, according to God's will. . . .

Knowing love for others and for all creation, knowing the Beatitude, "Blessed are the merciful, for they will achieve mercy"—that is the goal to which my idea of reverence for life is meant to call them. . . .

The Kingdom of God is great politics; the politics of personal and national freedom is the politics of this world. The latter politics may be justified, but it must not preoccupy our minds to the exclusion of all else.

~

To Wolfgang Lauterburg, Berne
Lambarene
2 March 1959

Dear Godchild,

I am writing you amid the great hustle and bustle of the large consulting room. Many, many thanks for the splendid beeswax candle that you prepared for me. This is a precious object here. Thanks for your letter with the news about you. When Latin class begins, pay attention, learn everything properly. It is not hard. If the beginning doesn't sit right, as if hewn in marble, you'll never get over your lack of a solid foundation. Follow my good advice. And it is wonderful to learn a language that has played such a major role in the world and in spiritual and intellectual life even in our day. I knew Herr Ganz as an adolescent when he was studying piano with Professor Blumer at the Strasbourg conservatory. You are right to think about the organ. There is something marvelous about playing on this large, perfect instrument. If I live long enough, I'll give you organ lessons, but not without cuffing you and poking your ribs. That's an old tradition in organ lessons. But for now, get used to memorizing everything for the piano: first at the keyboard; subsequently, repeat it mentally when you go to sleep and when you wake up, so you can virtually recite the piece by heart. And have your left hand study separately. That was how I did it, and still do it today. If you have studied properly, you can come to Lambarene.

With best regards to the entire family,

Your godfather,
Albert Schweitzer

～

To Rolf Steinwascher, youth leader in Stuttgart
[Lambarene]
17 March 1959

Dear Herr Steinwascher,

You have probably already given up expecting any response from me to your kind letter of 8 June 1958, but I have a need to answer you.

Through my vicarious experiences with today's young people, especially those having a particularly difficult time, I am worried about their losing their faith in mankind. That is why I am taking the liberty of saying to you: Hold on to it. Human beings cannot set aside their human sensibilities. Approach them with simple trust whenever you deal with them. They will then become different from what they appear. We must arouse compassion in the people we encounter. That is my experience. Such an approach works many changes.... Do not judge others; instead, try to be a just and natural person in any circumstances whatsoever. In our dark time, which is bleak in many respects, there must be a light within us, to bring back warmth and brightness. In order to be natural, you have to discard all hypersensitivity. Do not quarrel with people, do not apply a biased criticism and interpretation of their conduct; instead, tolerate them and wait for them to develop warmth and friendliness in some way.

If mankind is not to perish after all the dreadful things it has done and gone through, then a new spirit must emerge.

And this new spirit is coming not with a roar but with a quiet birth, not with grand measures and words but with an imperceptible change in the atmosphere—a change in which each of us is participating and which each of us regards as a quiet boon. Become quiet, capable, kindhearted people—striving for the spiritual piety to which Jesus' words show us the way.

I am writing this to your adolescents deep in the night, after a hard day. If I have started out awkwardly, please ascribe it to my fatigue and forgive me.

With best wishes to you and your boys,

Albert Schweitzer

To Robert F. Geheen, president of Princeton University, Princeton, New Jersey

[Lambarene]
27 March 1959

Dear President Geheen,

You have received my telegram informing you that I unfortunately cannot be in Princeton on 16 June 1959 to receive the honorary doctorate in law. A letter was supposed to follow my wire immediately, but I injured my right hand, which made it impossible for me to write for several days. But now the bandage has become so small that I can write again, albeit with a slight handicap. My injury is not dangerous, I have simply scratched the back of my hand, and it is healing nicely if slowly.

Now let me emphasize how deeply moved I am that Princeton University is being so kind to me and so interested in my work and myself. I first realized this years ago when I received an invitation from the Institute for Advanced Studies to spend some time in Princeton and have a professor's home and salary in order to have peace and quiet so that I might complete some books that I am working on. Back then, too, I had to turn down the very tempting invitation. My hospital has made me one of the unfreest of the unfree.

I would love to accept the kind invitations to speak throughout the world about the creation of a new civilization since this has been on my mind for years, but primarily I can use only my pen to speak and to associate with people. I do so conscientiously and zealously, day by day, usually until deep into the night.

Through letters I maintain contact with the people who are working to create the new, more profound civilization, and I am with them in championing this cause. Through my written speeches and my letters I have joined the fight against test explosions of atomic and nuclear arms and the struggle for the elimination of these weapons. Through letters I am trying to make known and effective the major argument that atomic and nuclear weapons violate international law. It is only when this elementary and irrefutable argument occupies and determines public opinion throughout the world that it will have the power to bring about the abolition of atomic and nuclear arms, thereby preventing the destruction of mankind. Until then we will be hovering on the verge of annihilation, which leading politicians incomprehensibly view and laud as wonderful behavior.

Such is the nonpublic work that fate prescribes for me and enables me to do. I can act along these lines and accomplish something. I am deeply moved by the fact that the idea of reverence for life is beginning to gain ground in the world and helping to pave the way for a civilization with a humanitarian conviction.

Thus, I have to forgo being in Princeton on June 16, although you cite Dr. Howard Rice, Dr. Nassau, Walter Lowrie, Adlai Stevenson, Karl Weinrich, Albert Einstein, and Robert Oppenheimer, and others to persuade me to come, which only makes my failure to do so more difficult than it already is.

Once again, many, many thanks to you and all members of the university faculty for the kind regard they are showing me. It means a great deal to me.

~

To Marie Woytt-Secretan, Strasbourg
Lambarene
5 April 1959

Many, many thanks for your letter of 22 March 1959.[1] Forgive me for not thanking you right away, but a lot of problems are over-whelming me here. The worst problem of all is that very little rice is now coming to Lambarene from Saigon because the people there would rather get dollars for their rice than [French] francs, which have already been devalued twice. Since we were not informed that Saigon was no longer sending adequate supplies, and the trading posts (which did not know either) kept putting us off from week to week, saying the rice was sure to come, I was suddenly unable to feed my hospital.

The administration lent me cars to obtain bananas in villages on the road to Libreville and on the road to Mouila. This was a complicated enterprise because no road for cars, much less heavy trucks, runs to the hospital. We had to unload the bananas far from the hospital, on both sides of the river, and then carry them, three tons at a time, to the hospital or else ferry them across the water in a canoe. These banana transports wrecked my boats. All three boats had to be pulled ashore and repaired, which took a number of days.

I then decided to build a truck turnoff for the hospital, partially using the road from Atouma to Maison Foing (Atadié)!! The road winds around the leper village and then curves steeply over a knoll, on to the plateau where the fruit trees stand, until it reaches our residence. The work was grueling. The road had to be covered with a dense surface of stones (big stones) for hundreds of square meters. Bringing the stones over was quite a job, and a long stretch of the road had to be raised two meters above the terrain level, which required huge transports of soil. Don't force me to describe all our strenuous efforts! And in the rainy season to boot! Four German boys, who are touring Africa in a Volkswagen, dropped by and labored along with us for three weeks. It was thanks to them that we managed to complete the project. But I had to be on the construction site all the time. Now the road is finished except for a few details. It would have been easier to build the road from Atouma along the river, but high water would have made it unusable. So once or twice a week we rent a truck and a driver; together with a native and a nurse, he drives about fifteen miles to the villages along the road to Libreville and returns with three tons of bananas. For the final part of the road construction, I only have to be present two or three hours a day.

Because of the road construction I am behind with all my mail. Furthermore, my correspondence has doubled in the past few months, and so has the number of visitors.

~

To the Congress of Japanese Physicians
                    [April 1959]

I welcome the news that the large meeting of Japanese physicians will be dealing with the creation of the spirit of humanity and the role played by physicians in this undertaking. How I wish I could attend the discussions. Unfortunately, I cannot leave Lambarene at this time.

It is my deep conviction that we doctors who strive to preserve life are called upon in a special way to educate mankind to have reverence for life and thereby achieve a higher spiritual and ethical stance, which will enable people to grasp and solve the difficult problems of our era.

~

To Prof. Dr. Hans Walter Bähr, Tübingen
Lambarene
[May 1959]

Dear Friend,

Many, many thanks for the information about the danger of radio-activity. Everything helps me in putting together as thorough a doc-umentation as possible. The explosions at a three-hundred-mile altitude constitute a major problem. As a result, the Americans in Geneva have now tried to limit the testing ban to an altitude of thirty miles. Tests are now to take place in the higher altitudes; nuclear bombs launched by rockets are to be warded off by devices produced by explosions. This is a new reason and a new motive for [their] blocking the testing ban agreement.... On the other hand, the American population has become aware of the danger of these tests because the United States is the country most vulnerable to stron-tium 90—oddly enough, three times more than other countries! So now their eyes are opening—and that includes the gentlemen in the Senate.

It is interesting to see that Americans are now starting to concern themselves with the issue of international law and atomic and nuclear weapons.... Oddly enough, the group around Nixon seems to be dealing with the question of international law.

~

To Albertine van Beek-Vollenhoven, Clinical Therapy Institute, Arlesheim by Basel
Lambarene
19 May 1959

If I were to accept all the invitations I receive, I would be constantly traveling and lecturing at universities. At present I am supposed to be in the United States at Princeton University, which has been very friendly to me for years. I am also supposed to visit South America and Japan. But I don't want to travel anymore. I want to work in peace and quiet. And the atomic cause requires so much correspondence. Our goal is to make it clear to people throughout the world that atomic and nuclear arms are against international law. Once public opinion has understood and recognized this, then those horrible weapons will be eliminated. Until then mankind will be living on a volcano that can erupt at any moment and wreak havoc, unstoppable havoc.

To Marcel Bodin, the Catholic Albert Schweitzer Boy Scout Troop, Marseilles

Lambarene

2 June 1959

Dear Marcel Bodin,

It's a good thing you wrote me. Thank you for the confidence you are showing me. I would gladly authorize the use of my name for the boy scout group to which you belong.

Don't choose to make your life into something great! Make your life good and true. Maintain your simplicity. Stick to the idea of always doing whatever is consistent with the spirit of the children of God. I don't see why your goal should disappear as you grow older. Staying young doesn't mean having the soul of a child, it means having the soul of a child of God, the soul of a man trying to be a child of God, animated by the spirit of God. Seek simplicity. *Read the Beatitudes of the Sermon on the Mount.* Learn them by heart, meditate on them, let them guide you, you will then be in profound and eternal truth, and you will fulfill what life asks of you.

With all my heart,

Devotedly,

Albert Schweitzer

To Ali Silver, Lambarene

Bordeaux
26 August 1959

Dear Ali,

Thank you so much for the construction reports. I assumed that it would take a week to erect the aluminum barracks, and now it is to take four weeks. As for the provisional use of this space, let's stay with my decision: half for the doctor, half for Catchpool. And naturally Catchpool should also put up patients of Dr. Lindner's in his half. The maternity ward remains just that! As soon as I arrive I'll make the concrete floor (all the people will have to be cleared out for a couple of days).

Well, yesterday we were in Garaison and Lourdes. Everything went very well, and the long train ride was restful. Just think: In Bordeaux, after a long search, I discovered the building in which my wife and I were imprisoned in 1917 when we arrived here. It's at 136 rue de Belleville. Its name was *caserne de passage* [barracks for temporary billeting] (for the military). It is now neglected and decaying but still in existence. The trees have gotten big in the barred courtyard, where I walked up and down. I was deeply moved when I walked up and down there again.

With fond thoughts,

Albert Schweitzer

~

To Ali Silver, Lambarene

Wetzlar
8 October 1959

Our trip is going well. I am welcomed everywhere with exquisite friendliness and festivities: in Copenhagen, in Hamburg, in Münster (Westphalia), in Dortmund. In Münster, where I was officially awarded an honorary doctorate, they had a poignant celebration. Today was a travel day. Tomorrow it's off to Frankfurt where (on the ninth) at 1100 A.M. I am to be made an honorary citizen of the town. More important than these honors was learning that the [concept] of reverence for life is far more widespread than I would have thought. The Albert Schweitzer schools have played a major part in propagating this idea. This is a grand experience for me.

I also have to visit Tübingen to thank the faculty for awarding me a doctorate.[1] From there I'll be traveling via Königsfeld and Freiburg to Gunsbach, where we'll be arriving on the fourteenth.

~

To Ali Silver, Lambarene

on the *General Leclerc*
15 December 1959

Dear Ali,

Tenerife now lies behind us. Tomorrow we'll be arriving in Dakar. We are bringing, I believe, 180 pieces of freight! This includes two pumps with long hoses; during the *saison sèche* [dry season] they can pump water from the river to the barrels in the garden. This was my idea, and it was approved by Michel and other experts. All the medicines from Specia in Paris are coming along!

The atomic situation is quite nerve-wracking. America still seems intent on carrying out nuclear tests because they feel that the Russians have better bombs than they do! Yesterday I wrote to Oslo that I am thinking of giving two or three new radio speeches.

Now on shipboard I am starting to deal with my huge correspondence, which has been piling up. I've lost track of it. And I have to write a lot of thank-you notes for all the friendliness I have encountered during my travels. I would never have expected to enjoy so much empathy in Belgium. And in Paris the workers were likewise very friendly. In any case, I have a lot of work for the second part of the trip. I don't have to tell you how eager I am to see you again.

Best,
Albert Schweitzer

Regards to all, and tell them whatever you feel is right.

~

To Fritz Studer, engineer, Glockenthal-Steffinsburg, Switzerland
19 December 1959

Dear Friend,

During the first war, the roof and the tower of the Gunsbach church were destroyed. Rain fell on the organ, and little by little it was totally ruined. In 1932 a new one was built according to my design and intentions by my dear organ builder, Härpfer from Bolchen. My friends and I enabled the parish to go through with this enterprise by means of donations. The organ builder did his job at cost in return for the many favors I have done for him over the years. This made it possible for me to fulfill my idea of a village organ, which I have developed during years of studying organ construction. Two keyboards, twenty-two registers; Bach and the moderns (Widor, César Franck, Reger) can all be played on it. The proof: The American sound engineer who came with the equipment to record my performances for Columbia inspected several other, larger organs; then, to my astonishment, he chose this village organ for the recording sessions! At a different time I'll explain the uniqueness of the sound produced by this organ. French, German, British, and American organists have recognized this as the very model of a village organ. However, since there wasn't enough money for new construction, they had to take over any still usable material from the old one. Under these circumstances I made up my mind to rebuild the organ: to make the action mechanical (without a Barker lever), to use slider chests, and to replace all the inferior pipes with good new ones. The work is being done by Kern, an organ builder in Strasbourg who used to be part of the Haerpfer [sic] firm; several years ago he went out on his own in Strasbourg. He is an outstanding tuner and in 1932 participated in the tuning of the present organ.

~

To Dr. Hans Hickmann, Polydor International—Deutsche Grammophongesellschaft, Archiv Produktion, Hamburg
[1959–60]

[Concerning the stereo recording of J. S. Bach's Brandenburg Concertos]
In Africa I have a chance to see what it means when the creations of the great masters of composition can be heard in a perfect rendering, anytime, anyplace, whenever the mood strikes us. How different it was in my youth when we sometimes had to wait months or years to reexperience an opus that appealed to our souls in a special manner.

This possibility of becoming familiar with the masterpieces of music is a spiritual advance that must be valued highly for our civilization. It is of special importance that Bach can now be revealed to us completely.

I must therefore thank you for making the treasures of music accessible to us.

≈

To J. D. Newth, A. & C. Black publishing company, London
Lambarene
1 January 1960

[*f*]

Dear Friend,

This is one of the first letters that I am writing in 1960. Please accept my good wishes for this year. I arrived in Lambarene yesterday afternoon. My stay in Europe was very full. I had to visit cities and universities with which I am associated. I was in Frankfurt, Dortmund, Hanover, Münster (Westphalia) with its big university, Copenhagen, and Malmö, where I met with my Swedish friends. After returning from the north I went to southern Germany, to Stuttgart and Tübingen. For years now I have had a special bond with Tübingen because my studies of Jesus and St. Paul directly continue the work of Ferdinand Christian Baur and his students.

After traveling to the north and through Germany, I spent a few weeks in Paris, resuming contact with the academy and my Parisian friends. I hadn't been there for four years. After that I visited Brussels and Holland. Back in Gunsbach and Strasbourg, I focused on purchases for my hospital, on packing them and preparing the customs documents. I traveled with nearly two hundred crates and baggage items weighing a total of three and a half tons. In Dakar, Clara [Urquhart] joined me and Fräulein Mathilde [Kottmann] on the boat. She enjoyed the trip very much.

She told me how deeply you mourned our friend Mettler who was taken from us so suddenly. They have attended to all the necessary matters in this case. I would like to tell you how touched I am by your loyalty to this dear and simple man. I am glad that I saw him in Gunsbach toward the end of summer.

≈

To G. Jahn, Nobel Prize Committee, and K. Fostervoll, Oslo
15 January 1960

To gain some insight into the process of the negotiations [on the atomic problem], one must thoroughly study large numbers of magazines and newspapers and also maintain personal relations with people involved in scientific and practical activities. This requires a great deal of reading, a large correspondence, and remaining in contact with many people in various countries. It also means taking a lot of notes on whatever is happening. Along with all my other work, I spend two or three hours a day on the cause of peace and nuclear arms. I have always wished to serve the cause of peace with the prestige and confidence that I enjoy in the world.

⁓

To the World Council of Churches, Geneva
                    20 January 1960

                                        [f]

The native pastor, Anatole Wora Reliva of Libreville, was selected by the Evangelical Church in Gabon to visit Europe in order to complete his training. He wrote me a letter informing me of this. He is also asking me for a recommendation to the World Council of Churches in Geneva. I am glad to recommend him. I am acquainted with his life and the background of his calling, and I believe that he will be a loyal servant of our Church and use his sojourn in Europe and his studies there to prepare for the activity that he will pursue in Gabon.

⁓

Letter to Europe, to the collaborators involved in the book *We Helped the Doctor in Lambarene*
                    [Lambarene]
                    23 February 1960

Well, on 1 January 1959 I returned to Lambarene, weary from my many travels and speeches in Europe, and during the first few days of January I took off with the whole gang and *avec tous les outils* [all the tools] to repair the road to Atouma, which had been impassable because of last autumn's flooding; we have to be able to use it for our huge five-and-a-half ton trucks. . . . We also had to widen and improve the Atadié-Atouma road. As a result, starting last fall, we could drive our truck toward Atouma, obtaining bananas on the Atouma-Libreville road.

During my travels through Europe last autumn I ascertained how deeply people now sympathize with this idea [reverence for life]. They expect it to help create a new spirit in our time. This is a necessity, after all. With the current spirit, we cannot possibly cope with the difficult and urgent problems facing us. It can only leave us with a lack of peace. It will not allow us to achieve the peace that we so badly need. . . .

~

To Prof. Dr. Hermann Mai,[1] Münster

Lambarene
25 February 1960

Dear Friend,

Many, many thanks for your dear letter. So you people celebrated my birthday! I am touched that you are so good to me and show me such friendship. I'm looking forward to the text of the speech. If you can come for Easter, you can do the work that you consider the most worthwhile.

And I have come back to a lot of work here (road repairs, bridge repairs, buildings, hospital work, and an inconceivable quantity of mail). I am coping with everything as best I can, but I long for a less crowded life. My experiences in Münster are still fresh in my mind. It was beautiful, but everything passed so quickly. Lack of time is a harsh poverty.

Best regards to all. And until Easter,

Sincerely,
Your old
Albert Schweitzer

~

To Prof. Dr. Hans Walter Bähr, Tübingen

Lambarene
29 February 1960

Dear Friend,

There is something very bizarre about making your way through opinions that are expressed about you [Schweitzer is referring to a collection of essays for his birthday in 1960].[1] You wonder if everything is correct: other people's views from the outside and your own view from the inside. But I felt that all the external views harmonize with my internal view. Now I can rejoice that my works on Jesus and Paul have convinced people, and that reverence for life is being seen as a basic element that we must again struggle for in our civilization. A lot of what I wanted to write has remained incomplete. I was prevented by the two wars, and now by the task of keeping up with the nuclear issue both scientifically and politically. I suffered from my failure, but I have now calmly resigned myself because I hear from others that I have recognized and expressed something that can advance us spiritually, something that is important to them.

What I had to offer found acceptance calmly and slowly while I was running my hospital in the stillness of Lambarene. I regard this as a great privilege that was bestowed on me.

~

To Joseph S. Whiteford, president of Aeolian-Skinner Organ Company, South Boston, U.S.A.

Lambarene
27 March 1960

[f]

Dear Mr. Whiteford,

Many, many thanks for your letter of March 18. I fully agree with you that the sound of the organ is seriously endangered in our time because church architects do not provide a place in which organs can have the best sound effect and because such vast amounts of noise-reducing material are being used in today's churches. This material swallows the sound and destroys the splendid resonance that stone lends to the organ sound. Yes, it is time that organists joined forces and confronted this danger. I would love to send you a short article on this issue, but my huge workload won't allow it. Still, you do have organists who could write a good article. And the issue is quite clear.

So I wish you the best of luck in your project of fighting for the organ and for church music.

~

To Pastor Emil Lind (retired), Speyer on the Rhine

Lambarene
12 June 1960

Dear Friend,

I was delighted to read what you wrote about your semester in Strasbourg. Some of this is new to me or else it has slipped my mind. I had forgotten that you discovered me when I was a hardworking hospital resident, nor did I realize what a poor examination applicant was risking if it came out that he had read my writings. Today, fifty years later, it is clear that theology cannot do without eschatology. In October I visited Baur's grave in Tübingen in splendid sunshine. . . . I was deeply moved that I had helped him gain his just recognition.

   With fond thoughts of you and yours,

                                        Albert Schweitzer

                              ∽

To Gerald Götting, Berlin

                              [Lambarene]
                              24 July 1960[1]

Dear Friend,

Many, many thanks for your friendly letter of 7 June 1960. I apologize that the echo is functioning so poorly. I am going through difficult times because of the necessary construction work. The concrete floor supporting the hospital motors (including a 46 H.P. diesel) is not high enough. During a severe flood, they would be standing in water, which would ruin them. Now I have to tear down the entire building near the river and replace it with a higher one. And since the ground lies very low, I have to cover it with 2.3 meters of concrete. The surface area is 6 × 12 meters. That adds up to a goodly number of cubic meters of concrete and a lot of cement, sand, and stones, and workers to break the stones for the concrete! Where am I to get it all? However, I have resigned myself to the fact that once a heavy job is done, another equally heavy and equally urgent job pops up, and so on, in my life in Lambarene until my earthly pilgrimage reaches its end.

   Thank you for the lovely color pictures of Lambarene. I have never seen such perfect color photographs. They are being sent to Gunsbach, where they will be stored with the things I hold dear.

   I am very worried about the political situation. Contrary to the agreement reached between Eisenhower and Khrushchev, the summit conference did not take place in early December 1959; instead, at the behest of other governments that wanted to lessen its impact, it did not come about until early May 1960. The results are disastrous. Had the conference taken place at the end of 1959, it would have created an atmosphere in which the events would have been less negative than was the case because of the subsequent lack of that atmosphere. At the point we have reached now, the political events no longer have their own meaning; they have been given a different meaning by the confrontation between East and West. The effect is that of a powerful loudspeaker transmitting a piece of music. I regard this state of affairs as extremely detrimental if not dangerous. I am deeply worried.

Best wishes,
Albert Schweitzer

~

To Tony van Leer, Amsterdam

Lambarene
7 August 1960

Dear Tony,

I am writing to extend my warmest congratulations on your birthday. My good wishes all have the same goal: the hope that you will regain your health completely and return to us. When I am sitting at my desk down in the pharmacy, I often yearn to hear your voice again.... Everything here is business as usual, and the number of patients keeps mounting, and we keep building.... We also have a new Swiss physician[1] who is very capable and very nice. I am still sitting downstairs in my place. Day after day. And when you come back, it will be a day of joy.

Give your mother my very best.

Sincerely,
Albert Schweitzer

~

To the Christian Peace Conference, Prague
[1960]

I hope that the peace conference in Prague this September will shake up those who are indifferent and point out that Christianity, by its very essence, has no choice but to demand the abolition of atomic weapons and to trust that God can protect us without atomic weapons, without our needing atomic weapons, if we follow the dictates of the spirit of our Lord Jesus. We cannot live with a weak faith. The times demand that we believe profoundly that God helps us if we allow ourselves to be guided by the Gospel.

~

To the director of the Association for the Prevention of Cruelty to Animals, Bonn

Lambarene

12 August 1960

Dear Sir,

Thank you for informing me that the animal shelter that is to bear my name will be dedicated in mid-August. Animal shelters are a grand achievement of the animal protection movement. This can truly be gauged right here in Africa where stray dogs run around in every locality, especially the towns and cities; they are nothing but skin and bones, suffering from scabies and their fur bloody from constant scratching.

My hospital has become a miniature animal shelter. Local Europeans who go on vacation or leave Africa hand their dogs over to me. They have no one else they can entrust them to. Sheltering them is no problem. They always find a place to creep into. There's no such thing as cold weather here. And poor cats also turn up. However, it is harder for them than for the dogs to be recognized and tolerated by the tribespeople residing here. Nevertheless, they manage to find refuge somewhere, under one of the numerous roofs, and to unearth some food. The natives of the surrounding area know that they can bring us orphaned jungle animals and receive a present in exchange. As a result, we are raising antelopes, wildcats, gorillas, and chimpanzees. When the gorillas and chimpanzees turn two, we try to find homes for them in European zoos.

Weaverbirds have forced themselves upon us as pushy guests. What lures them to settle down with us is the chicken feed, of which these uninvited diners partake by the score. They also find it practical to reside on the hospital palm trees, using the frond fibers to weave artful nests for their broods and hanging them from the branches. A palm tree hung with sixty or seventy nests and surrounded by the birds bringing chicken feed to their young offers a charming tableau, but the tree is doomed. Within a few years it will perish because the weaverbirds keep removing their nesting material from the fronds. They could get it from neighboring palms, but they find it more convenient to use their home tree.

The poor palm could be rescued only if we shot the birds, but we can't get ourselves to do that. As a result, we have lost dozens of trees.

During these weeks we often think about the poor pets left behind by the whites fleeing the Belgian Congo. Those starving creatures roam the cities, and their misery stops only when they starve to death. Your letter of January 25 arrived so late here that I cannot send you any contribution for the *Festschrift*. Perhaps you could use the short piece on the animal shelter in my hospital.

~

To Prof. Werner Ludwig, M.D., chairman of the Albert Schweitzer Committee of the German Red Cross, GDR [German Democratic Republic]

Lambarene

3 October 1960

Dear Professor Ludwig,

I am very grateful to you for your efforts in getting donations for my hospital so smoothly across the GDR border. This is almost a miracle in our time. I am deeply moved that the GDR is providing such great help to my hospital.

Our staff now has six physicians and fifteen nurses from Europe. Feeding our hospital is a constant problem for us. A new doctor cannot run the hospital even if he has the requisite knowledge. It also requires the authority that I have attained through long years in Africa. Construction is also a major problem for us. The hospital keeps growing year after year so that new buildings have to be added to the old ones every year—two or three or four. We do not have the wherewithal to assign the construction work to an outside firm, so we have to do it ourselves. That is a task I have to deal with. I am both architect and contractor. I have designed all the existing buildings and have overseen the construction work. The hospital is now a large village with some forty buildings.

It is a great comfort for me to remain healthy and able-bodied in my old age. I certainly appreciate this great privilege.

Once again, many, many thanks for your kindness.

With best wishes,

Albert Schweitzer

~

To Bruno Walter, Beverly Hills, California

Lambarene

8 November 1960

Dear Friend,

Much as I would like to, I cannot supply pieces that are not part of my normal program. That is why you have had to wait for my account of my experiences with Rudolf Steiner. Thank you for sending me all those writings about him. I have most of them in my library in Gunsbach, but it was easier getting them from you than having them sent to me from my library. The most valuable item was the auto-biography. The reader really gets to know him. Too bad death took the pen from his hand.

I will write about our meeting in Strasbourg, where Annie Besant introduced us. I can still remember our conversations. They inspired me to keep dealing with him and to remain cognizant of his impor-tance. What the two of us share is a desire to replace the uncivilized with civilization. In Strasbourg we both realized we had this rapport. He expected civilization to emerge from ethical thinking and from the insights of the humanities. In terms of my own character, I had to stick to having civilization come forth from an immersion in the true essence of the ethical. In this way I came to the ethics of the reverence for life—which, I hope, will instigate the emergence of civilization. I realize that Rudolf Steiner greatly regretted that I stuck to the old way of thinking, but we both felt the same obligation to lead people back to true civilization. I was delighted at what he managed to achieve in the world with his great personality and his profound humanity. Everyone should follow the road that is his. . . .

~

To Emmy Martin, Gunsbach

Lambarene
Sunday, 15 January 1961

I have Sunday duty and am spending the afternoon in the hospital. Since everything is quiet, I'll tell you about the birthday party. It was entirely dominated by the news that Prime Minister Léon M'Ba would be arriving at 11:00 A.M. to present me with the Grand Cross of the Order of Gabon.

So we had to forget about our usual warm and simple birthday party. The prime minister was accompanied by two native ministers and a whole set of V.I.P.s from Libreville, and they all dined with us! Twelve people! We also received numerous white people from near and far, so by eleven o'clock the courtyard was packed.

The prime minister stood by the steps to our house, I in front of it, police troops behind me, presenting arms when the order was hung around my neck. Then the prime minister gave a nice little speech about me, and I spoke about Gabon, which has become my second home.

Soon after lunch the visitors drove off. At dinner we celebrated my birthday quietly, in the usual way.

~

To I. A. Aler, director of K.L.M., Royal Dutch Airlines, The Hague
Lambarene
20 February 1961

Dear Mr. Aler,

Visitors have already traveled to my hospital by K.L.M., and now a new relationship has been created between K.L.M. and myself: The board of directors has decided that in 1962 a DC 8 jet plane, a modern giant of the air, will bear my name. I gladly accept this honor that you are bestowing on me. In my youth in France and Germany, the locomotives bore the names of mythological figures and deities. Around 1895 [that stopped, and] they bore only numbers. They did their jobs anonymously, which I greatly deplored. Thus, I am delighted that you are going back to the custom of names. I wonder why you don't also use names of deities and mythological figures rather than providing one of your modern giants of the air with the name of a country doctor who has written a few books. You impose his name on a giant of the air that cannot defend itself! But it is not up to me to try you for your mistake. I am too flattered by your decision, and so I'll let it be. I hope that this giant is a solid worker, like myself, and that it finds the approval from which, to my astonishment, I have benefited in my life.

Thank you from the bottom of my heart.

Albert Schweitzer

~

To the Mayor of Kaiserslautern
[Lambarene]
21 May 1961

Your Honor,

In your letter [of] 2 May 1961, you have informed me of the decision of the municipal senate to rename Ernst-Thälmann-Strasse after me. Thank you for the kindness you are showing me, but I cannot deprive a dead man of the honor that has been awarded to him.

Please forgive me for saying this to you, but I cannot act against my conviction.

I have known Kaiserslautern since my youth and have lovely memories of your city.

With best wishes to you and the members of the town council, I remain,

> Truly yours,
> Albert Schweitzer

~

To Lee Ellerbrock, Montecito Sierra Madre, U.S.A.
> [Lambarene]

Dear Friend,

Thank you so much for everything you are doing to foster the idea of reverence for life! It is so important for this idea to circulate broadly. People today live in an atmosphere of inhumanity. They are trapped in it! All the current atomic policies are a politics of inhumanity. People take for granted the possibility of a war with horrible nuclear arms. We now have to raise our voices for humanity so that we may become humane humans. The first utterances that Jesus made in Galilee included the Beatitudes concerning the merciful and the peace-makers, in which he proclaims humanity!

It was wonderful of you to come to Lambarene so that we could meet.

~

To Alfred Kern, organ builder, Strasbourg
> [Lambarene]
> 29 June 1961

Dear Herr Kern,

The organ [reconstruction of the organ at the church in Gunsbach] will be put to use as soon as Herr Dickert and you have jointly decided that the construction is completed and that it can be viewed as successful in every respect. I have to rely on both of you. I am also writing to Herr Dickert, asking him to send me a report on the completion of the organ. I have to count on your knowing my intentions in regard to the tuning and on your implementing the latter according to my wishes.

In your letter of May 29, you wrote that the wind conditions and the playing style are good. That is a basic premise for the success of the [re]construction. I wonder if you have managed to completely contain the noise of the wind production in the church tower. That is an absolute must.

Once Herr Dickert and you regard the work as finished, please send me a report of your joint decision.

And I would like you yourself to send me a bill that clearly indicates how much I still owe you.

~

To Prof. Dr. Herbert Spiegelberg, Appleton
                              Lambarene
                              17 July 1961

Dear Herbert,

Your letter was a great joy for me. It is a lovely present, which I owe to Miss Sörensen (please send her my regards). I was very interested to hear the news about your philosophical work. When Husserl was visiting Strasbourg around 1902, he personally tried to initiate me into phenomenology. But when it came to "parenthesizing," I always parenthesized the wrong thing. That is why I need your historical introduction to phenomenology, to get a better purchase on the essence of phenomenology.

I was interested to hear that the name "philosophy of humanity" is emerging for my philosophy. I am enclosing a photograph that was given to me. It shows the three islands in the Ogowe near the village of Igendja; it was here, after three days of difficult voyage up the Ogowe, that the phrase "reverence for life," which I had never seen before, came to me in a daydream. And you are right to demand reverence for phenomena. . . .

I often think about your parents and your dear, noble Uncle Heinrich [von Recklinghausen]. What an atmosphere that was in Strasbourg back then. I am homesick for those days. If your Munich lectures, or simply a report about them, are ever printed, please send me the publication.

                              Best,
                              Albert Schweitzer

~

To Naemi P. Raymond, Tokyo
Lambarene
[1961]

I am delighted that you wish to honor me by making me the patron of your animal protection society. I am very glad to give you my permission. As far back as my youth I was convinced that we should not behave heartlessly toward animals. Later it dawned on me that true religion and true philosophy demand a sympathetic and helpful attitude toward all creatures, and that ethics that does not deal with human behavior toward creatures is incomplete and inconsistent with life.

It is the great mission of our era that we come to true humanity from the inhumanity in which we are trapped and that we thereby turn back from unspiritual to truly spiritual human beings.

That is why it is highly important to acquaint children with reverence for life, which is already happening in many schools.

You can also imagine what it means to me that you have founded an animal protection society in Tokyo, asking people to have reverence for all life and to spread this idea.

In your letter you write about all the things that your group is doing for animals. I wish you constant success for your animal protection society, and I hope that you can induce many people to view animals as creatures that have a right to human kindness, which is what makes people human beings in the first place.

Please give my best regards to the members of your association, and please send me news of your activities from time to time.

~

To Pastor Lantos-Kiss, Sopron, Hungary
Lambarene
9 August 1961

Dear Pastor Lantos-Kiss,

Thank you for your kind letter of 16 February 1960. It touched me profoundly. You pray for me.... I am very interested in what you write about yourself and your work as a Catholic priest and about your studying me! I would greatly value your writing a biography about me in Hungary. I know that I have many friends in your country and that the idea of reverence for life means something to them. You are right to point out the significance of the fact that it was a priest who wrote the first book about me in Hungary. In my village of Gunsbach, the church is shared by both Catholics and Protestants. This had a deep impact on me in my childhood. I am always aware of the fraternity of the two churches, and I taught it to the children who attended my religious instructions when I was a preacher in Strasbourg. The idea of reverence for life is a late bloomer on a branch of what our Lord Jesus teaches us about love. I was profoundly shaken by the fact that I was found worthy to express that teaching. It is destined to help our time work its way out of the inhumanity into which it threatens to sink; in this way we can avoid waging horrible atomic warfare and bring permanent peace to the world. After all, we are in a dreadful historical situation. The danger of atomic war is much greater now than the people of our time realize. Nor are they aware of their inhumanity, which is shown by the very fact that they deal with the possibility of a nuclear war. They must be wrenched out of the heedlessness in which they are vegetating. May God grant success to this undertaking.

Please allow me, dear pastor, to dispense with explaining why the answer to your kind letter is coming so late.

Write me, even if it is only a few lines, to let me know that this letter of mine has arrived.

~

To Léon M'Ba, president of the Republic of Gabon, Libreville
1961

[f]

Dear Mr. President,

May I congratulate you on being elected president of the Republic of Gabon by the Gabonese people. It is my sincere wish that you may rule the destiny of this country for a long time and bring about whatever contributes to its development and its peace.

We owe it to you that peace reigns among us. Those who understand the role that you have played in establishing and maintaining peace are deeply grateful to you.

Best wishes,
Albert Schweitzer

~

To Prof. Dr. Martin Werner, Berne
Lambarene
20 September 1961

Dear Friend,

Forgive me for this belated response to your kind letter, but I have been [preoccupied] with building a bridge across a large creek that flows into the Ogowe on the terrain of our hospital. The bridge is twenty-three feet long, and it was very difficult to lay a good foundation for it in the clay soil. The bridge is made of steel and concrete. I'm a modern person in that respect! I had to build it in order to connect with the new government roads leading into the interior of the country. This enables us to do something we could never do before: drive inland patients to my hospital at any time.

I am delighted that your new, big book is completed.[1] I have to tend black patients and build bridges, and you keep watch in theology. So I can put my mind at ease. Six hundred and forty pages of sensible investigation of the life of Jesus—now that's something. So I didn't have to come into the world to do research on Jesus. You could have done the necessary work and led eschatology to victory! The eschatological knowledge of Jesus is pious because it allowed us to get to know Him as He is, with His piousness.

Your letter did not tire my eyes because you write legibly. I, on the other hand, am writing this letter poorly because I am writing it on the evening of a hard day.

With kind thoughts about you and yours,
Gratefully yours,
Albert Schweitzer

~

To Provost Matti A. Muskkonen, Pori, Finland
Lambarene
22 October 1961

Eminence,

Many thanks for your kind lines. It is inexplicable to me that the journalist Olavi A. can tell people in Finland that I said, "The Christian mission signified a great spiritual decline for Africa." I myself have joyfully and emotionally preached the Gospel at the Lambarene mission church. The Gospel has been a great spiritual boon for the natives. It has liberated them from the dreadful concepts of the heathen life they used to lead. It has freed them from the fear of magic and cruelty that the witch doctors practice! And it has brought them Jesus and the faith in the kind Father in heaven. I have heard the natives thank me for the tidings of the Gospel.

Whenever a visitor comes here, I am terrified that upon returning to Europe or America he will disseminate something that he has misunderstood here. I cannot understand the heedlessness of these people.

I am touched that ideas from my books are meaningful to you. What dismal times we live in! I am very worried about the future of mankind because of nuclear danger....

⌇

To Dr. Hermann Baur, Basel
[Chairman of the Swiss Society for the Lambarene Hospital]
Lambarene
20 November 1961

I find it touching of you to devote yourself so intensely to the affairs of my hospital.[1] It is wonderful that the people working for the hospital get together, meet one another, and also discuss practical issues concerning the supplying of the hospital.

We've had a big flood here. The water rose twenty feet, reaching all the way to the hospital buildings. Several buildings had to be cleared out. The water has been receding since yesterday. And this inundation came even though we had nice weather and only a minor thunderstorm every five nights, and otherwise nothing but sunshine!

Please let me know how your brother, the cellist, is getting on. I know nothing about him. And how is your mother? Sometimes I recall my visits with your family in the parsonage, when you and your brother were still in high school. What lovely times those were! Your father [Pastor Hans Baur] was hale and hearty and so kind to me. Several days ago a complete edition of my writings came out in Japan. I was reminded that your father was the one who first put me in touch with Uchimura, the leader of the Christians in Japan. That contact was of great importance for me.

⌇

To Wolfgang Voelter, student, Tübingen
Lambarene
21 November 1961

Dear Herr Voelter,

I was deeply moved by your letter. I had no idea that my thoughts could find such resonance in the heart of a young man.[1] Keep living in the spirituality in which you now exist; remain true to it.

We have to create a new spirit in our time. And you are sending my hospital a large donation from the first money that you have ever earned! Thank you from the bottom of my heart. If ever I am in your area, please do your best to come see me and remind me who you are. I would be delighted to make your acquaintance.

Best wishes,
Albert Schweitzer

~

To Heinz Sawade, organist, Mühlhausen, Thuringia
[Lambarene, 1961]

How good of you to enable me to hear the organ [tape recording, Bach organ, Mühlhausen]![1] Luckily, one of my doctors owns a tape recorder so I was able to listen to the sound of the organ that I have thought about so often in terms of Bach's wishes. I also listened to your clear and well-phrased playing and was overjoyed that the right Bach organist is sitting at this Bach organ. I was also interested in the taped comments. I don't know how to thank you. Please tell the Mühlhausen authorities and congregation how much pleasure they have given me by building the organ as it was conceived by Bach.

This means a great deal to the music world. And please convey my congratulations to the organ builder who did such a good job of building and tuning the organ in the spirit of Bach. On my trip to Copenhagen last October I had planned to take a detour to Mühlhausen while traveling back to Germany and to see the organ. Unfortunately, I could not do so because my schedule was too crowded and I could not take a day off for this detour. I was deeply sorry. Now I am somewhat comforted by the tape that you have sent me, except that I cannot see the people connected with the organ.

~

To Prof. Dr. Hans Walter Bähr, Tübingen
2 January 1962

Dear Friend,

Your big book reached me two days before the new year. I sat up half the night reading through it.[1] The thing that bowled me over was the statement that Indian and Chinese thinkers now write that I have completed the voyage which their thinkers started out on. I knew it, but I believed I would not live to see the day when this was acknowledged in the Orient.

I find it incomprehensible that I have actually lived to witness this recognition of my way of thinking. I already knew this or that about the recognition achieved by my outlook, but I would never have dared to imagine that it could be so unanimous.

Indeed, I find quite a number of things in my life incomprehensible. As a student I was already immersed in a critique of our civilization, and at the turn of the century I got to hear the title of this book, *We Epigoni,* at the Curtius publishing house [in Berlin]. The day I heard about the outbreak of the first war, I made up my mind to start writing this book since I was not permitted to work as a physician; however, I discarded the minor-key title *We Epigoni* and switched to one in a major key, *Civilization and Ethics*—with a constructive goal. All those developments were incredibly providential, and they were crowned by my experience on my river voyage in September 1915 when we came to the three islands facing the village of Igendja. Granted, I was determined to place much greater value on kindness to living creatures than was previously the case, but it was only the phrase "reverence for life," which surfaced mysteriously and unconsciously in my mind, that made me realize ethics would have a much deeper and greater energy by taking heed of all creation because it would put us in a spiritual relationship with the entire universe.

And then, in January 1920, Archbishop Söderblom, whom I didn't even know, invited me to deliver the Olaus-Petri lectures in Uppsala, even though, as I told myself later, I was really still far too young! He did so because he believed that I was still being detained by the French, and he wanted to obtain my release with his invitation (which he sent to the French government through the Archbishop of Canterbury). And so I came, as he put it, to the potter's wheel at a relatively early age. Indeed, a short time later Cambridge invited me to deliver those same lectures on civilization and ethics, and that was followed by similar invitations from other universities. Thus, I experienced the most favorable concatenation of circumstances to disseminate the ethics of reverence for life.

9 January 1962

Long days have passed since the start of this letter and its continuation. I've had to work in the hospital, supervise at construction sites, and devote small or large amounts of time to visitors, which I have done willingly, not viewing it as an obligation.

And now you've come and, from Tübingen, you've helped to gain recognition for my ideas. From Tübingen:—that means something to me. You know that my maternal ancestors come from Swabia. On the day after New Year's 1801, shortly after his birth, my grandfather, Schillinger, was carried across Kehl's Rhine bridge to Strasbourg, where his son eventually studied theology and become a pastor in the Vosges village of Muhlbach in the Munster Valley. My grandfather died before my birth, but ever since my childhood my mother has told me that he was a very important person who dealt not only with theology but also with philosophy, science, and astronomy. If there was anything to see in the sky, he would set up his telescope in front of the parsonage and let people peer through it, explaining to them what they should see. He was keenly interested in everything that went on in the world. When the Pope lost control of the papal states, my grandfather hoped that this would bring an end to papal power. He also concerned himself with organ building. He was friendly with all organ builders. If they had business anywhere near Gunsbach, Pastor Schillinger would invite them over. When a famous Swiss organ builder installed the grand and renowned organ in Lucerne, my grandfather traveled to Lucerne with my mother, who was a young girl at the time. Day after day, from morning until evening, he was up on the organ gallery with his daughter, following the construction. She got to see nothing of the town around Lake Lucerne. My grandfather had an organ built in Muhlbach, and I often played it as a boy and adolescent. It had a wonderful, mild sound. During World War I it was buried under the ruins of the bombed church. At the age of eight I wanted to know how an organ was built, and at nine I was already replacing the organist at the worship service; my mother was happy that my grandfather was living on in me. She also secretly enjoyed the fact that at the university I studied not only theology but also philosophy very seriously.

It was important for me that I became a student of Theobald Ziegler's in Strasbourg and that he was personally interested in me.

I frequented his home and learned a great deal from him about Tübingen's past. For my doctoral dissertation he assigned me an analysis of Kant's philosophy of religion, which was rather daring for such a young fellow like myself. Through Ziegler I became thoroughly familiar with Hegel, which meant a great deal to me. My most intimate relationship was with Fichte.

When I became director of Strasbourg's School of St. Thomas in 1902 (if I am not mistaken), the first thing I did was go to Tübingen with the first in the senior class; and there we got acquainted with the famous theological school, hoping to use our findings for our Strasbourg institute.

I already had great respect for Baur, although, as Holtzmann's pupil, I hadn't yet freed myself from the Markus priority. Nevertheless, I regarded Baur as a great scholar of earliest Christianity and the Synoptics.

And now, in Tübingen, you and others have expressed your recognition of my thinking—by people in Tübingen and outsiders involved in your enterprise. I cannot imagine how this has come about. Happy as it makes me, there is something mysterious about it. As a theologian and thinker, I am at home in Tübingen, but I owe it to you personally that I could live to see this day. Words fail me when I try to thank you for the work you have done on my behalf. I will never understand how you came to make this effort for me. I can only keep thanking you.

Best,
Albert Schweitzer

~

To Isabel Slater, M.B.E., Humane Education Institute of Africa, Dar es Saalam, Tanganyika

Lambarene
9 March 1962[1]

Dear Mrs. Slater,

Thank you for your letter of 24 January 1962. . . . True civilization begins with the knowledge of compassion. I wish you success in teaching compassion for all creatures.

~

To Dr. Willy A. Petritsky, Leningrad
                        Lambarene
                        26 March 1962[1]

Dear Mr. Petritsky,

Thank you for your friendly lines. My main work is a philosophical study, *Civilization and Ethics,* which came out in Germany during 1923 and in England shortly thereafter. This book deals with the problem of the ethical substance of our civilization. It was partly inspired by Tolstoy, who made a deep impact on me. In this book I stated that our civilization has too little of an ethical character, and I then focused on the question of why ethics has such a weak influence on our society. Ultimately I concluded that ethics does not have full energy because it is nonelementary and incomplete. After all, it deals with the way people relate to one another instead of having us concern ourselves with our relationship to all living creatures. This complete ethics is far more elementary and far more profound than the usual ethics. It brings us to a spiritual relationship with the universe. I first presented the idea of this elementary and profound ethics when I lectured at the University of Uppsala, Sweden, then Cambridge, then Prague; and I noticed that it found its way to people's hearts and minds. It is also being recognized in philosophy as well as religion. Now it is being taught in schools, and the children are taking it quite for granted.

The ultimate [goal] of philosophy and religion is to bring people to the deepest humanity. The deepest philosophy becomes deeply religious, and the deepest religion becomes thinking. They both fulfill their true destiny when they allow people to become human in the most profound sense of the term.

In 1913 I founded the hospital in the Equatorial African jungle of the former French colony of Gabon, which has recently become the Republic of Gabon. If you would like to find out more about my philosophy and myself, you can contact Herr Gerald Götting in the GDR [German Democratic Republic]. He is well acquainted with me.

Best wishes,
Albert Schweitzer

To Dr. Max Tau, Oslo

Lambarene

28 March 1962[1]

Dear Friend,

No matter what, I continue to work on a new [anti-atomic] appeal. But I won't be going public with it until a new situation is established. It makes no sense to keep reiterating that nuclear testing should stop and nuclear arms should be abolished if the situation remains as is, and no decision of any kind is reached. A decision has to be made.

We have to see how the new negotiations work out and what sort of position should be taken in an appeal. The situation in the world is very dismal, and it takes a lot of courage to keep hoping. . . . And yet, we mustn't give up.

～

To Wolfgang Lauterburg, Berne [On his confirmation]

Lambarene

10 April 1962

Dear Godson,

I have retained a clear memory of you. I can picture you, and I love you. In a letter from your mother I have learned some pleasing things about you. I feel it is important that you not go in for sports, which are such a mindless waste of time, and that you love hiking, which keeps you in a living rapport with nature. I also find it wonderful that you sympathize with my ideas. I regarded it as a privilege to concern myself in detail with spiritual matters, studying theology and philosophy for years and thereby forming views that are meaningful to some people and are gaining acceptance. My simple and yet deep and living ethics of reverence for life has found its way to people's hearts and minds.

My viewpoint that religion and thinking should get people to attain true and deep humanity is a highly important goal for us. Atomic bombs have launched the era of inhumanity, from which we must emerge if mankind is not to perish spiritually and indeed physically.

And, my dear godson, remain pious. Piety means being inspired by and remaining true to the spirit of Jesus, as expressed in His words and deeds. Don't forget to meditate in prayer and to read about Him in the Gospels. Paul also has a lot to say to us.

I would have told you these things in a quiet moment if I had been able to come to Europe for your confirmation. God bless you.

Your godfather,
Albert Schweitzer

~

To Dr. Gerhard Kühn, Oberkochen, Württemberg
Albert Schweitzer
Lambarene, Gabon
West Equatorial Africa
14 April 1962[1]

I wanted to try and keep the hospital going with the donations that came to me. My friends told me it was a crazy idea. And it *was* crazy. But it worked! I managed to build and run the hospital as a free man. This was given unto me. I went through times of great anxiety at the end of World Wars I and II, but I managed to keep going. He [Fritz Dinner] was one of my first friends in Switzerland; as a well-situated bank officer who was recommended to me on all sides, he offered to administer the hospital funds, which he has been doing for years with devotion and great expertise. He pays for the deliveries we receive from various countries; it is easiest to do this in Switzerland. We can't do it so well from Lambarene.

At present we have considerable expenses because of the necessary construction work.

Best,
Albert Schweitzer

~

To President John F. Kennedy, Washington
Personal

Lambarene, Gabon
West Equatorial Africa
20 April 1962

[e]

Dear President Kennedy,

Would you have the great kindness to forgive me, old as I am, for taking the courage to write to you about the tests, which the United States, together with England, wants to carry out [if] Russia does not accede to your request that an international inspection on their territory takes care that no tests will take place.

I take the courage to write to you about this as one who occupies himself since a long time with the problem of atomic weapons and with the problem of peace.

I believe that I may assure you that with the newest scientific inventions, each test carried out by the Soviets will be registered on the highly developed instruments which your country possesses and which protect the United States.

I also take the courage, as an absolute[ly] neutral person, to admit that I am not quite convinced that the claim that one state can oblige the other to tolerate an international control commission on its territory is juridically motivated. This right can only exist after the states agree on disarmament. Then a new situation will have been established, which will put an end to the cold war and which will give each state the right to know, through international inspection on each other's territory, that each country meets its obligations to disarm according to the agreement. The same international control will see to it that no tests can be carried out.

An urgent necessity for the world is that the atomic powers agree as soon as possible on disarmament under effective international control. The possibility of such disarmament negotiations should not be made questionable by not absolute[ly] necessary appeals for international verification of the discontinuance of testing.

Only when the states agree not to carry out tests anymore can promising negotiations about disarmament and world peace take place. When also this time this cannot be achieved, then the world is in a hopeless and very dangerous state.

Please do consider if you will take this responsibility by insisting on not absolute[ly] necessary conditions for the cessation of atomic tests, or if this terrible responsibility will move you to let the time come in which tests belong to the past and in which promising negotiations about disarmament and peace are at last possible.

[President Kennedy responded by writing a detailed letter to Schweitzer (6 June 1962, The White House, Washington). Kennedy first reported on the state of the test-ban negotiations, which then led to the agreement of 1963. He said that he himself had two children and knew what anxiety about the future felt like. Nothing was closer to his heart than hoping for complete and universal disarmament with the premise of international control. J. F. Kennedy wrote: "You are one of the transcendent moral influences of our century. I earnestly hope that you will consider throwing the great weight of that influence behind the movement for general and complete disarmament." Kennedy's letter was accompanied by documents.]

~

To Rabbi David Jacobson, San Antonio, Texas
Lambarene
1 May 1962

Dear Rabbi Jacobson,

Thank you so much for your letter of 26 March 1962 in which you tell me that you know and are sympathetic with my ideas. In my opinion, all religious and philosophical thinking must induce people to deal with themselves and to feel the need to attain true and profound spirituality and humanity. Today mankind is living in a state of inhumanity, into which it has sunk because of wrong thinking and thoughtlessness and also because of the two horribly inhumane [world] wars that were fought with horribly inhumane weapons. We must all jointly experience the yearning to become humane humans again. The Jewish and the Christian religions share the ideal of profound humanity. In the Jewish religion it is the prophet Amos who first demands humanity, and the prophet Hosea who first announces it as God's will in the verse, "I want mercy and not sacrifices," which is quoted by Jesus. All people belong together if they understand that the major problem of our time is that we [must] become truly human. They are heading toward the same goal in the history of mankind; they want to emerge from the darkness and walk in the light. If you feel that we have this goal in common, then you may regard me as an honorary member of your congregation.

~

To Bertrand Russell, London
Lambarene
18 May 1962

[*e*]

The world needs unyielding thinkers to make it aware of its possible annihilation by atomic weapons. Einstein was the first thinker in this line. He knew that others would continue this resistance after him. As one of the most important of these unyielding people, you, dear friend, have launched the struggle. You have the power to encourage the population to follow the path that you have smoothed. You have brought the anti-nuclear struggle in England further than it has advanced in any other country. You may be certain that this is important for any country where resistance is being waged against these weapons.

~

To Prof. Dr. Mayumi Haga, Tokyo
Lambarene
2 June 1962

Dear Dr. Mayumi Haga,

Thank you so much for sending me the offprint of your contribution to Bähr's book. I am deeply moved by what you write about the significance of my ethics, in which West and East meet.

By the time I completed my book on civilization and ethics, the chapter on Indian thinking had become so long that there was no room for it in that form. I therefore decided to publish it separately under the title *Indian Thought and Its Development*,[1] which was a gamble since I was not part of the group of European "indologists," the scholars of India thought. My book appeared, and Europe's indologists behaved indulgently toward the outsider and newcomer in indology.

After returning from Africa, I made contact with Gandhi through my dearest British friend, a reverend, who was also an intimate friend of Gandhi's and lived with him in India.[2] When I was visiting England, this mutual friend went through my book on Indian thinkers with me to make sure there were no errors. That certainly put my mind at ease.

How I would have loved to visit India, but I didn't have the money, much less the time. Ever since my hospital grew large, I have been able to take few vacations and no lengthy ones. However, for many years now I have maintained a spiritual rapport with India, and I have made the marvelous discovery that the idea of reverence for life has brought West and East together in a highly promising spiritual kinship. The kind essay on me that you have contributed to Bähr's book is vivid evidence of this unity.[3]

~

To Alfred Kern, organ builder, Strasbourg-Kronenburg
Lambarene
1 July 1962

Dear Herr Kern,

I am delighted that you have a chance of getting the Neudorf organ [project] and that my dear old organist friend from Paris likes the Gunsbach organ. May I ask you to begin installing the two pedal registers in the Gunsbach organ (dulcian 16 and furniture stop) as soon as possible. I expect the franc to fall, and I would not care to put up with a corresponding price rise. The price of the two registers together is 250,000 francs. I am delighted that Callinet organs are once more being expertly restored in Alsace and Switzerland. There is a Callinet organ in Rouffach. If it is restored, try to familiarize yourself with the work.

To the pediatricians in Münster, Westphalia
Lambarene
August 1962

Dear Colleagues,

Many, many thanks for your [donation for Lambarene]. Your help was a big and lovely surprise for me. I was deeply touched. As I am writing this to you, Professor Mai is sitting near me, explaining how this large collective gift came about.

It means a great deal to me to have him here in Lambarene. At the hospital everything is going smoothly except that it keeps growing and growing, which forces me to add another building or two every year. I have to supervise the construction work myself, which requires a great deal of time and effort. Assigning the work to a construction firm would be very expensive. Workers for the construction include the companions of patients being treated at the hospital. We can build here only during the dry season, our winter, south of the equator. This period begins in early July and ends during the first few days of October. It is absolutely impossible to build during the rainy season. We get only brief, heavy thunderstorms, no continuous precipitation. Totally rainy days are unknown here.

To G. Schirmer, music publisher, New York
Lambarene
27 August 1962

Dear Herr Heinsheimer,

At the moment my friend and colleague Edouard Nies-Berger is visiting me in Lambarene. We keep talking about the Widor/ Schweitzer edition of Bach's organ works,[1] the last two volumes of which have yet to be published. I am very anxious for them to come out. You have already printed the texts. All that is missing is the prefaces. The texts of the prefaces for the two volumes already exist. In 1951 and 1955 I completed the final drafts with my colleague Herr Nies-Berger, who was visiting me in Gunsbach. These texts, which are ready to go to press, are now in Herr Nies-Berger's hands.

Here in Lambarene I am in no position to deal with the publication. I am too deeply absorbed in running the hospital, and during those nocturnal hours when I can wield my pen, I have to do philosophical work.

Regarding the publication of the last two volumes of Bach's organ works, I suggest that you issue them with the help of Herr Nies-Berger. The two of us worked on the texts of the prefaces in Gunsbach, and I know that Herr Nies-Berger can assume responsibility for the printing. I propose to have him oversee the publication of those two volumes.

I regret that I am unable to collaborate because this edition of Bach's organ works is very close to my heart. I recall the many hours that my dear mentor Widor and I spent working together on this project.

It is a great satisfaction for me that the preface to the sixth volume could include my discussion on performing Bach's ornamentations, which offers musicians an authentic and simple solution to the problems.

⌒

To Prof. Dr. Hans Walter Bähr, Tübingen
Lambarene
24 November 1962

Dear Friend,

First of all, thank you for *The Voice of Mankind*.[1] This book preserves the spirit of people who continue to have something to say to mankind. This is a deeply moving work.

My loveliest correspondence was with Carmen Silva.[2] I also had interesting correspondence with Pauline Metternich, the widow of the Austrian envoy to the court of Napoleon III. I met her at an early point. She and Countess Pourtalès were intimate friends of Empress Eugénie. Countess Pourtalès, who lived near Strasbourg, gave me a great deal of help when I founded the hospital.

My religious views meant something to her. I also exchanged letters with Pauline Metternich after the first war. She was a noble and lively woman. It was she who persuaded Emperor Napoleon to have the Paris Grand Opera produce Wagner's *Tannhäuser*. However, the performance was hissed and hooted. . . . Pauline Metternich was so enraged at the cabal that she smashed her expensive fan on the edge of the imperial balcony. And when Wagner was utterly impoverished in Paris (he could never handle money), he stayed at the mansion of the Austrian legation, where he managed to compose again in peace and quiet. Both these women had an influence on me. When I left for Africa in 1913, I took leave of Countess Pourtalès in Paris. She was ill, and she said to me, "We shall never meet again, but I feel fine about letting you sail to Africa. I know that you will be successful in your undertaking. It is in your nature to achieve success and happiness."

I am constantly involved in fighting nuclear arms, chiefly through letters going to distant lands because distant lands are still completely uninterested in this issue. The people there feel that it does not concern them.

I maintain close and steady contact with Lord Russell, with whom I was friendly even before the atomic era. His Easter marches are a grand and highly effective idea.

Best,
Albert Schweitzer

~

To Gerald Götting, Berlin

Lambarene
10 December 1962

Dear Friend,

The hands of the clock are moving toward midnight. . . . What wonderful Christmas figures you have sent me! Genuine, noble carvings! Real traditional art. I don't know how to thank you for this splendid Christmas gift. Ah, and you went to such great expense for me. All I am sending you is a loving Christmas greeting. During these past few days I have had to work hard, with the pen and without it. The construction work is very demanding. I am adding a ten-room structure to the Sans-Souci building. This extension is in the very same style as the present Sans-Souci building.

And my correspondence keeps growing and growing. I am unable to cope with it, even with help from Mathilde [Kottmann] and Ali [Silver], and even if I devote myself to it every day until midnight and all of Sunday. And I receive such dear letters from people to whom the ethics of reverence of life means something. I simply cannot grasp the fact that I was privileged to take this step. St. Francis took it, but he expressed it in splendid poetry. People viewed it as poetry that belonged to history. I was privileged to announce it in ordinary words, as a demand made on thinking. But why was I granted this?

My deepest thanks for the many copies of our little book.[1]

Best,

Albert Schweitzer

~

To Prof. Dr. Robert Minder

Lambarene

20 December 1962

[On Minder's book, *Culture and Literature in Germany and France*,[1] with his discussion of the image of the parsonage in German literature, which he wrote for the Mainz Academy of Science and Literature]

Dear Friend,

Your essays are very solid and very interesting. I have enjoyed reading them and rereading them. The writing is also very beautiful and natural. I am delighted that you connect civilization and literature. They belong together, which is something that people have not always realized.

Your article on parsonages is very successful! I myself know what I owe to the parsonage and its atmosphere. . . . I was well acquainted with Christoph Schrempf. When we were children, our mother read aloud to us from Wildermuth's book on Swabian parsonages.

I witnessed the boy scout period because the boy scouts got in touch with me as someone who would understand them. There was something deeply poignant about the movement when it was still fresh. I was very close friends with René Schickele. He was noble and pro-

found, but very complicated. You know about my friendship with
Romain Rolland.

How kind of you to mention *Memoirs of Childhood and Youth* among
the parsonage books. This little book was written quite by accident.
I jotted it down within two weeks, during February 1924, shortly
before my second trip to Lambarene; I did it as a favor for a friend
of mine, a Swiss pastor.

Let me congratulate you on these essays on civilization and literature. Your wide readings and your sound judgment have empowered
you to create something that is both interesting and meaningful.

Your style is highly readable. I am proud of my pupil. Andler
[professor of German at the University of Paris], your predecessor,
whom I knew quite well, would be overjoyed.

~

To Abbé Pierre, Charenton [France; temporarily: Lima]
                        Lambarene
                        22 December 1962

[f]

Dear Abbé Pierre,

Thank you from the bottom of my heart for your fine letter. I am
glad to have an address in order to send you a sign of life no matter
what corner of the world you may find yourself in. So now you're in
Lima. My uncle[1] had a large business in Lima, La Casa Théodore
Harth. The current director, Monsieur Harth in Paris, is my kinsman
and my friend. Through my uncle I got to know the poverty in Lima,
which is the poverty of South America. And now you are fighting
that poverty and are awakening the younger generation.[2] As for me,
I am always at my post in the hospital and in the world, in my struggle
against nuclear arms. I'm still fit as a fiddle.

Come and vacation here whenever you like. And if you lack the
money for the trip, let me know. I'll manage to dig it up.

~

To Herr Elster

>   [Lambarene]
>   30 January 1963
>   [archival copy]

Dear Herr Elster,

Every morning life confronts me with realities that I have to cope with: making broken pumps work, improving roads, replacing walls that have become useless, conquering the weeds in the plantation, and keeping the hospital properly afloat. My heart has to make sure that it doesn't succumb to old age. . . .

Seldom has a human being been so fortunate. I am able to work day after day: in the hospital, on the construction site, in the plantation, with my mind, and with my pen. . . . I have twenty dear coworkers, and the common goal of our work is: helping to fight pain, saving lives. Sometimes I'm embarrassed at being able to do such beautiful work and having such a beautiful old age. April 18 will be the fiftieth anniversary of my life under equatorial palms.

~

To Mr. Jack Anderson, *Parade Magazine*, Washington
>   [1963]

It has been estimated that with the innumerable and tremendous atomic weapons that both East and West have at their disposal today, over 200 million people would be wiped out on the very first day of a nuclear war between these two [super]powers. This implies that no political problem existing between them and no political event can be important enough for them to wage an atomic war, in which both sides would be risking casualties and annihilation that would challenge their very survival.

Any policy that ignores the fact of the horrible destructive power of today's nuclear arms is nothing but nonsensical adventurism.

We have no choice but to recognize that in order to lead a humane existence again, we must mutually resolve to abolish atomic weapons, on which we have already spent and would like to continue spending billions upon billions.

The great problem in the negotiations on abolishing nuclear arms is that the two negotiating parties do not consider each other trustworthy enough to honor the agreement. Controls on their adherence to the agreements concluded in the negotiations cannot replace trust-worthiness. This is made obvious by the lengthy and fruitless nego-tiations. Trust between nations can be created only by a solid public opinion that demands the abolition of nuclear arms.

≈

To Prof. Werner Hartke, president of the German Academy of Sciences, Berlin

Lambarene
3 February 1963

Dear President Hartke,

Thank you so much for your kind lines regarding my eighty-eighth birthday. Please tell the members of the Academy that your con-gratulations have brought me a great deal of pleasure. It was a great experience for me, while still young, to become an honorary member of the Prussian Academy of Sciences at the suggestion of Professor Harnack.[1] I was not his student, he barely knew me (so far as I could see). How did he decide on me? I was unable to explain it. It was only afterward that we got to know each other properly. When I told him I was working on a book on the Apostle Paul's intellectual world, he said to me, "I'd like to read the galleys." He sent me the proofs, with his revisions, when I was in Lambarene. He had written on the last sheet, "Everything fine." Four weeks later he died. . . .

An American who had provided the wherewithal to rebuild the University of Heidelberg became an honorary member at the same time I did.[2] I found the thorough work done at the sessions very interesting.

As a student I was already at home in Berlin, in the home of Ernst Curtius. His son was district director of Colmar.[3] I was close friends with him and his wife. They and their children often visited the parsonage in Gunsbach.

At the moment we keep thinking about the great plight of people in Europe, who are suffering from the dreadful cold and the storms. We are downright ashamed that we simply live on without having to worry about weather. We are almost afraid to open the newspapers, which report on the crisis appearing from north to far in the south.

I am writing to you on this Sunday afternoon when I am on duty at my desk in the large consulting room.

Please extend my best regards to the members of the Academy.

~

To Fränzi Hunziker, high school student, Solothurn
Lambarene
9 February 1963

Dear Fränzi,

Thank you for your dear letter and for your thoughts on religion. I have read and reread what you have written, and I was delighted by your introspective conception of Christianity and the personality of Jesus. You are right in viewing Christianity as an introspective rapport with our Lord Jesus and with God. Christianity is introspectiveness. It is damaged by any exteriorization. And all introspective Christianity is active. This is what wins people's hearts.

And the Christian avowal of faith is the Lord's Prayer. How moving that Jesus taught us this prayer, which says everything that is important in the Christian religion.

I am fairly well acquainted with the world's religions, and none of them has a similar collective prayer such as the one proclaimed by Jesus.

Send me an occasional sign of life on your typewriter so that my overstrained eyes can read it without difficulty.

Yes, get your high school diploma. My best to your parents.

Best,
Albert Schweitzer

~

To Prof. Dr. Walter Bähr, Tübingen
Lambarene
4 March 1963

Dear Friend,

April 18 will mark the fiftieth anniversary of my arrival at the equator and the founding of the hospital. We are planning a quiet and modest celebration. I would be overjoyed if you could visit us at this time, so I am now inviting you to come for April 18 and to stay as long as you like and are able.

If for any reason you cannot make it by April 18, then come later. It is quite an experience getting to know life on the equator and in the jungle, and it is valuable for me to have you here to discuss a number of things with you.

Give my best to Spranger. How lovely it would be if he could come along. There is enough room because of all our construction work. I fondly recall that during my first year as a student it dawned on me that I belong to Tübingen theologically and philosophically.

Much love,
Albert Schweitzer

~

To Dr. Robert Weiss, Strasbourg

[Lambarene, 1963]¹

My strategy consists of never responding to any attack of any kind whatsoever. This has always been my principle, and I have stuck to it loyally. In the long run no one can fight against silence. It is an invincible opponent. Nor does anyone have to defend me. It is my lot to go my way without combat. It is my lot to pave the way for the spirit of reverence for life, which is also the spirit of peace. I am quite dumbfounded by the fact that I have been granted such a splendid calling; as a result, I go my way, spiritually unhindered. A grand, calm music roars within me. I am permitted to see the ethics of reverence for life starting to make its way through the world, and this elevates me beyond anything that anyone can reproach me for or do to me.

~

To Eduard Spranger, Tübingen

Lambarene
8 March 1963

Dear Friend,

Inspired by the Black Forest, you have responded to my letter with a poignantly loving letter. I do not know how to express what I feel. I, too, enjoyed the Black Forest. When I had the wherewithal, I built the house in Königsfeld for my wife [and] child. I wanted my daughter to grow up in the atmosphere of the Moravian Brethren. I spent two visits to Europe in the Black Forest, and I spent many lovely hours strolling through the woods. My book on the mysticism of the apostle Paul was written during my second sojourn in Königsfeld.

But the nicest coincidence is that you and I both advocated a humanitarian civilization before we ever met.

The buildings that are now being constructed under my supervision will contain four single rooms and three double rooms, as well as seven rooms for the staff, which has gotten larger. We also have to build storerooms for the medicines, for rice (twenty tons) and dried cod and all manner of things. I cannot leave such planning and building to anyone else. There can be no disorder in the hospital because we have no rooms for storing things, including the most unbelievable things. And along with all that, I have to find time to keep thoroughly abreast of the nuclear arms problem. To do so I have to set aside at least one and a half hours during the day or at night. Not only do I have to read letters and magazines, I also have to take notes (newspaper clippings or with my pen), so that I can remember the facts and the gist of speeches or explanations. One cannot talk about an issue without thorough knowledge.

I relax by keeping up with philosophy. I love the pre-Socratics. They are great men with their ideas and their plans. It was a tremendous intellectual event when the notion of the atom came up in their era.

As I write this at my desk in the large consulting room, a cat and her kittens are sleeping on the table. Peering through large palm trees, I can make out the Ogowe River 130 feet away.

Best,
Albert Schweitzer

~

To Queen Juliana of Holland, The Hague
Lambarene
26 April 1963

[f]

May I extend my profound gratitude to Your Majesty for her congratulations on the fiftieth anniversary of my arrival in Lambarene. I regard it as an advantage that I could establish this hospital during the period of the great struggle against sleeping sickness. The project has grown far beyond my expectations. It evolved because of donations from my friends and because of the doctors and nurses who came to help me. The capable Dutch nurses have played a major role in the history of the hospital because of the work they have accomplished and the spirit they have developed here. I owe Holland a great debt of thanks.

In my heart I also treasure the memory of your mother.

May I ask Your Majesty to accept my devotion and best wishes.

〜

To the Special School, Bad Freienwald, German Democratic Republic

[Lambarene, 1963]

I am delighted to authorize the use of my name for the special school. Thank you for your kindness and for the honor you are bestowing on me. As a doctor I know the importance of a special school. During my youth I witnessed the emergence of such institutions. . . .

〜

To Prof. Eduard Spranger, Tübingen
Lambarene
5 May 1963

Dear Friend,

This note is to tell you that I often think of you. I know that you are very worried about your sick wife and that you have found no possibility of a breather.[1] You are walking through the valley of darkness, and I can do nothing for you but think about you with deep friendship and deep sympathy.

I am writing to you at my table in the large consulting room. "The old man" is on duty on Sunday afternoon. That is an old law in my hospital.

Nature barely changes here in the course of the year. That is something wonderful and beneficial. The trees never lose their leaves. There is never a series of rainy days, indeed no rainy day at all. The tornadoes generally come at night and last for an hour. By 10:00 A.M. the ground is dry again: The powerful sun has lapped up the water.

I don't know when we shall meet again. Along with my duties in the hospital and at the construction site, I am constantly working with my brain and my pen. Day after day I am immersed in the problem of atomic weapons. We are in great danger. Kennedy feels it too: New nations have nuclear arms, and if an atomic war breaks out somewhere, the two great atomic powers might have to join the fray. Kennedy no longer regards the NATO countries with atomic weapons as fellow fighters and worthy allies but merely as minor powers with nuclear arms that can trigger an atomic war. As far as he is concerned, the devil can take their atomic weapons.

A further explanation has been fulfilled: Stockpiling nuclear arms today spells economic ruin, which cannot be prevented in any way.

≈

To Mr. R. J. Vogels, vice president of Royal Dutch Airlines, The Hague

Lambarene
8 July 1963

Dear Mr. Vogels,

I am deeply touched by your warm letter on the fiftieth anniversary of my hospital on the equator. Thank you from the bottom of my heart. I sometimes think about the large K.L.M. airplane that bears my name. How I would love to fly on it someday. But I don't know when this will be possible. I haven't been to Europe since 1959, and I have no idea when I will return. My huge workload in Lambarene does not allow me to travel.

≈

To Prof. Dr. Walter Bähr, Tübingen

Lambarene
25 July 1963

Dear Friend,

I am sending you a strange little book.[1] India is noting that the West is developing an ethics that overlaps with Indian ethics in that it deals not only with relations between humans but with making it a duty for humans to be good to all living creatures. The Indian thinkers developed this universal ethics by negating the world and life. I have reached this ethics by a deeper affirmation of life and the world. . . . They are delighted that West and East have joined in their ethics and share the common goal of creating a living ethical civilization. . . .

The Indian thinkers have been studying me ever since I published *Indian Thought and Its Development*.[2] Now they are astonished that the West is developing a philosophy that deals with our treatment of all living creatures. It is a great surprise for them that the Western affirmation of life and the world is coming to the same ethics as they are. They are welcoming this mentality. . . . I hope you are vacationing somewhere.

~

To Dr. Hermann Baur, Basel

Lambarene
[July 1963]

If ethics in its basic form is the manifested respect that we owe to other human beings, then it is inconceivable that it concerns only human beings. By its very nature, ethics refers to all living creatures. Only this broad ethics can be justified. Interhuman ethics alone cannot really be justified intellectually. This was sensed by Kant, who therefore characterized the ethical as an existing, categorical imperative. In so doing he posited it as something inexplicable. Positing ethics as inexplicable is merely a stopgap measure because ethics that concerns only interhuman relations cannot be justified. In contrast, a complete ethics, as the result of human thinking and feeling, can be understood and justified.

~

To John F. Kennedy, president of the United States; a parallel letter was sent to Nikita Khrushchev, secretary general of the Communist Party of the U.S.S.R.

[This letter was prompted by the American-Soviet pact of 1963, which was signed in Moscow that August.[1]]

25 August 1963

I am writing to congratulate you and to thank you for having the vision and courage to initiate a policy of world peace.

At last a ray of light is visible in the darkness in which mankind is seeking its path; this glimmer gives us hope that the darkness will yield to the light.

The East-West pact that bans nuclear testing in the atmosphere and under water is one of the greatest events in world history.

It allows us to hope that atomic war between East and West can be prevented.

When I heard about the Moscow agreement, I thought of my friend Einstein, with whom I was allied in the battle against nuclear arms. When he died in Princeton, he was in despair.

Thanks to your vision and courage, I am now in a position to observe that the world has taken its first step on the road to peace.

~

To Prof. Dr. Eduard Spranger, Tübingen
                    Lambarene
                    8 September 1963

Dear Friend,

This note is meant to tell you that I am with you in thought. I am devastated by the news that you are ill. I can never forget what you have done for me.

I have learned from your writings that you, too, see ultimate human perfection as the true spiritual goal and that this has been the essence of your work. Because of the way I have lived my life, we did not meet personally until a late point. It was a wonderful event for both of us. Together we raised our voices to educate human beings in humanity.

I had to say that to you once more. We have been brothers-in-arms. I cannot tell you how important it was for me to get to know you.

Now I think about you in your suffering. I wish I could be with you and tell you everything that you mean to me and how greatly I have appreciated and loved you. I will not give up hope that your condition can improve.

Ah, if only you could see the huge palms outside my window in the glow of the sun. I hope that you will not be denied the benefit of sleep and that I can keep sending you loving letters.

                    Devotedly yours,
                    Albert Schweitzer

~

To Dr. Hans Hartmann, Berlin
                    Lambarene
                    19 February 1964

Dear Herr Hartmann,

Nietzsche compelled me to keep being concerned with the problem of ethics and the emergence of an ethical civilization. Thus, by the fall of 1915, I developed the notion of an ethics of reverence for life. It dawned on me that European philosophy deals purely with half an ethics. All it demands is kind behavior and mercy toward other people. A complete ethics, however, requires kindness and mercy toward all life, for any living creature can suffer. Kindness knows no limits. It is boundless. Only a profound and complete ethics is able to create an ethical civilization. Through studying Nietzsche I came to realize that an ethics focusing solely on mankind is incomplete and cannot really be justified. Schopenhauer was right when he said, "Preaching ethics is easy, justifying ethics is hard." Only a complete ethics can be justified. There is no justifying the semi-ethics of European philosophy.

Please forgive this long disquisition. I felt that you'd be interested.

You are right: The Hartmanns come from Upper Alsace. I was close friends with the Hartmanns who owned large factories in the Munster Valley, since Gunsbach is near Munster. The factory still stands, but the family has died out. The Hartmanns of Munster were friendly with Napoleon [III], who came to visit them in Munster.

~

To Franz Ruh, Freiburg im Breisgau
                [Lambarene]
                26 March 1964

I was a great admirer of César Franck. He reacquainted French organists with the correct organ style.

I myself became a student of Widor's at the age of eighteen. I owe him a lot. I was also friendly with other Parisian organists, especially Vierne. As a student in Strasbourg I fought together with Rupp, the organist at the Garaison church, for the preservation of the Silbermann organs. The Alsatian organists were unaware of the value of these organs. The church authorities also felt that a modern organ had to be better than an old one, and they refused to have anything to do with Rupp and me. After all, we had no status, we were just simple organists. We were told that the church's organ affairs were none of our business. As a result, a number of Silbermann organs were lost, so we appealed to the towns and parishes that were supposed to subsidize the new organs, and we enlightened them. That put an end to ten years of fighting. Widor, who followed the trail blazed by César Franck, created marvelous symphonies for the organ. He was born in Alsace. His father worked for a competent organ builder in Upper Alsace. He had emigrated there from Hungary. Later on he moved to southern France, and Widor attended the Paris Conservatory. Eventually he became organist at the Church of St. Sulpice, whose organ was a masterpiece of the great Parisian organ builder Cavaillé-Coll, who also built the organ at the cathedral of Notre Dame. You could run into Cavaillé-Coll every Sunday on the organ loft of St. Sulpice. I learned a great deal from him.

Silbermann, while headquartered in Strasbourg, also built organs in Baden. They have been meticulously restored.

~

To Prof. Dr. Hans Besch

Lambarene
[1964]

Dear Professor Besch,

For years now I have stopped worrying about the chitchat that Bach wrote his works only because his position obligated him to do so, and not in a religious spirit. I assumed that this unfounded opinion would die out of its own accord. This struck me as self-evident since I had been dealing with Bach's works for many years. How childish the opinion that Bach had no heartfelt relationship to the organ and that the performance of the *St. Matthew Passion* was merely a burden for him. How can such foolish views endure in Germany? The more I immersed myself in Bach's works, the more I realized that he wrote them with his heart. Bach left us an inexhaustible wealth of profound religious music. We cannot make those who do not feel this understand, nor do we need to make them understand. I cannot believe that anyone can possibly go along with this frivolous opinion.

When I was an organist playing at performances of cantatas and passions in Germany and abroad, I never encountered an organist or soloist who was not convinced of the depth and piety of Bach's music. The Parisian organists were in awe of the deep spirituality of Bach's choral preludes. I simply cannot understand why anyone has to struggle for the recognition of the true Bach, especially in Bach's homeland.

Warmly and sorrowfully yours,
Albert Schweitzer

He who has ears to hear with understands Bach.

Dear Professor Besch,

You can do what you like with my letter. I know the passages that are cited to demonstrate Bach's worldliness. If the occasion demanded it, he would add new texts to the music, and whatnot. But this cannot persuade us to understand the depth and spirit of his music in any way. You may show my letter to the Evangelical Academy, and you can add my signature to the petition. I served you poorly in 1929 when I advised you not to write any piece on Bach's faith and piety. All I meant was that you should not try to prove Bach's piety by quoting his statements, for that would be a difficult task. I meant and still mean that his piety has to be proved on the basis of the works themselves and the impression they make on us. The rest of the world doesn't understand that in Germany the pious spirit of Bach's music is being challenged. If you can send me anything about the development of the debate, I would be delighted to see it.

Give my best to Professor Schering.

Don't add Dr. Dr. Dr. to my name. One is enough.

~

To Prof. Hermann Mai, M.D., Münster, Westphalia
Lambarene
4 May 1964

Dear Friend,

You write, "Is there enough room for me and could you stand my visiting you at Christmas and remaining until 15 January?" You, the hospital, and we belong together. It goes without saying that we should get together as much as possible and as long as possible. That is what logic and the heart say. I am delighted that it will be possible for you to visit me.

12 June 1964

After a long interruption I continue:

Now for the water pump issue. Your small motor is doing a marvelous job, as you have learned from Dr. Müller. We are happy that, as Dr. Müller tells us, you can also send us a large water pump. He recently gave you the necessary data. As far as water goes, we now have a pump on a raft on every level of water; the raft can be anchored, and water can be pumped from the river even when huge sandbanks emerge during the dry season. This is a great step forward.

We can thus get water from the river at every season of the year. After all, river water, taken at a certain distance from the shore, is the purest water. If pure river water can also serve as drinking water, then our water problem is solved in the simplest way. In regard to all water problems, please write directly to Dr. Müller, who will then tell me about the problem and discuss it with me.

With my deepest thanks to you and my best wishes to your family,

Albert Schweitzer

~

To Pastor Willy Bremi and Dr. Hermann Baur, Basel

Lambarene

12 June 1964

My sermons are somewhere in Gunsbach. I'll write Frau Martin and tell her to make them available to you. Incidentally, I'll be seeing her in Lambarene at the end of this month. But please be strict with me and publish only things that are really significant.[1] Many of the sermons were written at night because I couldn't get to them during the day. Here is something that may interest you.

When I was an auxiliary preacher at St. Nicholas's Church, I asked the old ministers at the church to allow me to remain at the altar after the service and to spend ten or twelve minutes reading my selections from the Old or New Testament out loud in order to make people more familiar with the Bible.

The ministers were kind enough to acquiesce, and both they and I were surprised that the congregation enjoyed it. After all, theoretically, we Protestants believe in the Bible, but we are unfamiliar with it because at services only the verses that the pastor wants to preach about are read aloud to the congregation. The worshipers greatly appreciated the reading of the Bible; some of them even complimented me by saying that they came more for the Bible reading than for my sermon. I am still convinced that the reading of the Bible gets short shrift in our Protestant services.

~

To Dr. Hermann Baur, Basel

Lambarene

12 June 1964

Let me tell you how deeply moved I am that you are dealing with the publication of [my] sermons![1]

It is so wonderful that Babel and Munz have joined the committee.

I set great store by Babel. I am delighted that active and competent people are on the committee. I am pinning great hopes on Dr. Walter Munz[2] for the continuation of the hospital. It is a great comfort for me to know that he is coming back.

What sort of creature is that Mr. Gerald McKnight with his book, *Verdict on Schweitzer!*[3] How utterly delightful. Sign nothing. Let the heathen rage. Send me the book.

~

To Pierre Leclerc, Adventist Youth, Rouen
                              Lambarene
                              12 June 1964

[f]

Dear Monsieur Leclerc,

You wish to give my name to your mission. It already bears a lovely name, which means "struggle for the advent of Jesus." Why give my poor name to your group if it already has the lovely name of "mission"? Your present name indicates that you are trying to make Jesus known. Why add a second name? Please forgive this old geezer for making these remarks. In true Christianity everything should be simple. We seek to win men's hearts for Jesus through our lives, through our love for Jesus. We await His coming into our hearts and into those of other men. May God grant us the strength to be faithful. You were kind enough to contact me. It is the spirit that is important. I feel that I am in contact with you through the spirit, through the nature of our Christianity. Let us remain united and faithful.

My heartfelt wishes, and my thanks for your message.

~

To Pastor Strege, Wülfrath, Rhineland
                              Lambarene
                              25 June 1964[1]

Dear Friend,

The book *Being in God* [by M. Strege, 1937] and the new *Reverence for Life* are lying in front of me. I have to thank you for the latter. It is very lucid and beautiful in its simplicity. I find it very valuable that friends have been advocating this complete ethics. Their efforts have greatly contributed to getting it recognized and gaining more and more recognition for it. It has even drawn the attention of Indian thinkers. They are of the opinion that this ethics is akin to Buddha's ethics, which is actually the case, for Buddha's ethics likewise demands compassion for all creatures. The Indians feel that a time will come, a philosophy will come, in which Indian and European thinkers will walk together because they share a deep common ethics.

I haven't been to Europe for years, and I will probably never go there again. The work I have to do here does not permit me to travel. Once again, many, many thanks for both books.

> Best,
> Albert Schweitzer

~

To Aymà, publishing house, Barcelona
> Lambarene
> 30 June 1964

Dear Sir,

Thank you for your letter of 17 June 1964. I am delighted that you intend to publish a Spanish translation of my book, *Indian Thought and Its Development*. No Spanish edition exists as yet. In regard to the negotiations for this publication, you do not have to contact any publisher or agent. Negotiate directly with me. That would be the easiest way. I would be delighted if a Spanish edition of this book came out.[1] When I was an organist, I visited Barcelona several times to play at recitals of the Orféo Català, and I still maintain contact [with] my Catalan friends.

~

To Prof. Dr. Helmut Thielicke, Hamburg
> [Lambarene]
> 20 July 1964[1]

You have compiled a vast amount of material, and you are allowing my opinion to be heard. What I found particularly significant was your way of coping with the issue of nuclear war and nuclear peace— a problem that has been occupying me for many years. In 1955, Einstein, with whom I was friendly, and I campaigned against atomic weapons. The deplorable thing is that people cannot be induced to deal with this issue. They refuse to realize the spiritual necessity of abolishing nuclear arms. They try to find solutions based on practical considerations—an approach that cannot succeed. It is my belief that we must first become more profound people, for whom military and nuclear weapons are no longer viable. That was also Einstein's conviction.

I was very interested to read and reread your discussion on the problem of war and peace. You focus on the issue of the right direction and analyze it in detail. This is a major undertaking and a necessary one. And you also make an effort to delineate this path rather than merely hint at it. I tend more to get people to think about who and what they are in order to find the road to peace. But I have not yet gotten the path clear enough in my own mind. How I would have loved to thrash out this major issue with you.

~

To Les Editions Vogel, Geneva
[Lambarene]
20 July 1964

Dear Sirs,

I was acquainted with Buddhism, which identifies ethics as boundless compassion. However, this compassion was not active. It was merely an object of meditation. It consisted of thoughts but not deeds. Schopenhauer wanted to implant this meditative compassion in Europe's ethics, but he failed. Having no roots in European ethics, this compassion withered. It had to sprout directly in the world-affirming ethics, deepening and ennobling it. Nevertheless, the emergence of a complete, world-affirming ethics was an event for Indian thinking.

The time has come for a universal philosophy, and it will deal with the fate of mankind. Meditation and collective activity will guide mankind to the right path.

~

To Prof. Dr. Hans Walter Bähr, Tübingen
Lambarene
29 August 1964

Dear Friend,

Many thanks for your letter. I am deeply touched that you again want to publish something about my ideas, as if you hadn't already sacrificed enough time for me! But do as you think best. I'll leave it up to you, for I have so much to do here that I don't see any light at the end of the tunnel. I like your plan.[1] So: "Good luck!"

I'm in good health except that I have to work more than I can. I have to work a lot with my pen, and I also have to build a lot. And the correspondence keeps growing by the month. My worn-out eyes cannot read everything. You must all be indulgent with me. The only reason I can scribble anything at all is that I use the steel nibs I've been sent from America. Writing a small but legible script is a major problem.

For several years now, summer and autumn, I've had a lot of visitors from all over the world, chiefly America, as well as all kinds of globe-trotters. And we have to feed and house all these people. Occasionally we have up to fifteen or twenty dinner guests. I have eight rooms for visitors. Some guests are very interesting, but I don't have enough time to converse with them.

Thank you for your clear presentation of the plan for the book. I was deeply moved by your study[2] on the ethics of reverence for life.

Best,
Albert Schweitzer

~

To an ecumenical Christian conference in Erfurt
Lambarene
9 September 1964

My heartfelt wishes for the Catholic and Protestant Christians gathered in Erfurt is that their efforts for peace may be crowned with success. We must not let ourselves be discouraged by the difficulties we are encountering. The Gospel commands us to advocate peace in all areas. We must strive in the spirit of Jesus to work for peace in everything. In this respect, our time is making greater demands on us than we have previously realized. The events of our time demand that we become conscious of that. A new age has to come, and new things must be accomplished by us and by those who come after us, through the spirit of Jesus, which is always powerful. It is only with this knowledge and with this desire and hope that we can take the right path.

May Jesus, our Master, illumine us on the road to peace.

~

To Pastor Dr. Hans Pribnow, Hanau
Lambarene
6 October 1964

Dear Friend,

I am very interested to hear your opinion that the portrait of Jesus is connected to the one in the Qumran texts. Jesus takes Peter and the sons of Zebedee along to Gethsemane because the three of them have said they could die with him. He takes them along to Gethsemane so that they, like Him, may ask God to also spare them this suffering and dying. That is the sense of what Jesus says to the three of them when He arouses them from their sleep: "Awaken and pray that *you* may be spared this test." I am deeply moved by your comments on the effects of this image of Jesus.

One more request: Please send three copies of the little book to Frau Emmy Martin, Gunsbach, Upper Alsace, France. She will forward them to friends of mine.

Best,
Albert Schweitzer

≈

To President M. Corneil, Section for Legal Affairs, European Council [Reply to a questionnaire of 1 October 1964 sent to Nobel laureates]

Lambarene
14 October 1964

[f]

Dear Monsieur Corneil,

I am against the death penalty. We have no right to kill a human being. We have only the right to deprive him of his freedom if he constitutes a menace to human society.

≈

To Dr. Hermann Baur, Basel
Lambarene
8 November 1964

Dear Friend,

I have just received the list of lectures about me[1] that are now being given in Basel. It comes as a shock to me that I can be celebrating my ninetieth birthday as a fully active man. I find it overwhelming that I was able to figure out the path of my life and follow it. . . . (A new and better pen from the United States. . . .) Naturally, I can't write as I used to in earlier times, but nevertheless I *can* write again to some extent, which I did not dare hope for. How modest a man becomes. I am also delighted that the lectures include one on the significance of the choir in church construction. I've had to suffer from seeing churches being built that had nothing churchly about them; they were simply auditoriums with belfries. I had given up trying to get architects to see the light, and now I may hope. . . . Thus there are rays of sunlight in my twilight years. . . . I am writing you from my desk in the hospital, with a view of the river.

≈

From Schweitzer's declaration, *Words to Mankind*
[Lambarene, 1964]

White and nonwhite must strive toward the goal of meeting in an ethical spirit. Only then will true understanding be possible. Working toward the creation of this spirit constitutes a highly promising policy.

≈

To Dr. Harald Steffahn, Hamburg-Niedorf
Lambarene
10 November 1964

I don't know how to thank you for completing "Evening on the Ogowe" [an essay] in time so it could appear in the twenty-fifth circular letter for the Circle of Friends for my ninetieth birthday.[1] I just don't know how to thank you for this piece. Whenever I hear that someone is planning to write about me, I worry that even with the best of intentions he will not hit the right note. But you play calmly and confidently in the right key. You tune your lyre with verses by Mörike, whom I have admired since my youth; indeed, I grew up in German Romanticism and am still living in it. . . . Yes indeed, the Mörike lines, "My heart, oh, tell me," do speak to me. My mother, whose father was a pastor in the Munster Valley, loved German poetry, especially lyrical verse. This was a spiritual treasure that made us happy. We felt at home in this poetic world. The same was true of Alsatians who lived in Paris. I was very close friends with Romain Rolland. The French were very hard on him because he opposed the war. The period of moral decay provided a direction for Romain Rolland's thinking and mine, except that I was lucky enough to live, work, and meditate far from Europe.

Mathilde [Kottmann] and Ali [Silver] are faithfully portrayed, but Ali does not just attend to correspondence, she also takes care of financial matters. She deals with the bank, she prepares the payroll, and the like. All this used to be my bailiwick. And she came at the right time to replace me with her magnificent memory. Your accurate depictions of our life here are true and lovely.

Now I can tell you that I regard what you write about my life and thought as the best that can be written about them. I am astonished that you have such great knowledge and that you know how to present it. I can imagine how much work it took to compile this material and shape it.

Best,
Albert Schweitzer

My regards to your mother.

⌒

To Arnold Krieger

[Lambarene]
20 November 1964

Dear Herr Krieger,

Both of us are striving to get the people of our time to once again become true and feeling human beings for whom the ideal of humanity means something. We are not spoiled by our contemporaries. They have trouble getting out of the old thoughtlessness. This should not discourage us. We are advocating the ideal that should be recognized as valid. We are looking toward a new era. . . .

~

To Prof. Dr. Werner Ludwig, board of directors of the German Red
Cross, Dresden[1]

21 November 1964

Dear Dr. Ludwig,

I don't know how to thank you and your friends for everything you
are doing for my hospital. Special thanks to the men who have taken
care of the packing. For many years I did that work whenever I was
in Europe. And my best regards to the women who help with the
packing. Thank you, dear Dr. Ludwig, for what you have sent me
from the German Red Cross in the German Democratic Republic.
This text gives me a picture of you. I found it worthwhile getting a
glimpse of the work being done by the Red Cross. My regards to the
women who work at the Red Cross.

Here, everything is going smoothly except that the hospital keeps
getting bigger and bigger, which forces me to do new construction
work every year.

Building on the equator has its peculiar features. The houses have
to face east and west. That is also the sun's daily route. As a result,
the sun continually shines on the roof. It can never hit the side of a
building. There is constant shade on both sides. . . . So the chief rule
is: Never use a square floor plan; always build in a line, one room
behind the other. In this way each room has a strong natural draft.
The interior remains cool even during the hot season. I have learned
such things from old black construction workers.

~

To Prime Minister Lal Bahadur Shastri, New Delhi

Lambarene

29 November 1964

Dear Mr. Prime Minister,

My nephew, Pierre Paul Schweitzer from Washington,[1] who recently
went on a world tour in regard to some financial matters, visited
India where, as he has written me, you spoke to him about me. Thank
you for being interested in me because my ideas are known in India
and are consistent with Indian ideas.

I did not know Gandhi personally, but I maintained contact with him through a mutual British acquaintance.[2] Back then I was spending some time in Lausanne, Switzerland. When Nehru[3] was released, he visited me in Lausanne for a while. Luckily my wife was fluent in English. He spent several days with us. He was like a dreamer, awakening very gradually. During the first few days he never spoke.

So those were my Indian friends. Little by little they were joined by others because I was seriously studying Indian thought, to which I felt drawn.

The main thing is that India and the rest of the world are getting closer and closer to a deep ethical civilization, bringing an era in which no more wars will be fought and no more nuclear arms will be built. An entirely different spirit must come into the world and illuminate human beings. It is the living spirit of reverence for life which imbued the great Indian thinkers.

~

To Hans Fleischer, Leipzig

[Lambarene]
30 November 1964

What counts is *true piety*. Jesus taught it to us in pure, simple, and moving words in the Sermon on the Mount, in the Beatitudes, where He teaches us to become God's children and to live and strive as God's children. That is what matters. We cannot peer into sunlight. Its brightness is too powerful. We can only live in God's spirit. That is what Jesus taught us. He demonstrated it to us. He is our spiritual guide. God sent Him to us.

~

To Hélène Kazantzakis, Geneva

Lambarene
Christmas, 25 December 1964
[f]

My dear Friend,

I've received your letter on Christmas Day, and I am responding on the same day. I am deeply touched by what you write. I frequently think about your husband [the writer Nikos Kazantzakis], and I wish that the two of us could speak jointly to the world. Knowing him was a godsend. Do you ever reside in Greece?

Christmas under palm trees has a special appeal. I always regret that I have never been to Greece, the country of the thinkers who created true civilization. I have to content myself with battling for that civilization.

≈

To Hans Margolius, Miami

Lambarene
7 February 1965

Dear Hans Margolius, Dear Friend,

I've spent Sunday afternoon reading your aphorisms.[1] I have Sunday duty in the hospital. I'm at my desk in the hospital, peering through the palms at the large river flowing past us. It is so wonderful to be living in grand natural surroundings day after day. I have the peace and quiet to read your aphorisms, which you and your wife sent me. How kind of you to think of me.

I spent my ninetieth birthday in good health, surviving nicely. I got to see old friends who took the trouble to come and visit me. I myself never travel.

I've read and reread your *Philosophical Notes.* Your aphorisms are lovely and lucid in their wording. I was especially impressed by the fifth aphorism because you mention living creation. It is only by getting to know and deal with living creatures that we can become true human beings. *"La destinée de l'homme est de devenir toujours plus humain"* [Man's destiny is to become more and more human]. . . . I came to this conviction as a POW in Africa back in 1915, and I have stuck with it. . . .

I completely agree with your aphorism, "All deep things are simple." I am pleased that you have detailed it. I like the fact that aphorism no. 33 deals with the meaning of memory.

[Aphorism] 61. I set greater store by the debates between thinkers than Bergson, the spread of whose philosophy I witnessed. He was important in his day. A return to simplicity. That was how we saw him.

65. While I love Hermann Hesse, I do not agree with his notion that ideas should not be pitted against each other as sharply as possible. Our goal is to seek the truth.

74. Friendship with animals is something deep and marvelous. Animal friendships thrive in the silence of Lambarene. Three hippos

sometimes spend the night on the shore by the hospital because they know they won't be bothered.

With loving wishes to both of you. I will keep the aphorisms.

Best,

Albert Schweitzer

~

To the Asiatic Society, Calcutta, India

Lambarene

10 February 1965

Dear Herr Gupta,

Your kind letter of 6 January arrived in Lambarene only on February 2. It was too late for any of us to go to Calcutta and accept the Rabindranath Tagore medal in my stead. I greatly admired this thinker. Unfortunately, I cannot send anyone to receive this medal. I suggest that you send it to my house in Europe, in France. Alas, this is not as solemn an approach as it should be. The address is: Madame Emmy Martin, Maison du Dr. A. Schweitzer, Gunsbach.

I studied Indian philosophy early on, when I was attending the University of Strasbourg, Alsace, even though no course was being given on that subject. But then, around 1900, Europe started getting acquainted with Indian thought. Rabindranath Tagore became known as the great living Indian thinker. When I grew conversant with his teachings, they made a deep impact on me. In Germany it was the philosopher Arthur Schopenhauer who first recognized the significance of Indian thinking. A pupil of Schopenhauer's was director of the Mulhouse Secondary School in Alsace, which prepared students for the university. His name was Deecke. In this way I got to know Indian thinking at an early date. And by the time I completed my doctoral examination in philosophy, I was familiar with Indian thought. By then I was teaching at the University of Strasbourg. Focusing as I did on the problem of ethics, I reached the conclusion that Indian ethics is correct in demanding kindness and mercy not only toward human beings but toward all living creatures. Now the world is gradually realizing that compassion for living creatures is part of true ethics. I regret that I have never found time to visit India. In 1913 I founded my hospital in Africa, so there was no question of my traveling to India. But through letters and through one of my British friends I became familiar with Indian thinkers, especially Gandhi, who was the same age as I. Forgive me for writing you all this. I believe it may interest you.

~

To Pablo Casals

12 February 1965

[f]

Dear Friend,

I often think of you. I cannot correspond as much as I would like, but I have to regard it as a privilege that I still enjoy good health at ninety and that I am able to do my work. I read the touching lines about me in the program of the Esterhazy Orchestra. Thank you, I am deeply moved. I will never travel to Europe again. I was last there in May 1959. My hospital has become a huge enterprise, and I have to run it as long as I live. The assistant who takes care of my correspondence suggests that I send you a photograph of me that was taken in England. Here it is.

~

To the schoolchildren of Gunsbach

Lambarene

19 February 1965

[f]

Dear Monsieur Hamm, Dear Children,

Thank you from the bottom of my heart for your letter on my ninetieth birthday. I attended school in Gunsbach for many years, first elementary school, then high school.

The schoolmistress at the elementary school was Miss Goguel, the schoolmaster at the high school was Mr. Iltis. Miss Goguel came from Neu-Breisach. Mr. Iltis came from the Munster Valley. I was very shy when I arrived at school. But my friend Jean Demangeat, who was older than I, defended me when the bigger boys tried to bully me.

At first I was a bad student but very well behaved. Jean Demangeat helped me with my homework. Each school day began with a hymn and a prayer. The hymn was accompanied by a pump organ. Miss Goguel had a hard time playing the hymn properly. One day, when the room was empty, I played the hymn myself without the sheet music. Miss Goguel caught me unawares. Rather than scolding me, she congratulated me on knowing the music so well. She would then frequently allow me to play the hymn in her stead.

At the high school I likewise started out as a mediocre pupil, but I soon gained a good knowledge of history. I was up on historical dates. I was also a good student in geography, but I still remained very shy.

I stayed at the Gunsbach school for four years. One autumn day, at the beginning of the school year, my father told me that I would have to transfer from the Gunsbach school to the Realschule [secondary school stressing modern languages] in Munster. I was very, very, very sad at having to leave my friends at the Gunsbach school, especially Jean Demangeat, who would no longer be helping me with my assignments. I then set out every morning at seven to go to the Munster school, and I came home every evening at five. Luckily I had a travel companion. He was the son of Mr. Scheer, the Gunsbach miller. In those days the Gunsbach mill worked very nicely. In Munster I always had lunch at the home of Miss Immer.

I spent only one year at the Munster Realschule, where I began to learn Latin.

My uncle and godfather, Louis Schweitzer, the director of the municipal schools of Mulhouse, told my father that I could live with him so I could attend the Mulhouse Gymnasium. My father was delighted. But a dismal time began for me. I was the worst student in my year, and I completely lost heart. The principal wrote to my father, telling him it would be best if he removed me from the school. My father earnestly begged him to let me spend a few more weeks there. At the same time a new teacher took over our class. During the very first weeks of his instruction, I began working hard. The new teacher felt sorry for me and gave me private tutoring. Three months later I was one of the best students in my year! This teacher's name was Wehmann; he loved me like a father. I remained in contact with him when I founded my hospital in Africa. He became a teacher at the Strasbourg Gymnasium. When I returned to Strasbourg at the end of the war, I learned that he had starved to death in Strasbourg during the war.

My dear children in Gunsbach, I have told you the story of my school years, and I hope that you will always find compassionate teachers and that you will always remain grateful to them.

To the Greek Orthodox Archbishop of Central Africa, Usumbura, Burundi

Lambarene, Equatorial Africa
20 February 1965

[f]

Your Eminence,

I don't know whether I have already thanked you for your very friendly letter and for the metal picture of Hippocrates, my honored master. It will have its place in our operating room, but for a while it will remain here on my desk. I have known the Greek language since my adolescence. I studied it at the gymnasium of the city of Mulhouse, Alsace, and then at the University of Strasbourg, where I studied Greek philosophy and also theology. Later on, for several years before leaving for Africa, I taught theology at the University of Strasbourg while practicing medicine.

You have informed me that Dr. Tassos Athanassiadis's biography of me has come out. The publication of some of my books in Greece is a major event for me. How I would have loved to visit Greece during this period! But I couldn't. I am unable to leave my hospital at this time because it has grown larger than I had imagined. We have an average of six thousand patients a year here. Our hospital is located directly on the equator on a strip of land between the jungle and a large river called the Ogowe.

I am deeply touched to learn that you plan to write a series of articles on my work and myself. I cannot tell you what it means to me that my ideas are becoming known in Greece. If you travel to Europe, I would be overjoyed if you stopped off in Lambarene. You can fly to us and then continue your journey to the north.

～

To the Protestant Congregation, Neudorf, Strasbourg

Lambarene
28 February 1965

I am deeply grateful to the members of the congregation for their best wishes on my ninetieth birthday. I was well acquainted, indeed friendly, with the pastors of the congregation. The Neudorf congregation has done a great deal for my hospital. Ah, how I would love to visit Strasbourg and also Neudorf. I visited Neudorf in 1959. Since then, I haven't traveled at all. My constantly growing hospital requires my presence.

~

To Manfred George, editor in chief of *Der Aufbau*, New York
[Lambarene, 1965]

I am delighted to have an opportunity to greet you. I am still constantly at work, and I have to forget all about taking a holiday. The last time I spent a vacation in Europe was during 1959. Since then, my hospital has grown so big that I have to constantly keep the reins in my hands. I can well endure this permanent residence on the equator, but of course I'm sorry that I can never see my friends in Europe and the rest of the world.

[An undated letter to Manfred George from years earlier:]

I have always regretted that the Christian church did not speak out on its own against this disgraceful treatment of the Jews. These two religions belong together, and the Old Testament also has its place of honor in the Bible. And now, in my old age, I am witnessing the fact that Christians are starting to become aware of their spiritual bond with the Jews.

I am glad that I have lived to see this. At the evening services of my hospital staff, we read books of the Old and the New Testament. It was easier to achieve a togetherness between the synagogues and the Christian churches on American soil. The prejudices toward the synagogue were not as deeply rooted there as in the historical soil of Europe. But here, too, a mutual understanding must be achieved.

~

To Nobel Peace Laureate Father Dominique Pire, Brussels
Lambarene
14 March 1965

[*f*]

Dear Father Pire,

You were kind enough to write the foreword to the book *L'Evangile de la Miséricorde* [The Gospel of Compassion].[1] I was deeply moved by this book, which is dedicated to me. Thank you for your kindness toward me. I am grateful to you for appraising my ethics of peace. How I would love to see you again. I am very touched that this big book is to honor me. It encourages me to continue on my path. I have read and reread this book over and over again. I hope that your work is progressing well. You probably have to travel a great deal.

~

To Prof. Dr. Hans Walter Bähr, Tübingen
Lambarene
2 April 1965

Dear Friend,

I apologize for writing you so tardily, but my ninetieth birthday has forced me to write masses of thank-you letters.

Thank you for everything you are doing on my behalf. I am eagerly looking forward to your compilation of texts on humanity and ethics. The ethics of reverence for life is gaining ground in the world, especially because it is being taught in schools. Something interesting has happened in India. The government is requiring schools to include Buddha's doctrine of kindness in their curricula. Previously, schools did not teach this to the children.

I am deeply moved by the news that a celebration for my ninetieth birthday took place at [Tübingen's] collegiate church. I have already thanked Dean K. Epting, and I will also be writing to Professor Achenbach.

~

To Prof. Dr. Herbert Spiegelberg, St. Louis, Missouri
Lambarene
4 April 1965

Dear Friend,

Many, many thanks for your two big books. I don't know English, but when I read philosophy, I understand a lot more than when I read a novel. So I have found a number of things in your writings that were instructive for me. I admire you for your fine overview of the entire area of philosophy. I was especially interested in your presentation of Sartre's philosophy. He is my cousin, you see. His mother is a Schweitzer, and his grandfather, Karl Schweitzer, is my uncle. I also knew his father, who was a naval officer. He was a noble and profound man. Sartre grew up in the home of my uncle, who spoke only German to him so that the boy would master the German language. I am telling you this because it may interest you. I am disturbed that Sartre has written such derogatory things about his grandfather. This man had a thorough knowledge of the German language and literature and deeply loved his grandson. I dealt with Sartre early on when he was still a baby. His mother and his grandfather lived near the Bois de Boulogne, and I, too, lived near the Bois de Boulogne with my uncle [Paul]. My cousin frequently asked me to replace her and take the baby in his carriage for a walk in the Bois de Boulogne, which I enjoyed doing. Supposedly, he penned his first writings, as a high school student, in the garden of the Gunsbach parsonage.

Many, many thanks for your book, *The Socratic Enigma*. It is greatly to your credit that you have put together all statements about Socrates! This book makes a tremendous impact.

~

To Dr. Max Tau, Oslo

Lambarene
6 April 1965

I have many letters to write in order to respond to gifts and congratulations for my ninetieth birthday, and this is made more difficult by the fact that I have to write very slowly.

How I would love to visit my friends in the north one more time, but the work I have to do in the hospital won't allow me to travel. I can never go to Europe again. Unfortunately, the hospital keeps growing. At first it had 50 beds, and we were proud of that. Now it has 560! There are six doctors and fourteen European nurses. I have to build a new house for the hospital almost every year.

I am sound and fit. At ninety I can still do my work at the hospital. This means a lot to me. I am still fighting against atomic bombs. Now that China has atomic bombs, no one knows what is to come next. Luckily, the Moscow Pact is still in effect, but China refuses to join. It wants to remain free.

With best regards to all my friends in the north,

Albert Schweitzer

I thank my friends in the north for everything they are doing for my hospital.

~

To the Reverend Timothy Yilsun Rhee, director of the Ullung-Do
Hospital, Ullung-Do Island, Korea

Lambarene
16 May 1965

Dear Friend,

I have learned from Mr. Chungoh Doh in Seoul that you invited him
to the celebration of my birthday. He did a wonderful bronze relief
of me, which is now in Lambarene. I consider it a great work of art,
but I am worried that it was too expensive for him. Mr. Chungoh
Doh studied theology. He writes me that he is now a soldier. I admire
this artist very much.

I constantly think of you.[1] If Mr. Chungoh Doh has trouble getting
together the money he spent for the relief, please write me so that I
can try to help him. I would be delighted if you wrote me from time
to time and let me know how you and your hospital are doing.

~

To Tomin Harada, World Peace Study Mission, Hiroshima, Japan

Lambarene
[May 1965]

Thank you so much for your letter of April 9. How I would have
loved to accept your friendly invitation to visit Japan in August. . . . I
am touched that you wish to make me an honorary member of the
World Peace Study Mission. The world must learn the historic significance of Hiroshima and Nagasaki. Please extend my best wishes
to the mayors of both cities.

~

To Patzer, teacher, Bondorf

Lambarene
26 May 1965

Dear Mr. Patzer,

I was very interested in the mission schools in Lambarene, both the
Catholic and the Protestant ones. They were very solid. The pupils
studied agriculture at these schools. Since they had to be fed, the
schools owned land, which the boys and girls had to work—one and
a half hours every morning, one and a half hours every afternoon.

By graduation they knew how to farm, and they loved it. I am writing this to you because I believe you are interested. The mission schools were very important for the land.

~

To Prof. Dr. Hermann Mai, Münster
                                        Lambarene
                                        9 June 1965

Dear Friend,

After making it through my ninetieth birthday, I am now trying to put order into my correspondence again. I have been feted in a manner that I did not expect. I was deeply moved by the fact that my ethics of reverence for life is making its way through the world.

My health is fine. I can do all sorts of work without straining myself. At the moment we are building a house for the patients. I began with a 50-bed hospital, now it has 560 beds. . . . Soon it will have 600.

But then I'll stop. When are you visiting us again?
                                        Best,
                                        Albert Schweitzer

~

To Dr. Zavarsky, Bratislava, Czechoslovakia
                                        Lambarene
                                        [July 1965]

Dear Dr. Zavarsky,

I have learned from Mr. Zeraski that you are working on a book on Bach in Slovak and that you wish to dedicate it to me.[1] It is, I feel, to your credit that you wish to make your compatriots more familiar with Bach. If this is your intention, then you may dedicate your book to me. Thank you. I regret that I am not in Europe and that I therefore cannot make your acquaintance.

I am still interested in everything concerning Bach.

NOTES

1905

9 July 1905

1. This letter, which is part of Schweitzer's correspondence with the Paris Mission Society, contained the suggestion that they send him to Africa. Alfred Boegner, the recipient of the letter, was director of the Paris Mission Society. His article, "Les besoins de la Mission du Congo" [The needs of the Mission in the Congo], appearing in *Journal des Missions Evangéliques* (June 1904, pages 389–93), was crucial to the path that Schweitzer chose. When he heard Boegner's appeal for help in the Congo, Schweitzer resolved to go to this Mission area in Equatorial Africa and begin his service there. The place he decided on was Lambarene, partly at the advice of Morel, a missionary. According to Schweitzer's book, *Out of My Life and Thought* (chapter 9), Boegner expressed the hope that this appeal would prompt those "on whom the Master's gaze already rests" to volunteer for this urgent work. Schweitzer then quotes Boegner's statement: "The Church needs people who respond to the Master's sign by simply answering, 'Lord, I am starting out.' "

2. Eugène Casalis, missionary of the Paris Mission Society. During Albert Schweitzer's adolescence, Casalis's accounts were quoted by Schweitzer's father during church services on Sunday afternoons in Gunsbach. As Schweitzer later wrote, those accounts made a deep impact on him.

3. Albert Schweitzer's parents, Pastor Louis Schweitzer (1846–1925) and Adele Schweitzer (1842–1916), originally resided in Kaysersberg, where Albert was born. That same year his father was chosen pastor of Gunsbach in the Munster Valley. Adele Schweitzer was the daughter of Pastor Johann Jakob Schillinger in Muhlbach in the Munster Valley. Philipp Schweitzer, the father of Louis Schweitzer, had lived in Pfaffenhoten as a teacher and mayor.

4. Friedrich Curtius (1857–1938), from Berlin, a lawyer, son of Ernst Robert Curtius, the classical philologist who headed the Olympia excavations. Friedrich Curtius, director of the district of Colmar, then chairman of the board at the Alsatian Church of the Augsburg Confession, was a close friend of Albert Schweitzer's. See the letter of 3 February 1963 and what it says about Curtius's relationship to Albert Schweitzer.

5. Albert Schweitzer, *J. S. Bach, le musicien-poète*, with the collaboration of Hubert Gillot; preface by C.-M. Widor. Breitkopf & Härtel, Leipzig, 1905, 455 pages. Regarding the revised German edition, see the letters of 1907.

6. Six months before he wrote this letter, Schweitzer's "Sermon on Mission Day" at St. Nicholas's Church in Strasbourg expressed his conception of help

in the Mission areas and advocated the Mission. This sermon was published in Albert Schweitzer, *Strasburger Predigten* [Strasbourg Sermons], edited by U. Neuenschwander, Verlag C. H. Beck, Munich, 1966, pages 47ff.

1905 (to J. C. B. Mohr publishing company)

1.   A. Schweitzer: *Von Reimarus zu Wrede: Eine Geschichte der Leben-Jesu-Forschung (The Quest of the Historical Jesus)*, J. C. B. Mohr, Tübingen, 1906, 418 pages (dedicated to Schweitzer's father, Pastor Louis Schweitzer). In 1913 the expanded edition came out. Its title, *Geschichte der Leben-Jesu-Forschung* [History of research on the life of Jesus], was retained for all German editions.

Schweitzer later repeated the words to which the book leads:

> *Because this became a certainty for me through investigating and thinking about Jesus, the history of the quest for the historical Jesus ends as follows: "He comes to us as an unknown and anonymous person, just as He came along the shore of the lake and approached those men, who did not know who he was. He speaks the same words, 'Follow Me,' and confronts us with the tasks that we must perform in our time. He commands. And for those who obey Him, the wise and the unwise, He will reveal himself in whatever peace, work, struggle, and suffering they may experience in His community, and they shall experience who He is as an ineffable mystery"* (Albert Schweitzer, Out of My Life and Thought, *chapter 6*).

1905 (to Anna Schäffer)

1.   Anna Schäffer, from Munster, Alsace, a teacher at the Finishing School in Mulhouse, lived in the home of A. Schweitzer's great-uncle, Louis Schweitzer, chancellor of the municipal schools. A. Schweitzer attended the Gymnasium [secondary school] in Mulhouse.

His religious teacher in Munster, Pastor Schäffer, Anna's father, was "an important religious figure and an outstanding speaker in his way" (*Memoirs of Childhood and Youth*). In the same book he writes that "intelligent and friendly as she [Anna Schäffer] was, she contributed far more to my education than she realized."

1906

April 1906

1.   Gustav von Lüpke, from Kattowitz (now Katowice, Poland), head conductor, received a number of letters from Schweitzer after reviewing the French edition of his Bach book (in: *Der Kunstwart*, second edition in April, pages 60–64). Schweitzer's letters are among the most important documents on his early years and his understanding of Bach. Von Lüpke, born 8 December 1875 in Hermannsburg, Hanover, was head of the Master Musical Institute in Kattowitz. During World War I he succumbed to a wound at the military hospital in Siedlce. Schweitzer's letters to von Lüpke suggested that the Bach

book be translated into German; Schweitzer then rewrote it entirely in German and sent von Lüpke several portions of the text for his advice, as this letter shows. In connection with these letters, the Central Archive would like to express its gratitude to Frau Christel Frank-von Lüpke in Darmstadt.

2.   See note 5 on the letter of 9 July 1905.

3.   Under the baton of Prof. Ernst Münch, the brother of Eugen Münch, Schweitzer's organ teacher in Mulhouse, the St. Wilhelm Choir in Strasbourg performed chiefly Bach's cantatas. Schweitzer first accompanied the choir on the organ at the age of nineteen in 1894 and then regularly played the organ part at their recitals.

4.   Albert Schweitzer, *Deutsche und französische Orgelbaukunst und Orgel-kunst* [The art of German and French organ building and playing], Breitkopf & Härtel, Leipzig, 1906, 51 pages; first printed in *Die Musik*, numbers 13 and 14, volume 1906; republished in 1962.

1907

1907 (to Gustav von Lüpke)

1.   During this period Schweitzer, age thirty-two, was working on the German edition of his Bach book (introduction by Charles-Marie Widor, 1908, 844 pages). The German version is almost twice the size of the French edition of 1905. The English translation (1911) is based on the larger version. This book has also been translated into a number of other languages: Italian (1952), Hebrew (1958), Spanish (1955), Hungarian (1974), Japanese (1955), Polish (1963), and Russian (1965).

Schweitzer's book is one of the fundamental works on Bach, not only because of the overall picture that it presents but also because of its insights into Bach's tonal diction and the problems of performing the passions, the cantatas, and the instrumental works.

1 November 1907

1.   "My mother and my sister": Adele Schweitzer, née Schillinger, and Luise Ehretsmann-Schweitzer (1873–1927), Colmar.

2.   Georg Walter (1875–1952), lieder and oratorio singer, known as a singer of Bach; married to Elsa Haas, who belonged to the Schweitzer circle in Strasbourg.

3.   Maria Philippi (1875–1944), concert and oratorió singer.

4.   For this winter semester at the University of Strasbourg, Schweitzer had announced that he would be lecturing on "Exegesis of the Catholic Letters, Part II" (2 Peter; Jude; 1, 2, and 3 John). The following term he again lectured on the quest for the historical Jesus.

1908

19 July 1908

1.   Hans Pfitzner, in Strasbourg, was a head conductor, the director of the conservatory, and conductor at the theater.

2.   Professor Ehrismann was the president of the Strasbourg Male Glee Club, which built the Sängerhaus concert hall (today's Palais des Fêtes) on Vogesenstrasse. The organ was built by Dalstein and Härpfer according to Schweitzer's plans.

3.   A. Schweitzer, *Deutsche und französische Orgelbaukunst und Orgelkunst,* op. cit.

22 October 1908

1.   Regarding the Bach singer Georg Walter, see note 2 on the letter of 1 November 1907.

2.   Hohnack is a mountain and fortress in the Munster Valley, Alsace.

23 October 1908

1.   Paul was Schweitzer's brother.

1909

1909 (to Gustave Bret)

1.   Gustave Bret, organist at St. Sulpice, Paris, and Charles-Marie Widor's deputy conductor, directed the Paris Bach Society, which he had founded; Schweitzer, a cofounder, took part as organist. This letter refers to the performance at the Salle Gaveau. In April 1912 the Paris Bach Society sponsored a benefit organ recital with Albert Schweitzer for the planned Lambarene hospital.

5 July 1909

1.   Fritz Härpfer, an experienced organ builder, worked closely with Albert Schweitzer. In his autobiography (1931), Schweitzer relates that it was possible for him to realize his ideal church organ in several new organs, thanks to Fritz Härpfer's "artistic talents" as well as the cooperation of church boards. Schweitzer's letters to Härpfer are to be found in the detailed analysis penned by Dr. Bernhard Billeter, "Albert Schweitzer und sein Orgelbauer" [A.S. and his organ builder]; it also contains F. Härpfer's letters. This thorough study—the first to present and examine Schweitzer's correspondence on the organ—was published in *Acta Organologica*, volume II, Berlin, 1977, pages 173–225.

2.   Dalstein was an organ builder with the firm of Dalstein & Härpfer, Bolchen.

15 August 1909

1.   The Lenel family—the historian Dr. Walter Lenel and Frau Luise Lenel—first met Schweitzer in Strasbourg, becoming friends with him. This letter was prompted by Edith Lenel's christening; it was made available to the editor in 1982 by Edith Lenel, Ph.D., in the United States. Schweitzer's letters to the Lenel family are now preserved at Princeton University Library; in 1964 and 1965, Edith Lenel visited Lambarene.

In regard to Dr. W. Lenel, see the depiction of his friend, the historian

Friedrich Meinecke, in F. Meinecke, *Werke*, volume 8, *Autobiographische Schriften* [Autobiographical writings], pages 149ff. The same volume also contains Meinecke's description of his meeting with Schweitzer during those years in Strasbourg.

1910

5 April 1910

1. The suggestion for the title of this book was originally "Paulinism as Eschatological Mysticism."

After Pentecost (to Edith and Luise Lenel)

1. Seventeen of Schweitzer's sermons from his Strasbourg period were published in 1966 by Prof. Dr. Ulrich Neuenschwander, *Strasburger Predigten* [Strasbourg Sermons], University of Berne, 169 pages; the French translation by Madeleine Horst was published in 1970 with an introduction by Georges Marchal. A second volume of sermons was edited in 1974 by Martin Strege and Lothar Stiehm, *"Was sollen wir tun?"* ["What ought we to do?"]. This cycle of twelve sermons on ethical problems dates from 1919, and the edition was reprinted in 1986. An English-language edition was published in 1988 under the title *A Place for Revelation: Sermons on Reverence for Life*. In regard to Schweitzer's thoughts about publishing his sermons, see his letter of 12 June 1964 to Pastor Willy Bremi and Dr. Hermann Baur, Basel.

Today the special significance of the sermons in Schweitzer's lifework is seen on the basis of those publications. In his 1966 afterword, Ulrich Neuenschwander says that the Gunsbach Central Archive contains some 150 of Schweitzer's sermons from his Strasbourg years, and he offers the presentation, "Schweitzer as Preacher." With his thorough knowledge of the context, Otto Spear concludes, in *Albert Schweitzers Ethik* (1978), that "in sermons that he gave at St. Nicholas's Church, [Schweitzer] expressed the ideas that crucially determined the entire course of his life (after 1905)."

1911

26 August 1911 (to J. C. B. Mohr publishing company)

1. *Geschichte der paulinischen Forschung von der Reformation bis auf die Gegenwart* (English: *Paul and His Interpreters*), J. C. B. Mohr, Tübingen, 1911, 197 pages. Second edition, 1933. (Based on a lecture series at the University of Strasbourg.)

2. The manuscript was not completed prior to Schweitzer's trip to Lambarene. It was two decades later, in 1930, that the book came out after further work on it: *Die Mystik des Apostels Paulus (The Mysticism of Paul the Apostle)*. See the letters of 11 December 1929 and 9 May 1930.

26 August 1911 (to Karl Leyrer)

1. Karl Leyrer (1875–1936), Schweitzer's university friend, read his manuscripts and galley proofs, as indicated by acknowledgments in several of

the books. The letter of 26 August 1911 most likely refers to *Paul and His Interpreters*.

18 November 1911 and "Sunday"

1. Tartarin de Tarascon is the title character of Alphonse Daudet's novel.
2. The colonial minister with whom Schweitzer spoke was Albert Lebrun, later a president of the republic.

1912

9 January 1912

1. Lluís Millet (1867–1941), Catalan composer and conductor, founded the Orféo Català Choir and was a pioneering performer of Bach's works in Barcelona. Schweitzer frequently played the organ for the choir. In regard to Millet, see M. Garçia Venao, *L. Millet*, Barcelona, 1951.
2. *Sic.*
3. The English translation of Albert Schweitzer's book on Bach (1908 German version) had come out in 1911.
4. Helene Bresslau, born in 1879, was the daughter of the famous historian Harry Bresslau. She first met Schweitzer around 1900. She actively participated in his literary oeuvre, editing his manuscripts. Initially working as an orphan welfare worker in Strasbourg, she studied nursing in Stettin and Frankfurt. After marrying Schweitzer in 1912, she accompanied him to Africa (until 1917) to work in the first Lambarene hospital, which she helped him build. Her health was greatly impaired by her long equatorial sojourn— due to World War I—and her subsequent internment. As a result, she had to spend years in sanatoriums and was no longer able to take her place at her husband's side in Africa. Shortly before Schweitzer's second trip to Africa, she and their daughter Rhena (b. 1919) settled in Königsfeld in the Black Forest. She made another attempt at living in Lambarene, but after three months she had to leave in 1930 for health reasons and seek a sanatorium. In 1935 she was forced to leave Germany because of her Jewish background. After spending some time in Switzerland, she lectured at the American Fellowship, which supported the Lambarene hospital during World War II. She then succeeded in getting to Lambarene, where she remained until 1946. Since her health had improved somewhat, she managed to revisit Lambarene several times and also attend the ceremony of the Nobel Peace Prize in Oslo. However, she repeatedly had to take special care of herself. After revisiting Lambarene, she died in Zurich in 1957. Regarding the phases of her life and her work, see the information presented by letters and notes in this volume after 1912.

1913

April 1913 (to Heinrich von Recklinghausen)

1. This refers to the picture of the S.S. *Europe* on this postcard, which Schweitzer wrote during his first voyage to Lambarene.

April 1913 (to Adele Woytt)

1. Adele Woytt, née Schweitzer (1876–1969), Schweitzer's younger sister, married Pastor Albert Woytt (1862–1942) in Oberhausbergen near Strasbourg; Pastor Woytt was treasurer of the Lambarene Project from 1924 to 1936.

2. Helene Schweitzer kept a diary in Lambarene during 1913–14, sending portions of it to her parents, partly so they could show them to friends and acquaintances.

3. The circle of Alsatian pastors whose meetings Schweitzer attended.

4. Albert Woytt wrote stories for the *Alsace/Lorraine Family Calendar*.

April 1913 (to J. C. B. Mohr publishing company)

1. The first trip to Lambarene, starting in Bordeaux, was described by Schweitzer in the circular letter he dispatched to Strasbourg just a few months later. Helene and Albert Schweitzer arrived in Gabon in mid-April and then reached Lambarene in a river boat on April 19; here they were greeted by missionaries. In Dakar, as Schweitzer notes, they had first set foot on African soil. Shortly before going to Lambarene he had obtained information about health conditions in the small villages. In 1921 the text of this letter was reworked into his book, *Zwischen Wasser und Urwald (On the Edge of the Primeval Forest*, chapter 2, "The Trip. Lambarene, early July 1913"; see the sections entitled "On the Ogowe to Lambarene"). Albert Schweitzer always traveled to Lambarene from Bordeaux, where the freight for the hospital was loaded on shipboard; this was his normal route to Africa.

2. During the first few days after his arrival in Lambarene, Schweitzer transmitted the list to J. C. B. Mohr, his publisher in Tübingen, who was to send out copies and galleys of the second German edition of *The Quest of the Historical Jesus*, which Schweitzer managed to complete in Strasbourg just before sailing to Africa. This roster contains the names not only of friends and relatives but of a general circle of readers whom Schweitzer wished to address as a theological scholar.

"Copies of the whole book are to be sent to Prof. Julius Wellhausen, Göttingen; Prof. Dr. W. Bousset, Göttingen; Prof. Dr. J. Weiss, Heidelberg; Prof. Dr. E. Tröltsch, Heidelberg; Prof. Dr. A. Harnack, Berlin; Prof. Dr. Arthur Drews, Technische Hochschule, Karlsruhe; Privy Councilor Prof. Wilhelm Wundt, Leipzig; Prof. William Sanday, Oxford; Prof. F. C. Burkitt, Cambridge; Prof. Maurice Goguel, Paris; Reverend [William] Montgomery, Cambridge; Albert Loisy, Ceffonds, Haute Marne; Prof. B. W. Bacon, Yale University; Prof. [Gustav Adolf] Anrich, Strasbourg; Megoz (instructor), Strasbourg; Dr. Walter Lenel, Strasbourg; Reverend [Karl] Leyrer, Schirmeck, Lower Alsace; Olympia Curtius, Strasbourg; Frau Prof. [Annie] Fischer, Strasbourg; Prof. Cahn, Strasbourg; Frau Dr. Roth, Strasbourg; Prof. Harry Bresslau, Strasbourg; Pastor Ludwig Schweitzer, Gunsbach, Alsace; Paul Ehretsmann, Colmar, Upper Alsace; Suzanne Ehretsmann, Colmar; Pastor [Albert] Woytt, Oberhausbergen near Strasbourg; Prof. Dr. Schorbach, Strasbourg; Paul Schweitzer, Vallerysthal near Saarburg, Lorraine; Library of the Collegium Wilhelmitanum, Strasbourg; University and

State Library of Strasbourg; Library of the Protestant Theological Seminary of the University of Strasbourg; Monsieur Théodore and Salomon Reinach, Paris; Madame Théodore Reinach, Paris."

18 May 1913 (to Anna Schäffer)

1. During 1913–14 in Strasbourg, Annie Fischer, née Stinnes, wife of Prof. Fritz Fischer, M.D., had a leading role in dispatching all the supplies to the Lambarene hospital. Some of Schweitzer's sermons have been preserved in her manuscript copies.

2. Great-aunt Sophie Schweitzer was married to Louis Schweitzer. Albert Schweitzer lived with them while attending the Gymnasium in Mulhouse, 1885–93.

18 May 1913 (to Suzanne Ehretsmann)

1. Suzanne Oswald, née Ehretsmann, writer and journalist, niece of Albert Schweitzer, knew her uncle in Gunsbach during her childhood. In 1971 she published her autobiographical book, *Mein Onkel Bery* (My uncle Bery), Verlag Rotapfel, Zurich/Stuttgart, 211 pages. It has been translated into French, Dutch, and Japanese.

16 June 1913 (to the Committee for the Lambarene hospital)

1. After Schweitzer's departure for Africa, the Strasbourg committee included August Ernst and Robert Will, both pastors and university friends of Schweitzer's; Friedrich Curtius, the chairman of the Church of the Augsburg Confession, Strasbourg; and Annie Fischer.

The text of the circular letter in this volume is taken from the original text, which Schweitzer subsequently presented to Lotte Gerhold-Schall in Königsfeld; L. Gerhold-Schall made it available to the editor.

16 June 1913

1. Pastors August Ernst and Robert Will: See the note to the preceding letter.

2. See note 3 on the letter of April 1913 to Adele Woytt.

23 July 1913

1. When the Orféo Català Choir performed J. S. Bach's mass in Barcelona in 1912, Schweitzer played the organ part. See the list of Schweitzer's overall recital activities, as drawn up in 1986 by H. Schützeichel; it is preserved at the Central Archive.

25 August 1913

1. Christol, a missionary, and his wife were stationed in Lambarene-Andende and welcomed Schweitzer on his arrival in 1913. They returned to France in 1927. Schweitzer maintained contact with the Christol family until the 1960s.

2. H. Champel, a missionary in Gabon. See the letter of 28 August 1938

to L. and G. Morel, which mentions the missionary conference in Samkita, north of Lambarene, during Schweitzer's first sojourn in Lambarene.
3. Soubeyran and Faure were missionaries in the Ogowe area.
4. La Belle Jardinière: department store in Paris.

Lambarene, 1913

1. This circular letter provides a more detailed account of the situation. It also contains "notices and explanations" with information about materials needed by the hospital. Further donations are required to "carry out the project." See *Mitteilungen aus Lambarene 1913–1914* (News from Lambarene, 1913–1914), Union Verlag, Berlin, 1983, edited and introduced by Gerhard Fischer.

15 October 1913

1. *Das Messianitäts- und Leidensgeheimnis*, 1901. English translation: *The Mystery of the Kingdom of God*, 1914.
2. Dr. Lowrie was rector of St. Paul's American Church in Rome.

1914

Postcard, 1914 (before August)

1. *IMG: Zeitschrift der Internationalen Musik-Gesellschaft, ZIMG* (Journal of the International Music Society).
2. Because of his work load in Lambarene, Schweitzer was unable to revise his Bach book.

5 August 1914

1. After the outbreak of the war, Robert Kaufmann—a Bach singer whom Schweitzer occasionally accompanied at the piano—transmitted Helene and Albert Schweitzer's letters to their families in Alsace. Kaufmann, "with the help of the Office des Internés Civils, Geneva, made a point of keeping me in touch with the world" (*Out of My Life and Thought*, chapter 13).

28 December 1914

1. Robert Kaufmann: See preceding letter.
2. After the outbreak of the war, Helene and Albert Schweitzer were interned in their Lambarene home since, as Alsatians, they were German citizens. They were allowed to resume their work in November.

1915

1915 (to Romain Rolland)

1. Rolland, a writer and scholar, winner of the Nobel Peace Prize, resided in Switzerland during the war and wrote pacifistic pieces against war and international hatred. When Schweitzer was about thirty, as he reports in *Out of My Life and Thought*, he met Rolland in Paris, and he is also mentioned in Rolland's book, *Musiciens d'aujourd'hui* [Musicians of Today, 1908]. In

1965, Robert Minder published "Albert Schweitzer et Romain Rolland" (with some of Rolland's letters to Minder) in *Europe*, November-December 1965.

August 1915

1. See the letter of 15 October 1913, note 1: Dr. Lowrie translated Schweitzer's work of 1901, which had been put out by J. C. B. Mohr.

2. This refers to the work on the philosophy of civilization and the writing of manuscripts for this book in the summer of 1915.

A few weeks later, in September, Schweitzer coined the phrase "reverence for life," which was then elaborated. Here, as he explains in his autobiography, he found "the elementary and universal concept of the ethical." In summarizing he states: "The ethics of the reverence for life comprises everything that can be called love, devotion, compassion, shared joy, and cooperation. . . . It is the ethics of Jesus, which has been recognized as essential for thought."

The manuscript for the philosophy of civilization that Schweitzer wrote in Africa during 1914–17 could not be taken along when he and his wife were transferred to internment in France. He left the papers with Ford, an American missionary, who mailed them to him after the war. See the letter of 12 February 1920 to Ford.

1916

26 May 1916

1. H. Goldschmidt's book, *Musik-Asthetik des 18. Jahrhunderts* (Musical aesthetics of the eighteenth century), which Schweitzer mentions here and which he was reading in Lambarene, had been published one year earlier and sent to him via Switzerland.

July 1916

1. These lines, dated "July 1916," are repeated in *On the Edge of the Primeval Forest* (section x), in the discussion of the work and the situation in the hospital during the war years (until 1916). Otherwise he wrote about the developments and experiences in the hospital before and after the war in his circular letters for the patrons and friends of the hospital.

1917

24 December 1917

1. Helene and Albert Schweitzer were transported from Africa to France as civilian internees—first to Bordeaux, where they arrived on 12 November 1917. On November 21 they were brought to the Garaison detention camp in the Pyrenees. There, on December 24, Schweitzer wrote to the director of the camp. Three months later, on 26 March 1918, Schweitzer and his wife were brought to the St. Rémy camp in Provence, which was meant exclusively for Alsatians. (See the catalog for the Albert Schweitzer exhibition, Strasbourg, 1975.)

2. Refers to the relatives in Paris, Auguste Schweitzer and Prof. Charles Schweitzer. No direct correspondence was possible with their families in Alsace.

1918

June 1918

1. J. S. Bach's cantata, *Gottes Zeit ist die allerbeste Zeit* (BMV 106).
2. During his internment, Schweitzer traced out organ keys on a table top and pedals on the floor in order to practice.
3. Daughters of F. Curtius.

2 August 1918

1. Through an exchange of internees, Helene and Albert Schweitzer returned to Alsace like other Alsatians, traveling from the south of France via Zurich. This exchange was implemented by a neutral Switzerland during 12–17 July 1918.
2. During the war, when Schweitzer and his wife were interned, Prof. Dr. Jean Strohl, zoologist, and his wife sent them literature.
3. Paul François Mathieu, a religion teacher in Zurich, was friendly with Schweitzer.

29 September 1918

1. Ernst Kurth, *Grundlagen des linearen Kontrapunktes: Einführung in Stil und Technik von Bachs melodischer Polyphonie* (Foundations of linear counterpoint: Introduction to the style and technique of Bach's melodic polyphony), Bern, 1917; fourth edition, 1946.
2. Schweitzer was unable to carry out his plan of revising his Bach book for a new edition—even after the war.
3. At this time Schweitzer was vicar of the Church of St. Nicholas and a physician at the dermatological clinic of the Strasbourg Civic Hospital.

1919

7 December 1919

1. Rhena Schweitzer, Albert Schweitzer's daughter, was born on 14 January 1919. Her first husband was Jean Eckert, an organ builder. When their four children reached adulthood, she became a laboratory technician and worked for her father in Lambarene. In his will Schweitzer gave her sole responsibility for the hospital and made her executor of his writings and manuscripts. In 1970 she married David Miller, a physician from Atlanta, Georgia. The two of them devoted themselves to social and medical care for children in developing countries. In 1984–85, together with her husband, she worked at a refugee camp in Pakistan.

Alongside this charitable work, Rhena Schweitzer-Miller also lectures, writes essays, and talks about her father's lifework.

1920

12 February 1920

1.   See the account that Schweitzer wrote during the war about the manuscript of his philosophy of civilization in note 2 on the letter in August 1915 to the publisher J. C. B. Mohr.

Ford, the American missionary in Gabon to whom the letter of 12 February 1920 was addressed, is also mentioned in chapter 14 of Schweitzer's autobiography. He safeguarded the manuscript and sent it to Schweitzer after the war.

1920 (for readers of *Kirchenbote*)

1.   During that period, *Kirchenbote*, the Evangelical gazette for Alsace and Lorraine, was edited by Schweitzer; he also ran a number of his own pieces in it.

16 March 1920

1.   Prior to Schweitzer, Gustav Adolf Anrich was director of the St. Wilhelm Studienstift, where students lived and had study rooms and which also supplemented the university curriculum. G. A. Anrich taught church history at the University of Strasbourg; he later became a professor at Bonn and Tübingen.

2.   See Schweitzer's account in chapter 16 of *Out of My Life and Thought*.

13 May 1920

1.   These were the Olaus-Petri lectures, which Schweitzer delivered in Uppsala from mid-April to about May 10.

2.   The student Elias Söderstrom, who accompanied Schweitzer, became a missionary.

3.   In regard to the relationship between Schweitzer and Archbishop Söderblom, who was an ecumenical pioneer, his son, J. O. Söderblom, a minister of state, wrote the essay "Bishop Söderblom and Albert Schweitzer," in *In Albert Schweitzer's Realm*, edited by A. A. Roback, Cambridge, Massachusetts, 1962.

1921

19 September 1921

1.   Charles-Marie Widor, Albert Schweitzer's organ teacher in Paris, a composer and important French organist, performed at the Church of St. Sulpice, Paris. He greatly respected the young Alsatian and his new interpretations of Bach's choral preludes. Widor suggested and wrote

a detailed introduction for Schweitzer's book on Bach. The time will come, Widor wrote in that introduction, "when Bach will be one of the most popular composers in France. He expresses the pure feeling of religion."

2. Schweitzer and Widor edited the American edition of J. S. Bach's organ works. Each volume contains commentaries on the structure and performance of the compositions.

This vast undertaking, proposed by Schirmer, New York, and developed during the years before Schweitzer's first trip to Lambarene, is discussed in his autobiography (chapter 12). The Bach edition was launched in three languages: English, French, and German. Volumes one to five of the American edition were published in 1912–14. After 1950, Schweitzer resumed work on volumes six to eight—the choral preludes and the organ chorales—in collaboration with Edouard Nies-Berger. Volume six, which came out in 1954, includes Schweitzer's discussion of Bach's ornamentations. Volumes seven and eight followed in 1967. So far, volumes one to five of the German edition and volumes one to three of the French edition have been published.

American edition: *J. S. Bach, Complete Organ Works*, a critico-practical edition in eight volumes. It contains a preface with general observations on the manner of performing the preludes and fugues and suggestions for the interpretation of the compositions contained in each volume. By Charles-Marie Widor and Albert Schweitzer, volumes one to five. Albert Schweitzer and Edouard Nies-Berger, volumes six to eight.

4 October 1921

1. Prof. Dr. Martin Werner, a theologian at the University of Berne, was a close friend of Schweitzer's for decades. Werner was pastor of Krauchthal; that was where this letter was sent. As a pastor he completed his *Habilitation* (a German postdoctoral degree) in 1921; in 1927 he became professor of dogmatics and symbolism at the University of Berne. In 1924 he published *Das Weltanschauungsproblem bei Karl Barth und Albert Schweitzer* (The problem of a world view in Karl Barth and A.S.). Werner's fundamental scholarship eventually produced other works; see *Der protestantische Weg des Glaubens* (The Protestant path of faith), volume I, 1955; volume II, 1962. In 1948 the University of Berne elected the theologian and veteran professor as its president, and the University of Chicago awarded him an honorary doctorate for his significant theological work. Concerning Werner, see *Weg und Werk Martin Werners: Studien und Erinnerungen* (Martin Werner's path and work: Studies and reminiscences), edited by Francesco Sciuto, Paul Haupt, Berne, 1968.

2. Paul Haupt, Berne: the publisher of Schweitzer's *Zwischen Wasser und Urwald* (*On the Edge of the Primeval Forest*), 1921, 165 pages. Countless translations have appeared, in France (1923), England, Italy, Taiwan, Czechoslovakia, Yugoslavia, Finland, Japan, Holland, Denmark, Norway, Poland, Sweden, Spain, Portugal, Hungary, and Greece.

8 December 1921

1. In October, Schweitzer had given an organ recital in Saanen, Switzerland. Dr. Marc Lauterburg, the son of Pastor Lauterburg, did his residency with Schweitzer in Lambarene during 1925.

1922

5 January 1922

1. Baron Lagerfelt and Greta Lagerfelt founded the Swedish circle of friends of the Lambarene hospital; in 1921, G. Lagerfelt translated *On the Edge of the Primeval Forest* into Swedish.
2. Swedish student who accompanied Schweitzer on his trip through Sweden.

25 March 1922

1. The lectures appeared as *Das Christentum und die Weltreligionen*, Munich, 1922. They have been translated into several languages, including English: *Christianity and the Religions of the World*.

The book is dedicated "to the dear friends of the Swiss Universal Evangelical Mission Society." In these lectures, Schweitzer tries to show what "constitutes the uniqueness of Christianity." The audience was made up chiefly of missionaries or guests who wanted to be trained for the Mission. At one point Schweitzer says that, although in different fields of the Mission, "we are bound in spirit as people who wish to enter God's will and who see their calling in kindling the yearning in people to experience such things." One year earlier Schweitzer had described what he viewed as the tasks of missionaries in *On the Edge of the Primeval Forest* (chapter 10: "On the Mission").

8 April 1922

1. In 1920, at the initiative of W. Gurlitt, the Praetorius organ in Freiburg was reconstructed according to the specifications in Michael Praetorius's *Syntagma musicum* (1618). The goal was to perform organ music of the seventeenth century. Schweitzer's letter to Gurlitt, a musicologist and organ expert in Freiburg, refers to that instrument. The organ was built for the Musicology Institute of the University of Freiburg.

27 September 1922

1. This letter provides insight into the genesis of Schweitzer's *Memoirs of My Childhood and Youth* (1924), which has been translated into numerous languages. He reported in his 1931 autobiography: When he was visiting the pastor and psychologist Dr. O. Pfister, the recipient of this letter, in Zurich, Schweitzer told him about his childhood. Pfister recorded the information in shorthand for a children's magazine. Schweitzer then rewrote the text and sent it to Dr. Pfister. Shortly before sailing to Lambarene, he added a few summarizing sections.

1923

22 September 1923

1. *The Philosophy of Civilization: I. The Decline and Restoration of Civilization. II. Civilization and Ethics.* The original German edition was published in Munich and Berne in 1923. Albert Schweitzer's philosophical magnum opus has been translated into a number of languages.

1923 (to Noël-Alex Gillespie)

1. During 1924, Gillespie, a student, spent a few months with Schweitzer in Africa. Eventually he taught college in Madison, Wisconsin. Schweitzer remained in contact with him. Gillespie's epistolary account of his experiences with Schweitzer was later included in *In Albert Schweitzer's Realm*, ed. A. A. Roback, Cambridge, Massachusetts, 1962. Schweitzer's letters to Gillespie were published in *Cahiers de l'Association française des Amis d'Albert Schweitzer*, 1971–72 (contribution by Erwin R. Jacobi). The German translations were published in *Rundbriefe* (Circular letters), Dresden, German Democratic Republic, 1972–73.

1924

13 January 1924

1. Mrs. Reider was Noël-Alex Gillespie's mother.

1 March 1924 (to Archbishop Söderblom)

1. Schweitzer is referring to Bad Nauheim in Hesse.

1 March 1924 (to Otto Heuschele)

1. The writer Otto Heuschele, an expert on contemporary and classical literature, wrote this article on Schweitzer's *Philosophy of Civilization* right after the publication of the book; he understood the concept at an early date. His article, "Verfall und Wiederaufbau der Kultur" (Decay and restoration of civilization), came out in *Heilbronner Blätter für Kunst und Wissen*, number 3, 16 January 1924 (supplement to the *Neckar-Zeitung*).

2 March 1924

1. Pastor Hans Baur (1870–1937), a close friend of Schweitzer's, pastor of St. Leonhard, developed and directed the Swiss assistance for the Lambarene hospital, starting with the preparations for the postwar reconstruction, which was launched in 1924. The enormous Swiss contribution was due chiefly to Baur's initiative: Advocating the idea of the hospital as a work of Christian charity, he supplied the hospital with goods, medicines, and requisite funds. Baur's parsonage became a center for assistance to the hospital. That was why Schweitzer's letters refer to his friend as a "helper in need" for Lambarene. In 1949, Baur's work was posthumously extended with the founding of the Swiss Relief Organization for the Albert Schweitzer Hospital in Lambarene.

Schweitzer tells about the phase of the 1920s in *Out of My Life and Thought* (chapter 19): After he resumed his work in Africa, "Emmy Martin in Strasbourg, Pastor Hans Baur in Basel, and my brother-in-law, Pastor Albert Woytt in Oberhausbergen by Strasbourg, did the work that had to be done in Europe for my hospital. Without the self-sacrificing help of these and other volunteers, the greatly expanded enterprise would not have survived."

April-May 1924 (to Clement Chesterman)

1. Clement Chesterman, M.D., a British physician, subsequently played a major role in Dr. Schweitzer's Hospital Fund in England.

20 July 1924

1. This letter concerning orders and transportation, with its specifications about materials, packing, and shipping, is typical of numerous Schweitzer letters in the hospital's business correspondence. It is included as an example of this group of letters. Some of them have been preserved in duplicating pads. See note 1 on the letter of 25 October 1937.

All Saints' Day 1924 (to Martin Werner)

1. Dr. Victor Nessmann was the first physician who went to Lambarene to help Schweitzer; he subsequently remained in contact with him (see the references to him in *The Forest Hospital at Lambarene*). In 1944, in France, Nessmann died after being tortured by the Gestapo when he refused to reveal names of resistance fighters. His account of his experiences in Lambarene and the treatment of patients is to be found in *Rayonnement d'Albert Schweitzer* (Radiance of Albert Schweitzer), Colmar, [1975], pages 217ff.

1925

9 February 1925

1. This motorboat was donated to Schweitzer by Swedish patrons of his work.
2. In 1925, during the rebuilding of the hospital, Mathilde Kottmann, from Molsheim by Strasbourg, came to Lambarene as Schweitzer's first coworker. For some forty-five years she performed various duties. She handled significant and detailed work that he assigned to her; his letters often reveal how important she was for his project. Working day by day with Schweitzer, she conscientiously fulfilled her responsibilities with patients and problems in the hospital. Letters came to Lambarene from all over the world, and in her wide correspondence she provided detailed and sympathetic responses about Schweitzer's deeds and thoughts. In this way, especially as an overall helper in the hospital, she played a special part in Schweitzer's lifework in Africa.

Palm Sunday 1925

1. Along with Dr. Nessmann (see the note to the 1924 letter to M. Werner), Dr. Marc Lauterburg joined Dr. Schweitzer at the hospital (1925–28, 1929–

30). Both physicians arrived in Lambarene at an early point of the reconstruction of the hospital—Dr. Nessmann from Alsace, Dr. Lauterburg from Switzerland. They were followed by Dr. Fritz Trensz from Strasbourg; the first female physician, Dr. Ilse Schnabel from Germany (1928–30); Dr. Ernst Mündler (1927–29); Dr. Hans Stalder (1928–29); Dr. Karl Hediger (1927–29); Dr. Oskar Zähner (1929); Dr. Anna Schmitz (1929–32); Dr. René Meyländer (1930–31).

Until 1965 various physicians kept offering Schweitzer their services for the hospital whenever their obligations at home permitted it. Up to and during World War II, that is, 1933–46, Dr. Ladislas Goldschmidt of Hungary was able to join Schweitzer in Lambarene. Subsequently, the number of physicians kept growing with the hospital's mounting needs. Along with these doctors who spent several years in Lambarene, other physicians came as visitors. Dr. Takahashi from Japan worked for a number of years in the hospital's leprosy ward.

5 May 1925

1. Treating sick lumber workers in the Gabon region was one of Schweitzer's constant tasks in Lambarene, especially during the first few decades. The overworked laborers at the concessions for the lumber export companies contracted serious diseases. Schweitzer writes about them in *On the Edge of the Primeval Forest*—specifically the chapter on social problems.

Also see the references to Schweitzer's discussion of the situation of the lumber workers in Hans-Otto Neuhoff, *Gabun—Geschichte, Struktur und Probleme der Ausfuhrwirtschaft eines Entwicklungslandes* (Gabon—history, structure, and problems of the export trade of a developing country), Berlin, 1967, pages 59, 69.

18 September 1925

1. Siegfried Ochs (1858–1929), founder of the Berlin Philharmonic Chorus, directed it jointly with the Berlin Philharmonic Orchestra. His Bach performances were brilliant, and he published some Bach cantatas. For his correspondence, see Anton Bruckner's edition of Ochs's letters (1974), which includes letters to Ochs. His connection with Schweitzer was established, as the physician points out in chapter 7 of his biography, by Schweitzer's Bach book, which led to their friendship during the 1920s.

1926

1926 (to C. F. Andrews)

1. The lines describing Schweitzer's faith and religious feelings are a crucial document for understanding the course of his life. The full text was published in *The Visvabharati Quarterly*, founded by Rabindranath Tagore, Andrews Number, volume 36, edited by Sisirkumar Ghose. The text, in German probably, was translated into English, as Schweitzer explains at the outset, by Emma Haussknecht in Lambarene.

23 February 1926

1. Albert Schweitzer, *Deutsche und französische Orgelbaukunst und Orgelkunst*, op. cit.

2. Albert Schweitzer and F. X. Mathias, *Internationales Regulativ für Orgelbau*. Drafted and reworked by the Organ Construction Section at the third congress of the International Music Society, Vienna, 1909.

7 April 1926

1. *Briefe von und an Malwida von Meysenbug*, the correspondence of a pioneer of women's emancipation, was issued by Berthel Schleicher in 1920. Schleicher also wrote *Malwida von Meysenbug* (third edition, 1923) about the woman whose encounters with Nietzsche and Romain Rolland are mentioned in this letter.

7 May 1926

1. Like Schweitzer, Oswald Spengler, a philosopher of civilization, was published by C. H. Beck in Munich.

2. Emma Haussknecht, initially a teacher in Alsace, went to Lambarene in 1925, becoming a close colleague of Schweitzer's, and was active in various areas of the hospital, from nursing problems to economic issues, administration, and the plantations. In this versatile work, Haussknecht, as an experienced assistant, devoted herself to the needs of the project, confident of its meaningful function in Africa. Schweitzer's letters often express his appreciation of her contributions. In 1931 she wrote an article about her participation in the expedition across the savanna and the jungle in search of a location for the hospital. During World War II she continued as a member of the small staff. In Lambarene she also concentrated on preserving objects of regional arts and crafts.

In the second issue of *The Forest Hospital at Lambarene*, Schweitzer wrote that Emma Haussknecht was the second nurse to arrive in Lambarene (1925). "I have known her for a long time. She offered to work with me many years ago."

3 September 1926

1. Prof. Dr. Robert Minder, a close friend of Schweitzer's, taught German language and literature at the universities of Grenoble and Nancy before becoming a professor at the Sorbonne and then at the Collège de France. Early on he became Schweitzer's colleague in Strasbourg. Minder worked in many capacities for Schweitzer's humanitarian and intellectual projects. His essays and articles on Schweitzer are important interpretations written on the basis of special knowledge. For many years he edited the *Cahiers de l'Association française des Amis d'Albert Schweitzer* (Journal of the French association of the friends of A.S.) in France. Minder was also chairman of the commission for Albert Schweitzer's Intellectual Work from its establishment until 1980. Minder's publications include the documentary volume *Rayonnement d'Albert Schweitzer: 34 Etudes et 100 Témoignages* (Radiance of A.S.: 34 studies and 100 testimonies) (Editions Alsatia, Colmar, 1975, 301

pages). Earlier, in 1966, he had issued his study, "Albert Schweitzer, humaniste alsacien et citoyen du monde" (A.S., Alsatian humanist and citizen of the world) in *Saisons d'Alsace* (Alsatian seasons), Strasbourg. The book *Albert Schweitzer: Sein Denken und sein Weg* (Tübingen, 1962) contains Minder's essay, "Albert Schweitzers Begegnung mit Goethe" (A.S.'s encounter with Goethe).

2. Henri Lichtenberger, a French scholar of German studies, wrote scholarly works on German literature and international understanding; he founded the Institut d'Etudes Germaniques at the Sorbonne.

3. *Kranopel* is the Alsatian pronunciation of *Grenoble*.

4. In 1920, Minder had been accepted by the Ecole Normale Supérieure in Paris.

1927

7 January 1927

1. Lilian Marion Russell (1875–1949) got to know Schweitzer's writings during the 1920s and then frequently visited Lambarene as an assistant between 1927 and 1939. She translated the first part of his philosophy of civilization and, in England, she lectured on the hospital. An animal lover, she wrote *My Monkey Friends*.

2. IHIM stands for International Hout-Import Maatschappij, a Dutch lumber company located chiefly in Asia and Africa.

3. SHO stands for Société du Haut Ogooué, a trading company in the Ogowe district.

10 February 1927

1. This refers to the move to the new hospital, which Schweitzer had built nearby during the preceding months. This new location, above the Andende mission station, offered more favorable possibilities of accommodation.

20 February 1927

1. Martin Werner and Pastor Julius Kaiser issued a book for confirmands, *Alles Leben strömt aus Dir* (All life flows from thee), Berne, 1926; fourth edition, 1957. Kaiser, as Dr. Gertrud Hofer-Werner reveals, was pastor of the Lucerne congregation.

3 March 1927

1. With the preparations for the reconstruction of the Lambarene hospital, Emmy Martin, who was married to Pastor Wilhelm Martin (1878–1923), began her many years of service for Schweitzer's lifework. In 1929 she began running the newly built house in Gunsbach as a center with far-reaching tasks for the hospital and for Schweitzer's cultural activities. She developed and carried out her duties steadily through five decades. In Gunsbach she also corresponded with important people who were interested in Schweitzer's work. Her overall contributions are treated in

Emmy Martin—die Mitarbeiterin Albert Schweitzers (Emmy Martin—Albert Schweitzer's coworker), Tübingen, 1964. Along with "Emmy Martin," a detailed article by Robert Minder, this book included texts by authors in various countries. She also published reports on Lambarene: See her contribution to *Begegnung mit Albert Schweitzer* (Encounter with A.S.), Munich, 1965; also in Spanish and English. Emmy Martin also published *Tiergeschichten um Albert Schweitzer* (Animal stories about A.S.). Told for young people in the form of letters to Johannes Bähr, this collection appeared as a special issue of the German Circle of Friends of Albert Schweitzer (1975) and in *Berichte aus Lambarene* (Reports from Lambarene), Vevey, Switzerland, 1976, 1979. In Gunsbach, Emmy Martin built up the vast and fundamental collection of books, papers, documents, and writings about Schweitzer. She gave shape to this archive in addition to her comprehensive efforts for Lambarene.

12 March 1927

1. Dr. Fritz Trensz worked as a physician at Lambarene during 1926–27; in Strasbourg he promoted Schweitzer's work for decades. Trensz wrote "A. Schweitzer, le Médecin" (A.S., the doctor), with a detailed account of illnesses and treatments at the hospital, in *Rayonnement d'Albert Schweitzer*, Colmar, [1975].

23 March 1927

1. See the letter to Oskar Kraus, 7 November 1931.

Before 1928

1. Alice Ehlers, a musicologist and harpsichordist, taught at the University of Southern California. She wrote, among other things, "Musical Days with Albert Schweitzer," in *The Albert Schweitzer Jubilee Book*, edited by A. A. Roback, Cambridge, Massachusetts, 1945.

1928

20 July 1928

1. Dr. Hans Stalder, physician in Lambarene, 1928–29.

8 August 1928

1. Schweitzer's speech for the Goethe Prize ceremony in Frankfurt, 1928, was published as *Goethe: Vier Reden* (Goethe: Four speeches), C. H. Beck, third revised edition, 1950; also in English and Japanese.

1928–29 (to Max Drischner)

1. Max Drischner, musical director at St. Nicholas's Church in Brieg, Silesia, and a composer, wrote organ pieces. He had conversations with Schweitzer in Königsfeld and Strasbourg and also in Herrenberg (1951) where Drischner spent some time as a refugee and where Schweitzer visited him.

14 September 1928

1.   Julius S. Bixler, later president of Colby College, collaborated on *The Albert Schweitzer Jubilee Book*, Cambridge, 1945. During World War II, he was already one of the leading members of the Albert Schweitzer Fellowship in the United States.

1929

March 1929 (to Adolf von Harnack)

1.   Wilhelm von Bode (1845–1929) was an art historian, general director of the Berlin Museums, a collector and scholar. The editor of this volume obtained Schweitzer's letters to A. von Harnack with the help of Dr. Axel von Harnack, library director. The originals are in the German State Library, Berlin.

11 December 1929

1.   The family of Dr. Eugen Jacobi (1877–1933), an engineer and political scientist in Frankfurt am Main, had been friendly with Schweitzer back in Strasbourg. After World War I the family moved to Frankfurt where Schweitzer occasionally visited them, for instance, when he received the Goethe Prize. The son, Erwin Jacobi, a musicologist, was very intimate with Schweitzer's work. Schweitzer's letters to the Jacobi family are preserved at the Schweitzer Archive of the Zurich Central Library. The editor is grateful to the musicologist Dr. Bernhard Billeter, Zurich, for transmitting several copies from this collection. Some of the correspondence between Schweitzer and Margit Jacobi (1881–1943) were published in 1976 by Erwin Jacobi in *Librarium: Zeitschrift der Schweizerischen Bibliophilen-Gesellschaft* (volume 19, number 1, pages 2–21).

1929 (to Hans Martin)

1.   Hans Martin (b. 1910), son of the pastor Wilhelm Martin and Emmy Martin (Schweitzer's colleague), was a lawyer who acted as consultant for various projects in Schweitzer's lifework. He also published several articles, including "Der Musiker Albert Schweitzer (The musician A.S.), in *Die Gegenwart*, 1946, and in *Begegnung mit Albert Schweitzer*, 1965.

1930

10 January 1930

1.   This was Helene Schweitzer's first return trip to Africa. She wanted to see the new hospital, and she assumed she could endure staying in the equatorial region. However, after a brief visit she returned to Europe where she spent years in sanatoriums.

27 April 1930

1.   The German text of *The Mysticism of Paul the Apostle* was first published in 1930 by J. C. B. Mohr, Tübingen, and then translated into English, French, and Japanese. After Schweitzer's *Paul and His Interpreters* (1911), this book was meant to spread the apostle's teachings. In its fourteen chapters, this

presentation of Paul develops a fundamental insight "that the realization of the Kingdom [of God] began with Christ." This book, the author explains, "establishes the complete consistency of Paul's teaching" with the Gospel of Jesus Christ.

2.   A revised version of *Mitteilungen aus Lambarene* (News from Lambarene) for 1925–28 was planned but never implemented. Instead, *Mitteilungen aus Lambarene*, 1928, was published by C. H. Beck as *Briefe aus Lambarene* (Letters from Lambarene).

13 July 1930

1.   Lotte Gerhold-Schall, as Schweitzer's colleague, repeatedly performed tasks for his work and the hospital. She frequently visited Lambarene and handled all kinds of correspondence for him. A large group of letters that Schweitzer wrote her from Lambarene has been preserved. Frau Gerhold-Schall was kind enough to make several of these letters available to the editor of this book.

1931

14 January 1931

1.   These two chorales were sung by the hospital staff on the mornings of birthdays of staff members.

2.   *Out of My Life and Thought*. The German edition was published in 1931 by Felix Meiner, Leipzig. The original version had been published by Felix Meiner in 1921 as *Schweitzer: Selbstdarstelling* (Self-Presentation). The 1931 volume, which has been translated into nineteen languages, has contributed enormously toward explaining Schweitzer's path, from the earliest phases until 1931. In a letter to Albin Michel, the publisher of the revised French translation, Schweitzer says that this book permitted him to "present my religious, philosophical, and artistic ideas." He states that he spent five months writing it. For a new German edition in 1975, Rudolf Grabs updated the text by adding, "Die weiteren Jahre" (The later years).

3.   Anna-Elysabeth Schmitz, M.D., was Schweitzer's assistant in Lambarene during 1929–32. In 1931, together with Emma Haussknecht, she went on the arduous trek into the southern jungle of the region in order to plan better routes for patients.

1931 (circular letter before Palm Sunday)

1.   In October 1929, Dr. Erich Dölken, a physician from Thun, Switzerland, who wanted to assist Schweitzer at the Lambarene hospital, succumbed to a heart attack aboard the ship bound for Africa.

23 November 1931

1.   The recipient of this letter, an English composer, conductor, and organist, was the subject of *Donald Francis Tovey: A Biography Based on Letters*, 1952, edited by Mary Grierson, Oxford University Press; this book contains letters from Schweitzer. Tovey, who in the early thirties dedicated his edition of

J. S. Bach's *Art of the Fugue* to Schweitzer, wrote chamber music and orchestral works.

2.   Margaret Deneke, in England, lectured and worked for the Lambarene hospital. She visited Lambarene in 1926 and 1931.

1932

30 March 1932

1.   At the invitation of the city of Frankfurt, Schweitzer delivered his addresses for the Goethe celebration on 22 March 1932. Four years earlier he had received the Goethe Prize of the City of Frankfurt on Goethe's birthday. The two Frankfurt speeches were published in A. Schweitzer: *Goethe*, C. H. Beck, third expanded edition, 1950. In English: *Goethe: Two Addresses*. Translated by Charles R. Joy and C. T. Champion, with an introduction by Charles R. Joy, Beacon Press, Boston, 1948, 75 pages.

24 May 1932

1.   Emmy Hopf, organist in Berne, assisted at Schweitzer organ recitals and gave benefit concerts for the Lambarene hospital.

3 December 1932

1.   Schweitzer maintained contact with Martin Buber for several decades. In February 1933, Buber visited Schweitzer in Königsfeld to discuss biblical writings. In regard to Schweitzer, Buber has said: "It was owing to him, to his personality and his life, that I first became directly acquainted with the openness to the world and thereby the unique closeness to Israel that is possible for the Christian and also the Christian theologian (which Schweitzer never stopped being). My heart will never forget the hours of our stroll through the Königsfeld countryside and through the landscape of our minds" (M. Buber: *Zwei Glaubensweisen*, Zurich, 1950, pages 12ff). The extant correspondence between Buber and Schweitzer was published in *Martin Buber: Briefwechsel aus sieben Jahrzehnten*, edited with a biographical introduction by Grete Schaeder, 3 volumes, Lambert Schneider, Heidelberg, 1972–75.

The relationship between Buber and Schweitzer is detailed by Otto Spear in *Albert Schweitzers Ethik: Ihre Grundlinien in seinem Leben und Denken* (Schweitzer's ethics: Its foundations in his life and thought), Evangelischer Verlag Herbert Reich, Hamburg, 1978, pages 75ff: "Buber und Schweitzer" (Buber and Schweitzer).

2.   M. Buber, *Das Verborgene Licht* (The hidden light), Frankfurt am Main, 1924 (Chassidic tales and teachings).

3.   This refers to the three volumes of Buber's translation of the Old Testament that came out during 1930–32, volume 10 in collaboration with Franz Rosenzweig; volumes 11 and 12.

4.   Regarding Buber's *Zwiesprache* (*Dialogue*, 1932), see the new German edition edited by Lothar Stiehm, Lambert Schneider, Heidelberg, 1978.

19 December 1932

1.   Arthur Honegger (1892–1955), one of the most important composers of

our century, was, like Schweitzer, a pupil of Widor in Paris. Honegger penned a contribution for the French festschrift on Schweitzer's eightieth birthday (see the letter to Robert Minder, 10 March 1955). The symphony that was sent to Schweitzer in 1932, as mentioned in the letter, was Honegger's First Symphony (1931).

1933

28 April 1933

1. This account is typical of Schweitzer's circular letters orienting the friends and patrons of his work. This is the first excerpt from those circular letters in this book. Printed in Strasbourg and sent out from there, these letters deal with developments, and they express appreciation for Schweitzer's fellow workers; they are also important as source material. In their style and arrangement, they belong to the group that includes the *News from Lambarene*. The circular letters went on until 1938. See the various texts in this volume.

2. The verse from I Thessalonians 5:18 goes: "In every thing give thanks: for this is the will of God in Christ Jesus concerning you." Schweitzer discussed it in connection with gratitude in two sermons he gave at St. Nicholas's, Strasbourg, 1919. These sermons were published in Schweitzer: *Strasburger Predigten* (Strasbourg sermons, titled *A Place for Revelation* in English-language edition), 1966.

11 July 1933

1. Schweitzer's *Indian Thought and Its Development* was first published in German by C. H. Beck, Munich, and Paul Haupt, Berne, 1935. It has been translated into English, French, Dutch, Italian, Japanese, and Swedish.

27 December 1933

1. Maud Royden was also active at the City Temple. In addition to her theological and social work, she implemented various forms of charitable assistance through the Guildhouse in London. A constant supporter of the Lambarene hospital, she propagated Schweitzer's lifework in England. Glasgow University awarded her an honorary doctorate. Maud Royden wrote "Dr. Albert Schweitzer" for *Man of Turmoil: Biographies by Leading Authorities of the Dominating Personalities of Our Day*, New York, 1935.

1934

26 May 1934

1. Because of anti-Semitic persecution during the Nazi dictatorship, Helene Schweitzer and their daughter Rhena left Königsfeld and were now living in Lausanne. Her brother Ernst Bresslau, a professor at the University of Cologne, emigrated to Brazil.

1935

12 January 1935

1. *Die Hilfe*, a weekly journal of politics, literature, and art, was founded by Friedrich Naumann. Theodor Heuss, one of its editors from 1905 to 1909, later became its publisher. On 11 April 1908, Heuss and Elly Knapp (the daughter of G. F. Knapp, professor of economics at the University of Strasbourg) were married by Schweitzer at St. Nicholas's Church, Strasbourg. From 1900 to 1908, Elly Heuss belonged to the same circle of friends in Strasbourg as Schweitzer.

In her book, *Ausblick vom Munsterturm* (View from the cathedral tower, 1934, reprinted in 1952, with drawings by Theodor Heuss), Elly Heuss tells about her encounters with Helene Bresslau and Schweitzer; like Helene Bresslau, Elly Heuss was a social worker in Strasbourg. Her book provides informative depictions of cultural events in Strasbourg and its university during that period.

2. Schweitzer, *Indian Thought and Its Development*, 1935.

10 February 1935

1. Müller, an engineer and the son of a Gunsbach pastor, donated his house in Gunsbach to the Protestant church; that was the parsonage in which Schweitzer grew up. See A. Schweitzer, *Memoirs of Childhood and Youth*.

2. The family of Hindermann, a baker in Gunsbach, was friendly with Schweitzer's family. Like Albert Schweitzer, Louise Hindermann had attended the Gunsbach school.

18 February 1935

1. These were the "Gifford Lectures, Part I." Schweitzer was too overworked in those years to complete the manuscript.

1936

1936 (to Margit Jacobi)

1. Because of his Jewish background, Erwin Jacobi had to leave Germany, settling in Palestine in the fall of 1934. After World War II he studied harpsichord and musicology, first in the United States, then with Paul Hindemith in Zurich. Later on, Jacobi taught musicology at the University of Zurich, issuing fundamental editions. A friend of Schweitzer's, he published various scholarly and biographical writings about him. See Erwin R. Jacobi, *Albert Schweitzer und die Musik* (A.S. and music), Breitkopf und Härtel, Wiesbaden, 1975, as well as the piece on Schweitzer's Bach book in the 1975 *Bach-Jahrbuch* [Bach yearbook].

15 August 1936

1. For the English edition of *Indian Thought and Its Development* (London and New York, 1936), Schweitzer added material on Gandhi, which was then incorporated in the new German edition of 1965. (The galley proofs of

the French edition contain Schweitzer's note, "revised by [Robert] Minder.")

This edition triggered a detailed critical response in S. Radhakrishnan, *Eastern Religions and Western Thought*.

11 October 1936

1. The recordings for Columbia Records (as mentioned in this letter) were played by Schweitzer on the organ of All Hallows, London. They were published in 1936: Bach Organ Society, Album I; rerecording, 1964 (EMI). Details can be found in E. R. Jacobi's catalog of Schweitzer's concerts (at Zurich's Central Library). Further recordings (see the letter) in Strasbourg are to be found in Bach Organ Society, Albums II and III; later rerecording for EMI.

6 November 1936

1. Edouard Nies-Berger, from Strasbourg, became an organist in the United States. A professor at the Baltimore Conservatory, he accepted the position of honorary organist at the New York Philharmonic with concerts at Carnegie Hall. Starting in 1950 he joined Schweitzer in the edition of volumes 6 to 8 of J. S. Bach's organ works (begun by Schweitzer and Charles-Marie Widor; see note 1 on the letter of 19 September 1921 as well as Schweitzer's letters to Schirmer, New York). Nies-Berger then became coeditor of this edition after thorough joint analyses of performing, above all, the choral preludes. He also performed other services for Schweitzer's lifework.

2. Gerhard Herz, *J. S. Bach im Zeitalter des Rationalismus und der Frühromantik* (Bach in the age of rationalism and early romanticism), Paul Haupt, Berne, 1936.

1937

1937 (to the president of Harvard University)

1. Regarding the philosopher H. Spiegelberg, see the note on the letter of 25 July 1938.

3 May 1937

1. SHO: Société du Haut Ogooué—a trading company in the Ogowe region.

20 June 1937

1. Chargeurs Réunis, a French shipping concern that plied the African coasts.

26 September 1937

1. Refers to the manuscript mentioned in the letter of 26 June 1937, to Prof. Dr. Oskar Kraus, Prague.

25 October 1937

1. This letter, like the letter of 3 June 1937, is characteristic of many letters

of recommendation that Schweitzer wrote for African patients in his hospital. He also wrote such letters to native administrations.

The Central Archive in Gunsbach contains numerous carbon pads that Schweitzer used for various sorts of correspondence, especially regarding the medical and business sectors of the hospital, in order to have copies of his handwritten letters. It is owing to Ali Silver that several years of these pads, including this letter, were preserved and then stored at the Central Archive.

7 December 1937
1. Prof. Albert Fraenkel, M.D., had inquired about the occurrence and use of strophanthus. Fraenkel contributed enormously to the development of strophanthin and its therapeutic use.

1938

25 July 1938
1. Herbert Spiegelberg, philosopher, was confirmed by Schweitzer in 1919 at St. Nicholas's Church in Strasbourg. Because of his Jewish ancestry, he had to leave Germany in the 1930s. Schweitzer provided recommendations for him in the United States, as shown by his letter of 1937 to the president of Harvard University.

Spiegelberg wrote a number of pieces about Schweitzer, including "Good Fortune Obligates: Albert Schweitzer's Second Ethical Principle," in *Ethics*, 85, 3 (1975), University of Chicago.

28 August 1938
1. Léon Morel (1883–1976), a missionary, and his wife Georgette Morel spent many years at various stations of the Paris Mission in Gabon. According to Schweitzer's account in *Out of My Life and Thought* (chapter 13), Morel advised him, before 1913, to pick Lambarene as the site of his hospital. Later on, after Schweitzer's second arrival in Lambarene, Morel also indicated the place where the hospital was erected in 1926. Morel wrote various pieces, including "Au Gabon avant l'arrivée du Docteur Schweitzer" (In Gabon before the arrival of Dr. Schweitzer), in *Rayonnement d'Albert Schweitzer*, Colmar, 1975.

April 1938 marked the twenty-fifth anniversary of Helene and Albert Schweitzer's arrival in Lambarene. For this occasion missionaries collected funds for the hospital.
2. L. and G. Morel had their station in Samkita, where the Missionary Conference took place during Schweitzer's first sojourn in Lambarene; Samkita is located above Lambarene, on the Ogowe River.

1939

April 1939 (to Jeannette Siefert)
1. When Albert Schweitzer arrived in Strasbourg in 1939 for a visit to Europe, he decided to return to Africa within barely two weeks because of

the political situation. At this point, nine months before Hitler began World War II, Schweitzer felt it was absolutely urgent to hurry back to Lambarene so that he would be able to run the hospital during the coming developments and tend the patients.

Regarding this letter, see Siefert, *Meine Arbeitsjahre in Lambarene 1933–1935* (My years of working in Lambarene, 1933–1935), A. Schweitzer Archive, Frankfurt am Main, 1986, edited by M. Hänisch.

2 April 1939

1. For decades, Fritz and Anita Dinner-Obrist worked in the Swiss Relief Organization for the Lambarene hospital, first as accountants and then, after Pastor Hans Baur, as directors until 1976. They also took care of forwarding the numerous donations of goods from Switzerland.

21 July 1939

1. Jürgen Gerhold is now a doctor in Graz, Austria.
2. Schweitzer's daughter Rhena first visited Lambarene in 1939.

1941

9 January 1941

1. During World War II the Lambarene hospital received donations of goods and funds from the United States.
2. During the war, Prof. Everett Skillings, of Middlebury College, Vermont, later one of the founders of the Albert Schweitzer Fellowship, collected American donations for Lambarene.

1942

February 1942

1. In 1942, Helene Schweitzer did manage to reach Lambarene via various countries. See her letter of March 1945.

10 August 1942

1. The American organist and choir director Gardner Evans had written to Schweitzer on 29 June 1942 explaining his approach to performing the tempi in Bach's organ works. This wartime inquiry from the United States reached Lambarene very quickly, inducing Schweitzer to make his basic statements when he replied on 10 August 1942 from Lambarene. The correspondence was published in *The Diapason*, Chicago, Illinois, 1 November 1950.

1943

25 October 1943

1. Hudson Shaw, a pastor in London, married Maud Royden in 1944.
2. Dr. Anna Wildikann, from Riga, Latvia, was a physician at the Lam-

barene hospital from 1935 to 1937; at the start of World War II she managed to travel from Riga to Lambarene via Germany. In Schweitzer's *Ein Pelikan erzählt sein Leben* (A pelican tells its story, second edition, Hamburg, 1954, 64 pages), the forty-eight photos of a pelican were taken by Dr. Wildikann. The series, meant as a birthday present for Schweitzer, inspired him to write this little story.

1944

25 November 1944

1.   Regarding Schweitzer's parents and their forebears, see the information in note 3 on the letter of 9 July 1905. Schweitzer's grandfather, Philipp Schweitzer, in Pfaffenhofen, kept a diary on events during the second half of the nineteenth century with critical comments. Thanks to G. Woytt, the diary is now at the Central Archive in Gunsbach. Regading the importance of Pastor Johann Jakob Schillinger, Schweitzer's maternal grandfather, see the letter of 2 and 9 January 1962. A family history is included in *Rayonnement d'Albert Schweitzer*, op cit.: Robert Minder and Marie-Paule Stintzi, "Origines de la famille" (Origins of the family). This essay is followed by Minder's piece on Philipp Schweitzer and his diary. Also see *Les ancêtres d'Albert Schweitzer* [A.S.'s ancestors], 1978, 92 pages, Cercle Généalogique d'Alsace. This booklet points out that Schweitzer's ancestors came from France; Johann Nikolaus Schweitzer, later a pastor in Kork, moved to Strasbourg.

1945

January-February 1945

1.   On 14 January 1945 the British Broadcasting Corporation, London, aired a program for Schweitzer's seventieth birthday. The broadcast was beamed toward Africa and could be heard in Lambarene.

2.   Emil Mettler, a Swiss in London, maintained a friendship of many years with Schweitzer. The proprietor of a hotel/restaurant, he played a major role in the English relief organization for the Lambarene hospital. It was at his home that Schweitzer conversed with Bertrand Russell and, in earlier years, with other important people.

27 January 1945

1.   Frau Ochs knew Schweitzer since she was the wife of his close friend, Siegfried Ochs, in Berlin (see Schweitzer's letters to her husband). The unknown place to which Frau Ochs was taken during the war, as Schweitzer writes in this letter, was Terezin. In 1947, Schweitzer was informed that Frau Ochs did not survive.

23 March 1945

1.   George K. A. Bell, D.D., bishop of Chichester, member of the British Committee for Dr. Schweitzer's Hospital, worked persistently for ecumenism

and international understanding. One of his books was *The Kingship of Christ*, 1954.

March 1945 (letter from Helene Schweitzer)

1.   Dr. George Seaver, pastor and rector at St. Patrick's Cathedral, Dublin, wrote *Albert Schweitzer: The Man and His Mind*, 1947, one of the first major biographies of Schweitzer. Helene Schweitzer's letter to Seaver is taken from this book. Seaver used to work for the native population of Rhodesia.

12 June 1945

1.   During the war Frau Margit Jacobi, because of her Jewish background, was taken to Terezin, where she died. Prior to 1939, Schweitzer had offered to house her in Gunsbach. She became a victim of the Nazi dictatorship's persecution of Jews.

2 July 1945

1.   Borelli and Galley: missionaries and their families.
2.   This hotel was located on the other side of the Ogowe.

1 November 1945

1.   Dr. Charles R. Joy, *Albert Schweitzer: An Anthology*, New York/Boston, 1947; expanded edition, 1960. These people were also acquaintances of Helene Schweitzer, thereby promoting knowledge of Schweitzer's work.

16 November 1945

1.   In regard to Dr. Victor Nessmann, see the information in note 1 on Schweitzer's 1924 letter to M. Werner.

1946

1946 (to George Seaver)

1.   In regard to Dr. George Seaver, see note 1 on Helene Schweitzer's letter of March 1945. This 1946 letter from Schweitzer to Seaver is likewise taken from the latter's biography.

20 January 1946

1.   Schweitzer received the Goethe Prize of the City of Frankfurt in 1928.

1947

13 January 1947

1.   In 1936, in Strasbourg, Charles Michel replaced Pastor Albert Woytt as accountant for the hospital project. Until the 1970s, Michel was entrusted with responsible tasks for the hospital, collaborating and consulting on various issues. He was also in charge of forwarding goods from Alsace to the Lambarene hospital.
2.   Charles Michel, in Strasbourg, had sent Schweitzer a birthday present:

several drawings filled with proverbs, apparently in German, the Alsatian dialect, and French.

14 October 1947

1. Prof. Dr. Fritz Buri, theologian, issued *Christentum und Kultur bei Albert Schweitzer* (Christianity and civilization in A.S.), 1941. It was followed by several more of his writings on Schweitzer, including *A. Schweitzer's Wahrheit in Anfechtung und Bewährung* (A.S.'s truth challenged and proven), Artemis Verlag, Zurich, 1960, 47 pages. The correspondence between Schweitzer and Buri, some of it in copies, is preserved at the Central Archive in Gunsbach. Buri also edited *Ehrfurcht vor dem Leben* (Reverence for life), in celebration of Schweitzer's eightieth birthday, Paul Haupt, Berne, 1955. As a prolific scholar and author, Buri worked in many theological areas.

December 1947 (to Elsa Reger)

1. Max Reger's wife had written to Schweitzer in 1947. This response was made available to the editor by the Reger Archive, Bonn.

1948

7 February 1948

1. Dr. Emil Lind, a pastor, later a pastor in Speyer, studied theology under Schweitzer in Strasbourg and was friends with him. Lind wrote several books on Schweitzer, including *A. Schweitzer: Aus seinem Leben und Werk* (A.S.: Out of his life and thought), Paul Haupt, Berne, 1948.

1949

18 March 1949

1. Dr. Max Rehm met Schweitzer in Strasbourg and heard his performance of Bach. Later, as an author, he dealt with cultural developments in Alsace and wrote about Schweitzer and also about Eduard Spranger. (See his reminiscences of Schweitzer in volume 4 of the studies of the Erwin von Steinbach Foundation, 1975.)

19 March 1949 (to Rudolf Grabs)

1. Of all the scholars in East Germany, Dr. Rudolf Grabs, a pastor in Dresden and an expert on Schweitzer's work, contributed the most in analyzing and treating Schweitzer's creativity and writings. His anthology, *Albert Schweitzer: Denken und Tat* (A.S.: Thought and action), which is mentioned in this letter, came out in German during 1950 and has been translated into Norwegian and Swedish. It was followed by further writings, including *Sinngebung des Lebens: Aus Geist und Gedankenwelt Albert Schweitzers* (Meaning of life: From A.S.'s spirit and thought), 1950, 157 pages; *Albert Schweitzer: Denker aus Christentum* (A.S.: Christian thinker), 1958, 208 pages; and the five-volume edition of Schweitzer's writings, with introductions by R. Grabs. This edition came out in Berlin in 1971 and then in Munich and Zurich in

1974 for the centennial of Schweitzer's birth (*Gesammelte Werke*, Collected works). As a scholar, Grabs, who was friends with Schweitzer, penned important studies and other writings.

19 March 1949 (to Margarethe Klinckerfuss)

1. Margarethe Klinckerfuss, *Aufklänge aus versunkener Zeit* (Echoes from a distant past), second edition, 1948, Port Verlag, Esslingen.
2. Dr. Carl Schleich, physician and author.

1 July 1949

1. The tall tale shows Schweitzer's love of story telling and his sense of humor. The recipient of the letter, Jean Baptiste Kempf, a master tailor in Gunsbach, had been friends with Schweitzer since childhood and had likewise attended the village school. Born in Gunsbach in 1870, Kempf became the village tailor with a large clientele in the Munster Valley.

2 July 1949

1. Schweitzer delivered this talk on Goethe in July 1949 at the International Symposium for Goethe's two-hundredth birthday, Aspen, Colorado. His address was translated into English by Thornton Wilder. The event was cosponsored by the University of Chicago, which documented it in Arnold Bergstraesser, *Goethe and the Modern Age*, Chicago, 1950, 402 pages. Schweitzer's German text was published in A. Schweitzer, *Goethe*, third edition, 1950.

In July 1949, Schweitzer spent four weeks in the United States, participating in this symposium and conversing with friends who had long since been collecting donations for the Lambarene hospital and/or belonged to the committee of the hospital's supporters in the United States. During those days Schweitzer received his honorary doctorate from the University of Chicago.

3 July 1949

1. Dr. Emory Ross, an American friend and helper of Schweitzer's, played a crucial role in building up the Albert Schweitzer Fellowship in the United States. This group, initially inspired by Helene Schweitzer's lecture tours of the United States, was founded in 1946.

On 21 April 1948, the Fellowship was legally recognized as a charitable organization; on 29 November 1955, Schweitzer, in Gunsbach, issued a document designating the Fellowship as the only official American group collecting donations for his work.

29 September 1949

1. In regard to this play, see note 5 on the letter of 23 July 1950 to Gustav Woytt.

6 December 1949

1. Ernest Ansermet, a writer and composer, was conductor of the Orchestre de la Suisse Romande, Geneva.

1950

21 February 1950

1. Richard Kik and Mine Kik, the founders of the German Relief Organization for the Lambarene hospital, were active in various ways, supplying medicines to the hospital, attending to financial matters, and promoting Schweitzer's ideas. Richard Kik, who gave numerous lectures on Schweitzer, collaborated with his wife in publishing the Circular Letter for the Friends of Albert Schweitzer, which he developed. He thereby created important documentation on Schweitzer and his hospital. After Richard Kik's death, this literary contribution was continued and directed by his widow together with Dr. E. Mitschischek as editor. Since 1977, Schweitzer's hospital and his spiritual legacy have been helped immeasurably by the circular letter Professor Manfred Hänisch has published every six months.

11 March 1950

1. The sixth German edition of *The Quest of the Historical Jesus* was published by J. C. B. Mohr in Tübingen, 1951. It included Schweitzer's new foreword dated 19 August 1950.
2. This refers to Georg Siebeck.

3 May 1950

1. Schweitzer gave this speech in Aspen, Colorado, in 1949 at the celebration of Goethe's two-hundredth birthday. See *Goethe*.
2. Only the French edition was reworked; the German edition of *Zwischen Wasser und Urwald (On the Edge of the Primeval Forest)* was left as is.
3. The Berne publisher Paul Haupt put out the first German edition of this book in 1921.

23 July 1950

1. Gustav Woytt, the son of the pastor Albert Woytt and Schweitzer's sister Adele, translated a few of Schweitzer's writings, some in collaboration with André Canivez. This letter provides some insight into Schweitzer's work methods: Instead of translating his own German text, he revised someone else's translation, applying his own style. Today, on behalf of Rhena Schweitzer-Miller, G. Woytt administers Schweitzer's literary estate.
2. Introduction to the new edition of *A l'orée de la forêt vierge (On the Edge of the Primeval Forest)*, Albin Michel, Paris, dated 15 December 1951.
3. Canivez, professor of philosophy at the University of Strasbourg, was also called "Chavez" by Schweitzer. He penned "Raison, éthique et vie dans la philosophie d'Albert Schweitzer" (Reason, ethics and life in the philosophy of A.S.) in *Rayonnement d'Albert Schweitzer*, Colmar, 1975.
4. The first German edition of *The Kingdom of God and Primitive Christianity*, edited by Ulrich Neuenschwander, was published by J. C. B. Mohr, Tübingen, in 1967. See the note on the letter of 4 January 1951.
5. The play *Il est minuit, docteur Schweitzer*, later made into a movie, was

written by Gilbert Cesbron. Its premiere took place in Colmar in 1949; this passage in the letter refers to a radio adaptation.

27 July 1950

1.   The Central Archive in Gunsbach contains some information about Madre Maria, a Franciscan nun in Umbria. Mother Sorella Maria (Pignetti from Turin) founded a Franciscan sisterhood, "demonstrating the simple life of the Gospel," following, we are told, St. Paul's precepts in his Epistle to the Philippians.

10 October 1950

1.   Pastor Robert Charles Hirt (1872–1957) studied theology in Strasbourg together with Schweitzer and was pastor of the parish of Hohweiler-Hermesweiler, Alsace. Schweitzer visited him in Hohweiler during the 1950s.

13 November 1950

1.   During the early 1950s, Erica Anderson, an American film expert and photographer, visited Lambarene several times, where, with Schweitzer's permission, she shot her widely circulated documentary. The photos she took in Lambarene have been frequently published. She herself issued two large photo books on Schweitzer's work (S. Fischer, New York and Frankfurt, 1955; New York, 1965). Later, in Great Barrington, Massachusetts, she founded a library and conference center containing a large collection of audiovisual materials on Schweitzer.

1951

4 January 1951

1.   Schweitzer, *Reich Gottes und Christentum*, edited and introduced by Ulrich Neuenschwander, J. C. B. Mohr, Tübingen, 1967. The manuscript was published posthumously. According to the introduction, the four chapters of this book, based on examinations of the Bible, "sum up the biblical faith in the Kingdom of God" (page vii). Schweitzer concludes: "We have to take the road that is thus opened" (page 204).

1951 (to Minoru Nomura)

1.   Minoru Nomura, M.D., chairman of the Schweitzer Society in Japan, founded the Japanese circle of friends of the hospital. During the 1950s, he visited Lambarene several times and over the years helped circulate Schweitzer's books.

In regard to Japanese encounters with Schweitzer's work during 1913–60, see Nomura's contribution to *A. Schweitzer: Sein Denken und sein Weg*, op. cit., page 412. The major Japanese efforts and initiatives include those of T. Kagawa and K. Uchimura; the latter's son, Prof. J. Uchimura, of the University of Tokyo, worked at the Lambarene hospital in 1954.

2.   At Nomura's suggestion a complete nineteen-volume Japanese edition of Schweitzer's work was published by Hakusuisha, Tokyo, 1956–61.

15 April 1951

1. In regard to the genesis of *The Kingdom of God and Primitive Christianity*, see the letter of 4 January 1951.

11 June 1951

1. The Hebel Prize, named after the theologian and author Johann Peter Hebel, is awarded for cultural achievements.

5 August 1951

1. Refers again to the work on *The Kingdom of God and Primitive Christianity* (see the letter of 4 January 1951) and the third volume of the philosophy of civilization.

2. From 1934 to 1936, Helene Schweitzer and her daughter Rhena lived in Lausanne.

Summer 1951

1. Dr. August Heisler, physician in Königsfeld, recipient of the Paracelsus Medal, wrote the widely circulated book *Dennoch Landarzt* (Still a country doctor) and made lasting contributions to issues of medical treatment. Schweitzer was friendly with Heisler and his family. Prior to his second trip to Africa, Schweitzer built the house in Königsfeld for his wife and his daughter.

11 August 1951

1. Schweitzer first met Cosima Wagner in Strasbourg. He played some Bach organ works for her and discussed features of Bach's and Wagner's art. In regard to Wagner's music, also see the passages in chapter 20 of Schweitzer's Bach book.

In 1933, Schweitzer wrote the essay, "Mes souvenirs sur Cosima Wagner" (My memories of Cosima Wagner), *L'Alsace française*, pages 124–25; English translation in *Music in the Life of Albert Schweitzer*, New York and Boston, 1951; second revised edition, London 1953. See Erwin R. Jacobi's presentation, *Albert Schweitzer und Richard Wagner: Eine Dokumentation* (A.S. and Richard Wagner: A documentation), Michelsen, Zurich, 1977.

1951 (to Christoph Martin)

1. Christoph Martin was the son of Hans and Lore Martin and grandson of Pastor Wilhelm Martin and Schweitzer's associate Emmy Martin.

27 October 1951

1. Edouard Nies-Berger. See note 2 on the letter of 19 September 1921.

2. Schweitzer received the Peace Prize of German Booksellers in 1951. The address was delivered by his friend, West German president Theodor Heuss.

3. In 1951, Schweitzer recorded Bach organ works. The information in this letter concerns the large group of recordings for Columbia. Schweitzer also recorded works by César Franck, Charles-Marie Widor, and Felix Mendelssohn-Bartholdy.

1952

15 February 1952

1.   Pierre Count Sovorgnan de Brazza (1852–1905), whom Schweitzer discusses in this epistolary speech from Lambarene on the occasion of the centennial of the count's birth, was an African explorer and government commissioner (naval officer). As a geographer he explored the Ogowe region; he also fought against slavery and later against the exploitation of the natives by concession companies. The city of Brazzaville, which was named for him, was made the capital of the Congo Republic. See S. de Brazza, *Conférences et lettres sur les trois explorations dans l'Ouest Africain* (Lectures and letters on the three expeditions in western Africa) by N. Ney, 1888.

   Fundamental for the exploration of de Brazza's expeditions and accounts is *Brazza et la fondation du Congo Français* (De Brazza and the foundation of the French Congo), I–III, in *Documents pour servir à l'Histoire de l'Afrique Equatoriale Française* (Documents concerning the history of French Equatorial Africa), I, Paris, 1966; II, Paris, 1972; III, Paris, 1969. Volume 1, which deals with de Brazza's exploration of the Ogowe region (1875–1879), was published by Henri Brunschwig.

8 July 1952

1.   Queen Elisabeth of Belgium visited Schweitzer in Gunsbach several times; a violinist herself, she discussed problems of musical style with Schweitzer.

on the *Foucauld* [1952]

1.   SHO stands for Société du Haut Ogooué, a trading company in the Ogowe district.

15 August 1952

1.   In regard to Elly Heuss-Knapp, see the letter of 12 January 1935 and note 1 on Theodor and Elly Heuss.
2.   Luise Hoff, wife of Ernst Bresslau, the brother of Helene Schweitzer-Bresslau.

26 September 1952

1.   In regard to this speech in Paris, see note 2 on the letter of 18 March 1953 to the Schirmer publishing house.

15 November 1952

1.   Ali Silver, the Dutchwoman who was a close long-term associate of Schweitzer's, first arrived in Lambarene in 1947 and worked there until 1965. Schweitzer assigned her numerous tasks in the hospital, where she also answered many of the letters. During those eighteen years she made a major contribution to Schweitzer's lifework and helped him with many problems. Since 1972 she has been in charge of the Albert Schweitzer House in Gunsbach and the Central Archive; on the basis of her knowledge and great

experience, she has also helped authors and friends of Schweitzer's work. Ali Silver and her work for Schweitzer have been treated in the collection *Akewa*, edited by M. Abé, F. C. Braun, Tübingen, 1986.

28 December 1952

1.   After a visit to Lambarene, Stefan Zweig, in the course of his biographical writings, penned the essay "Unvergessliches Erlebnis: Ein Tag bei Albert Schweitzer" (Unforgettable experience: A day with A.S.). His text is included in Stefan Zweig, *Begegnungen mit Menschen, Büchern, Städten* (Encounters with people, books, cities), Verlag Reichner,Vienna, 1937, pages 118ff. Since then, his essay has been reprinted in other publications.

1953

18 March 1953 (to Jacques Feschotte)

1.   Jacques Feschotte, a French expert on music and a friend of Schweitzer's, wrote the book *Albert Schweitzer*, published by Editions Universitaires, 1952, 129 pages (Classiques du XXe siècle); it has been translated into English, German, Italian, and Spanish.

18 March 1953 (to the Schirmer publishing house)

1.   In regard to the American edition of J. S. Bach's organ works, edited by Schweitzer and Charles-Marie Widor, and in regard to Nies-Berger's collaboration on the three volumes of the chorale compositions, see note 2 on the letter of 19 September 1921.

2.   Schweitzer was elected to the Académie des Sciences Morales et Politiques. His acceptance speech has been published: "Le problème de l'éthique dans l'évolution de la pensée humaine" (The problem of ethics in the evolution of human thought), Paris, Recueil Sirey, undated, 11 pages, 1952; it has been translated into English.

5 November 1953

1.   The 1952 Nobel Prize was awarded to Schweitzer in 1953. Gunnar Jahn, on behalf of the board of directors of the Nobel Foundation, delivered the address at the ceremony on 10 December 1953 in Oslo; the text is preserved at the Central Archive in Gunsbach. The German text of Schweitzer's speech, "The Problem of Peace in the World Today," was published by C. H. Beck, Munich, 1954, and has been widely translated.

19 December 1953

1.   Dag Hammarskjöld, secretary general of the United Nations, corresponded with Schweitzer, thanking him in a personal letter of 21 July 1955 for his thoughts and actions in the cause of international understanding. The letter was published in *Rayonnement d'Albert Schweitzer*, op. cit.

23 December 1953

1.   Max Tau was one of the important men in Norway who supported the

awarding of the Nobel Peace Prize to Schweitzer. See the information on
Tau in the note on the letter of 28 March 1962.
2.   Refers to the edition of Bach's organ works. See the letter of 18 March
1953 to Schirmer.

1954

14 February 1954 (to Richard Kik)
1.   In regard to Kik, see the letter of 21 February 1950. After World War
II, Kik, in Heidenheim, put together the circular letters; consisting of correspondence from Schweitzer and his assistants and physicians, they were
sent out to many patrons.
2.   Hartmann was a pharmaceutical firm that made donations to the Lambarene hospital.

June 1954 (to Abbé Pierre)
1.   Abbé H. A. Grouès, known as Abbé Pierre, founded the Emmaus
Brotherhood, which performs far-reaching charitable services in France and
non-European countries. He visited Schweitzer in Lambarene in order to
get to know him and his work. When Schweitzer wrote to him in 1962 (see
the letter of 22 December 1962), Abbé Pierre's efforts had gained international
importance in the struggle against hunger and poverty in the Third World.

[Lambarene] (to a handicapped woman)
1.   Schweitzer based a few sermons on this biblical verse about peace, from
Philippians 4:7. See *Strasburger Predigten* (Strasbourg Sermons), Munich,
1966; and a crucial passage in his autobiography, *Out of My Life and Thought*
(chapter 21).

December 1954
1.   Ernst Beutler (1885–1960) received this letter from Schweitzer on his
seventieth birthday; Beutler was the director of the Freies Deutsches Hoch-
stift and the Goethe Museum in Frankfurt. He is the editor of the Artemis
edition of Goethe's works.
2.   The picture was painted by Ada von Erlach in Strasbourg during 1905.

1955

20 February 1955
1.   *The Problem of Peace in the World Today*, Harper & Row, New York,
1954.
2.   Albert Einstein wrote "Schlichte Grösse," published as "Out of Inner
Necessity," in *To Dr. Albert Schweitzer: A Festschrift Commemorating His
Eightieth Birthday*, edited by Homer A. Jack, Evanston, Illinois. In Switzerland, Einstein's text was included in *Ehrfurcht vor dem Leben* (Reverence
for life), edited by Fritz Buri, Paul Haupt, Berne, 1955, and in Germany, it
was included in *Albert Schweitzer: Sein Denken und sein Weg*, op. cit.

10 March 1955
1. Association Française des Amis d'Albert Schweitzer.
2. Along with the authors mentioned in this letter, contributions to the French festschrift, Hommage à Albert Schweitzer (eightieth birthday), came from André Canivez, Pablo Casals, Alfred Cortot, and Gustave Bret. This book was published in 1955 by Le Guide.

29 June 1955
1. The Greek writer Nikos Kazantzakis wrote an afterword for Jean Pierhal's book *Albert Schweitzer*, Verlag Kindler, Munich, 1955. The English-language edition, *Albert Schweitzer: The Story of His Life*, was published in New York in 1957.

31 August 1955
1. The Albert Schweitzer Settlement is located in Hamburg. Schweitzer visited it while traveling in 1955.

8 December 1955
1. The title of the book by Sigurbjörn Einarsson is *Albert Schweitzer: Aevisaga*. It was published in Reykjavik in 1955.

1956

1956 (to Howard Rice)
1. In 1952, in Paris, Robert Amadou published *Albert Schweitzer: Eléments de Biography et de Bibliographie* (A.S.: elements of biography and bibliography), 148 pages.
    In the United States, *Albert Schweitzer: An International Bibliography*, listing works on Schweitzer, was published by G. K. Hall in 1981. It was edited by Laura Person, librarian at the Mission Research Library of Union Theological Seminary, New York, and Nancy Snell Griffith, likewise a librarian in New York.

1 March 1956
1. Karel Reichel, bishop of Nové Paká, Czechoslovakia.

11 May 1956
1. Arthur Piechler, cathedral organist and composer in Augsburg, Germany, wrote choral works, organ works, and chamber music. See *Das praktische Orgelbuch* (The practical organ book), 1952, 1959.

8 December 1956
1. J. S. Bach's organ report was published in *Bachdokumente*, volume 1, pages 152ff.

1957

2 January 1957
1. During that period Dr. M. Nomura in Japan worked persistently, prop-

agating the ideas of this work, partly in connection with the nineteen-volume Japanese edition of Schweitzer's writings; he himself translated several of the volumes. The Central Archive in Gunsbach contains a new survey of the Japanese translations and editions, expertly compiled by Makoto Abé in 1983.

2. Tony van Leer of Laren, Holland, who worked with Schweitzer in Lambarene for more than ten years, devoted herself to his assignments and the total idea of his work. Since 1971 she has shared the administration of the Albert Schweitzer House in Gunsbach, making a valuable contribution. She is also employed at the Central Archive, having actively participated in its development and its collections.

12 April 1957

1. After meeting Schweitzer in Lambarene and discussing world peace, Norman Cousins suggested that he publish an appeal. Cousins wrote *Dr. Schweitzer of Lambarene*, Harper, New York, 1960, 254 pages. In 1985, Cousins edited *Albert Schweitzer's Mission, Healing and Peace*, which chiefly documents the problem of peace.

2. This radio address, aired internationally by Radio Oslo, was printed several times as *Appell an die Menschheit* (Appeal to Mankind). It was also included in a German edition of Schweitzer's selected works, *Ausgewählte Werke* (volume 5), edited by Rudolf Grabs. See the publication in the eleventh circular letter, published by Richard Kik.

6 June 1957

1. Soon after returning to Zurich from Lambarene, Helene Schweitzer succumbed to illness. She died in Zurich on 1 June 1957. Tony van Leer had accompanied her back to Europe.

July 1957

1. This letter shows the direction in which Schweitzer felt the ecumenical rapport of the churches can develop.

1957 (to Eduard Spranger)

1. This letter was written for the birthday of Eduard Spranger, a philosopher and pedagogue in Tübingen. For the Spranger festschrift, *Erziehung zur Menschlichkeit* (Education toward humanity), Tübingen, 1957, Schweitzer contributed "Wie mein Lebenswerk entstand" (The genesis of my lifework). After World War II, Spranger became the first president of the University of Berlin and, like Schweitzer, was a member of the Prussian Academy of Sciences. After their initial encounter in 1959, Spranger and Schweitzer remained friends.

2. A. Schweitzer, "Le problème de l'éthique dans l'évolution de la pensée humaine," op. cit.

18 November 1957

1. The ceremony took place at Schweitzer's home in Gunsbach on November 24.

The diploma that Otto Michel, dean of the Theological Faculty, handed to Schweitzer states that the University of Tübingen has awarded an honorary doctorate in theology to Schweitzer, "who has taught us to hear anew the testimony of the New Testament as the tiding of the imminent Kingdom of God; who, in philosophy and theology, has dedicated himself to the value of ethical deeds and vicarious sacrifice; who, through the power of the living example, has called upon mankind to show brotherly responsibility."

31 December 1957

1. The correspondence between Bertrand Russell and Schweitzer, lasting form 1959 to 1965, was issued by Herbert Spiegelberg with an introduction: *The Correspondence between Bertrand Russell and Albert Schweitzer* in *International Studies in Philosophy*, volume 12, 1980.

1958

4 April 1958

1. Schweitzer was a guest at a Lindau meeting of the Nobel laureates in physics. Here, after an evening stroll through the town, he played some works of Bach's for Werner Heisenberg and a small group of physicists, on the organ of the Stiftskirche. In 1957, Heisenberg published an account of that recital (fortieth circular letter). He writes that Albert Schweitzer also talked about Bach's compositional technique and the various readings of his ornamentations: "It became absolutely clear to us that his careful approach to Bach's music and his careful dealings with people sprang from the same root."

2. Göttingen scientists published a manifesto against atomic weapons.

28 July 1958

1. Schweitzer's three speeches against nuclear testing were broadcast in countless countries. These addresses convey his argumentation and his urgent warnings against the consequences of the test explosions. During subsequent years he devoted himself intensely to this problem, approaching it from various angles. The speeches were published as *Peace or Atomic War?* The titles of the individual speeches are "Forgoing Test Explosions," "The Danger of an Atomic War," and "Top-Level Negotiations."

The three talks, read by G. Jahn of the Nobel Prize Foundation, were Schweitzer's contributions to the worldwide discussion, both oral and written. In his book, *Die Ethik Albert Schweitzers* (A.S.'s ethics) (1977), Otto Spear investigated and systematized the problems of nuclear weapons and peace in Schweitzer, developing his insights into an appeal. (See the section "Sorge um Menschheit und Friede" [Concerns about humanity and peace], pages 21ff.) We should also mention Benedict Winnubst, *Das Friedensdenken Albert Schweitzers* (A.S.'s ideas about peace), Amsterdam, 1974—a dissertation in Brussels with a detailed analysis and documents. In the collection *Albert Schweitzer: Sein Denken und sein Weg*, op. cit., with contributions by several authors, see "Albert Schweitzer und das Atomproblem" (A.S. and the atomic problem), pages 437–91, with a detailed introduction by Friedrich Wagner.

14 August 1958

1.   In 1960, Carl J. Burckhardt wrote an appreciation of Schweitzer (published in *Universitas*, number 1, 1960); and in 1966 he delivered the memorial speech for Schweitzer in the peace class of the West German Pour le Mérite medal (published in *Universitas* number 8, 1966) as well as in the book *Orden Pour le mérite für Wissenschaft und Künste: Reden und Gedenkworte* (Pour le mérite medal for science and art: Addresses and memorial speeches), volume 7, Lambert Schneider, Heidelberg, 1967.

23 August 1958

1.   Timothy Yilsun Rhee, Korean theologian and physician, worked at the lepers' village in Lambarene. Christened as an adult, he took the name of Timothy. After returning to Korea he opened a hospital on the Korean island of Ullung-Do. In 1975 he published *Reverence for Life and World Peace: Dr. Albert Schweitzer's Centennial Birth Anniversary Commemoration Address*, Seoul, Korea. In his homeland Rhee is considered the "Korean Schweitzer." His publications include *Albert Schweitzer: The Man and His Thought*, Sasangesa Publishing Co., Seoul, 1954, 155 pages.

5 October 1958

1.   Pastor Georges Marchal issued several publications on Schweitzer's work and also worked on behalf of his project. He wrote the introductions for the French translations of *The Mysticism of Paul the Apostle* and *Strasbourg Sermons*.

13 October 1958

1.   J. Lefftz, *Elsässische Dorfbilder* (Alsatian village tableaux), Wörth, 1958, 301 pages.

19 November 1958

1.   Ulrich Neuenschwander, who posthumously published the German editions of Schweitzer's *The Kingdom of God and Primitive Christianity* (see the letter of 4 January 1951) and *Strasbourg Sermons*, taught theology at the University of Berne after practicing as a pastor in Olten. He spent years researching Schweitzer's unpublished manuscripts and then made a major scholarly contribution by drafting the plan and structure of a multivolume edition of Schweitzer's theological and philosophical writings. Together with Johann Zürcher, he prepared the first volume. In 1977, while serving as Rector designatus of the University of Berne, he succumbed to a sudden illness. His work on the Schweitzer edition was taken over by Zürcher.

16 December 1958

1.   The sculptor Fritz Behn created the Albert Schweitzer statue that now stands on the Kanzrain in Gunsbach.

1958 (to Martin Niemöller)

1. Niemöller had been planning a donation from the Church of Hesse-Nassau to the Lambarene hospital.

1959

24 January 1959

1. During this period, as since 1923, the publisher Dr. Heinrich Beck and his editor Dr. George Sund were issuing works of Schweitzer's at the C. H. Beck publishing house. The selection titled *Selbstzeugnisse* (Self-Documentation) was widely circulated (sixty thousand copies).

5 April 1959

1. Marie Secretan, who later married Gustav Woytt, worked at Lambarene from 1929 to 1932 and wrote informatively about Schweitzer and his work. Next to his own accounts, her book *Albert Schweitzer baut Lambarene* (A.S. builds Lambarene) is the most important depiction of the early years; she expanded both the text and the pictures for the new edition in 1979, *Albert Schweitzers Lambarene lebt* (A.S.'s Lambarene lives). In 1947 she published a biography, *Albert Schweitzer: Der Urwalddoktor von Lambarene* (A.S.: The jungle doctor of Lambarene). Her reminiscences of Lambarene are likewise treated in her contribution, "Souvenirs d'une infirmière" (A nurse's memories) in *Rayonnement d'Albert Schweitzer*, op. cit.

8 October 1959

1. On 11 and 12 October 1959, Schweitzer visited Tübingen to thank the university for the honorary doctorate in theology (1957) and to engage in discussions. See the note on the letter of 18 November 1957 containing the text of the diploma.

1960

25 February 1960

1. Prof. Dr. Hermann Mai, a close friend of Schweitzer's, chairman of the German Relief Organization for the Lambarene hospital from 1971 to 1981, often practiced medicine in Lambarene, concentrating on children. The development of Lambarene's pediatric clinic during the 1960s and 1970s was mainly his doing. Professor Mai was also elected vice president of AISL, the International Association for the Lambarene Hospital. He has dealt with Lambarene and Schweitzer's work in lectures and articles as well as important analyses of tropical illnesses that occur in Gabon. All his dedication to Schweitzer's work and thought has evolved as a far-reaching achievement for Lambarene and Schweitzer's ethics. His publications in this area include not only the treatise "Uber vierzig Jahre Urwaldhospital Schweitzer" (Over forty years of Schweitzer's jungle hospital), 1962, but also *Das Albert Schweitzer-Spital Lambarene* (The Albert Schweitzer Hospital in Lambarene), H. Kunz, Kelkheim, 1984.

29 February 1960

1. The special issue of *Universitas* (volume 15, number 1, 1960) for Schweitz-er's eighty-fifth birthday contained a number of papers by various scholars.

24 July 1960

1. Gerald Götting, chairman of the Christian Democratic Union in the German Democratic Republic, was elected deputy chairman of the city coun-cil. He visited the Lambarene hospital twice and helped it by promoting donations of goods from East Germany. His publications include *Zu Gast in Lambarene* (A guest in Lambarene), 1964, and *Albert Schweitzer—Pionier der Menschlichkeit* (A.S.—pioneer of humanity), Union, Berlin, second edi-tion, 1979, 191 pages. This volume also contains the Schweitzer-Götting correspondence, which began in 1959. Götting, in contact with Schweitzer, compiled and published the anthology *Die Lehre der Ehrfurcht vor dem Leben* (The doctrine of reverence for life), which has been translated; Schweitzer reviewed his 1952 academy address for inclusion in this volume.

7 August 1960

1. The physician Rolf Müller came to the Lambarene hospital in July 1960, treating a wide variety of patients until September 1964.

1961

20 September 1961

1. Martin Werner, *Der protestantische Weg des Glaubens*, volume 2, Paul Haupt, Berne, and Katzmann, Tübingen, 1962, 620 pages.

20 November 1961

1. Dr. Hermann Baur, chairman of the Commission for Albert Schweitzer's Spiritual Work since 1980, has been doing fundamental work for Schweitzer's ideas and the Lambarene hospital. Through his contacts with important groups and persons devoted to Schweitzer's work, he has helped enormously to spread information about Schweitzer's spiritual and intellectual creations and the Lambarene hospital as a symbol of Schweitzer's theological and philosophical ideas. In his publications, Baur, a medical doctor, has contrib-uted to a solid presentation of Schweitzer's lifework. Baur's writings include "Albert Schweitzer als Arzt" (A.S. as physician), in the 1959 festschrift for Schweitzer's eighty-fifth birthday, and "A. Schweitzer und unsere Zukunft" (A.S. and our future) in circular letter number 34.

21 November 1961

1. The student W. Voelter had donated some money that he had earned. Today he is professor of biochemistry at the University of Tübingen, and he has also implemented a series of important measures in the area of scientific and educational help for developing countries.

1961 (to Heinz Sawade)

1. A delegation of guests from the German Democratic Republic brought

along tapings of the Bach organ in Mühlhausen, Thuringia, thus enabling Schweitzer to hear the sound of the organ.

1962

2 January 1962

1. Hans Walter Bähr, ed., *Albert Schweitzer: Sein Denken und sein Weg* (A.S.: His thought and his path), Tübingen, 1962, 578 pages; Dutch edition, Haarlem, 1963.

9 March 1962

1. In the sentence quoted, the letter, concentrating on reverence for life and basic ethical direction, shows the connection to the idea of civilization.

26 March 1962

1. Dr. Willy A. Petritsky did scholarly writings on Schweitzer and his ethics. As a specialist he made a valuable contribution to propagating Schweitzer's ethics in the Soviet Union and Eastern Europe. His publications include "The Development of the Principle of Reverence for Life in Albert Schweitzer's Philosophical-Ethic Teachings" in *Didactic Letters of the Chair for Social Sciences of the Leningrad College*, 1965; "Albert Schweitzer's Ethical Teachings—Conclusions of Critical Analysis" (publishing house of Leningrad University, 1970); "The Right to Address our Souls" (in *Literary Issues*, Moscow, 1976, number 5); and his article in the *Great Soviet Encyclopedia*, volume 29, Moscow, 1978.

28 March 1962

1. In Oslo, Norway, Max Tau, a German emigré, spent over a decade propagating Schweitzer's work, his hospital, and his conception of peace. That is the context of this letter. In 1955, Max Tau published *Albert Schweitzer und der Friede* (A.S. and peace); in 1956, together with Lotte Gerhold, he put out *Albert Schweitzer—Veien til deg selv*, a collection available only in Norwegian. His writings on Schweitzer's ideas and accomplishments have appeared in both Norway and Germany. His other writings deal with issues and possibilities of international understanding. He was one of the Norwegian friends of the Lambarene hospital who obtained donations for it.

14 April 1962

1. Dr. Gerhard Kühn frequently wrote about Schweitzer's ideas and actions; he started, and shaped the contents of, a major series of publications in connection with the Albert Schweitzer Archive and Center, Frankfurt (directed by E. Bomze). Kühn likewise published the picture book *Ehrfurcht vor dem Leben* (Reverence for life). He also helped with the allocation of instruments and funds for the Lambarene hospital.

2 June 1962

1. Schweitzer here quoted the French title of his book on Indian thought.

2. C. F. Andrews.
3. M. Haga, "Albert Schweitzer—Brücke zwischen Ost und West" (A.S.—bridge between East and West) in *Albert Schweitzer: Sein Denken und sein Weg*, op. cit.

27 August 1962

1. In Lambarene, during 1962, Albert Schweitzer, in long-distance collaboration with Edouard Nies-Berger, edited the publication of volumes 7 and 8 of the American edition of Bach's organ works. They appeared in New York during 1967 (see the note on the letter of 19 September 1921).

24 November 1962

1. *Die Stimme des Menschen*, a collection of letters and other writings from around the world, 1939–45, edited by Hans Walter Bähr, Munich, 1961; sixth edition, 1981: Zurich and Vienna, 1962; Tokyo, 1962, 1963; Haarlem, 1964; Milan, 1964.
2. The queen of Romania, née Princess zu Wied, wrote under the pen name of Carmen Silva. The letters mentioned by Schweitzer have not been located.

10 December 1962

1. Albert Schweitzer, *Die Lehre der Ehrfurcht vor dem Leben (The Teaching of Reverence for Life)*, Union Verlag, Berlin, 1962, 80 pages. This anthology was originally suggested by G. Götting.

20 December 1962

1. Robert Minder, *Kultur und Literatur in Deutschland und Frankreich*, Insel Verlag, Frankfurt, 1962. The essay on the parsonage in German literature was first published in the Protocols of the Mainz Academy.

22 December 1962

1. Schweitzer's uncle was Auguste Schweitzer, the older brother of Schweitzer's father, partner of the firm of Harth & Co., Paris. It was Auguste's wife Mathilde, née Härtle, who introduced Albert Schweitzer to Charles-Marie Widor. Schweitzer's Bach book, with an introduction by Widor, was dedicated to Schweitzer's aunt Mathilde Schweitzer.
2. Groups that were part of Abbé Pierre's Emmaus movement, Paris (see Schweitzer's letter in June 1954 to Abbé Pierre), went to developing countries to provide aid; these mostly young volunteers work in poor areas.

1963

3 February 1963

1. See the March 1929 letter to the theologian Adolf von Harnack about Schweitzer's election to the Prussian Academy of Sciences.
2. Schurman, the American ambassador to Berlin.
3. In this letter Schweitzer goes into his close ties with the Curtius family—

a relationship that began during his early years in Strasbourg when he became friends with Friedrich Curtius, district director of Colmar and later chairman of the board of the Alsatian Church of the Augsburg Confession (see the letter of 9 July 1905, note 4). Friedrich's father, Ernst Curtius, likewise mentioned in this letter of 3 February 1963, was a classical scholar in Berlin. Schweitzer, in the second chapter of *Out of My Life and Thought*, writes that his friend Friedrich, during their student days in Berlin, introduced Schweitzer into the Curtius home. "I thus got to know and love Berlin in its most beautiful time."

1963 (to Robert Weiss)

1. For decades Dr. Robert Weiss, a pharmacist in Strasbourg, helped Schweitzer procure medicines for the hospital; he visited Lambarene in 1952. He is the author of *Albert Schweitzer als Arzt und Mensch* (A.S. as physician and human being), Morstadt, Kehl, 1976.

5 May 1963

1. In 1959, Susanne Spranger (1890–1963), wife of Eduard Spranger, participated with Schweitzer in the Tübingen talks.

25 July 1963

1. The reference is to T. L. Vaswani, *Albert Schweitzer*, Gita Publishing House, Poona, India.
2. *Die Weltanschauung der indischen Denker (Indian Thought and Its Development)*, Munich and Berne, 1935.

25 August 1963

1. A German version of the letter to J. F. Kennedy is extant. Concerning the text of the letter to Nikita Khrushchev, see G. Götting, *Zu Gast in Lambarene* (A guest in Lambarene), Berlin, 1964, page 129.

1964

12 June 1964 (to Willy Bremi and Hermann Baur)

1. This suggestion culminated in the collection of the Strasbourg sermons, edited by U. Neuenschwander (1969), who supplied an introduction, "Albert Schweitzer als Prediger" (A.S. as preacher). A friend of Schweitzer's, the Berne professor describes the manner, themes, and language of the sermons. Neuenschwander (who subsequently edited an edition of Schweitzer's manuscripts published posthumously) writes: "The sermons show us the unity of this man's theology, faith, and life." The texts are imbued with "a deep Christian piety that lives from the both powerful and intimate rapport with Christ."

12 June 1964 (to Hermann Baur)

1. See the note on the preceding letter.
2. Dr. Walter Munz, a Swiss physician, began working in Lambarene

during 1961. In 1965 he became head physician of the hospital. The Swiss writer Henry Babel, a pastor in Geneva, is the author of *La pensée d'Albert Schweitzer: Sa signification pour la théologie et la philosophie contemporaines* (A.S.'s thinking: Its significance for contemporary theology and philosophy), 1954, 239 pages.

3. Gerald McKnight, *Verdict on Schweitzer: The Man Behind the Legend of Lambarene*, F. Muller, London, 1964, 254 pages.

25 June 1964

1. Pastor Martin Strege, a scholar of theology, wrote and lectured on Schweitzer's work. In 1937, Strege published *Zum Sein in Gott durch Denken: Eine Darstellung der ethischen Mystik Albert Schweitzers* (On being in God through thinking: A presentation of A.S.'s ethical mysticism). In 1955 he published *Das Eschaton als gestaltende Kraft in der Theologie: Albert Schweitzer und Martin Albertz* (The eschaton as a shaping force in theology: A.S. and Martin Albertz); in 1956, *Das Reich Gottes als theologische Problem im Lichte der Eschatologie und Mystik Albert Schweitzers* (The kingdom of God as a theological problem in the light of A.S.'s eschatology and mysticism). This was followed in 1965 by *Albert Schweitzers Religion und Philosophie* (A.S.'s religion and philosophy), a methodical investigation of the sources. Strege also meticulously probed into Schweitzer's Strasbourg sermons. In 1974, Lambert Schneider, Heidelberg, issued Martin Strege and Lothar Stiehm, *Albert Schweitzer, "Was sollen wir tun?" Zwölf Predigten über ethische Probleme* (A.S., "What ought we to do?" Twelve sermons on ethical problems), second edition, 1986.

30 June 1964

1. The Aymà publishing house did not issue this book; instead it eventually published the translation of *Out of My Life and Thought*.

20 July 1964 (to Helmut Thielicke)

1. This refers to Thielicke's statements, which, as this letter shows, were read by Schweitzer during the 1960s debates on nuclear weapons. Thielicke also wrote the multivolume magnum opus of contemporary theology, *Theologische Ethik* (Theological ethics), which also discusses problems of ethical conduct in society. For Schweitzer's ninetieth birthday the author wrote an essay that was reprinted in circular letter 40, 1975.

29 August 1964

1. The suggestion pertained to the edition of Schweitzer's writings on the ethics of reverence for life, 1919–63. This goal was realized by a book planned chiefly as a study edition: H. W. Bähr, *Albert Schweitzer: Die Lehre der Ehrfurcht vor dem Leben (The Teaching of Reverence for Life)*, C. H. Beck, Munich, 1966, third expanded edition, 1981; fourth edition, 1984.

2. The title of H. W. Bähr's study, mentioned here by Schweitzer, is "Die universelle Erweiterung der Ethik im Denken Albert Schweitzers" (The universal expansion of ethics in A.S.'s thinking). It was published in *Albert*

Schweitzer: Sein Denken und sein Weg, op. cit. (translated into English, French, Dutch, and Romanian). See also H. W. Bähr, "L'Ethique cosmique d'Albert Schweitzer et les problèmes de l'éthique naturelle" (A.S.'s cosmic ethics and the problems of natural ethics). This lecture, delivered at the University of Strasbourg in 1975 for what would have been Schweitzer's hundredth birthday, was published in *Revue d'Histoire et de Philosophie Religieuses*, Presses Universitaires de France, Paris, 1976, pages 97ff.

8 November 1964
1. In 1964, in Basel, Dr. Fritz Buri and Dr. Hermann Baur organized a lecture series on Schweitzer and his work for Schweitzer's upcoming ninetieth birthday on 14 January 1965.

10 November 1964
1. Dr. Harald Steffahn, a writer and journalist, visited Schweitzer in Lambarene, was friendly with him, and published a number of articles on his life and thought. In 1974 he published *Du aber folge mir nach: Albert Schweitzers Werk und Wirkung* (But thou follow me: A.S.'s work and impact). Steffahn is the author of the widely circulated pictorial biography *Albert Schweitzer* (Rowohlt) and also *Das Albert Schweitzer-Lesebuch* (The A.S. reader). 1984; second edition, 1986.

21 November 1964
1. As this letter shows (see the letter of 3 October 1960 to W. Ludwig), Werner Ludwig, chairman of the Albert Schweitzer Committee of the German Red Cross, German Democratic Republic, sent valuable and helpful East German donations to the Lambarene hospital. Because of its steady and coordinated activities, the committee (which includes S. Lange) has maintained a relationship with Lambarene and with Schweitzer's ideas about civilization and peace.

29 November 1964
1. Pierre Paul Schweitzer (b. 1912 in Strasbourg), son of A. Schweitzer's younger brother Paul and Emma Schweitzer, née Münch, was director of the International Monetary Fund, Washington, D.C. from 1963 to 1973; their trip mentioned in the letter was taken in that connection. Since 1980 he has been vice chairman of the Commission for Albert Schweitzer's Spiritual Work.
2. C. F. Andrews brought about the connection between M. Gandhi and A. Schweitzer in his correspondence, but these two men never met. See the sections on Gandhi in the English translation of *Indian Thought and Its Development* and the second German edition.
3. Prime Minister Jawaharlal Nehru; see Nehru's "A Letter and a Cabled Greeting to Dr. Schweitzer," in A. A. Roback, ed., *In Albert Schweitzer's Realm*, Cambridge, Massachusetts, 1962.

1965

7 February 1965

1. Hans Margolius, philosopher, wrote systematically about philosophical scholarship. In the realm of ethics he wrote meticulously about Schweitzer's work. Margolius is also the author of philosophical aphorisms; he sent Schweitzer the manuscript of the aphorisms by various hands, mentioned in this letter.

14 March 1965

1. Schweitzer's ninetieth birthday was celebrated with the book *L'Evangile de la Miséricorde—hommage au Dr. Schweitzer*, edited by Alphonse Goettmann, Rome, with contributions by countless theologians of both churches (Paris, Les Editions du Cerf, 1965, 445 pages). The authors include M. Boegner of the Protestant Church, France, and Cardinal Eugène Tisserant of the Catholic Church; the introduction was written by Nobel Peace Laureate Father Dominique Pire. This collection treats Jesus Christ's Gospel of mercy ecumenically in essays on the New Testament tiding and its consequences for the present day. The book points to the basic idea of Schweitzer's lifework in Lambarene as an act of Christian faith.

16 May 1965

1. Timothy Yilsun Rhee, a theologian and physician (see the letter of 23 August 1958), worked in Lambarene and modeled a hospital after it on the Korean island of Ullung-Do.

July 1965

1. Dr. Ernst Zavarsky, a Czechoslovakian musicologist and author who asked Schweitzer for permission to dedicate his Bach studies to him, wrote on modern music and music history; he was also interested in organ building and the organ movement.

INDEX